An Extraordinary Time

AN EXTRAORDINARY TIME

*The End of the Postwar Boom
and the Return of
the Ordinary Economy*

MARC LEVINSON

BUSINESS
BOOKS

1 3 5 7 9 10 8 6 4 2

Random House Business Books
20 Vauxhall Bridge Road
London SW1V 2SA

Random House Business Books is part of the Penguin Random House group of companies
whose addresses can be found at global.penguinrandomhouse.com.

Penguin
Random House
UK

First published in Great Britain by Random House Business Books in 2016

www.penguin.co.uk

A CIP catalogue record for this book is available from the British Library.

ISBN 9781847941893 (hardback)
ISBN 9781847941909 (trade paperback)

Printed and bound by Clays Ltd, St Ives Plc

Penguin Random House is committed to a sustainable future
for our business, our readers and our planet. This book is made
from Forest Stewardship Council® certified paper.

To Kay, for everything

Contents

Introduction   1

1 | The New Economics   15

2 | The Magic Square   27

3 | Chaos   47

4 | Crisis of Faith   57

5 | The Great Stagflation   65

6 | Gold Boys   81

7 | Quotas and Concubines   99

8 | The Export Machine   115

9 | The End of the Dream   133

10 | The Right Turn   155

11 | Thatcher   179

12 | Socialism's Last Stand   199

13 | Morning in America   219

14 | The Lost Decade   239

15 | The New World   257

Acknowledgments 271

Notes 273

Index 313

Introduction

On Sunday, the fourth of November, the traffic stopped.

University students spread blankets on the motorway and picnicked to the sounds of a flute. Young children raced through stoplights on their roller skates. From Eindhoven in the south to Groningen in the north, the streets of the Netherlands were nearly free of cars—aside from those of German tourists and of clergy, who, by special dispensation, were allowed to drive to church. Abandoning her Cadillac limousine, Queen Juliana, age sixty-four, cheerfully hopped on a bicycle to visit her grandchildren. To those uninvolved with the difficult decisions behind it, Holland's first car-free Sunday of 1973 was a bit of a lark.[1]

Four weeks earlier, Egyptian and Syrian armies had burst through Israel's defensive lines, routing Israeli troops and threatening to overrun the entire country in what became known as the Yom Kippur War. When the United States and the Netherlands funneled weapons to Israel, Arab oil-producing countries retaliated. Led by Saudi Arabia, they had already been demanding more money for their oil, raising the official price from $3.20 per barrel in January to $5.11 on October 16. Now they turned the valves even tighter and cut off the Netherlands and the United States altogether.

Gloom descended across Europe. As storage tanks were drained, the Belgians, the Swiss, the Italians, the Norwegians, even the auto-obsessed West Germans soon faced car-free Sundays of their own. Speed limits were lowered, thermostats turned down, diesel supplies rationed. Indoor swimming pools in Stockholm were closed to save the energy required to heat them, and the Tour de Belgique auto race was called off. Permits for Sunday driving became coveted status symbols. West Germany, imagining itself to be a socially conscious market economy, was challenged by a gas station manager's brusque explanation of her method for allocating petrol: "People I don't know don't get any."[2]

Across the Atlantic, there were no car-free Sundays. Instead, there was panic. The United States was consumed by the price of oil, and Richard Nixon was consumed by the treacherous politics of high oil prices. "We are headed into the most acute energy shortage since World War II," the US president warned in a televised address on November 7. He asked Americans to lower their thermostats and unveiled Project Independence, a fanciful scheme to end oil imports by 1980. Congress debated whether to ration gasoline and, unbidden, authorized Nixon to allocate petroleum supplies among refiners, bus companies, service stations, farmers, and anyone else with a special claim. As cold weather arrived, truck drivers blocked highways to protest the soaring price of diesel fuel, and homeowners unplugged their Christmas lights in sympathy—or, perhaps, to avoid the opprobrium of their neighbors. Texas, a state floating on oil, gave birth to a popular bumper sticker urging, "Freeze a Yankee." Gas lines, clogged with drivers desperate to top off nearly full tanks while the precious liquid was still available, symbolized the collapse of the American dream.

The oil shock upset the equilibrium in Canada, setting off a boom in oil-rich Alberta while crippling import-dependent Quebec. The reverberations were even more disquieting in Japan. As petroleum prices rose through 1973, the Japanese did not anticipate serious trouble; their country had little engagement with the Middle East, and many Japanese companies had even complied with the Arab boycott against Israel. But Japan's neutrality in Middle Eastern affairs did not spare it from pain when oil prices spiked. The Japanese did not block highways or threaten gas station attendants, but anxiety over the end of cheap petroleum ran very deep: every drop used to fuel Japan's huge industrial base was imported. As the government slashed its economic growth forecast by half, it rationed oil and electricity to factories and instructed families to extinguish the pilot lights on their water heaters.[3]

As tumultuous as it was, the shock was short-lived. By December 1973, it was clear that crude oil was not at all in short supply. Storage tanks at European ports were overflowing, and tankers lined up in the Atlantic waiting their turn to dock at US refineries. Higher prices and conservation measures had cut demand, so some oil exporters, desperate for cash, set their pumps at top speed to raise production and keep their incomes steady. January 1974 brought the last of Europe's car-free Sundays. In February, Nixon released gasoline from government stockpiles, and the lines at gas stations went away. On March 18, the Arab producers, eager for US help in mediating the withdrawal of Israeli troops, officially abandoned the embargo and turned their attention to averting a price collapse as oil flooded the markets.

The global oil crisis had passed.[4] But from its embers, a crisis that would endure far longer and cause infinitely greater upheaval was just beginning to smolder.

FROM AN ECONOMIST'S PERSPECTIVE, THE SECOND HALF OF THE twentieth century divides neatly into two. The first period, which began in the rubble of World War II, saw an economic boom of extraordinary proportions across much of the world. A host of new international arrangements to assure steady exchange rates, ease restrictions on foreign trade, and provide economic aid to the poorest countries pointed to an era of global cooperation. As economic growth exploded, people could feel their lives improving almost by the day. New homes, cars, and consumer goods were within reach for average families, and a raft of government social programs and private labor contracts created an unprecedented sense of personal financial security. People who had thought they were condemned to be sharecroppers in the Alabama Cotton Belt or day laborers in the boot heel of Italy found opportunities they could never have imagined.

The second period, from 1973 almost to the end of the century, was dramatically different. In Japan, North America, and much of Europe and

Latin America, the warmth of prosperity was replaced by cold insecurity. International cooperation turned to endless conflict over trade, exchange rates, and foreign investment. White-collar workers grew nervous. Blue-collar workers could feel themselves slipping down the economic ladder. From the steel towns of Pennsylvania's Monongahela Valley to the coal-mining districts of northern Japan to the brutal high-rises in the Northern Quarter of Marseilles, communities emptied out as people fled economic devastation. Repeated economic crises devastated countries from Mexico to Russia to Indonesia, destroying the value of old-age pensions, wiping out families' savings, and slashing the buying power of an hour's wage. Labor shortages turned into chronic unemployment, and young people were hard-pressed to find anything beyond temporary work. It was an age of anxiety, not an era of boundless optimism.

This depiction may seem puzzling. After all, the 1950s were the years when primary-school students learned to duck and cover in the event of nuclear attack, when much of Europe was imprisoned by an Iron Curtain, when war in Korea brought armies from fifteen countries face to face with Chinese troops, when war in Algeria destroyed the French Republic. In the 1960s, the United States was convulsed by protests against racial discrimination and the Vietnam War, the Troubles turned Northern Ireland into a war zone, and student revolts and labor unrest shook governments around the globe. Inflation became a worldwide concern in the early 1970s, and workers took to the streets to protect their hard-won gains. These were not years when farmers peacefully tended their flocks and grapevines, satisfied in their blessings.

Yet the turbulence of those decades can be understood only if we remember that economic conditions were getting steadily better in many parts of the world—not just for the rich, but for almost everyone. The very fact that life was so good—that jobs were easy to find; that food was plentiful and decent housing commonplace; that a newly woven safety net protected against unemployment, illness, and old age—encouraged individuals to take risks, from marching in the streets to joining the antimaterialist counterculture. Rising living standards and greater economic security made it possible for many people in many countries to join in the cultural ferment and social upheaval of the 1960s and early 1970s, and arguably engendered the confidence that brought vocal challenges to injustices—gender discrimination, environmental degradation, repression of homosexuals—that had long existed with little public outrage.

Then, quite unexpectedly, growth stalled. As economic conditions turned volatile, the sense of limitless possibilities gave way to fear about the future. Turning on, tuning in, and dropping out were unaffordable luxuries; now it was time to get a job and cling to it. If technology entrepreneurs and Wall Street buyout artists were getting ahead, everyone else seemed to be treading water. The public mood turned cynical and sour.

The divide between these two eras is stark. Between 1948 and 1973, the world economy expanded faster than in any similar period, before or since. According to the careful estimates of British economist Angus Maddison, income per person, averaged across all residents of Planet Earth, grew at an annual rate of 2.92 percent from 1950 to 1973, enough to double the average person's living standard in about twenty-five years. Certainly, prosperity was far from universal; in numerous countries a tiny proportion of the population captured most of the gains, and many individuals were left behind. Even so, never before in recorded history had so many people become so much better off so quickly.[5]

In wealthy countries, the trend was even more remarkable. Employment, wages, factory production, business investment, total output: almost every measure of vitality increased year after year, at a rapid rate, with only brief interruptions. Bank failures were rare, bankruptcy rates low, inflation restrained. Societies seemed to be growing more equitable, income more evenly shared. "A continuation of recent trends will carry us to unbelievable levels of economic activity in our own lifetimes," a top official of the US Census Bureau pronounced in 1966, joining the many serious thinkers who were genuinely worried that society might not offer sufficient opportunity for consumers to spend their rising incomes.[6]

The amazing trajectory of the postwar economy reached its apogee in 1973, when average income per person around the world leaped 4.5 percent. At that rate, a person's income would double in sixteen years, quadruple in thirty-two. Average people everywhere had reason to feel good.[7]

And then the good times were over. The world would never again approach the economic performance it had enjoyed in 1973. Volatile conditions became the norm, stability the exception. In Europe, Latin America, and Japan, average incomes would grow not even half as fast through the end of the twentieth century as they had in the years leading up to 1973, and the steady improvement in living standards was no longer so readily apparent. In much of Africa, incomes would hardly grow at all, and the same was true for much of that period in North America. The almost universal feeling of prosperity faded quickly. As economies sputtered, jobs grew scarce, and inflation raged, confidence in the ability of governments to make life better began to melt away.

That confidence had been grounded in the evident ability of economists, planners, and operations researchers—technocrats, in the lingo of the time—to steer their countries along a path of steady economic growth. Their increasingly sophisticated models, depicting entire national economies as a lengthy series of equations, spat out policy prescriptions, and for a quarter-century it seemed that politicians merely needed to follow their instructions to assure everyone a job. But as full employment vanished and incomes stagnated, the technocrats lost much of their stature. The standard remedies that had, by all appearances, kept the major economies in rude health since the late 1940s—raising interest rates a bit, or lowering them; cutting back on taxes, or increasing them; building some dams or highways to deal with a bit of unemployment—no longer had curative power. Politicians, unable to deliver prosperity, were left to rail haplessly against currency speculators, oil sheikhs, and other forces they could not control.

In earlier years, no one would have blamed public officials for failing to keep everyone employed, for that had never been seen as the responsibility of governments. Emperors and presidents were not assumed to have the least control over the droughts and floods, much less the bank failures and bubbles of overinvestment that, when they eventually popped, could spread misery and bring commerce to a halt. When the economy turned down, government officials could do little more than offer inspiring speeches while praying the gloom would pass. Difficult times were the norm, not the exception: between October 1873 and June 1897, the US economy spent more months contracting than expanding, even if the overall trend was positive growth.[8]

It was during the Great Depression of the 1930s that governments first took on responsibility for economic revival. Masses of jobless workers threatened political instability, making it imperative to create employment quickly. Travelers to the Soviet Union, where everyone worked for the state, reported zero unemployment in a communist economy; idealists imagined that job creation by government could have the same benefits elsewhere. And a new development of the Depression era, the creation of statistics to describe unemployment and national income, made government intervention unavoidable. Once unemployment was reported as a percentage of the labor force rather than simply as a nebulous problem, politicians came under immense pressure to demonstrate their effectiveness by driving the rate lower. They could no longer stand on the sidelines and wait for the problem to solve itself.

So when the world economy abruptly took sick late in 1973, democratic nations looked to their leaders for a cure. The truth, though, was that neither the politicians nor their economic counselors had any idea what was causing the ailment. They acted because they were under pressure to act, not because they had confidence in their prescriptions. From a political perspective, doing something, anything, was better than admitting ignorance about what to do. Predictably, their actions failed to bring back the world that had been, the world in which jobs were a birthright and prosperity a constant.

Many factors that might have caused this downshift in the world economy were readily apparent: the cost of energy, a critical input for industry, was sharply higher; exchange rates were quite volatile, adding to business uncertainty; consumer demand for cars, homes, and appliances suddenly weakened; population growth was beginning to slow. But beyond these obvious factors lurked a more pernicious problem. Productivity, the efficiency with which economies put resources to use, was no longer advancing smartly year after year. Fast productivity growth, the result of better-trained workers, heavy business and government investment, and technological innovation, had made the postwar boom possible. If productivity growth was lagging, then economies would be less able to raise families' incomes and create new jobs.

There was no handbook for fixing the productivity problem, which left the door open for politicians of every stripe to tout their favored tax and spending policies as solutions. Tax breaks for factories and equipment to stimulate business investment and help families with education costs, stronger patent protection to encourage inventors to come up with ideas that would make the economy flourish, greater spending on scientific research, more seats at universities, expanded vocational training: all were repackaged as measures to make productivity grow faster by speeding the pace of innovation, said to be the critical factor in economic growth.[9]

In the political arena, meanwhile, governments came under conservative fire for causing the productivity slowdown by disrupting market forces. Venerable small-government policies were now promoted as solutions to the problem. Regulations concerning pollution, occupational safety, working hours, business licensing, initial stock offerings, and dozens of other matters came under heavy attack for making the economy less efficient. Introducing competition into state-dominated sectors like railroads and telecommunications sectors would enable their customers in the business world to cut costs and improve productivity. Laws protecting labor unions and some social insurance programs, notably unemployment benefits, were criticized for interfering with an efficient labor market. Yet where such purportedly onerous policies were reformed, any salutary effects were hard to find in the productivity data. Political measures were of little help against a problem whose fundamental cause, technological change, was beyond government control.

During the 1970s and 1980s, as more frequent job loss, slower wage growth, and pockets of seemingly intractable unemployment became the norm, elected officials and economic-policy bureaucrats alike flailed ineffectually. Despite stacks of policy memos and a great deal of fancy mathematics, understanding of why the good times disappeared has not increased with time. Back in the 1990s, the American academic Paul Romer revolutionized thinking about economic growth by insisting that innovation and knowledge matter far more than labor and capital; "endogenous growth theory," the unwieldy name attached to his work, taught that strengthening education, supporting scientific research, and making entrepreneurship easy would do more to improve economic growth than fretting over budget deficits and tax rates. Three decades after his theory swept through economics departments everywhere, Romer was no longer sure he was right. "For the last two decades," he admitted in 2015, "growth theory has made no scientific progress toward a consensus."[10]

Such a statement is shocking to modern ears. The idea that the economy is not an instrument that can be carefully tuned, that its long-run course is determined largely by forces not under the control of government officials and central bankers, contradicts the lessons absorbed by generations of students since World War II. More upsetting still is the possibility that the volatile trends after 1973 marked a return to normal, a reversion to the time when productivity, economic growth, and living standards improved haltingly, and sometimes not at all. Political conservatives, whom we might expect to be especially attuned to the power of markets and to be particularly skeptical of government's ability to control economic outcomes, turn out to be just as infatuated with the power of the government's hand as progressives. "Making slow growth normal serves the progressive program of defining economic failure down," the conservative US political commentator George F. Will asserted in a 2015 critique of President Barack Obama's policies, as if the rate of economic growth were a matter of presidential discretion.[11]

IN CHRONOLOGICAL TIME, THE GOLDEN AGE WAS BRIEF. BARELY a quarter-century elapsed from its blossoming out of a world in ruins to its sudden end amid unimagined prosperity, steadily rising living standards, and jobs for all. Scholars have spent the past fifty years struggling to understand what went wrong and how to set it right. But it may be that there is nothing to fix, that the long boom was a unique event that will never come again. Harvard University economist Zvi Griliches, a pioneer of research into productivity, concluded as much. "Perhaps the 1970s were not so abnormal after all," he mused after decades studying productivity change. "Maybe it is the inexplicably high growth rates in the 1950s and early 1960s that are the real puzzle."[12]

Our inability to restore the world economy to its peak condition has had long-lasting consequences. It radically changed social attitudes, engendering a skepticism about government that has dominated political life well into the twenty-first century. With that change came a shift away from collective responsibility for social well-being; as state institutions were allowed to wither, individuals were asked to assume more of the costs and risks of their health care, their education, and their old age. It is fair to say that the economic changes of the 1970s turned the world to the right. The global political climate warmed to market-oriented thinking because other ideas appeared to have failed. The demand for smaller government, personal responsibility, and freer markets transformed political debate, upended long-established public policies, and swept conservative politicians like Margaret Thatcher, Ronald Reagan, and Helmut Kohl into power.

In the rich world, the postcrisis years brought a massive shift in income and wealth in favor of those who owned capital and against those whose only asset was their labor. In the poor world, they fueled a boom and subsequent bust among countries eager to join the advanced economies. Anger and frustration fed by stagnant wages, rising inequality, and the fecklessness of public officials swept country after country, reshaping culture, politics, and society. International finance grew explosively, far outpacing governments' ability to regulate it and, within a decade, bringing economic collapse to emerging economies from Peru to Indonesia. Trade unions lost bargaining power in almost every country, and abrupt shifts in international trade patterns reverberated through industrial towns, decimating the industrial working class that had prospered in the years since the war. Gaping holes opened in the safety nets that had only recently been woven to protect families against risk and offer hope of upward mobility.[13]

These developments have been the subject of an outpouring of literature and history, music and film, from the forty or more biographies of Silvio Berlusconi, the Italian media magnate and prime minister, to the angry, poignant songs of Bruce Springsteen, an icon of America's working-class past. Yet with few exceptions, these works treat the unpleasant changes that began in the 1970s as the product of domestic forces. As the US journalist George Packer described the decade, for example, "What happened, we now know, was the collapse of the American consensus, the postwar social contract founded on a mixed economy at home and bipartisan Cold War internationalism abroad."[14]

This focus on the local news is perhaps unavoidable: few of us are truly globalists, and our understanding of events is shaped by the news reports, political campaigns, and intellectual debates in whatever country we call home. The politicians whose utterances shape the news, of course, often blame other countries for domestic ills. This happened in the 1980s, when US politicians frequently accused Japan of destroying American manufacturing by trading unfairly, and in the 2000s, when immigrants from Poland and then Syria stood accused of causing unemployment in Western Europe. But political leaders frequently understate the connection between large global trends and individuals' well-being, first so they do not seem hapless while in power and second so they can blame the incumbents for economic troubles while in opposition.

Approaching economic and social change in this way means we tend to ascribe causality to factors within the control of a national government, whether a tax provision or a tariff reduction, a welfare program or the electoral rules that allowed a particular leader to gain power. Clearly, such things matter. But it is equally clear that the economic stagnation and political reaction of the late twentieth century were not just the consequences of domestic conditions and choices. Social contracts were rewritten not just in the United States, but in Japan and Sweden and Spain and dozens of other countries, each following its own mix of social and economic policies. The forces at work transcended national borders, and we can understand the era only by viewing them in a global context.

"Globalization," a word not yet coined, was both a cause and a consequence of the harsher economic climate that developed after 1973. An unimaginable increase in the amount of money moving around the globe vastly complicated governments' efforts to control exchange rates, inflation, and unemployment, not to mention the stability of the banking system. As economic growth slowed, politicians spent freely to create jobs and stimulate consumer spending, assuming that the downturn would be brief. When that failed, they desperately agreed to try measures that would have been labeled radical only a few years before. The regulatory strings that had given governments tight control over the transportation, communications, and energy sectors were gradually cut away. Steps to dismantle state-owned monopolies and sell off state-owned companies soon followed. Deregulation and privatization left no end of losers among workers who had enjoyed ironclad job security in communities that thrived in the presence of state-owned factories, but they opened the way to a faster-changing, more innovative economy. The state got the Internet started, but had it been left up to the established telephone monopolies to administer, we would still be waiting to reap the rewards.

The world, of course, does not revolve around money alone. Many factors influenced the development of the late twentieth century, from the worldwide movement for gender equity to an intense East-West confrontation that spawned proxy wars across the globe, from the revival of religious fundamentalism to the reunification of Europe following the collapse of the Iron Curtain in 1989. And, of course, every country had its unique political and social concerns. It is these—affirmative action in the United States, the battles over language and separatism in Canada and Spain, the re-establishment of democratic governments in Korea and across South America—that tend to fill the airwaves and the history books. Yet in a way that has generally gone unappreciated, these factors played out in the wake of sweeping changes that buffeted the global economy and left citizens anxious and ill at ease.

These pages trace a transformation that was neither swift nor painless. In the third quarter of the twentieth century, even the most calcified companies prospered; in the fourth, venerable manufacturers and banks would meet their end in large numbers, unable to adjust to the changing times. Workers' professional capital, the skills acquired over decades of labor, was valued and sought-after in the 1950s and 1960s; a few years later, that knowledge would become all but worthless as technology transformed the workplace. Regions that flourished in the industrial expansion of the post-war years would struggle to adjust to new conditions in which the ability to deliver services and ideas mattered more than the ability to weave cloth and stamp metal. In some eyes, a merit-based society that rewarded creative ideas and an appetite for risk replaced a stultified society that encouraged passive acceptance of the established order. In other eyes, a postwar social contract binding business and government to improve the welfare of average people was shredded, replaced by coldhearted market relationships that offered far less protection against job loss, illness, or old age.

Perhaps the most important thing that vanished along with the Golden Age, though, was faith in the future. For a quarter-century, average people in every wealthy country and in many poorer ones had felt their lives getting better by the day. Whatever their struggles, they could live confident that their sacrifice and hard work were building a strong foundation for their children and grandchildren. As the Golden Age became a memory, so did the boundless optimism of an era of good times for all.

CHAPTER 1

The New Economics

Only a real optimist would have thought that Arlington, Texas, had particular promise. Straddling the Texas & Pacific Railroad line between Dallas and Fort Worth, on the plains above the winding Trinity River, Arlington was still a dusty farm town after World War II. Its best-known landmark was a gazebo, erected in 1892, sheltering a mineral water well at the intersection of Main and Center. Its best-known business, Top O' Hill Terrace, was famed far and wide for its high-class entertainment and its illegal basement casino, replete with hidden rooms and passage-ways offering escape in the event of a police raid. Arlington was not a notably poor town, but it was certainly not notably rich. A third of all adults had left school by the end of eighth grade. The men worked construction, welded metal, and clerked at the retail stores, while the women mostly kept house. One home in four lacked a private bathroom.

Save for the little airstrips where pilots in training had practiced take-offs and landings during the war, Arlington in 1946 wasn't all that different from Arlington in the 1920s. It had grown a bit, to around five thousand people, and Franklin Roosevelt's Depression-fighting programs had paved a few streets. But not even a promoter with a Texas-size imagination would have bet that by the early 1970s this dusty burg would boast an automobile plant, a vast amusement park, a four-year state university, and a major-league baseball team—much less that pastures and pecan orchards would give way to street upon street of ranch houses with brick facades and two-car garages to accommodate a 2,000 percent increase in population.[1]

Such transformations were not unusual in the years after the Second World War. The French called this period *les trente glorieuses,* "the thirty glorious years." The British preferred "Golden Age"; the Germans, *Wirtschaftswunder,* or "economic miracle"; the Italians, simply *il miracolo,* "the miracle." The Japanese, more modestly, named it "the era of high economic growth." In any language, economic performance was stellar.

It was, in fact, the most remarkable stretch of economic advance in recorded history. In the span of a single generation, hundreds of millions of people were lifted from penury to unimagined riches. At its start, two million mules still plowed furrows on US farms, Spain lived in near-total isolation, and one in 175 Japanese households had a telephone. By its end, the purchasing power of the average French wage had quadrupled and millions of passengers were jetting across the ocean each year, some of them in supersonic jets that made the trip in less than four hours. The change in average people's lives was simply astounding.[2]

TO UNDERSTAND THE MAGNITUDE OF WHAT WAS TO FOLLOW, IT is worth considering the starting point. As World War II drew to a close in 1945, prospects were grim. Over vast stretches of Europe and Asia, refugees wandered the roads by the millions, seeking a future amid the rubble of shattered cities. Between widespread miners' strikes and worn-out machinery, just producing enough coal to provide heat through the winter was a challenge everywhere, and in the chaos that prevailed in lands torn by war, producing anything else was almost impossible. Many nations lacked the foreign currency to import food and fuel to keep people alive, much less to buy equipment and raw material for reconstruction. France's farms could produce only 60 percent as much in 1946 as they had before the war. In Germany, many of the remaining factories were carted off to the Soviet Union as reparations. Inflation ran rampant in Europe and Japan as mobs of people competed to buy the few goods that were to be had. Even in North America, where there was no physical destruction, turning bomber plants back into automobile plants would take years, not months. As shoppers mobbed stores seeking nylons, coffee, and real cotton underwear, prices soared, decimating the buying power of workers' pay and bringing yet more labor unrest. By one estimate, 4.5 million US workers were on the picket lines in 1946. And while most of the shooting had stopped, tensions between the Soviet Union and its former allies raised the specter of another conflict. The postwar world was not a hopeful place.[3]

Yet in many countries, those austere, even desperate years ushered in a political sea change: the welfare state. The idea that governments should be responsible for their citizens' economic security was not new; German Chancellor Otto von Bismarck had introduced a national pension scheme in the 1880s to stave off socialist demands for more radical social change. Sixty years later, though, hundreds of millions of people in the advanced economies still lacked old-age security, medical insurance, and protection against unemployment or disability. War fundamentally altered the politics. As they entered coalition governments or resistance organizations in the name of national unity, socialist and Christian parties insisted that citizens who had been asked to sacrifice in war now share the benefits of peace. An official 1942 report by British economist William Beveridge set the tone, calling for the United Kingdom to establish a comprehensive system of social insurance "to secure to each citizen an income adequate to satisfy a natural minimum standard." Beveridge proposed no fewer than twenty-three different programs, from training benefits for displaced workers to universal funeral grants, all to be financed by contributions from workers, employers, and the state. "A revolutionary moment in the world's history is a time for revolutions, not for patching," he declared.[4]

Such programs blossomed even before the war's end. In 1944, the Canadian Parliament authorized a "baby bonus" to be paid monthly for every child up to age sixteen—Canada's first nationwide social-welfare program. A December 1944 law in Belgium, approved as the Battle of the Bulge raged almost within earshot of the legislators convened in the Palace of the Nation, created national pension, health, unemployment insurance, and vacation pay schemes and provided cash allowances for families with children. France's postwar coalition government enacted family allowances and old-age pensions within months of the German Army's withdrawal. The British Parliament agreed in 1945 that every family should receive five shillings per week for each child after the first, and in 1946 it added unemployment insurance, old-age pensions, widows' benefits, and a national health service. In the Netherlands, a "Roman-Red" coalition of Catholic and socialist parties created a universal old-age pension and a national program of relief for the poor. In Japan, a 1947 law proclaimed, "national and local governments shall be responsible for bringing up children in good mental and physical health, along with their guardians," inserting the state deeply into what had always been private affairs.[5]

The birth of the welfare state did not magically create prosperity in a shattered world, for overwhelming problems stood in the way of recovery. Haunting images of ruined cities notwithstanding, physical destruction was not the main obstacle to revival. The war had done no damage to factories in the Western Hemisphere and surprisingly little in Europe. Even in Japan, where 90 percent of chemical-making capacity and 85 percent of steel capacity had been destroyed by US bombing, most of the railroads and electric plants still functioned. The urgent need to rebuild roads and bridges, restore farm production, and house millions of refugees and demobilized soldiers meant no lack of work. But three daunting factors stood in the way of economic recovery. The costs of battle and occupation had exhausted the reserves of gold and dollars once owned by European countries and Japan, leaving them unable to import machinery to restart factories or meat and grain to feed their people—and depriving the United States and Canada of export markets. Price and wage controls, imposed during the war to stanch inflation and channel resources into critical industries, discouraged farmers and manufacturers from bringing goods to market and led to endless labor unrest as workers agitated for pay raises that employers were not permitted to grant. Political turmoil deterred investment that might have revived growth, especially in Europe, where Communist parties directed by the Soviet Union squeezed out democratic parties from Poland to Yugoslavia and tried to do the same in Greece, Italy, and France. Wherever the Communists took power, expropriation of privately owned businesses and farms soon followed. The world seemed poised to follow a global war with a global depression.[6]

And then, in the first half of 1948, the fever broke. In January, US officials, worried about economic stagnation in occupied Japan, announced a new policy, soon dubbed the "reverse course," that emphasized rebuilding the economy rather than exacting reparations. In February, a Soviet-backed uprising ousted a democratic government in Czechoslovakia, installing a brutal Communist regime and turning the country into a Soviet satellite. In April, US President Harry Truman signed a law authorizing the economic aid program that would be known as the Marshall Plan—aid the Soviets and their client states promptly rejected. In June, the American, British, and French military authorities proclaimed a new currency, the deutsche mark, to be the legal tender in the parts of Germany not occupied by the Soviet Union. Three days later, the Soviets responded to the evident threat to separate the three western zones from the east by blocking road access from western Germany to West Berlin, taking the world to the brink of nuclear war.

Paradoxically, the clang of the Iron Curtain falling across the heart of Europe, dividing the postwar world into East and West, dictatorship and democracy, was also the signal for renewal. The Soviets and their bloc of captive allies had literally fenced themselves off. Investors and corporate managers were freed from worry about whether France or Japan would end up on the Soviet side. The huge amounts of aid flowing into Europe, the "reverse course" that brought Japan's inflation under control and allowed factories to import raw materials, and the promise of stable currencies and lower trade barriers all contributed to a surge of confidence. In West Germany, where people could finally return to doing business with cash instead of through barter, factories erupted into life. Industrial production rose at an astonishing annual rate of 137 percent in the second half of 1948. As dormant economies in Europe and Asia awakened, export demand brought "help wanted" signs out of storage across North America.[7]

IN MANY WAYS, THE WORLD ECONOMY OF 1948 WAS FAR FROM modern. Imports were tightly controlled almost everywhere; in much of the world, nothing was so coveted as an illicit carton of American-made Marlboros. Capitals across Europe burned with debate about whether advanced countries could prosper without colonial empires, and colonies seethed with revolt against the imperialists. Barely half of all Americans turning seventeen in 1948 graduated from high school—and in a country where racial segregation was rampant, half of black adults had less than seven years of schooling. In Tokyo, on average, three people had to cook, eat, relax, and sleep in an area the size of a parking space. One French household in thirty owned a refrigerator. The average Korean lived on less than half the calories required by an adult doing physical labor. In Spain, the land of olive trees, housewives needed ration books to buy olive oil. Infectious diseases still ran rampant, even in wealthy countries like Australia. For the vast majority of human beings, work, whether farming a rice plot, tightening bolts in a factory, or hauling wood and water in a village a hundred miles from the power grid, involved constant physical labor.[8]

Then, in 1950, the eruption of war in Korea sent military orders coursing through factories on every continent. After years of depression, destruction, and desperation, the world economy began to boom. And the boom fed on itself, as reviving factories hired more workers whose increased buying power created yet more demand for goods and services of every sort. From 1948 to 1973, Japan's economy doubled in size, doubled again, and then again, raising the average person's income almost 600 percent. West Germany's economy grew four times over during those same years, France's a bit less, Greece's even more.

Homes sprouted from rubble and farmland by the tens of millions. In the United States, the number of housing units increased by two-thirds in the span of twenty-five years, and twenty-two million American families became homeowners. More than half of British families owned their own homes by the early 1970s, twice the proportion of 1950 (which helps explain why eight out of ten Britons questioned in 1972 were satisfied with their living conditions). In Rome, quaint bicycles yielded to ear-splitting scooters, which were soon nudged aside by tiny Isetta cars. People in remote French villages installed electric wiring and indoor plumbing. Waves of demand for copper, iron, and other industrial commodities rippled across the world, raising living standards from Brazil to Thailand. Those gains meant not just more income, but also less work and greater opportunity. The average Frenchwoman retired at age sixty-nine in 1950; twenty years later the figure had dropped to sixty-four. Millions of people who had envied the Americans were soon living nearly as well as Americans, with claims to social benefits, like six-week vacations and tuition-free universities, that Americans could only envy.[9]

The long sweep of history, of course, brushes over important details. There were better years and worse years, and that went for countries, too. In the United States, eight million jobs vanished in 1948 and 1949, and Great Britain's economy barely grew in the mid 1950s. Chinese starved by the tens of millions between 1958 and 1962 amid Mao Tse-tung's barbaric campaign to impose his version of socialism, and the average Indian, subject to a less oppressive version, was barely better off financially in 1973 than at independence in 1947. And even powerful economic performance could not inoculate societies against the discontents that erupted in 1968, when students around the world protested their parents' materialism and a wall at the Sorbonne sprouted the epigram, "You can't fall in love with a growth rate."[10]

Yet the tenor of the times was unmistakably positive. Unemployment, ubiquitous in 1950, had all but vanished in the wealthy economies by 1960. Work was so plentiful that when the new mechanical cotton picker destroyed the livelihoods of perhaps a million semiliterate tenant farmers in the late 1940s and early 1950s, the Great Migration from the American South was absorbed almost effortlessly by factories in Detroit and Chicago. Thanks to government programs, a pensioned retirement at age sixty-five or even earlier replaced painful work into old age and relieved children of the burden of supporting their aging parents. People could feel their lives changing, their circumstances improving, from one day to the next. Even in Great Britain, far from the most dynamic of economies, "You will see a state of prosperity such as we have never had in my life-time—nor indeed in the history of this country," Prime Minister Harold Macmillan trumpeted in July 1957. "Let us be frank about it: most of our people have never had it so good."[11]

In much of the world, the postwar boom was the first long stretch of prosperity since the 1920s. Its causes were many. One was surely pent-up demand after years of austerity. Another was that wartime controls had set artificial limits on normal business investment, leaving companies rich with stored-up profits that could finance new buildings and equipment. Many of the factories that survived World War II were old buildings designed around steam engines, not electric motors, and were ill-suited to modern production methods. The opportunity to build from scratch allowed manufacturers to replace multistory plants with assembly lines arranged carefully on a single level, using the latest technology imported from the United States. Thanks to the "baby boom" that began around 1948, the demand for new homes, new furniture, and new clothes was almost insatiable. And diplomacy helped fuel the boom, too. Six rounds of global trade negotiations between 1949 and 1967 slashed import tariffs, expanding international trade and thereby pressing manufacturers to modernize in the face of foreign competition.[12]

The net result of all these changes was remarkable growth in productivity for reasons that had nothing to do with the physical task of rebuilding from the war. Starting in the late 1940s, millions of workers made the leap from agriculture to industry. Though unskilled and often illiterate, they were eagerly swept up by factories that retooled after making little for the civilian market during years of depression and war. Industry's need for new equipment fed on itself, creating yet more jobs and more demand for machines employing the latest technology. The amount of factory equipment in the United States nearly quadrupled between 1945 and 1973. Investment spending in Great Britain, 14 percent of the economy's total output in the early 1950s, topped 21 percent in the late 1960s. Yet even with all the high-efficiency machines, output was rising so fast that there was a constant need for more workers. Manufacturers in Japan employed 6.9 million workers in 1955 and 13.5 million in 1970. Starting in 1947, when its assembly lines turned out all of 8,987 cars, West German motor vehicle production increased for twenty-six consecutive years. As workers shifted from tending sheep and hoeing potatoes by hand to using expensive machinery, they were able to produce far more economic value, contributing to a rapid increase in national wealth.[13]

The manufacturing boom largely involved private investment. But it was fostered by government policies to lower trade barriers. When the war ended, tariffs were so high that they typically increased the cost of imports by one-fourth or more. A meeting of twenty-three countries in Geneva in 1947 began the process of rolling back tariffs and doing away with some of the other obstacles, such as quotas and permits, that were used to discourage imports. Four years later, six European countries—Belgium, France, Italy, Luxembourg, the Netherlands, and West Germany—agreed to free trade in coal and steel, the first step in what would become a single market covering most of Europe. These changes brought a massive increase in cross-border trade; according to one study, exports by five European countries rose 700 percent between 1946 and 1957. Greater trade goes hand in hand with greater productivity: firms that export successfully tend to be far more efficient and expansion-minded than firms that are driven out of business by import competition.[14]

Quite separately, in the 1950s governments began investing large sums to build high-speed roads. Those motorways could safely accommodate much larger vehicles than older roads, which required many tight turns as they passed through cities and towns. With a single driver able to move more freight over longer distances in a day, the productivity of transportation workers rose dramatically. Faster, cheaper ground transportation, in turn, made it practical for farms and factories to sell their goods not just locally, but regionally or nationally. Small plants based on craft methods gave way to large ones making heavy use of machinery to produce more goods at lower cost.[15]

In the twenty-five years ending in 1973, after adjusting for inflation, the average amount produced in one hour of work roughly doubled in

North America, tripled in Europe, and quintupled in Japan. Better education certainly played a role in this growth, and investment in new capital equipment helped, too. The driving force, though, seems to have been technological advancement, which offered more efficient ways for workers to do their jobs. After years of growing in fits and starts, the world took advantage of innovation to make itself rich.

And it did so in a most remarkable fashion. Rapid economic change often leaves many workers behind: think of the English farmers displaced as common land was enclosed by private owners in the eighteenth century, or of the newspaper workers whose industry all but vanished as news shifted to the Internet. But in the postwar world it was not just the wealthy who prospered. Farmhands and street cleaners saw their pay packets growing heavier year by year. Unions won not only better pay and benefits for industrial workers but also better job security, as laws and labor contracts made it steadily harder for employers to put unneeded workers on the street. Circumstances improved for almost everyone.[16]

Economic moderation went hand in hand with political moderation. Nowhere did conservative parties attempt to disassemble the welfare state. In many countries, they avidly supported it, whether out of a religious commitment to social justice, a fear of renewed class conflict, or a genuine belief that public spending would create a healthier economy. When Senator Robert A. Taft, an outspoken critic of Franklin Roosevelt's Depression-era social reforms, ran for president in 1952, his own party roundly rejected his extremism in favor of Dwight D. Eisenhower, the Allied commander in World War II, who went to great lengths to portray himself as a centrist. Eisenhower may not have embraced programs for the aged and the poor, but he did nothing to dismantle them. And neither he, nor Harold Macmillan in Britain, nor Charles de Gaulle in France, nor Konrad Adenauer in West Germany, nor Alcide de Gasperi in Italy, nor John Diefenbaker in Canada—conservative leaders all—subscribed to the idea that government should abandon its leading role in the economy and let market forces hold sway.

ECONOMIC PERFORMANCE THAT AT FIRST SEEMED MIRACULOUS was soon seen as normal. Year after year it went on: Australia, Austria,

Denmark, Finland, France, Germany, Italy, Japan, Norway, and Sweden all experienced a quarter-century with only the briefest of economic doldrums. The volatility that had always marked economic life had seemingly been consigned to the dustbin of history. How had this miracle happened? In most countries, there was little doubt of the answer. Economic success was attributed not to the animal spirits of capitalism but to careful economic planning.

In most countries, with the notable exception of West Germany during the 1950s, economic planning was very much in vogue in the postwar era. To some extent, planning was unavoidable: where foreign currency to buy imports was scarce at the war's end, someone had to decide whether importing fuel or food was more essential. But the planning bureaucracies that developed in the late 1940s were meant to be anything but temporary. Skilled in new quantitative tools such as linear programming and equipped with the techniques perfected by operations researchers to plot bombing runs, the planners claimed to know which industries, if properly fostered, could do the most for economic growth. Following the advice of economists, France's government laid out *grands plans* for new auto plants and steel mills. In Japan, the Ministry of International Trade and Industry, the awesome bureaucracy known as MITI, wielded life-and-death power by controlling individual companies' imports and exports, their investments in new factories, and their licensing of foreign patents.[17]

If planners could figure out how to manage key industries, why not entire economies? By the final months of World War II, a large majority of Americans, and nearly one-third of business leaders, told pollsters that it was government's role to maintain full employment. Among Americans with college degrees, a stunning 70 percent concurred that "Full employment is something we should try to get, and it will require government action as well as planning by industry to get it." When the US Senate, dominated by conservatives, considered the Full Employment Act in September 1945, seventy-one senators agreed that the government should ensure full employment when the private sector fell short, and only ten voted no.[18]

Although the Full Employment Act was much weakened before Congress finally approved it, support remained strong for the idea that government should, and could, ensure jobs for all. In the late 1940s, a US business organization, the Committee for Economic Development, proposed writing full employment into the federal government's budget. Its idea was that the budget should be crafted so that receipts would equal expenditures if the economy were operating at full capacity—a moment when, presumably, tax revenues would be high and payments to unemployed workers low. This new understanding of fiscal responsibility supplanted the idea that the budget should be in balance every year. Now, the thinking went, government deficits were tolerable, and even desirable, when unemployment was high, but should vanish at full employment. No one seemed to notice that the "full-employment budget" created perverse incentives for elected politicians everywhere. Agreeing to more government spending at times of high unemployment was easy enough, but reducing spending during economic upturns was far less attractive. Deficit spending would become the norm.

The well-intentioned idea of a full-employment budget, like many well-intentioned ideas, had unforeseen consequences. Economists became arbiters, specifying what unemployment rate would constitute "full employment" and then calculating how much government spending would be required to reach that target. "Conceptual advances and quantitative research in economics are replacing emotion with reason," Walter Heller, formerly the chief economic adviser to presidents John F. Kennedy and Lyndon Johnson, insisted in 1966. With better statistics and computer-assisted forecasting methods, Heller asserted, the government could know exactly how to adjust spending and taxes to vanquish unemployment without pushing up inflation. Heller called this idea the "new economics."[19]

CHAPTER 2

The Magic Square

Walter Heller's promise of rational governance was congenial to thinkers of many ideologies, from the Communists who were influential in Italy and France to the free-market monetarists whose voices grew steadily louder in America. All preached that good government—as they defined it, of course—could keep the economy on a steady tack. All would be surprised, puzzled, and remarkably unrepentant when, after 1973, the world stubbornly failed to conform to their expectations.

Perhaps the foremost prophet of this new economic religion was a self-sure West German politician named Karl Schiller. Born in 1911 in Breslau, in what was then the southeastern corner of Germany, Schiller grew up in Kiel, in the far north, where his divorced mother worked as a housekeeper to pay his school fees. A Protestant with strong views about the social responsibility of a Christian, he joined the Socialist Students' League, an organization close to the Social Democratic Party, when he entered the university in 1931. Both organizations were repressed after Adolf Hitler came to power in 1933. Schiller then switched sides, joining several pro-Hitler organizations, eventually including the Nazi Party, to smooth the way for an academic career. He earned a doctorate in economics in the Nazi era, writing his dissertation on the German government's job-creation policies between 1926 and 1933, and then spent four years in the German army.

At the war's end, the ambitious young economist remade himself again, rejoining the Social Democratic Party and establishing himself as an advocate of careful economic planning. Although he became a professor at the University of Hamburg, where his students included future West German Chancellor Helmut Schmidt, Schiller's true passion was politics. In 1946, he won a seat in Hamburg's state parliament and became the economy and transport minister. He gained fame for reviving the moribund commercial shipbuilding industry and spearheading the effort to restore Hamburg's historic role as Germany's main international trading center.

The year 1948 turned out to be pivotal in the development of Germany's economy. The country, within its pre-1938 borders but shorn of eastern regions that were transferred to Poland, had been divided into four zones at war's end, occupied respectively by the Soviet, British, American, and French armies. That division was replicated in Berlin, deep within the Soviet zone. The reichsmark, Germany's official currency since 1924, circulated everywhere, alongside Allied military currencies. But the four occupying powers had no agreement about managing the money supply, and they printed so many reichsmark that the currency was nearly worthless. Much of Germany's domestic commerce was conducted by barter, not with cash.

In June 1948, in the face of intense Soviet opposition, a new currency, the deutsche mark, was introduced in the American, British, and French zones, overseen by a new central bank system, which would develop into the German Bundesbank. At the same time, many regulated prices were set free, forcing the economy to adjust quickly to market conditions. With a stroke, the market-oriented economy of the western states was decoupled from the economy in the Soviet-occupied eastern states, where large private enterprises had been all but eliminated. The following year, after air forces from six countries mounted an airlift to overcome the Soviet blockade of the land routes between western Germany and Berlin, Germany was formally divided into two. The Soviet zone, including the Soviet sector of Berlin, became the German Democratic Republic, a police state of great equality but little opportunity, in which citizens were penned in by concrete and barbed wire, the communist Socialist Unity Party had a monopoly on wisdom, and the prosperity of their cousins to the west lay tantalizingly out of reach. The western zones became the Federal Republic of Germany.

Schiller, still in the Hamburg state parliament, was named to the advisory council of the new federal economy ministry, a position that offered him an unusual opportunity to shape the West German economy from its earliest days. He stood apart both from those who favored extensive government intervention in the economy, especially in shaping investment decisions, and from those who thought private choices about saving and investment would meet West Germany's needs. Schiller's advice called for "a synthesis of planning and competition." His notion of planning, though, was quite different from the ideas that prevailed in France and Italy, where governments determined that a new steel mill should be built here or an automobile plant there. Schiller wanted the government to plan the broad direction of the economy, but to leave business decisions to market forces. He defined his philosophy thus: "As much competition as possible, as much planning as necessary."[1]

The Social Democrats were a union-backed socialist party that had been viciously attacked under Nazi rule. After capturing less than 30 percent of the vote in West Germany's first two postwar elections, the party spent much of the 1950s plotting a new strategy. The electorate was strongly anticommunist. More than eight million West Germans had fled or been expelled from Central and Eastern Europe, and they blamed the communist governments now ruling their former homes in Poland, Czechoslovakia, Hungary, and the Balkans. Millions more were intimately familiar with the grim repression in East Germany. The Social Democrats' traditional support of state-owned industry—not to mention the open sympathy of some Social Democratic leaders with the communist states to the east—had very little appeal in the new, democratic Germany.

Schiller offered an alternative perspective. The economy, he insisted, was "a rational whole." The government's job was not to run it, but to use its tax and spending powers to fine-tune it for optimal performance. This would be accomplished with techniques such as input-output analysis, which showed how a million marks of government spending on highways would trickle through the economy, and linear programming, which could reveal which type of tax cut might create the most jobs. Highly trained experts conversant with new methods of statistical analysis would evaluate the data and make the critical decisions.

In 1956, Schiller put forth his ideas in legislation requiring the government to maintain full employment and steady economic growth while keeping prices stable. He called this wondrous combination the "magic triangle." With the Social Democrats in the minority, Schiller's bill was rejected. But his ideas had legs. In January 1958, six countries—Belgium, France, Italy, Luxembourg, the Netherlands, and West Germany—signed the Treaty of Rome, the founding document of what would eventually become the European Union. Its text, heavily influenced by faith in the ability of governments to regulate economic performance, required each member country to commit to maintaining high employment, steady growth, and stable prices, while keeping its international trade and investment in balance. With these four obligations, the magic triangle became a square.[2]

On its face, the magic square was hard to criticize. It fit nicely with Social Democratic ideals but also appealed to Europe's dominant Christian Socialist parties, such as the ruling Christian Democratic Party in West Germany. The Christian Socialists, while less keen on government spending and high taxes than the Social Democrats, drew on a religious tradition emphasizing government's obligation to help the humble, and they warmed to the idea that the government could assure jobs for all. Even West German chancellor Ludwig Erhard, a trained economist and an ardent proponent of free-market economics, found something to like in Schiller's thinking. Before taking over as head of government, Erhard had served as economy minister from 1949 to 1963 and received much of the credit for the German miracle. He worried openly about the growing influence of interest groups in German politics, and he came to see rational planning as a way to keep the special interests in their place.

After Erhard's government fell in 1966, the Christian Democratic, Christian Social, and Social Democratic parties formed a coalition in which Schiller became the economy minister. Schiller's rise to power marked the triumph of what West Germans referred to as "scientific government." No longer would politicians have to make decisions based on selective information supplied by lobbyists, industrialists, and self-interested labor leaders. Now, expert specialists, especially economists, could be called upon to assemble factual information and offer objective, authoritative advice about optimal policy choices—although, as political scientist Tim Schanetzky later observed, politicians tended to embrace the expert advice only when it meshed with their electoral calculus.[3]

In 1967, Schiller's magic square was enacted into law, assigning the government the legal obligation to foster growth, eliminate unemployment, avoid inflation, and keep the country's international accounts in balance, all within the framework of a free-market economy. Following Schiller's interpretation of the precepts of British economist John Maynard Keynes, federal and state governments were to plan their budgets with the goal of achieving "equilibrium of the entire economy."[4]

At the time, West Germany had just entered its first postwar recession. Schiller unveiled a program of spending and tax cuts to stimulate the economy. In his mind, he was following the advice Keynes had delivered in the 1930s, when he asserted that troubled economies might require a shot of stimulus in the form of higher government spending to escape the Depression. Keynes, alas, had said nothing about how quickly the economy could be expected to respond to such medicine. When hiring and business investment failed to respond quickly, the cabinet agreed to Schiller's proposal for a second stimulus program. Several months later, he offered a third stimulus plan, which was rejected. Luckily, the effects of the two earlier rounds of stimulus kicked in soon thereafter. The economy roared, cementing Schiller's reputation as an economic wizard.

At the ministry, Schiller created an elaborate planning exercise to build the magic square. Each year, teams of economists determined how the economy was to perform over the next five years. He and his "team of eggheads" worked late into the night, fueled by sandwiches and Johnnie Walker, evaluating how such factors as population growth, increased foreign trade, and environmental regulations might affect the economy's growth potential. After crunching the numbers, they specified the most desirable rate of economic growth. The first projection, released in the spring of 1967, called for economic growth averaging 4 percent through 1971, an average unemployment rate of 0.8 percent, along with 1 percent inflation and a 1 percent current account surplus. The economy ministry's experts calculated that reaching those targets would require faster growth in business investment, slower growth in consumer spending, and an increase in the government's budget deficit. The finance ministry, which had authority over taxes and the federal budget, was advised to adjust its policies accordingly.[5]

But in an economy that was overwhelmingly privately run, government alone could not reach perfection. Many of the crucial choices were up to private companies, self-employed workers, farmers, and labor unions. "The achievement of an optimal combination of these four macroeconomic goals under today's conditions can be attained only by the deliberate cooperation of all government bodies and nongovernmental groups," Schiller insisted.

The vehicle for that cooperation was a Schiller creation known as "Concerted Action." Four or five times a year, he summoned selected notables to a conference room in the ministry, where tables were arranged in a square. The ministers of agriculture, economy, finance, interior, and labor and a board member of the Bundesbank sat on one side, joined by their deputies. To their left were the heads of employer groups, such as the Federal Association of German Industry. To their right, facing the bosses, were an equal number of labor union presidents. The fourth side of the square was occupied by the chiefs of other organizations, such as the farmers' association and the association of savings banks. Over the course of an entire day, the dignitaries offered their views in turn. The star of the show, though, was Karl Schiller, who handed out packets of statistics, described the economic outlook, and announced how fast wages could rise without disfiguring the magic square. Of course, he would add, wage bargaining was a private matter between employers and unions, but he hoped the government's guidelines would contribute to "collective rationality."[6]

Schiller was not a man to suffer fools, even when those he considered fools were also union leaders, corporate executives, or cabinet members. Based on the work of his staff experts, he knew what was best for the world's third-largest economy, and he did not hesitate to instruct the captains of labor and industry. "An almost prophetic image, a very emotional speech," one high-ranking official scribbled on his copy of the text during a typical Schiller performance. The union leaders who joined in Concerted Action were willing to trust him, because they knew he would blunt the power of business; the business leaders across the table were reassured by the importance Schiller attached to profits and by his insistence that labor not demand more than the economy could afford.

His cabinet colleagues were less impressed. Infuriated that Schiller was announcing tax and budget changes that they had not approved, several ministers threatened to boycott Concerted Action. In 1967, Chancellor Kurt Georg Kiesinger, a Christian Democrat, was forced to intervene directly, insisting that Social Democrat Schiller seek approval from the coalition cabinet before telling labor and management what the government would do to keep the economy on track. Two years later, Kiesinger had to order the attendance of Finance Minister Franz Josef Strauss, head of the conservative Christian Social Party, who protested that he did not have time for a meeting likely to last six to ten hours.[7]

Schiller was unrepentant. Using every tool at his disposal—cutting taxes on investment to raise business profits; persuading unions to cap wage hikes; increasing outlays for research and infrastructure to boost the economy's growth potential; attacking price-fixing to stimulate competition—he was certain he could build a stable economy with jobs for all. His optimism was contagious. A prominent and highly visible figure, always impeccably dressed, Schiller frequently addressed business groups and appeared on television news shows. He developed an immense following that crossed party lines. His colorful personal life, which would eventually include four marriages, did his reputation no harm. In 1969, the Social Democrats outpolled every other party for the first time since the war in what was known as the "Schiller election." *Stern*, one of West Germany's most widely read magazines, selected him as man of the year.

To the Social Democrats, collective rationality was more than just a compromise among interest groups. It was the result of democracy in action. "We're not at the end of our democracy. We're just beginning," Willy Brandt, the first Social Democrat to lead West Germany's government, proclaimed on taking office in 1969. Democracy required constructing what the party termed the "empowered society," in which average citizens would have their say. This was to be neither the top-down democracy ostensibly practiced by the Christian Democrats nor an anarchic democracy of the sort favored by West Germany's vocal student movement, which had no respect for hierarchy and largely ignored its constantly changing collective leadership. In the empowered society, individuals would make their voices heard by actively participating in groups that were engaged in the planning process. By bringing those groups together, Concerted Action offered a vehicle for the masses to shape economic policy.[8]

The masses, in the Social Democrats' view, wanted higher federal spending for income security and education, never mind that education was the responsibility of the states. Schiller was not opposed, judging that higher spending in those areas might sustain growth without fueling inflation. Yet events stubbornly refused to conform to his expectations. The economy veered badly off course late in 1969, with the trade surplus growing far too large and prices rising much faster than the 1 percent inflation rate his experts' models had promised. Rounds of unauthorized strikes followed, as workers rejected the pay raises union leaders had agreed to through Concerted Action, which now lagged far behind inflation. Puzzled by the unanticipated jump in inflation, Schiller ordered his aides to redo their calculations, searching for errors in their forecasts. When they found none, he accused companies of driving up inflation by illegally conspiring to raise prices. If the economy was acting irrationally, something, or someone, must have led it astray.[9]

Only belatedly would he accept that the magic square was a technocrat's fantasy. Of the variables for which his ministry had set five-year targets in 1967, only the unemployment rate behaved as instructed. The other three corners of the square, economic growth, inflation, and the international balance of payments, stubbornly refused to conform to the government's dictates. The five-year targets set in 1968, 1969, and 1970 proved no more attainable. Even after Schiller took on the additional post of finance minister in 1971, becoming "superminister" with the power to turn his planners' recommendations into spending plans and tax laws, he could not produce the promised combination of fast economic growth, full employment, low inflation, and international balance. There were simply too many unpredictable events—such as America's decision to allow the fixed exchange-rate system to collapse—and too many political considerations for which Schiller had no patience. In 1972, angry that Chancellor Brandt denied him control over the exchange rate, he stormed out of the cabinet and left elected office for good.[10]

Later, after a brief flirtation with the Christian Democratic opposition, Schiller would pin the blame on his own Social Democratic Party. The party had mistakenly assumed that the postwar economic miracle, the *Wirtschaftswunder*, would go on forever, he said. But it was Schiller and his fellow economists, the dispassionate technocrats, who had created such expectations. When Schiller wrote that the German economy had reached "a sunny plateau of prosperity," that inflation and unemployment were permanently vanquished, people believed him, just as Americans had given credence to Walter Heller and the Japanese had bowed to the wisdom of their finance ministry. The long boom had created a near-universal faith in the capacity of governments to keep their economies on a steady course, with jobs for all.[11]

DESPITE HIS EXTRAORDINARY AMBITION, KARL SCHILLER ASSIGNED a relatively modest role to government when he drew his magic square. Unlike his counterparts in France and Italy, he did not want the government to own companies or appoint business executives; he thought that the state could best assure a healthy economy by adjusting taxes, spending, and interest rates while gently guiding the private sector. In Africa, Asia, and Latin America, meanwhile, technocrats and politicians were embracing far less subtle theories about government's proper role.

The "developing countries," as they were called in those days, undertook a forced march to modernity orchestrated by their governments.

Societies in which most people farmed small plots of rice, millet, or corn were transformed in short order into urbanized industrial economies. For a quarter-century, rapid industrialization, led by the state, seemed to be the solution to the poor world's problems. As in Germany, the answers came from the top, from government planners in collaboration with the heads of the organized interest groups considered important enough to matter: the national chamber of industry, the metalworkers' unions, the confederation of large farmers, the bankers' association. These officially recognized groups were deemed to represent all the businesses and workers in their sectors, whether or not those individuals agreed with their assigned leaders. The idea that preferences might be revealed more accurately by the discrete choices of millions of workers and businesspeople than by the wisdom of anointed representatives was not an idea that was common in the developing world, where representative democracy rarely functioned smoothly and autocrats were often in charge.[12]

The intellectual godfather of this statist movement was a man without a country named Raúl Prebisch. Largely unknown in the great financial centers, he became an economic superstar in the developing countries. In the 1950s and 1960s, he would come to have more influence on how governments pursued economic growth than any other economist in the world.

Prebisch, born in 1901 in the bustling provincial capital of Tucumán, in the northwest of Argentina, grew up in a prosperous nation that was seething with social unrest. Years earlier, his mother's father had been a senator. But by the time of Prebisch's youth, the glory was long gone; the family still had influential relatives in Buenos Aires, but neither money nor prestige. At seventeen, Prebisch enrolled in the economics department at the University of Buenos Aires. He briefly flirted with the Socialist Party but withdrew his membership application when his first article for the party newspaper brought condemnation for failing to conform to party policies. Prebisch would never again associate himself with a political party. Instead, he would always define himself as a technocrat, an expert on economic matters unencumbered by political affiliations.[13]

Argentina was then one of the world's wealthiest countries, but like every other country in Latin America, its economy was heavily based on the production of one or two commodities. In Argentina's case, those commodities were beef and wheat, almost all of which were exported to Great Britain. British investors controlled most of Argentina's railroads and many of its farms and slaughterhouses. Argentina's economy boomed when international wheat prices were high and suffered when they were low, just as Brazil's did with coffee and Chile's with copper. Armed with only an undergraduate degree, Prebisch began studying the relationship between his country, thinly populated and heavily reliant on agriculture, and the advanced economies of Europe and North America. Argentina, he discovered, was far more prone to boom-and-bust cycles than Europe because of its dependence on foreign borrowing and its undiversified, resource-driven economy. He concluded that Argentina's distinct conditions required unorthodox economic policies rather than the classical free-market ideas preached—although not necessarily practiced—in more industrialized countries.

A formal man who detested sports and had no hobbies, Prebisch threw himself into economics, working first for a powerful farm lobby and then government. After a rocky start to his career—twice, while on official business abroad, he was forced to pay his own way home when a change in government terminated his appointment—Prebisch's wide contacts led to a position as undersecretary of finance at the age of twenty-nine. In 1935, he advised the government on the creation of an independent central bank, an Argentine version of the Bank of England or the Federal Reserve. He was named its first general manager. As one of the youngest central bankers anywhere, he earned an international reputation for righting Argentina's economy. After World War II broke out in Europe, Prebisch was intimately involved in the delicate negotiations that reoriented Argentina away from Great Britain and toward the United States.

But his star fell as dramatically as it had risen. Argentina industrialized rapidly in the 1930s, thanks largely to a sharp increase in import tariffs that protected domestic industries at the expense of farmers and ranchers. The growing number of urban workers and factory owners had interests very different from those of the wheat growers and sugar barons who had traditionally dominated political life, and the conflict grew explosive. Seeing himself as an apolitical specialist in economic policy, Prebisch failed to understand that his diplomatic activities associated him with a government widely accused of electoral fraud and corruption. In 1943, following a coup d'état, the central bank's independence from the government proved illusory. Prebisch, accused of being too close to the United States and too hostile to Germany, was driven from office.[14]

With no personal wealth and no income, the famed central banker was forced to sell his Packard, rent out his house, and move into a small cottage. A few consulting jobs followed, but the United States and Brazil rejected his appointment to an important post at the International Monetary Fund, the Washington-based organization created to help manage exchange rates. The military government in Buenos Aires made it clear that he was not welcome at home, while also doing its best to keep him from finding work abroad. His career seemed to be over.

With few other options, Prebisch signed on as a consultant to the Economic Commission for Latin America, or ECLA, in March 1949. Calling ECLA an obscure organization would have been generous. Based in Santiago, Chile, about as far from the centers of world power as it was possible to be, ECLA was a newly minted agency of the United Nations with a tiny budget and no particular responsibilities. Prebisch's first assignment was to prepare an economic survey of Latin America for an upcoming meeting. The report, kept confidential until Prebisch presented it in Havana, Cuba, in May 1949, would shake the world.

The speech was an attack on the doctrine of free trade—specifically, on the venerable claim that each country would be best off if it produced those goods it turned out most efficiently and traded them for its other needs. This might be true for the large industrial countries, Prebisch said. But there were many other countries, those "on the periphery of the world economy," that had failed to prosper by engaging in international trade. Exporting their abundant raw materials and importing manufactured goods had not made the countries on the periphery wealthy, Prebisch argued, because the prices of their exports were in a long-run decline relative to the prices of the manufactured goods they bought abroad. They were on a treadmill, needing to produce more and more copper or bananas to buy the same amount of imported machinery and medicine.

The peripheral countries' inferior position in trade, Prebisch contended, kept them from amassing the profits necessary to finance investments that could make their workers more productive. Unequal trade was thus the fundamental cause of Latin America's poverty. "The enormous benefits that derive from increased productivity have not reached the periphery in a measure comparable to that obtained by the peoples of the great industrial countries," he said. Improving productivity, he insisted, required the peripheral countries to build strong manufacturing sectors. "Industrialization is not an end in itself, but the principal means at the disposal of these countries of obtaining a share of the benefits of technical progress and of progressively raising the living standards of the masses," he proclaimed.[15]

Prebisch was neither a Marxist nor an isolationist. In contrast to the populists who took power in many developing countries after World War II, he did not consider foreign capital exploitative; he thought poor countries needed more of it, not less. He opposed government ownership of farms and factories, and he understood how international trade brings mutual benefits and improves economic efficiency. In some ways, his ideas about the state's role in the economy echoed Karl Schiller's. But where Schiller considered it the private sector's job to assemble capital and choose which industries deserved investment, Prebisch saw a far more active role for government planning. He argued that governments might have to give priority to imports of capital goods such as factory equipment, even if that meant reducing imports of nonessential goods. Those nonessential goods, such as consumer products, could be made locally in factories protected from foreign competition by high tariffs. And they could be exported to the wealthy countries he referred to as the "center," allowing countries on the periphery to raise their people out of poverty and reduce their exposure to swings in commodity prices.

THE SPEECH IN HAVANA TURNED THE AUSTERE ECONOMIST INTO a celebrity. Even Washington agreed that Prebisch should be ECLA's permanent head. He mounted the bully pulpit, traveling across Latin America to preach the importance of industrialization. "The forced march of the first countries in the Industrial Revolution has created an economic firmament with a sun composed of the developed economies at the center, around which the peripheral countries rotate in their disorganized orbits," he wrote. To escape those orbits, he advised, the peripheral countries should undertake careful planning to determine which domestic manufacturing industries were most promising, and should then establish import restrictions to assure investors, including foreign companies, that they would be able to sell locally made products at a profit without being undercut by cheaper imported versions. This policy of deliberately replacing certain imports with goods made domestically came to be called "import substitution."[16]

Although Prebisch's work focused on Latin America, his ideas found a receptive audience around the world. Decolonization was in full swing: countries from the Philippines to Libya were shedding their colonial masters in the decade after World War II, and revolts were underway in dozens of British, French, Belgian, Spanish, and Portuguese possessions. By and large, the departing colonial powers assumed that their newly independent outposts would remain economically subservient, supplying the mother country with raw materials and buying its manufactured goods. Prebisch offered an alternative vision in which the ex-colonies could become industrial powers. Countries from India to Brazil set up planning ministries to decide which industries they should develop and how those industries should be fostered, overseeing the creation of textile industries, steel mills, and that most prestigious investment of all, automotive assembly plants.

Amid the intensifying Cold War, that alternative vision had implications outside the economic sphere as well. Countries in Asia, Africa, and Latin America were increasingly pressed to choose sides, either accepting foreign aid, military assistance, and economic advice from the Soviet Union or throwing in their lot with the United States and its allies. Many of them chafed under the pressure to enlist in the struggle between communism and the "free world," a struggle they considered remote from their own needs. Prebisch's contention that developing countries were fundamentally different from the far wealthier countries of the "center," that they should follow a third way, naturally led to the idea that they should present a common front.

This idea came to fruition in April 1955, when the leaders of twenty-nine African and Asian countries convened in Bandung, Indonesia, for the African-Asian conference. With swarms of reporters and photographers watching, Chinese premier Zhou Enlai, Indian prime minister Jawaharlal Nehru, Indonesian president Sukarno, Egyptian prime minister Gamal Abdel Nasser, and dozens of other notables condemned colonialism and emphasized their distance from the United States, which sent no official observers, as well as from the Soviet Union. In addition to calling for greater economic assistance from the wealthy countries, the delegates at Bandung set forth some economic principles Prebisch himself could have written. Their declaration urged Asian and African countries to process their raw materials before exporting them. It emphasized that "in view of their prevailing economic conditions," some countries would have reason to regulate the flow of trade, and proposed "collective action . . . for stabilizing the international prices of and demand for primary commodities." This program, the developing world's leaders imagined, might alter the global balance of economic power.[17]

The assertion of a commonality among developing countries redrew the map of the world. One new model of the globe had a "core," encompassing the Soviet Union and its client states as well as Western Europe, North America, Australia, South Africa, and Japan, and a "periphery" that included almost everyone else. Another version replaced the Cold War division of East and West with the economic division between a wealthy, "developed" North and an "underdeveloped" South, or a "Third World" whose needs differed from those of both the "capitalist world" and the "socialist economies." A more political version might show the "Communist Bloc" and the "Free World," along with a large number of countries that considered themselves "nonaligned." Although their economic conditions varied widely, the countries and colonies that formed the poorer three-quarters of the world almost uniformly blamed their economic backwardness on their unequal relationship with the core. For the next three decades and more, the lens of "dependency theory" would shape the way these countries were seen by others, and the way they viewed themselves.[18]

The basic policies advanced by dependency theorists, government intervention to steady prices of raw materials and to foster manufacturing, were strongly opposed by the high-income countries, where businesses wanted access to cheap raw materials and open markets abroad. But while the high-income countries preached freer trade, there was more than a bit of hypocrisy involved. Most of them protected their own manufacturers behind high tariffs and low import quotas. Many also imposed steep tariffs on sugar, coffee, and other tropical products to help their farmers, to favor their remaining colonies over other sources of imports, or simply to raise revenue. The manufactured goods most likely to come from low-income countries, such as clothing and processed foods, often faced especially high trade barriers.

Prebisch's work laid the foundation for a reassessment of the conventional economic wisdom by the high-income countries. The General Agreement on Tariffs and Trade, the international organization charged with making trade freer, asked four of the world's best-known economists to look into Prebisch's ideas. "We think that there is some substance in the feeling of disquiet among primary producing countries that the present rules and conventions about commercial policies are relatively unfavourable to them," the scholars concluded in 1958. In an astonishing departure from past norms, the economists admitted that countries that specialized in agriculture or mining might be better off trying to stabilize the prices of export commodities rather than passively enduring the brutal volatility of the international market.[19]

The mechanics of stabilizing commodity prices seem tantalizingly simple. According to the Old Testament, Joseph accomplished it in ancient Egypt by setting grain aside through seven years of plenty and selling it during seven years of famine. The 1960s version was called a buffer stock. A government that wanted to create one had to set a target price first. When the world market price of the commodity fell below the target, the government would buy and store the commodity, removing supply from the market and thus driving up the price. When the world price went above the target, those stored commodities would be sold, pushing the market price back down. The promise was that if a country's economy depended heavily on exporting one or two commodities, as was the case with Chile's copper and Ghana's cocoa, a steadier price might mean smoother economic growth and fewer crises caused by abrupt drops in the value of exports.[20]

This vision of stability was so alluring that seventy-seven countries—a group inevitably known as the G-77—asked the United Nations to help bring it about. Over European and American opposition, they got their wish. In 1964, the United Nations Conference on Trade and Development, or UNCTAD, was created to look after the international economic concerns of developing countries. Raúl Prebisch, arguably the developing world's most prominent economist, was named to lead the new agency.

In his address to UNCTAD's first international meeting, Prebisch laid out the case for what would later be called the New International Economic Order. The economies of the developing countries, he said, still depended primarily on exporting commodities, but global demand for commodities was growing too slowly to keep workers employed. Further, the buying power of those exports was falling relative to the prices of machinery and other vital imports, meaning that developing countries could not afford the equipment needed to operate new factories and provide jobs. Cooperation to stabilize commodity prices, import substitution to bolster domestic production, and greater financial assistance from foreign countries were essential to help developing countries amass the resources they needed to grow.[21]

Prebisch's vision proved enormously influential. Import substitution became all the vogue: dozens of countries used import licenses, cash subsidies, tax breaks, grants of monopoly, and a basketful of other measures to put themselves on the path to industrialization. Countries exporting tin, coffee, sugar, oil, and other commodities tried forming cartels to control supplies, and in some cases they succeeded in pushing up prices. Governments started banks, ship lines, and airlines to provide highly paid jobs at home and plant their country's flag abroad. A new order seemed to be in the making.[22]

IN MANY CORNERS OF THE DEVELOPING WORLD, THE THIRD quarter of the twentieth century was a truly terrible time. Tens of millions in China died in famines between 1959 and 1961, and many millions more saw their lives destroyed in the Cultural Revolution between 1966 and 1971. War devastated the Korean Peninsula (1950–1953), Vietnam (1946–1975), southeastern Nigeria (1967–1970), Algeria (1954–1961), and many other places. In East Pakistan, now Bangladesh, a cyclone that may have killed half a million people (1970) was followed by a murderous civil war (1971). Independence struggles culminated in rebellions with uncountable death tolls in places like Kenya (1952–1960), Congo (1960–1964), and Mozambique (1964–1974), and repressive governments from Guatemala to South Africa to Iran killed opponents, peasant and trade union leaders, and mere bystanders with impunity. Even where war and natural disaster were absent, hundreds of millions of families lived on the edge of economic catastrophe, barely earning enough to stay alive and far too little to educate their children or care for their health. There is no sugarcoating the brutality that, for many people, was part of everyday life.

Yet hardship was only part of the story of that quarter-century. During the same period many developing countries turned in impressive records of economic growth, as governments tried to wean their countries from dependence on crops or minerals and push them down the road toward industrialization. Newly independent Kenya grew at an annualized rate of more than 6 percent between 1960 and 1975, Pakistan and Bolivia almost as much. Collectively, the developing countries outperformed North America and Europe by a considerable margin. Even with rapid population growth, income per capita in many poor countries rose by more than half over those fifteen years. In the fifty-eight countries the World Bank designated as middle-income countries, manufactured goods accounted for a scant 5 percent of exports in 1960. In just over a decade, that share tripled. The urban slums mushrooming around every major city were the best indicator of success; for the landless peasants who fled penury in the countryside to take jobs in new factories, city life, with all its filth, crime, and tension, was immeasurably better than village life.[23]

On the surface, Prebisch's formula seemed to work. But over time, in important ways, it began to go terribly wrong. Prebisch had envisioned ministries of wise technocrats administering beneficent policies and promoting competition within the economy even as they protected it against imports. Almost everywhere, the reality was very different. Planning ministries assumed life-or-death power over the private sector, deciding what the country should import and what it should export, where its new factories should be located and what they should produce, and, critically, which individuals would receive coveted permits. The endless need for permits—"the license raj," as Indians called it—stifled competition as leaders' family members and key supporters won the right to run lucrative monopolies, no matter what the cost to poor consumers. Foreign investment was deemed suspicious and kept under tight control, offering corrupt officials yet more opportunity to extract under-the-table payments and favors. And whereas Prebisch had envisioned import substitution as a short-term policy, to be phased out as industries in developing countries began to take root, investors and industrial workers inevitably took a different view, demanding that the import barriers remain in place, protecting their income and wealth at the expense of everyone else.[24]

As it turned out, the impressive economic growth in developing countries after 1960 had less to do with dynamic new industries than with the old standby, raw materials. After languishing in the wake of World War II, the price of foodstuffs exported by developing countries rose 346 percent between 1965 and 1974. UNCTAD's minerals price index doubled within a decade, and palm oil, worth $252 per ton in 1967, reached $1,041 seven years later. Buoyed by these price increases, even the most corrupt, mismanaged countries saw increases in life expectancies, higher school attendance, and the proliferation of such luxuries as flashlights and transistor radios. But many other things did not change. The economies of many countries were dominated by monopolies, often owned by the state, whose high prices were a tax on every family and private business. The state's heavy hand made it hard to start a company, install a telephone, or, in many places, legally build a house. Instead of providing the foundation for steadier, more diversified economic growth, the commodity boom offered the irresistible temptation to get rich quick.[25]

And then the boom was over. As the economies of the high-income countries faltered after 1973, global demand for raw materials fell back. Prices dropped, revealing the developing countries for what they were: places with low productivity and very high obstacles to starting businesses and promoting new ideas. The very policies that the planners had introduced to drive their economies to new heights, policies that favored certain sectors and certain well-connected individuals, stood in the way of economic growth. As in Karl Schiller's Germany, so, too, in Mexico and Brazil and Indonesia: the idea that government planning could assure prosperity and rising living standards for all proved to be a cruel hoax.

CHAPTER 3

Chaos

Richard Nixon wasn't much for economics. Politics aside, the interests of the thirty-seventh president of the United States ran more to realpolitik: war and peace, nuclear deterrence, and the strategic balance of power. The economic realm, by contrast, offered too few opportunities for political advantage and too many problems a president could not fix. Inflation worries, budget deficits, and the concerns of US allies about trade and exchange rates meant that Nixon could not avoid dealing with economic policy entirely, but such issues truly engaged him only when they involved political considerations. Unstable exchange rates, important as they were becoming to many countries, were not a matter he deemed worthy of presidential time and attention. Nixon left the details of economic policy to the experts, and in his eyes, the leading economic expert was Arthur Burns.

Burns, sixty-four years old at the time of Nixon's inauguration in 1969, was among the most renowned economists in America. Born into a Jewish family that had fled the Austro-Hungarian Empire at the start of the First World War, Burns grew up in Bayonne, New Jersey, where his father earned a living painting houses. The precocious young man won a scholarship to

Columbia University in New York, where he discovered economics. When he returned to Columbia for doctoral study, Burns became the protégé of Wesley Mitchell, a prominent professor who had pioneered the study of business cycles—the economy's irregular ups and downs. In the late 1930s Burns himself became a Columbia professor and later succeeded Mitchell as head of the National Bureau of Economic Research, the foremost institution for the study of the US economy. In 1953, he signed on to head the Council of Economic Advisers under President Dwight Eisenhower.

As Eisenhower's vice president, Nixon saw up close Burns's skill as a teacher and his ability to deliver succinct, practical advice. When Nixon ran for president in 1968, he relied on Burns to oversee the teams that fleshed out his policy proposals. Upon his inauguration, Nixon brought Burns into the White House as counselor to the president with cabinet rank. The fact that his favorite economist was a Democrat bothered the Republican president not at all.[1]

The new counselor's academic expertise was in US economic policy—inflation, unemployment, and efforts to steady growth by smoothing the business cycle. But Nixon had other economists for that. Burns was instead given charge of a ragbag of domestic issues, from antipoverty programs to tax reform to oil import quotas. His main role, though, was professorial. With his white hair neatly parted in the middle, his rimless glasses, and his ever-present pipe, he became a familiar figure on the evening news. In his high-pitched voice, he spoke slowly, in short, clipped phrases, patiently explaining economic principles and defending Nixon's program from critics right and left. Burns dreamed of becoming secretary of the Treasury, but in October 1969 he was offered a job that would prove far more consequential. Nixon named Burns chairman of the Federal Reserve Board of Governors.

Burns was the first professional economist ever to take the helm of the central bank. His expertise in business cycles was sorely needed. In the mid-1960s, Nixon's predecessor, Lyndon Johnson, had offered America "guns and butter," building up military forces in Vietnam without raising taxes or curtailing social programs. The Fed had loyally supported Johnson's policies by making sure that short-term interest rates stayed low so that the government could borrow cheaply to fund the war. In the short term, this mix of policies had ensured jobs for almost everyone and rapidly rising wages. But it had also pushed up the demand for goods and workers faster than the economy could sustain, driving up consumer prices and eating away at the value of workers' pay and retirees' pensions.

By the time Burns moved into the Fed's marble edifice a few blocks from the White House, in January 1970, the inflation rate was poised to break 6 percent, the highest level in two decades. In late 1969, as Nixon began to scale back the US role in Vietnam, factory production began to fall. But even as layoffs became a front-page story, wages continued to rise. The unhappy combination of higher unemployment and higher inflation threatened Nixon's hopes of re-election in 1972. The president expected his new Fed chairman to solve the problem. He appeared to have the right man: no economist in the world had thought more carefully about how governments should deal with economic downturns than Arthur Burns.

Yet Burns, his immense prestige notwithstanding, was not the ideal general to fight the economic battles of the 1970s. He did not see himself as the independent leader of the most critical US economic institution, an institution deliberately designed to be sheltered from political pressure. He was Nixon's man, with a responsibility to meet the president's political needs. "I'm counting on you, Arthur, to keep us out of a recession," Nixon told him. Burns valued his proximity to the president, and to maintain it he was more than willing to bend with the political winds. Unfailingly calm and polite in public, he could be dramatic and even temperamental when his fellow Fed governors dared challenge his wishes. He used his knowledge of the administration's tax and spending plans to argue for one or another policy around the massive mahogany table in the Fed's two-story Board Room.[2]

THE FED, IN THOSE DAYS, WAS AN IMPORTANT INSTITUTION, BUT it was not the Delphic temple it later became. Economic thinkers had yet to acknowledge monetary policy—the Fed's basic instrument for moving the economy—as central to the core economic goal of keeping inflation in check. Monetary policy mainly involves trying to move the price of short-term loans to business borrowers and consumers. If the Fed "tightened" policy, it was trying to raise the cost of loans: fewer buildings would be built and fewer cars purchased, so there would be less buoyant demand for materials and labor, making it harder for businesses to raise prices and for workers to demand higher wages. Sooner or later, tighter money would cause inflation to subside—but in the short term, unemployment was all but certain to rise. If, on the other hand, the Fed was "easing" policy, loans would become cheaper: business activity would pick up, and unemployed workers would be recalled, but the lessened slack would make it easier for businesses to push through price increases and workers to win higher pay.

The Fed had several valves it might twist to tighten or ease the flow of money into the economy, and how it should do its day-to-day work was a matter of intense dispute. One school of thought, generally associated with political liberals, held that the Fed should focus on what mattered most to average Americans, jobs; keeping the unemployment rate around 4 percent should be the Fed's main goal, regardless of inflation. An opposing school, populated mainly by political conservatives, asserted that the Fed was unable to stimulate investment or create jobs except in the very short run; therefore, the sole purpose of monetary policy should be to stabilize prices, regardless of the unemployment rate. Most politicians shied away from those extreme positions. Like Nixon, they wanted the Fed to deliver both low inflation and low unemployment, and they expected it to do so without causing their constituents pain.

Burns was squarely in the economic mainstream. Like other leading economists of his day, he attributed inflation to a number of factors not within the central bank's control, from unions' wage demands (the Labor Department) to steel companies' price hikes (the Commerce Department) to government deficits (the Office of Management and Budget) to exchange rates (the Treasury Department). Burns did not think the Fed's monetary policy contributed to rising prices, and he told Americans worried about inflation to look elsewhere for help. "It would be unwise to depend on the Federal Reserve System as our sole or principal guardian of the stability of the dollar," he had said in 1957, and as Fed chairman he continued to emphasize the powerlessness of the institution he led. The minutes of the Fed's secret policy meetings, kept confidential for decades, confirm that Burns had real doubts that the central bank could stanch inflation if it tried.[3]

So how could inflation be stopped? Burns's answer was that the government needed to influence "public psychology." This was, to say the least, an unorthodox idea for a central banker; Burns's counterparts at the Bank of England and the German Bundesbank assuredly did not see their role as national psychologist-in-chief. But in Burns's conception, inflation-fighting required the president, his cabinet, and the independent central bank to tell unions to limit their wage demands, to weigh in against price increases, and to urge businesses to invest when the economy needed a boost rather than when it was overheating. In many ways, his views were strikingly similar to those of West German economy minister Karl Schiller, especially in his belief that the government's words should guide the actions of millions of private decision-makers in the interest of economic stability. Burns's conviction that the government should frequently adjust spending plans, taxes, and interest rates to mold public psychology fit neatly with Nixon's view of monetary policy as a tool that could be used to slow or speed up the economy at will.[4]

So it was that one of the most prominent economic thinkers of his day came to preside over an economic disaster. Early in 1970, Burns's Fed tightened policy to fight inflation; a few months later, it reversed course, aggressively easing in hopes of lowering the unemployment rate. In May 1970, warning that using monetary policy alone to choke off inflation would cause "a very serious business recession," he urged Nixon to create a board to review wage and price increases, but not to regulate them. Watching this bizarre economic comedy, it was easy to conclude that Washington was unwilling to pay the political cost of subduing inflation. After dipping briefly in the first half of 1971, the US inflation rate began to climb again.

BURNS'S INABILITY TO BRING INFLATION UNDER CONTROL WAS more than a domestic problem. The United States was by far the world's largest economy, and the US dollar was the linchpin of international trade and investment. The inflation that undermined the value of the dollar also upended a quarter-century of international economic calm.

That calm had arisen from the ashes of World War II. In July 1944, with Allied armies squeezing Germany and pressing north across the Pacific toward Japan, delegates from forty-four countries met at Bretton Woods, New Hampshire, to lay plans for the postwar economy. Rules for the new international financial system were the main point of discussion. The delegates agreed that other countries would keep their exchange rates steady against the US dollar. If currency traders pushed a currency's exchange rate away from the official rate, the government concerned was obligated to bring the market rate back into line. It could do that by controlling the movement of money into and out of the country; by having its central bank manipulate interest rates to change investors' desire to own the currency; or by buying or selling enough of the currency to move the market rate. In extreme cases, a government could ask permission of a new organization, the International Monetary Fund, to change its exchange rate. The one thing countries were meant not to do, except in dire circumstances, was restrict imports to prop up their currencies. The goal was to encourage international trade, not block it, as had occurred during the Great Depression.[5]

The Bretton Woods agreement, which stabilized exchange rates and lowered trade barriers, helped make the Golden Age possible. The great virtue of this system was that it handcuffed politicians. If a cabinet minister demanded lower interest rates to give the economy a temporary boost ahead of an election, the head of the central bank could aver that this might destabilize the currency and anger other countries. Similarly, if a legislator called for a lower exchange rate to help a company that wanted to increase its exports, the government could reject that request out of hand. But the system had some critical flaws. If a country had high inflation, its central bank could not easily raise interest rates to address the problem, because higher interest rates would likely attract money from abroad and drive up the local currency against the dollar. If an economy was dead in the water, the central bank could not simply lower interest rates to revive it because investors would dump the currency and shift their money back into dollars, causing the exchange rate against the dollar to fall. And everything depended on the United States, which agreed to buy other countries' surplus dollars with gold at the rate of $35 per ounce—an arrangement that would work only as long as the United States owned a large stockpile of gold and other countries did not hoard dollars that could be exchanged for US gold at any time.[6]

By 1968, other countries held so many US dollars that the Americans' ability to buy them with gold was no longer certain. As the financial system began to quake, the Bretton Woods rules made the situation worse. In 1969, as the Fed pushed up US interest rates to deal with rising inflation, the rules forced other countries to raise their own interest rates to keep exchange rates stable—even if their inflation rates were under control, as was the case in West Germany. And in 1970, when Arthur Burns began to lower US interest rates, other countries had to go along in order to hold their exchange rates steady against the dollar—even if lower interest rates were the last thing their overheated economies needed, as was the case in Japan. The United States' cheap money policy set inflation roaring around the world.

To quench the fire, governments turned to an anti-inflation policy so magical that it was expected neither to anger voters nor to move exchange rates: they simply ordered prices to stop rising. Norway imposed price freezes three times in three years. Austria slapped fines on businesses that raised prices too high. Belgium ordered companies to notify the government of price increases. Spain empowered cities to decide how much food should cost in local shops. Great Britain froze prices, wages, rents, and dividends. Canada created a national commission to approve wage and price increases. Even the United States joined in. Central bankers normally frown on the idea that government bureaucrats can determine the appropriate price for a bag of cement or a cup of coffee. But on August 15, 1971, with Burns's blessing, Nixon went on national television to announce a ninety-day freeze on wages and prices. The president also unexpectedly declared that foreign governments could no longer exchange their dollars for gold—an announcement that would be known as the Nixon Shock.[7]

Price controls made great theater, and the public invariably cheered. In the United States, even the *New York Times,* Nixon's arch-critic, applauded the president's "boldness" in applying them. In the short term, controls seemed to stop inflation in its tracks. But controls did not address the problems caused by central banks pumping out money, and they blocked the sorts of adjustments that routinely occur when a poor corn harvest drives up the cost of raising cattle or when retailers run low on air conditioners during a heat wave. The longer controls stayed in place, the more the resentment mounted, as voters asked why some workers were granted larger pay hikes than others and why some price increases won government approval while others were denied. Price pressure mounted too, threatening to explode the moment controls were lifted.

Meanwhile, the Americans' decision to stop buying dollars with gold did nothing to stabilize the volatile exchange rates that were upsetting the financial markets and making it impossible for businesses to plan ahead. The obvious alternative to the crisis-prone Bretton Woods system was to leave it up to the market to decide how many marks or francs it would take to buy a dollar. Many economists of a free-market bent loved this idea. As millions of individuals and companies made judgments about the relative value of dollars and deutsche marks, they promised, exchange rates would naturally move toward an equilibrium much steadier than what agreements among governments could attain. Burns, like most central bankers, was strongly opposed to allowing currencies to float to whatever values the market might take them; in his opinion, central bank guidance about the appropriate level of exchange rates was essential to keep the world economy on an even keel. But there was no getting around the fact that fixed exchange rates centered on the US dollar could survive only if countries other than the United States were willing to commit their monetary policies solely to that goal, regardless of the hardship that might cause their citizens.

There were endless summit meetings to try to patch up the system. A conference at the Smithsonian Institution in late 1971 led to a curious compromise under which the dollar was devalued against all other major currencies, which would henceforth be allowed to move a bit more freely in the currency markets. The Smithsonian agreement, Nixon declared, was "the most significant monetary agreement in world history."

Like the Bretton Woods agreement before it, the Smithsonian agreement left the US dollar at the center of the world monetary system. The United States could run its economy as it wished; other countries were supposed to adapt to US policies to hold their currencies within the allowable range. But the ink was barely dry before the new pact came under attack from currency traders smelling blood.

By late 1971, Burns, under pressure from Nixon, was calling for lower interest rates to give the US economy a boost ahead of the 1972 election. His Fed colleagues, most of them appointed by Nixon's Democratic Party predecessors, overwhelmingly agreed that rates should be lowered to bring unemployment down, and influential members of Congress urged the same. Almost all of them accepted the widespread belief that there was a trade-off between unemployment and inflation, and they were willing to accept higher inflation in order to put people back to work. Countries whose inflation rates were already higher than America's were reluctant to go along; Burns's West German counterpart, Bundesbank president Karl Klasen, refused to cut interest rates despite appeals from Schiller, who resigned as finance and economy minister after the cabinet refused to endorse his stance. Amid the disarray, currency traders had a field day, dumping dollars and buying marks. As exchange rates blew past the agreed limits, secret tape recorders in the Oval Office captured Nixon's eagerness to wash his hands of the entire matter; when his chief of staff, H. R. Haldeman, told him of the currency crisis shaking Italy, the president fired back: "I don't give a shit about the lira."[8]

Arthur Burns's easy money reverberated around the world, turbocharging economic growth. In several countries, short-term interest rates fell so low that after figuring in inflation, businesses could repay loans for less than the cost of borrowing—a strong incentive to erect buildings, buy equipment, and hire more workers, if any were to be found. Construction boomed, and auto sales set records. In 1972, after taking inflation into account, the average citizen's buying power rose more than 3 percent in France and Germany, more than 4 percent in the United States and

Canada, and about 7 percent in countries as far-flung as Japan, Finland, and Spain. Once again, well-timed action by governments and central banks seemed to have delivered prosperity. Nixon, for one, considered Burns's first years at the Fed a stunning success. With unemployment falling and a weak Democratic challenger, the president cruised to re-election in November 1972, winning forty-nine of the fifty states.[9]

But the bill would soon come due. A change in monetary policy, as economists were fond of pointing out, was not a switch central bankers could throw to produce an immediate economic result. Its effects spread gradually, with an unpredictable lag. The easier monetary policies of late 1971 and early 1972 took several months to be felt in prices and wages. By the time of Nixon's re-election, inflation was rising sharply in every major economy in the world.

CHAPTER 4

Crisis of Faith

While resurgent inflation and exchange-rate chaos roiled the financial markets, the chattering classes had a different preoccupation. Their concern was not that the world was about to fall into an economic abyss. Rather, they worried that times were simply too good, that the successful drive to create an unimagined level of wealth was causing economic and environmental collapse. The new environmentalism would have profound implications for the way people thought about economic growth in the early 1970s. For its adherents, a group decidedly more affluent and economically secure than the population at large, rising incomes and greater material well-being were problems to confront, not accomplishments to praise.

In March 1972, a little-known New York publisher issued a frightening book called *The Limits to Growth*. Written by academics from the prestigious Massachusetts Institute of Technology and carrying the imprimatur of an obscure organization called the Club of Rome, the book employed computer modeling to analyze "the predicament of mankind." The language was clear and ominous, expressing a confidence to match that of any well-schooled economic planner: "If the present growth trends in world population, industrialization, pollution, food production, and resource depletion continue unchanged, the limits to growth on this planet will be reached sometime within the next one hundred years. The most probable result will be a rather sudden and uncontrollable decline in both population and industrial capacity."[1]

The Limits to Growth was a worldwide sensation. Translated into thirty-seven languages, it eventually sold more than twelve million copies. Page after page warned that the world would soon grind to a halt because of human excess, the result of humanity's endless quest for economic growth. "[T]he great majority of the currently important nonrenewable resources will be extremely costly 100 years from now," the study asserted; even assuming huge new discoveries of copper, soaring demand would exhaust the world's supply in forty-eight years. Population growth would lead to a "desperate land shortage." The rate at which mankind was emitting virtually every pollutant "appears to be increasing exponentially." And while the authors were careful to qualify their forecasts with caveats, their tone was decidedly apocalyptic: "When there is plenty of unused arable land, there can be more people and also more food per person. When all the land is already used, the trade-off between more people or more food per person becomes a choice between absolutes."

Warnings about a world unable to feed its population were nothing new; the English cleric Thomas Malthus had predicted much the same in 1798. But Malthus had fallen out of favor, largely because, nearly two centuries on, the anticipated catastrophe had not happened. *The Limits to Growth* went beyond Malthus in predicting a world short of oil to heat its homes, metals for its factories, and even clean water to drink. Its real innovation, however, was its scientific gloss. With forty-eight charts and six tables, and discussions of computer runs and positive feedback loops, the study seemed to have a quantitative rigor Malthus lacked. Just as economists like Walter Heller and Karl Schiller had learned to use computers to forecast the economic future, the scientists were wielding computers as a tool to foretell the world's destiny.

The Limits to Growth was deliberately provocative, and the critics were brutal in denouncing its flaws. "Never mind that hardly a reputable economist can be found who thinks these projections amount to more than a fascinating exercise in model-making," *Science* thundered. William Nordhaus, later to be known as one of the world's leading environmental economists, pointed out that the model underlying the book's projections contained forty-three variables, of which "Not a single relationship or variable is drawn from actual data or empirical studies." An influential French government council asserted, "This analysis takes no account of . . . the reserves of human ingenuity." A group of scientists at the University of Sussex, in England, wryly pointed out that had *The Limits to Growth* been written a century earlier, its authors would not have worried about impending oil scarcity, as oil was hardly used.[2]

Whatever its shortcomings, *The Limits to Growth* presented a challenge to the politicians and central bankers who were overwhelmingly obsessed with jobs, inflation, and consumer spending. The remarkable growth of the postwar world was not just unsustainable; it was unconscionable. The world had grown wealthy by plundering its own resources. Now there was a balance to settle. "The earth is finite," the authors intoned, and so long as the world's population kept expanding, each person would have to learn to live with less. Attempts to maintain the prosperity to which millions had grown accustomed were doomed to failure. A brutal adjustment to lower living standards could not be avoided: "The basic behavior mode of the world system is exponential growth of population and capital, followed by collapse." That collapse, the authors said, might well occur soon.

THE LIMITS TO GROWTH WAS NO ISOLATED EVENT. IT APPEARED AS a new cause, environmentalism, was sweeping the world.

In the desperate early years of postwar reconstruction, environmental concern had been an unaffordable luxury. Providing shelter and food for hundreds of millions of people had been the priorities, and plumes of smoke from rebuilt power plants symbolized success. As prosperity returned and pollution worsened, catastrophes like the 1948 air inversion in Donora, Pennsylvania, and London's Great Smog of 1952 forced attention to the health risks of pollution. Great Britain tried to move coal-burning power plants away from big cities starting in 1956, and in 1961 California required new cars to come with devices to reduce smog. But in 1962, when Rachel Carson's best seller *Silent Spring* linked insecticides with harm to both birds and humans, public awareness of environmental issues was still very low.[3]

So was scientific understanding of how a multitude of human activities, from draining coastal wetlands to burning coal in power plants, could harm plants, animals, and human beings. Hundreds of new plastics and chemicals were invented in the two decades after the war. Government agencies lacked the money to investigate their safety, and the companies that produced them had no interest in independent scientists doing so, reasoning that "so long as people die from unknown causes, pollution will be blamed." Authorities still relied widely on the Ringelmann Scale, invented in 1888, to measure air pollution: an inspector would compare the darkness of a smokestack's emissions with the shades of gray on a printed card, and pollutants that did not darken the sky were disregarded. Pollution control, in many places, meant raising smokestacks so the winds could carry pollutants further away and extending pipes so sewage would be dispersed farther out to sea.[4]

The increasing sense of urgency about the environment in the early 1970s was directly related to another emerging concern: overpopulation. Words like "explosion" were used to describe postwar population growth, and they weren't completely wrong. The world added more than a billion people between 1950 and 1970, increasing the total population nearly by half. Demographic growth was fastest in the poorest countries of Africa, Asia, and Latin America, some of which were no better off in 1970 than they had been two decades earlier. It seemed obvious that rapid population growth was causing dire poverty and starvation in the countries broadly known as "the South." The more modern insight that the causal chain might run the other way—that is, that poor people in countries lacking social-welfare systems needed offspring to support them in old age—had not yet sunk in.

Worse was thought to lie ahead. Demographers projected another two billion people by the end of the century, with unavoidable catastrophic consequences. "The battle to feed all of humanity is over," Stanford University biologist Paul Ehrlich proclaimed in his 1968 book *The Population Bomb*. "In the 1970s hundreds of millions of people will starve to death in spite of any crash programs embarked upon now."[5]

Ehrlich's ideas became the new conventional wisdom. Governments and international institutions, such as the World Bank, embraced family planning as a means of forestalling environmental disaster. Environmental organizations moved population growth higher on their list of concerns. The environmental movement and the related movement for zero population growth transcended political boundaries to a remarkable degree. When millions of Americans rallied for a cleaner environment on the first-ever Earth Day, in April 1970, the parades, speeches, and teach-ins united college students wanting a better world, hunters worried about wildlife habitat, mothers concerned about their children's health, and corporate executives who loved weekend hikes in the woods. Quite suddenly, green was good.[6]

Even Richard Nixon bought in. Nixon had no use for environmentalists. "What they're interested in is destroying the system," White House tape recorders captured him saying in 1971. But with his acute political antennae, he realized that overpopulation worried even Americans who were indifferent to the fate of endangered lizards and had no desire to go camping in the wilderness. Nixon asked Congress to establish a population commission. Congress agreed, specifying that the commission should study the environmental effects of population growth. The resulting report, released just as *The Limits to Growth* appeared in 1972, found that "no substantial benefits would result from continued growth of the nation's population." This was an astonishing conclusion for a country in which towns boasted of their populations on highway signs. It threatened the prospects of homebuilders, appliance manufacturers, and thousands of other businesses that had prospered by serving a fast-growing population. Having reaped credit for commissioning a serious look at the population issue, Nixon announced his opposition to many of the report's findings and then ignored it.[7]

Across the Atlantic, *The Ecologist,* a new and influential magazine in Great Britain, called in 1972 for reducing that country's population from fifty million to less than thirty million. A third of Swiss voters supported an initiative to limit the number of immigrants to prevent "the overpopulation of Switzerland." The new United Nations Environment Program held its first conference that June, agreeing on a declaration endorsing governments' right to try to limit their countries' populations. Those needing a break from political arguments about zero population growth could drop by the cinema to take in *Z.P.G.,* an Anglo-Danish sci-fi film about a hellacious twenty-first-century world in which authorities deal with overpopulation by decreeing the death penalty for anyone bearing a child.[8]

The political response to the burgeoning environmental movement was swift, and not just in the United States. Within two years of that first Earth Day, Canada adopted a clean water law; the United States remade its feeble Clean Air Act; California imposed the first limits on auto emissions; and France, Switzerland, Canada, Great Britain, Japan, and the United States all set up national environmental agencies. Yet while Earth Day had been a fundamentally positive event, a hopeful joining together to make a better world, *The Limits to Growth* injected a decidedly negative message into the intense global debate over environmental policy. Humans were destroying their planet, the new narrative went, and the ceaseless quest for economic growth and higher incomes, as measured by the gross national product, was likely to make matters worse. Laws and regulations were unlikely to do much about the problems. It was already too late.

THE NEW ENVIRONMENTAL MOVEMENT REPRESENTED A DIRECT challenge to the reigning economic orthodoxy. As many commentators observed, traditional economic measures, such as growth of per capita income or gross national product, accounted for environmental considerations in perverse fashion. Greater output from smelters and refineries registered as an unalloyed plus, with no subtractions for the harm caused by the resulting increase in pollution. Nonsensically, however, if businesses or governments spent money to clean up dirty water after the fact, that counted as economic growth, too. The environmentalists' complaint that polluting more could make the economy seem to grow faster was right on target.

But from that fact came an entirely false conclusion: that economic growth was merely a fiction—or, worse, that prosperity was the enemy. "One-third of humanity—the developed world—has fallen prey to hedonistic tendencies, worshipping the idol of consumption and status symbols and enslaved to a multiplicity of modern gadgets, turning its back on human and spiritual values," a diplomat from Israel, then a relatively poor country, lectured his counterparts in 1971. Growth, in this new conception, meant intolerable pollution, immeasurable environmental damage, and the reckless depletion of natural resources. "If you accept this idea, then you will find it difficult to deny the conclusion that population, energy production, and consumption of material goods must eventually be limited," two young Yale University scientists wrote in 1971. Wealthy countries should not strive to grow wealthier; instead, their goal should be a "stationary-state economy" in which neither the population nor the stock of physical goods increases.[9]

This was more than environmentalism. It was a flat-out rejection of the goals pursued by every non-communist country since World War II. In the early postwar years, amid destruction and dislocation, what had mattered above all was growth. Economic growth had provided food and housing for millions of displaced people, built support for democratic governments to replace wartime dictatorships, and raised living standards so quickly that voters in Western Europe and Japan rejected the allure of Soviet-style communism. But by the early 1970s, when almost all of those voters had cars, well-built homes, and opportunities to get an education, an influential portion of society was renouncing the work of the postwar generation. Prosperity was passé. The gross national product was irrelevant. As the futurist Herman E. Daly summed up the situation, "for the poor, growth in GNP is still a good thing, but for the rich it is probably a bad thing."[10]

As events transpired, new laws and technologies would postpone the day of reckoning far longer than the alarmists anticipated. When *The Limits to Growth* came off the press, the average US corn farmer harvested eighty-eight bushels per acre; forty years later, unforeseen by the model, the average yield was two-thirds higher thanks to genetically modified crops, precision irrigation, and computers that told tractors how much space to leave between rows. While the amount of bauxite in the earth's crust was fixed, higher prices encouraged the search for new materials to replace aluminum and also gave rise to a lively trade in recycled beer cans. Vehicles, buildings, and electric generating plants all made far more efficient use of fossil fuels, and manufacturers needed far fewer raw materials to produce each unit of output. The fashionable claim that innovations and regulations could not shift the computer-drawn trend lines indicating impending disaster would be proven quite wrong.[11]

But all that would come later. In 1972, the issues at hand were cleaning up the emissions pouring into the skies, rivers, and oceans and dealing with the legacy of millions of tons of hazardous waste deposited recklessly all over the planet. Much of the cost would fall on manufacturers and electricity generators, which faced new mandates to scrub harmful gases and particulates from the exhaust leaving their smokestacks, and to treat wastewater before pumping it into the nearest lake. In the past, they had largely avoided such costs, arguably pushing the burden of environmental damage onto the public at large. Now governments required them to pay their fair share through environmental permits for new facilities and fines on illegal pollution.

Environmental regulation eventually brought widespread benefits in the forms of better human health and a cleaner environment. But it also diverted an increasingly large share of businesses' investment spending from new plants and production machinery toward the installation of pollution-control equipment. It would be one more drag on growth as the world's run of economic good luck came to an end.[12]

CHAPTER 5

The Great Stagflation

As 1973 dawned, a leading economic consultant expressed no doubts about the future. Alan Greenspan, a former student of Arthur Burns and a campaign adviser to Richard Nixon, urged his clients to be confident. Greenspan's political ambitions gave him reason to support the Fed chairman and the president. Rising prices and shaky currencies notwithstanding, he could find no fault with Burns. His forecasts offered no hint of a looming crisis. "It's very rare that you can be as unqualifiedly bullish as you can now," he said.[1]

Greenspan was not an outlier. The general consensus was that, once again, astute management by governments and central banks had brought the world economy through turbulent waters back to a course of strong, steady growth. "Advanced countries facing biggest boom for 20 years," Britain's *Guardian* reported. Consumers were spending like there was no tomorrow, secure in their jobs and confident in their rising incomes. In the United States, where purchasing managers complained that shortages of everything from truck parts to glass and lumber were interfering with plans to increase production, Nixon's Council of Economic Advisers forecast the economy to grow by almost 7 percent, with inflation slowing.

"The business upswing has been steadily gathering momentum," the Bank of Japan observed, and the Bank of England foresaw a "continued fast rise in output." Although a handful of gloomy forecasters sensed trouble ahead—Henry Kaufman of the New York investment bank Salomon Brothers warned that "1974 will see a mess of problems"—most business economists were more in tune with Charles Reeder of the chemicals behemoth DuPont, who told his company's directors, "The present boom appears to have a long way to go."[2]

The most obvious threat to this sunny forecast was the chaos in the currency markets. Every new economic report only further encouraged the smart money to bet against the exchange-rate agreement reached at the Smithsonian barely a year before. The pact Nixon had hailed as "the most significant monetary agreement in world history" was coming unglued. As it fell apart, some currencies were gaining in value and some were losing—and no one wanted to be stuck with the losers. Headlines told of exchange rates going haywire. Anxiety was contagious, made worse by signs that inflation was rising once again. Shortly after New Year's Day of 1973, stock prices began a long and painful decline around the world. From Great Britain to the United States to Hong Kong and Japan, more than half the value of investors' holdings of corporate shares would be wiped out within two years.[3]

Economic forecasters simply closed their eyes to the stock market's decline, taking comfort in the American economist Paul Samuelson's quip that "Wall Street indexes predicted nine of the last five recessions." In the early weeks of 1973, the market's message of impending collapse was not only unwanted but completely unbelievable. Things were simply too good. January 1973 was the second-busiest month ever for US home-builders, and home prices were rising smartly in Great Britain and Japan. A West German government study judged that 1973 was "the beginning of a new cyclical upturn," with the economy likely to grow by 6 percent. The forecasts from Japan were even better: Mitsui Bank predicted an astounding 12 percent growth pace, even if the yen climbed against the dollar. At that rate, Japan's economy would double in size in just six years. And why not? After more than a quarter-century of postwar reconstruction, three out of four Japanese households still lacked flush toilets. There was plenty of construction to be done.[4]

So it was that despite the euphoria in the real economy, where factories were running overtime and households were spending money as never before, the financial markets were in a tizzy in early 1973. In January, nervous Italians rushed to spirit their lira across the border and exchange it for Swiss francs, driving the price of the franc so high that the Swiss had to unlink it from the dollar. Then the markets turned on the dollar, as investors dumped it to buy deutsche marks and yen. For a brief moment, even the normally flaccid French franc looked strong. It was a speculator's dream: central bankers around the world sold their currencies to buy more than eight billion US dollars at the official exchange rates in a futile effort to hold the fixed-rate system together. By February 12, the speculators had claimed victory. Japan decided to stop holding the yen fixed to the dollar and allowed it to float as market forces dictated. Traders immediately drove the currency higher. The main Western European currencies rose, too. When the carnage was over, one dollar bought only half as many deutsche marks as it had six years earlier, and just two-thirds as many yen. The dollar-based Bretton Woods system of fixed exchange rates was dead.[5]

Central bankers were prominent among the mourners, for many of them held a nearly religious belief in the importance of fixed exchange rates. "The Sunday meeting of the governors was marked by an atmosphere of gloom that could not be wholly attributed to the weather," US Federal Reserve governor Jeffrey Bucher reported after meeting with his counterparts in Switzerland. But the central bankers' concerns didn't much matter: the decision to abandon Bretton Woods was irreversible. More consequential was the displeasure of the oil-exporting countries. They had always priced their product in US dollars, but the dollar's collapse meant that each million barrels of oil would buy fewer German trucks and Japanese I-beams. The exporters' querulous cartel, the Organization of Petroleum Exporting Countries, known as OPEC, demanded still higher prices to make up for the dollar's decline. As it did, Ahmed Zaki Yamani, hitherto a little-known Saudi Arabian official, became a household name.[6]

YAMANI, FORTY-TWO YEARS OLD AT THE START OF 1973, WAS AL-
ready familiar to oil-market insiders, but he was a mystery to almost everyone else. The son of a jurist, which in Saudi Arabia meant a religious
scholar, he had grown up in Mecca before studying law at the University
of Cairo. After a few years as a low-level bureaucrat in the ramshackle
Saudi finance ministry, he was sent by the government to the United
States, where he earned law degrees at New York University and Harvard.
Back home, he opened one of Saudi Arabia's first law practices, advising
foreign companies that wanted to do business in what was still a poor and
isolated country. Then came a stint as legal adviser to the crown prince,
who clearly appreciated Yamani's brilliance and discretion. In 1962, at the
age of thirty, he was named minister of petroleum, a crucial and powerful
post in a kingdom whose economy was built entirely on oil.

Yamani cut a most unusual figure. He was a commoner in a country
where almost every ministry was run by a royal relative. He was fluent in
English and French, liked opera and cross-country skiing, was at home in
New York and Vienna as much as in Riyadh. An unfailingly polite man
known for his extensive personal network and his constantly ringing telephone, Yamani moved easily between meditation in his private room at
the Grand Mosque in Mecca and dinner aboard his yacht in Sardinia.
Away from Saudi Arabia, he preferred Savile Row suits to the Arab *dish-
dasha*, and he kept his wavy black hair and his goatee and mustache perfectly trimmed. Telegenic in the extreme, Yamani could look straight into
a camera and speak slowly and briefly, with a gentle tone. When a reporter
asked about a newspaper article claiming he spent each summer living in
a desert tent, Yamani cast an amused glance around his vast suite on the
top floor of Geneva's Intercontinental Hotel and rejoined, "Do you see me
living in a tent?"[7]

In the 1960s Saudi Arabia produced more oil than any country save
the United States and the Soviet Union. When Yamani became minister
in 1962, though, the oil exporters were both poor and powerless. The oil
business was dominated by the Seven Sisters, a group of US and European
companies that controlled more than three-quarters of the world's oil reserves. The foreigners ran the show; they owned the drilling rigs, the pipe-

lines, the pumping stations, and the tankers that conveyed the oil to refineries abroad. Few Saudis, Libyans, Iranians, or Venezuelans held management posts with the oil companies, and their governments were short on both technical knowledge and financial expertise. In Saudi Arabia, Aramco, the US-owned consortium that pumped the kingdom's oil, paid a royalty of about thirty cents per barrel during the 1960s, plus an "income tax" of thirty-two cents per barrel. This would have provided the Saudi government with well below $1 billion per year.[8]

Saudi Arabia and four other countries had established OPEC in 1960 to wrest a better deal from the Seven Sisters, but the organization was unsophisticated and riven by internal disagreements. On behalf of the Saudi king, Yamani tried to mediate among its members. This was no task for the faint of heart. Some states had urgent need of oil revenue to pacify their young, fast-growing populations. Others, with small populations or other sources of money, could afford to wield oil as a political weapon against imperialism, Zionism, or other opponents, both imagined and real. In June 1967, as Israel went to war with Egypt, Jordan, and Syria, some Arab governments called for suspending oil shipments to Israel's allies in the United States and Europe. Yamani, who prided himself on his calm demeanor under fire, unsuccessfully advised against the radical move, knowing full well that many of the countries that promised publicly to curtail oil output would break their promises on the sly. He was right. The oil kept flowing, and the embargo proved a humiliating failure.

But nationalist and socialist tendencies were strengthening in the Arab world, manifesting themselves in the demand that Arabs should reclaim their mineral wealth. Fearful of being sidelined, the Saudis decided to get out in front of the trend. Yamani announced in June 1968 that his government wanted "participation" in Aramco. He made the rounds of world capitals, emphasizing in his deliberate way that "participation" was a far cry from "expropriation," but warning that some governments might simply seize foreign-owned oil companies if they could not buy ownership. "Participation is our substitute for nationalization," he insisted. Experts in the US State Department slammed the proposal as "more of a ploy than a program," and Aramco rejected it out of hand. The United States leaned heavily on the Saudis to leave Aramco alone. Yamani's diplomacy won out. In late 1972, after four years of stalling, the US and European oil giants agreed to sell Saudi Arabia, Kuwait, Abu Dhabi, and Qatar one-fourth ownership of each country's respective oil company immediately, and majority control within a decade. The Arab countries finally had a seat at the boardroom table.[9]

OPEC'S GROWING INFLUENCE WAS WATCHED WARILY IN NORTH America, Europe, and Japan. "The bargaining strength of the Arabs and the other oil producers is increasing," Secretary of State William P. Rogers warned Nixon in March 1972, shortly after six Arab nations won a small price increase to offset the falling international buying power of the dollar. Ever-rising oil consumption in the wealthiest countries increased the exporters' clout. Evidence of this appeared in September 1972, when Yamani told an audience at Georgetown University in Washington that his country was prepared to meet America's need for oil; in return, the Saudis wanted the United States to exempt their oil from import taxes and to let them buy refineries and chemical plants. When US officials failed to respond, Yamani granted an interview to *Newsweek* in which he said, "Don't forget that Saudi Arabia has the jewel in its hand." It was a less-than-subtle warning that the Saudis now had power over the price of oil.

In January 1973, Kuwait's rubber-stamp parliament passed a resolution urging Arab states to use oil as a weapon "the moment the armed struggle against the Zionist enemy is relaunched." Other Arab governments made similar pronouncements. Accordingly, anxieties about oil grew in Washington, London, and other major capitals through the early months of 1973. Then, in April, Yamani and Prince Saud, an oil ministry official and son of King Faisal, journeyed to Washington to convey a simple message: if the United States could not help resolve the Arab-Israeli conflict, Saudi Arabia's desire to act as a leader of the Arab world would require it to join with other countries to drive up the price of oil. When Henry Kissinger, Nixon's national security adviser, asked Yamani to keep their talks secret, Yamani grew concerned that his message would not reach President Nixon. A pro when it came to dealing with the news media, Yamani promptly leaked word of his mission to the *Washington Post*. After US officials insisted that Yamani was speaking only as a private citizen, the Saudi government repeated the message. Faisal himself met with Aramco executives in May to declare that it was "absolutely mandatory" that the United States change its policy toward the Middle East to take the Arabs' concerns into account. A few weeks later he met with the heads of Aramco's parent companies to warn that they would "lose everything" if the United States was not more forthcoming. The king granted an unusual interview to a US television network to reaffirm his warning.[10]

Even if the wealthy oil-importing countries had taken the threat seriously, it is not obvious how they could have responded to it. All had supported United Nations Security Council Resolution 242, passed to end the 1967 Arab-Israeli war, which called upon Israel to withdraw from "territories occupied in the recent conflict" but notably omitted the phrase "all territories." Most had good relations with Israel and were not inclined to support the Arabs' demand that it evacuate East Jerusalem and some other areas it had taken over. An alternative approach, reducing the oil exporters' leverage by sharply raising taxes on gasoline and diesel fuel, was blocked because of domestic political considerations. Bureaucrats and diplomats churned out copious memoranda and diplomatic notes about "energy shortages," the "energy problem," and the "energy crisis," but there was little action anywhere. Even the United States and Canada, peaceful neighbors and close allies, could not agree to cooperate in the event of an oil emergency.[11]

The thinking behind the blizzard of policy papers was remarkably muddled. The energy experts and foreign policy thinkers took it for granted that the prosperity of the industrial world was entirely dependent on cheap oil. It seemed indisputable to them that dearer oil would bring yet more inflation, as if central banks were powerless to limit any inflationary consequences. The universal assumption was that OPEC's aggressiveness would bring about not just higher prices but physical shortages of gasoline, jet fuel, and heating oil. The possibility that oil users might adjust quickly to sharply higher prices was not even considered. Perhaps the greatest worry was the possibility of a massive outflow of money from importing countries—a balance-of-payments crisis, in economist-speak—as if Iran and Kuwait and Libya might simply capture the world's dollars and store them in gigantic vaults without spending any of their new-found wealth.[12]

Tensions mounted by the week. In March 1973, a few weeks after the Bretton Woods agreement was buried for good, eleven OPEC countries made known they wanted a 15 percent increase in oil prices. The official line was that a price hike was needed to make up for the decline in the dollar. The United States tried to organize its allies in opposition, but Japan, France, and Italy were inclined to agree to OPEC's demands. Amid warnings of impending gasoline shortages, the contentious price negotiations between exporting countries and oil companies dragged on, moving from Tripoli to Beirut to Vienna to Cairo. Each failed meeting led to a new round of alarming headlines. In early June, a deal was finally struck. After starting the year at $2.59 a barrel—6.2 cents per gallon—the official benchmark price would now be $2.90, with the prices charged for crudes from specific places a bit higher or lower, depending on transport costs and the characteristics of the oil. Moreover, the benchmark would henceforth be pegged to the US dollar's value against a basket of eleven other currencies. Should the US currency weaken further, the dollar price of oil would automatically rise.[13]

Yet while OPEC's threats stressed diplomats and spooked stock market investors, oil users seemed hardly to notice. US consumer spending grew at a 15 percent annual rate in the first quarter of 1973, and businesses' spending on buildings and equipment soared at a 20 percent annual rate. Factories in Great Britain were running at 94.7 percent of capacity, an all-time record. Surveyed in May, Japanese manufacturers predicted sharp growth in sales through early 1974. Economic officials around the world seemed to share that sanguine outlook. The German government's revised forecast, issued in May, was rosy. So was the Federal Reserve Board's; the minutes of that spring's Fed policy meetings reveal no discussions about oil. When it published its semi-annual forecast in June, the Organisation for Economic Co-operation and Development, the Paris-based think tank of the wealthy countries, judged that "expansion . . . is likely to remain generally strong over the next twelve months, making further inroads into unemployment in most countries."[14]

Three months later, the world economy was still roaring. "The general picture that emerges is one of an exceptionally strong economy with demand for almost everything outrunning supply," DuPont economist Charles Reeder told his company's directors. In Japan, a survey found manufacturers making plans to increase investment by 29 percent over the coming year to cope with strong demand. In West Germany, the government was expecting economic growth to top 4 percent, with negligible unemployment. When the news arrived in mid-September that oil exporters were trying to flex their muscles once again, there seemed to be no particular cause for alarm. The consensus held that economic growth would slow gently in all the main economies through the end of 1974, with inflation gradually abating and labor markets holding strong. There was no sense that the world economy was about to take a drastic turn for the worse.[15]

OCTOBER 6, 1973, WAS YOM KIPPUR, THE DAY OF ATONEMENT, THE most sacred day on the Jewish calendar. If the long postwar run of economic growth could be said to have reached its apex on a single date, there is no better candidate than that Yom Kippur.

At two o'clock that afternoon, Egyptian aircraft struck at Israeli air bases, missile batteries, and radar stations. A few minutes later, thousands of troops began to climb Israeli fortifications along the Suez Canal, which had been closed to shipping since the 1967 war, even as Syrian troops and tanks attacked Israeli positions on the occupied Golan Heights. Within forty-eight hours, six Middle Eastern countries had backed Egypt and Syria by proposing to double the price of oil. After negotiations with a committee of oil company officials stalled, the exporters acted on their own. On October 16, they announced a new benchmark: $5.12 per barrel. "It was the day that OPEC seized power," Yamani said later. In the span of nine months since the start of 1973, the price of the world's most important energy source had nearly doubled. A day later, the Arab countries belonging to OPEC agreed to cut oil production by 10 percent, with a further 5 percent cut for each subsequent month.[16]

The threat was well timed, for the world was dealing with an unusual problem: scarcity. The boom of 1973 had sent consumers on a spending binge, and mines, farms, and factories simply could not produce enough to satisfy the growing demand. Japanese manufacturers reported shortages of everything from electric power to iron ore. The Federal Reserve's confidential "Redbook," a discussion of regional economic conditions sent to policymakers on October 10, described "a very strong economy with widespread shortages of manpower and materials." North Carolina textile mills discontinued nighttime shifts for lack of workers, and paper manufacturers in the Midwest turned away business. Also stamped "Confidential" was the West German economy ministry's caution that the country did not have enough workers to keep its industry running at full capacity. The Bank of England opined that shortages of oil and gas and coal "could create many imbalances in demand, and complicate the task of keeping the economy in balance." Scarcity of workers and goods meant upward pressure on wages and prices, adding to an inflation problem that simply refused to go away.[17]

Well before OPEC began to force up oil prices, surging inflation was seen as the pre-eminent economic problem of the 1970s. Already in 1970, consumer prices in Sweden had jumped 8.1 percent, the highest inflation rate in two decades. A year later, Portugal, which had enjoyed one of the world's lowest inflation rates before 1967, saw prices rise 15 percent. By 1972, the United States was the only major economy with an inflation rate below 5 percent. And this was without a drastic change in the price of a product fundamental to the world economy. Inflation had taken on a life of its own.

The effort to combat inflation was complicated by the widespread belief in a construct called the Phillips Curve. Named for the New Zealand–born economist A. W. H. "Bill" Phillips, who first traced it, the Phillips Curve suggested that countries faced a basic economic trade-off: if they wanted to provide jobs for everyone, they would need to accept higher inflation, and if they wanted to lower the inflation rate they would need to accept higher unemployment not just temporarily, but over the long term. Phillips based his curve solely on data from Great Britain, but the notion that a somewhat higher inflation rate was the permanent price of a full-employment economy quickly became the conventional wisdom among economists everywhere. The lesson the experts drew was that central banks could not go all-out against inflation; if they succeeded in bringing the inflation rate down, they could end up raising the unemployment rate for years to come.[18]

The Phillips Curve was not universally applauded. The American economists Edmund Phelps and Milton Friedman had launched separate attacks on Phillips's theory a few years earlier, insisting that the inflation rate and the unemployment rate were related only in the short term. But their views were decidedly on the fringe. Most leading economists of the day, including Fed chairman Burns, believed that the cost of taming inflation was unacceptably high, because political leaders would not tolerate the massive unemployment they expected to ensue if inflation were brought down. As the American scholar Charles Schultze, who would soon become chief economic adviser to President Jimmy Carter, interpreted the state of affairs: "We know how to get to full employment. That's not the problem. We know how to do it with the old, standard, tried and true techniques: tax cuts, easy money, putting more money into certain government programs. But when we do that, we set off the inflation." So instead of treating inflation as an urgent problem that could corrode an economy, most governments and central banks regarded it as an unwanted but unavoidable nuisance. Their response was to manage inflation as best they could without slowing down the economy and throwing people out of work.[19]

The effort to control inflation was confused by an understanding of the problem that, only a few years later, would strike a listener as bizarre. The widely accepted view in the 1970s was that there were various strains of inflation, each requiring a different sort of treatment. There was monetary inflation, which meant that the central bank was pumping too much money into the economy. There was "demand-pull inflation," which meant that consumers and businesses were trying to buy more than the economy could supply, giving sellers the ability to demand higher prices. And there was the "cost-push inflation," considered the most pernicious variety. This type of inflation was supposedly caused by the suppliers of inputs to businesses, such as raw materials, industrial goods, and labor. If mine owners, steelmakers, and trade unions demanded higher prices or higher wages, the businesses that used those inputs would be forced to raise their own prices, and inflation would move higher still.

Friedman insisted that all inflation was monetary inflation; if only the central bank would restrain the growth of the money supply, inflation would go away. Just a few years later, Friedman's dictum, "Inflation is always and everywhere a monetary phenomenon," would be treated as gospel. But in 1973, most influential economists lost sleep over the forms of inflation Friedman deemed fictitious. Demand-pull inflation was thought to be controllable by higher taxes, lower government spending, higher interest rates, or restrictions on bank lending, any of which would leave consumers and businesses with less money to spend, bringing demand back in line with supply. The Japanese government pursued such policies with a vengeance, directing steelmakers, aluminum smelters, and chemical manufacturers to defer capital spending while ordering banks to cut back on installment loans, all to lower demand for machinery and labor in the hope that price rises would subside.

Cost-push inflation was seen as a trickier problem. Governments usually addressed it with a combination of political pressure and price controls. It seemed entirely normal for government ministers to declare how large an industry's wage or price increases should be and then to press labor unions and employers to obey such "voluntary" guidelines, a technique Americans came to know as "jawboning." A more conciliatory approach involved creating a government commission to judge how much a given wage or price should rise. Either way, the assumption was that if grocery clerks or tire builders received only the pay increases that outside experts deemed justified, the government could slowly ratchet down the inflation rate without upsetting the economy.[20]

Jawboning and price controls usually met with loud applause, at least at first: it was popular to criticize big business for raising prices unfairly and to attack irresponsible unions for demanding more than their fair share. In most cases, when controls were put in place, prices stopped rising and the inflation rate measured by government statistics began to recede. But then reality would set in. A retailer would introduce a dress with pleats, contending that this complicated feature justified a higher price than it charged for last season's dress. A food processor would insist that after drought decimated the tomato crop, it needed to charge more for ketchup. Dockworkers would assert that their improved productivity entitled them to larger pay hikes than aircraft mechanics or sales clerks. Within a few months, complaints about unfairness would burgeon, and energy that could have gone into creating new goods and services was instead spent circumventing the controls to squeeze out higher profits or higher pay.

By late 1973, inflation seemed to have developed resistance to all of these courses of treatment. Central banks were paralyzed. On October 2, two weeks before the Arab oil producers jacked up prices, the Federal Reserve considered whether to lower short-term interest rates—and split, six in favor, five against. Private forecasters were also on the fence, Burns told his colleagues two weeks later. One reason for the uncertainty, a top Fed economist explained, was that the computer-driven models used by some forecasters had difficulty "taking appropriate account of the recent wild gyrations in prices, which were without precedent in modern experience." The experts were stumped.[21]

In hindsight, given the essential role of oil in running factories, vehicles, and generating plants, it seems obvious that the sharp price rise proclaimed by the Arab exporters on October 16 would lead to severe economic disruption in countries that imported large quantities of oil. But somehow this risk initially passed unnoticed. On the contrary, the mood in all the high-income countries remained optimistic. After the embargo was announced, the British and French governments both predicted robust economic growth in 1974. As late as November 14, even though oil was now selling for $5.12 a barrel instead of $2.90, the Federal Reserve raised its forecast of US economic growth while lowering its forecast of unemployment.[22]

Only in late November, six weeks after the oil shock, did the reality sink in. In September, the Japanese economy had been so hot the government took special measures to slow it down; in November, the same officials slashed their forecast of economic growth for the coming months to zero. French economists warned that growth could plummet. At the Fed, the optimistic November 14 forecast was consigned to the dustbin. One Fed economist predicted on December 12, "Income will be destroyed, business and consumer psychology will be dampened, and the upward momentum the economy still has at this point in the cycle may well be lost." In West Germany, where inflation was at the highest rate since 1952, a secret economics ministry forecast estimated that two million jobs could vanish in 1974. Chancellor Willy Brandt was blunt, telling parliament: "Things are bad and could get worse."[23]

THE PHILLIPS CURVE MADE NO ALLOWANCE FOR A COMBINATION of persistent inflation and economic stagnation. Inevitably, this unexpected threat took on a name of its own: stagflation. By driving up consumer prices while choking off economic growth, the oil price shock of 1973 threatened to bring stagflation even to countries renowned for both low unemployment and a commitment to low inflation, notably West Germany and Switzerland. Stagflation was a problem beyond the experience of central bankers and finance ministers. But for all the debate about whether it was more important to raise interest rates to stop inflation or lower them to save jobs, stagflation would prove to be merely a symptom of a far more intractable challenge, which received little notice at the time. The entire economic model that had brought the world a quarter-century of unprecedented prosperity was broken.[24]

That model was based on the remarkable growth of productivity. Productivity may be one of the most complex concepts in economics. The basic idea is that the more an economy can produce from a given quantity of labor, capital, and raw materials, the wealthier that economy will be. Since there are physical limits on the amount an individual worker can accomplish with muscle power, raising productivity involves making better use of machines, technology, and business methods. Productivity can be measured in a variety of ways, and these measurements can become exceedingly abstruse. But there is little dispute about the underlying idea that a healthy economy makes steadily better use of the resources it has at hand.

Rapid productivity growth brought very healthy profits for businesses in the postwar period. As profits grew, so did employees' wages, shareholders' dividends, business tax receipts, and investments in new capacity to produce yet more goods and services. It was this virtuous circle that put the glow on the Golden Age. But without much public notice, by the time the oil crisis arrived in October 1973, slower growth of productivity was already bringing the long run of global prosperity to an end.[25]

The oil crisis that arrived in October 1973 did not cause the productivity problem. It simply added one more item to the list of factors that were weighing on productivity around the world. Higher oil prices threatened to render obsolete an entire industrial infrastructure built on the assumption of cheap oil. The world would face a difficult and costly adjustment that would last for many years. As West Germany's council of economic advisers laid out the situation, "The reduction in petroleum imports thus confronts the economy with new difficulties, difficulties that cannot be resolved with the traditional methods of economic management."[26]

The productivity bust would have profound implications. Governments and central bankers knew, or thought they knew, how to use "traditional methods of economic management"—raising and lowering interest rates, taxes, and government spending—to restore an economy to health. When it came to fixing declining productivity growth, however, the economists' toolbox was embarrassingly empty.

CHAPTER 6

Gold Boys

Sentiment at the start of 1973 had been buoyant. A year later, as the oil shock reverberated through the world economy, the atmosphere was vastly different. Inflation continued to rise. West Germany had just banned the importation of immigrant workers, on which its industries had relied since 1955, and Austria was about to follow. As "Help Wanted" signs were taken down across Northern and Central Europe, families in Turkey, Yugoslavia, Portugal, and Greece, which together supplied Germany with workers by the millions, began to feel the pain. The mood grew even more somber on the other side of the English Channel, as factories were put on a three-day workweek after a strike by coal miners led to power cuts. In Japan, ministers were struggling to deal with a situation that the influential daily *Mainichi* described as "catastrophic."[1]

It was difficult, in the midst of crisis, to look beyond the imminence of unemployment lines and stagflation. But the dramatic changes in the international economic environment, with exchange rates gyrating and commodity prices highly volatile, would have larger, longer-lasting ramifications. Their impact would be felt most directly in the global financial system, the increasingly intricate web of banks and brokerage houses that transformed

workers' savings and oil exporters' earnings into the new factories, highways, and houses so essential to raising living standards. The banks were
bloated with oil money, and their decisions about how to use it were creating risks that few bankers had ever experienced. Among the first to foresee
the looming financial danger was a tall, commanding Englishman named
Gordon Richardson, the governor of the august Bank of England.

Richardson had more in common with Arthur Burns than casual observers might have suspected. Although he seemed every inch the English
aristocrat, he was nothing of the sort. Like Burns, he had propelled himself across a longstanding class divide by the sheer force of brains and
ambition.

Born in 1915, the son of a Nottingham grocer, Richardson had become
head boy at Nottingham High School, a prestigious independent boys'
school, and then won a scholarship to study law at Cambridge. After World
War II, he climbed to prominence as a corporate lawyer at a London firm.
He was recruited to join J. Henry Schroder & Co., one of the most venerable merchant banks in the City of London, and became chairman in
1962. Known for his immaculate appearance, his regal bearing, and his dry
martinis made "the way they mix them in New York," Richardson built the
sleepy family-owned Schroders into the most international of financial institutions, handling mergers and takeover bids from America to Australia.
In July 1973, at age fifty-seven, he reached the pinnacle of British public
life when Edward Heath, the Conservative prime minister, asked him to
become the 116th governor of the Bank of England.[2]

The world's oldest central bank, where visitors were greeted by a door-
man clad in a pink frock coat and top hat, sat at the heart of the British
economy, with extraordinary powers. It managed the borrowings of Her
Majesty's government. It decided which companies could obtain foreign
currency to import goods or invest abroad. It governed interest rates to
regulate the amount of credit available to businesses and homebuyers. And
it formally oversaw the two main types of financial institutions in Great
Britain: the accepting houses, merchant banks that traded the government's
gilt-edged bonds, and the high street banks in which most Britons deposited their savings, like Barclays and National Westminster Bank.

Because London's merchant banks organized share offerings and bond issues for companies and governments around the world, the governor's influence resonated far beyond the British Isles. Senior Bank of England officials often were recruited away to run commercial banks, cementing the central bank's influence over the City. Much of the governor's remit was not laid out in law, and the very vagueness of his powers made him all the more powerful. From his ornate ground-floor office in Threadneedle Street, opening onto the monastic stillness of an interior garden planted with mulberry trees, the governor of the Bank of England may have exercised greater authority than any other central banker in the world.[3]

But as Richardson took charge at the Bank, that authority was under threat. Under the Bretton Woods system, governments had maintained a host of regulations to control interest rates and limit the movement of money in order to keep exchange rates fixed. As Bretton Woods blew apart in the early 1970s, however, many of those restrictions were abandoned. Disregarding national borders, money began flowing to places where it could earn higher returns or go untaxed. Much of it ended up in London, the premier international banking center, in accounts denominated in US dollars.

A large portion of that money was owned by the oil states of the Middle East and North Africa, which were taking in unprecedented quantities of dollars as they pushed up the price of oil. The inflow of petrodollars helped the big London banks register an astounding 80 percent increase in profits in the first half of 1973. The foreign loans of the main British banks tripled between 1970 and 1974. Banks from every corner of the world set up shop in London to get a piece of the action.[4]

So much money was coming in that the big banks could not lend it all. The British government encouraged them to channel their excess cash through "secondary banks," obscure institutions that were allowed to lend money on much easier terms than the big banks. Many of the secondary banks' loans were used for property speculation, which had been an easy, low-risk way to profit from the boom. The party abruptly ended in November 1973, when a secondary bank called London and County Securities collapsed. Its failure, the result of fraud on the part of its managers, quickly triggered others. Bankers desperately tried to call in loans to stay afloat, but many borrowers, their money tied up in real estate, lacked the cash to repay. The secondary banks were small by the standards of international banking, but they had borrowed heavily from London stalwarts like National Westminster Bank, one of the largest banks in the world. Legally, Richardson and the Bank of England had no responsibility. Richardson charged into the void nonetheless, forcing Britain's big banks to pay into a fund that wound down the secondary banks in an orderly way.[5]

The secondary banking crisis exposed an uncomfortable secret: in the world's most important international banking center, no one kept a close watch on the banks. As of November 1973, the latest financial information the Bank of England had received from London and County Securities was a balance sheet dated March 31, with no details about loans, deposits, or other obligations. Far larger banks were overseen with the same informal methods applied in Victorian times. No examiners visited banks' offices to scrutinize their records and pore over their financial reports. "We didn't even have to show a full profit and loss account," a director of the merchant bank Kleinwort Benson recalled later. Once every six months or so, executives of each bank would call on the principal of the Bank of England's Discount Office to present their accounts. Once a year, the chairman of each major institution was invited to tea with the governor, who might wonder aloud whether the visitor's bank had sufficient short-term funding or whether it might be wise to cut back on property lending. When the governor raised his eyebrow, it was said, then bankers knew to pay heed.[6]

Exactly *how* bankers were to pay heed was deliberately unclear. The Bank of England had always preferred to be inscrutable. Its leaders avoided giving speeches. The job of the press office, insiders joked, was to "keep the press out of the Bank and the Bank out of the press." As the bank's official historian commented, "anyone looking at the annual report prior to 1980 would not even be able to identify who the executives were, let alone what they did." It issued almost no detailed regulations like those that governed banks in France, Canada, West Germany, and the United States. A London bank called out for, say, excessive foreign lending was expected to return in a few months and show that it had responded to the governor's concerns, but whether the governor wanted to see the foreign loan book shrink by 5 percent or 20 percent was anyone's guess.[7]

This approach to bank supervision had its merits. In the days when London had been a much cozier place, the deputies to the principal of the Discount Office spent their days taking tea with bankers and collecting gossip about their competitors. If the Discount Office got wind that a lender was dumping French bonds on the market or that a client of a certain institution was in distress, the principal, or even the governor, could call in the bankers and demand action. The Bank of England had no power to impose fines or injunctions, but it had enormous moral suasion. No one would do business with an institution rumored to be in the bank's bad graces. The mere possibility that word of the governor's unhappiness might leak out was enough to bring the most recalcitrant banker to heel.

By the time of Richardson's appointment in 1973, the Bank of England was struggling to keep pace with the financial revolution. Although it had individually approved each of the foreign banks that opened in the City to trade currencies and capture petrodollars, it usually based its assent on little more than assurances from the institution's home country that the bank was legitimate. Too often, the old-guard bankers on whom the Bank of England relied for market gossip and timely warnings were only vaguely acquainted with the foreign institutions that had settled in their midst. More worrying still, the Bank of England knew almost nothing about the new banks' business practices—their accounting, their procedures for approving loans, their methods for managing risk. Over the years, largely from personal contacts, it had amassed thick files on Great Britain's established banks. About some of the banks that were new to London, the Bank of England was very nearly blind.

Richardson was a novice when it came to bank supervision, but the frenetic developments in his first few months as governor made him acutely aware of the Bank of England's shortcomings. In the winter of 1974, with no public notice, he took two steps that were little short of revolutionary. One was internal: Richardson replaced the Discount Office with a new department of bank supervision. Whereas the Discount Office had a staff of only twenty, none of whom had routine responsibility for inspecting banks' records, the department of bank supervision would be larger and more professional. Bankers would no longer come by for tea; henceforth, banks were to submit detailed data about loans, deposits, and borrowings on a regular basis, and the head of supervision would send in examiners to comb their files, interview their staff, and review their policies. No law gave the Bank of England the right to do such things, but Richardson rightly figured that any institution that declined to be supervised by the Bank of England was likely to be shunned in the City.[8]

Richardson's other step was international. In their quiet, understated way, central bankers had begun to call attention to the fact that the international banking boom was creating new and unforeseen risks. Otmar Emminger, an influential vice president of the German Bundesbank, warned in November 1973 that in bankers' scramble to capture foreign deposits, "It appears that the financial interest of individual firms runs into conflict with the greater interests of the credit industry as a whole." Richardson, in private conversation with Federal Reserve chairman Arthur Burns, went further, raising the possibility that the influx of foreign dollars, exchanged for other currencies and lent out around the world, could destabilize the entire banking system. He proposed that this problem should be discussed in Basel.[9]

BASEL, A QUIET SWISS CITY NESTLED ON THE RHINE RIVER, IS THE home of the Bank for International Settlements, an obscure institution comprised of the world's most important central banks. Founded in 1930 to handle the German reparation payments required under the Versailles Treaty, which ended World War I, the bank served in the 1960s mainly to move money between central banks, a job so technical and boring that few nonspecialists could describe it. This obscurity had its advantages, as journalists were normally not on hand to keep tabs on visiting dignitaries.

In the 1970s, central bankers convened there roughly once a month to talk shop, which usually meant discussing economic conditions. In March and April 1974, the topic was how to handle the oil exporters' ballooning wealth. To profit from the dollars flooding into rich-country banks, the banks would have to exchange them for other currencies and lend out the proceeds. This created a variety of risks, even if the borrowers paid their loans on time. If exchange rates moved the wrong way, the loan repayments could be worth less than the banks' dollar obligations to their depositors. And should an oil sheikhdom suddenly demand its dollars back, a bank that had used them to make five-year loans in British pounds or Dutch guilders could find itself desperate for cash.

This was a frightening prospect, for in the new world of global finance and floating exchange rates, banks were more intimately connected than ever before. They not only lent one another money and joined forces to make loans, but also traded currencies to meet their customers' needs. In many cases, those trades involved betting on an exchange rate at some future date. For example, a Spanish textile company expecting to receive one million West German deutsche marks in six months could lock in the value of that sum in Spanish pesetas, with its bank assuming the risk if the exchange rate on that date turned out to be different from what it anticipated. The bank, in turn, might hedge its risk by arranging similar contracts with other banks. With thousands of such trades open at any one time, the failure of a single big bank, no matter where it occurred, could cause trouble for banks and economies around the world. Yet no central banker had authority over the new world of global banking. As Federal Reserve governor Henry Wallich dryly reported to his colleagues after the Basel meetings, "the lines of responsibility in this regard will need to be clarified."[10]

There was no time for clarification. In May 1974, crisis was at hand.

It struck first in a most unlikely place: not one of the great globe-striding banks in New York, London, or Tokyo but at a middling American institution, the Franklin National Bank.

Franklin, rooted in the suburbs of New York City, had seen its cozy franchise squeezed as bigger banks expanded, and its managers decided to seek higher profits abroad. In 1969 the bank won permission from the Fed to open a branch in the Bahamas. Although its examiners fretted over the troubled loans on Franklin's books, the Fed authorized a branch in London in 1971. Having gained the stature of an international bank, Franklin won the most coveted prize of all. On June 1, 1972, the Bank of England approved it to deal in foreign exchange, certifying Franklin's arrival in the big leagues. One month later, an Italian lawyer named Michele Sindona acquired 21.6 percent of Franklin's stock.[11]

Sindona, then fifty-two, had climbed from poverty in rural Sicily to the pinnacle of the Italian business world. The son of a vegetable seller, he won a university scholarship to study law and made his first fortune smuggling vegetables during World War II. An immaculate dresser with a white handkerchief always peeking out of the breast pocket of his tailored suit, he cultivated ties to the Mafia, the Catholic church, and the Italian political elite. In addition to handling investments for the Vatican bank, he owned a web of holding companies that controlled banks in Italy, Germany, and Switzerland, along with a variety of property and manufacturing interests. He had never done much business in America, where Franklin would give him a foothold.

Sindona's lawyers, though, insisted that his shareholding would not give him control of the bank—an important claim, because seeking control would have entitled the Fed's examiners to look into Sindona's other business interests. Buying Franklin shares strictly as an investment, as Sindona claimed to be doing, required no Fed approval.

Sindona proved to be far from a passive shareholder. He pushed the bank to step up its dealings in the currency market. Soon he installed longtime associates to run the international department. They began making large loans to Sindona's companies, ignoring regulations meant to limit banks' lending to their own investors. Franklin's currency traders lost large sums making bad bets on exchange-rate movements, but Sindona's minions covered up the losses by transferring money back and forth across his empire—and because no single banking supervisor had jurisdiction over all the Sindona banks, none caught on to the deceit. The rumor mill seemed to know: some banks were so concerned that they stopped trading currencies with Franklin in the autumn of 1973. None of this was yet visible to outsiders. In December 1973, at a dinner at New York's St. Regis Hotel, Italian prime minister Giulio Andreotti made a point of praising Sindona's currency trading, hailing him as the "savior of the lira." A month later, John Volpe, the US ambassador to Italy, named Sindona "man of the year."[12]

On May 3, 1974, after a London bank passed market gossip to the authorities, investigators in New York found evidence of unauthorized trading and undisclosed losses. On May 10, the Federal Reserve took control. But Fed officials saw immediately that they could not simply close Franklin down. It was a party to hundreds of currency trades, some of which would not mature for months. If Franklin were abruptly shuttered, some of the banks with which it had traded stood to suffer crippling losses. Fearful of unleashing a worldwide financial panic, US authorities kept Franklin on life support, gradually unwinding its positions before selling off its remains.

FRANKLIN WAS ONLY THE FIRST SIGN THAT THE ERA OF FINANCIAL stability was over. As the Americans were struggling to contain the damage, West German officials confronted an eerily similar crisis. This latest threat came from Cologne, where problems at a little-known bank suddenly overwhelmed financial markets half a world away.

Bankhaus Herstatt, a privately owned institution catering to Cologne's financial elite, used the slogan "Saving should not be a gamble," but it acted otherwise. Its boss, Iwan Herstatt, allowed his young team of currency traders, his "Gold Boys," to circumvent internal controls and gamble freely in the foreign-exchange markets. Herstatt's financial statements, certified by a leading accounting firm, showed ample resources to cover potential trading losses, including deposits at Econ-Bank in Switzerland. That country's tight bank secrecy laws would have barred Econ-Bank from confirming the size of Herstatt's deposits to any third party, which may be why neither Herstatt's auditors nor German bank examiners tried to verify the information. If they had, they would have discovered that Econ-Bank did not exist. When examiners finally closed Herstatt down on June 24, its losses had ballooned to nearly five hundred million marks, six times the funds it had available to repay depositors.

That was minor compared to what followed. German authorities seized Herstatt on a Thursday at 4 p.m. in a move *Der Spiegel* described as a "lightning strike . . . to avert financial chaos." But unlike in the United States, the German supervisors had given little thought to the fact that

Herstatt traded heavily with banks abroad. The closure came after it had received payments from banks in other time zones but before some of its corresponding payments to foreign banks had been sent out. Those outgoing payments were blocked, causing losses at banks around the world and creating months of chaos in the currency markets.[13]

The shockwaves from the Herstatt debacle set off a third cross-border banking collapse that was less publicized but in some ways even more frightening. The failure of Israel-British Bank did not come close to threatening the world economy, but it revealed dangerous gaps in the procedures established to keep the banking system stable.[14]

Israel-British was the sixth-largest bank in Israel, but by international standards it was a minnow. Founded by Polish emigrants as Palestine-British Bank in 1929, it was controlled by the heirs of Walter Nathan Williams, a leader of Great Britain's Jewish community. The Williams family was influential in the Zionist movement and well connected in right-wing Israeli political circles. By 1974, the bank had eight branches in Israel and a subsidiary in London. One of Williams's sons-in-law, a Welsh-born accountant named Harry Landy, was chairman. Another son-in-law, Joshua Bension, was vice chairman and general manager. From Williams National House, their headquarters in London's Holborn, the two men also ran a string of other companies, from British insurers to an Israeli vineyard.[15]

Insider lending—loans by a bank to its own directors and officers—is among the most insidious of banking practices, because it offers shady bankers a way to loot their institution. In 1970, the Israeli bank supervisor had ordered Israel-British to limit its lending to the Williams companies for precisely that reason. But Landy and Bension would not be denied. They found a way around the restrictions by having the Tel Aviv bank pledge some of its assets to two Swiss banks. The Swiss banks then lent $75 million to various companies controlled by Landy and Bension in Switzerland and in the tiny principality of Liechtenstein, with the assets pledged by Israel-British serving as collateral. These arrangements also offered Landy and Bension a way to move money out of Israel in violation of that country's foreign-exchange regulations.[16]

The Herstatt affair brought this chicanery to light. With the financial markets in turmoil, banks hastily scaled back their international commitments—including their deposits in Israel-British Bank of Tel Aviv. In July 1974, two weeks after the collapse of Bankhaus Herstatt, the Tel Aviv bank found itself short of cash to repay foreign depositors. Bension asked Israeli authorities for an emergency loan backed by assets in Switzerland. Only as they prepared the loan papers did the lawyers from the Israeli central bank discover that those assets were already tied up, pledged as collateral for the secret loans to Landy's and Bension's companies. The Israeli authorities thereupon closed down the Israeli operations, leaving Israel-British Bank of Tel Aviv unable to repay its loans from Israel-British Bank of London. The London bank failed two days later, despite Harry Landy's promise that "We will be carrying on."[17]

An investigation revealed that Israel-British was no innocent victim of the Herstatt crisis. The bank had thrived by deceiving regulators. Monday through Friday it kept ample cash in London to please the Bank of England. The London subsidiary then lent money to its parent bank in Tel Aviv over the weekend, giving the Tel Aviv bank sufficient short-term funding to meet Israeli requirements. The loans were repaid on Monday morning, again making the London bank look strong. When the music stopped, Israel-British was far more stretched than it had appeared. The bank's business proved to be so convoluted that a team of forensic auditors spent months disentangling it. Among the losers was the US government, which was on the hook for $2.1 million Israel-British owed to Franklin National Bank. And Israel-British was a small and relatively simple bank. If supervisors were blind to the goings-on at a bank with a mere nine offices in two countries, what might they not know about a giant stuffed with petrodollars, like Dai-ichi Kangyo in Tokyo or Chase Manhattan in New York?[18]

Michele Sindona would eventually be convicted of sixty-five felony counts in Franklin National's collapse; after serving four years in a US prison, he was imprisoned in Italy, where he died after drinking coffee laced with cyanide in 1986. Whether he committed suicide or was murdered to keep him from implicating politicians like Prime Minister

Andreotti in the scandal has never been conclusively resolved. Iwan Herstatt was twice convicted of fraud before being declared mentally incompetent in 1991. Joshua Bension, accused in Israel of stealing $47 million, received a twelve-year prison sentence in 1975 despite appeals for clemency from Israel's two chief rabbis; he was released from prison by Prime Minister Menachem Begin in 1977. Harry Landy's five-year prison sentence for fraud was overturned by a British court in 1979. The suave Sindona, the corpulent Herstatt, the pious Bension, and the voluble Landy were very different men, but all had exploited the same yawning gap in bank oversight. If a bank's activity crossed international borders, no banking supervisor in any country had a clear and complete view of its affairs.[19]

Gordon Richardson raised this issue with Arthur Burns, and they laid it in front of their fellow central bankers early in 1974. Problems in cross-border banking, even those involving tiny banks, they argued, had the potential to turn into massive economic crises far from where they began. In December 1974, the central bankers requested that their countries' banking supervisors figure out how to keep such frightening international contagion from happening again.[20]

DECADES LATER, IT IS DIFFICULT TO RECAPTURE THE MIND-SET that prevailed when the bank supervisors convened in a drab meeting room above Frey's Confectionery in Basel in February 1975. The participants were technocrats—anonymous bank regulators, not prestigious central-bank governors. Most did not know one another. Nor did they have a common language. In the meeting room, the delegates wore headphones as interpreters rendered the proceedings into English, Japanese, Italian, and French. During coffee breaks, they chatted with difficulty.

The men were uncertain about their legal authority and their ability to share information. Some had domestic political concerns to weigh, and the officials around the table did not necessarily have full authority over their countries' banks. The Fed could not speak for the US comptroller of the currency, which was not represented in Basel, and the Bank of Japan was famously estranged from the absent Ministry of Finance.

Diplomatic considerations interfered; France, in particular, preferred to treat financial regulation as a European matter, without the involvement of the United States, Canada, and Japan. Nor was it clear what this new Committee on Banking Regulations and Supervisory Practices was meant to do. The agenda would largely be determined by its chairman. After some discreet maneuvering, Richardson won the job for a colleague with little experience dealing with banking problems: George Blunden of the Bank of England.[21]

Blunden, then fifty-two years old, was the ultimate Bank of England insider. The son of a career Bank of England employee, he had been hired following his military service in World War II and studies at University College, Oxford, and had been in the bank's employ ever since. By the early 1970s he had worked his way up to chief of management services, overseeing administrative offices and computer systems. He was not an expert in banking supervision, but no one else at the Bank of England was, either; its oversight of the City, after all, was based more on social codes than on accounting standards. Blunden's organizational skills more than made up for his lack of supervisory background. He homed in on the near-total lack of data about the banking system, ordering bankers to submit monthly and quarterly reports detailing foreign-currency deposits, property loans, and loans to related companies. With those figures, Blunden's supervisors could compare one bank to another and lay down firm rules to govern their behavior.[22]

At that first meeting in Basel, Blunden announced that the central bank governors wanted the committee to devise a system to provide early warning of potential banking crises. This project was quickly abandoned as unrealistic. Instead, after several months of discussion, the supervisors decided to focus on the single issue that concerned all of them the most: oversight of banks' foreign offices.

Banks, to simplify, had three ways to set up shop outside their home countries in the 1970s. The first, a subsidiary, was like a local bank in the foreign country, subject to all the host country's regulations. Among other things, a subsidiary was required to have its own financial resources—capital, in bank-speak—so it could make good on its obligations even if the parent institution were to fail. A branch, on the other hand, was merely a local outpost of a foreign institution, with little or nothing by way of independent resources. If the branch was unable to pay depositors, the home office might make good on its obligations, or it might not; Canada and Sweden regarded foreign branches as so potentially troublesome that they did not allow them. The third type of cross-border arrangement was a joint-venture bank in which two or more foreign institutions owned shares. The issue with these was whether any of the foreign co-owners would take responsibility if something went wrong.[23]

Everyone could agree that these foreign-owned operations posed a potential problem. Foreign outposts were everywhere—the number of foreign-owned branches in the major European financial centers had risen from 303 in 1971 to 472 in 1974—but the supervisors' ignorance about them was shocking. They knew little or nothing about what their own country's banks did in other countries, and laws in many countries barred supervisors from sharing information across borders. German banks lent heavily to Poland through Luxembourg subsidiaries about which German overseers knew nothing, yet the collapse of Dresdner Bank's subsidiary in Luxembourg could have crippled one of the world's largest banks and hundreds of important institutions that did business with it. Japanese banks were expanding rapidly in Europe and North America, but the Bank of Japan admitted that it had conducted "very few" examinations of those banks' foreign branches. The Federal Reserve Board, which oversaw most of the big US banking companies, had no foreign-based examiners at all. Although US banks engaged in business practices abroad that were prohibited at home, such as arranging bond issues and trading commodities, US supervisors had no ability to keep an eye on them.[24]

After a year studying these issues, the supervisors reached consensus. In September 1975, they recommended that countries change their laws to allow supervisors to share information internationally. Home-country supervisors, they believed, should be allowed to examine their banks' branches in other countries, and host-country supervisors should be authorized to examine a foreign-owned branch in their country at the home country's request.

This well-intended agreement, christened the Basel Concordat, was celebrated as proof that outdated ideas about national sovereignty were yielding to a more enlightened understanding of the need for international cooperation. Yet the most difficult issue, final responsibility for financial institutions operating across international borders, was left unsettled. "It is not possible to draw up clear-cut rules for determining exactly where the responsibility for supervision can best be placed in any particular situation," the supervisors concluded. Nothing in the new agreement would have prevented crises like those caused by Franklin and Herstatt, much less a scam like the one that brought down Israel-British Bank. The issue of how to use national powers to regulate international banks was so politically fraught that the supervisors decided to drop the entire subject. In the new world of global finance, by default, there would be no one in charge.[25]

THE LONGER THE BANKING SUPERVISORS TALKED, THE MORE money poured in to the oil exporters' accounts. The official price of light crude from Saudi Arabia, $5.12 per barrel in October 1973, reached $11.65 in January 1974 and $12.37 in 1975, when the OPEC countries' receipts reached $135 billion. As that money coursed through the banking system, banks from around the world opened their doors in Frankfurt and New York, Beirut and Atlanta, jockeying for deposits and offering loans to borrowers with whom they previously had no contact. Many of the banks crowding into the business were novices at international lending, and they were unfamiliar with their new customers. This was a time bomb, and the supervisors knew it. The more they talked things over in Basel, the more worried they grew about a problem the banks preferred they ignore—the banks' lack of capital.[26]

Capital has a critical role in banking. In the most basic terms, it represents the resources available to repay depositors and trading partners in the event the bank sustains large losses. Banks raise capital by selling shares to investors, setting aside a portion of their annual profits, or building up a reserve of money in expectation that certain loans will turn sour. The common thread is that a bank's capital cannot be lent out to customers; it sits idly in the form of cash and short-term securities just in case it is needed. In the ideal world, the more loans a bank makes, the more capital it should set aside to protect against nonpayment. But bankers are painfully aware that holding more capital can lead to lower returns for shareholders. By the mid-1970s, many banks had almost no capital. Walter Wriston of Citicorp of New York, arguably the most influential banker in the world, argued that sophisticated management rendered bank capital less necessary, and he made it clear that his bank would hold as little of it as possible. As big banks' lending and trading business flourished, their capital did not increase accordingly.[27]

It was Arthur Burns who first sounded the alarm publicly. Burns had been shocked to find the Fed forced to rescue Franklin and to manage the fallout from Herstatt. When he addressed the American Bankers Association in Honolulu in October 1974, he did not bother with pleasantries. Banks, he said, were growing far too quickly. They were collecting short-term deposits too aggressively and lending them out with too little attention to the length of the loans and the likelihood of repayment. As they expanded, "the capital cushion that plays such a large role in maintaining confidence in banks has become thinner, particularly in some of our largest banking organizations." Regulators, he announced, were imposing a "breathing spell," delaying banks' expansion until the banks put themselves on a sounder footing.[28]

The general public knew virtually nothing about these problems, for bank supervisors almost everywhere kept the key measure of a bank's strength—the ratio of its capital to its loans and other assets—confidential. On those rare occasions when word got out, supervisors dissembled. After the *Washington Post* revealed in January 1976 that First National City Bank and Chase Manhattan, the second- and third-largest banks in the United States, were on an official list of problem institutions, their supervisor, Comptroller of the Currency James E. Smith, averred that they were "among the soundest banking institutions in the world." How they could be so sound when large numbers of borrowers were evidently failing to repay loans, Smith did not explain. The situation in other countries was even worse. Many French and Japanese banks had scarcely any capital, effectively leaving their governments on the hook if borrowers failed to repay their loans.[29]

The issue of how much capital banks should hold was so sensitive that the supervisors' committee decided in October 1976 not to discuss it. It was left up to each country to address the matter on its own. No country could afford to do so aggressively. If a bank were required to hold significantly more capital than its foreign competitors, it would be at a competitive disadvantage. When Paul Volcker, who became president of the Federal Reserve Bank of New York in 1975, and John Heimann, who became comptroller of the currency in 1977, instructed US banks to issue new shares or set aside profits in order to raise their capital levels, they ran into heavy resistance; even a small increase in capital levels took several years to accomplish. And so, as the petrodollars kept flowing and international lending boomed, the banks' impressive growth masked their increasingly fragile foundations. As Gordon Richardson had feared, international finance would expand far faster than the ability of supervisors keep it safe and sound. In a few years there would be serious consequences, as reckless banking fueled by greed and petrodollars would bring the world financial system to its knees.[30]

CHAPTER 7

Quotas and Concubines

So long as the world economy boomed, politicians and government officials happily claimed the credit. As boom turned to bust, starting in the final months of 1973, they were left with the blame; the same laws and policies that had seemed so instrumental in creating jobs and raising living standards during the Golden Age now were held up as obstacles to economic progress. Government regulators, who had styled themselves as professional, nonpartisan public servants working for the common good came under attack as self-serving bureaucrats protecting their power by stifling innovation and preserving inefficiency. The notion that greater competition might be the key to economic revival was gaining traction, and as it did it would power a worldwide movement for deregulation.

The early push for deregulation, though, had less to do with long-run economic concerns than with Richard Nixon's political problems. When the oil crisis struck in October 1973, the United States was poorly equipped to deal with higher prices and shortages of gasoline and diesel fuel. As a result of suburban sprawl, most homes, and a growing number of office buildings and shopping centers, were in low-density areas beyond the reach of mass transit; outside of a few big cities, almost everybody drove to work alone. Americans' love of large cars was legendary, and the introduction of massive V-8 engines and power-draining air conditioners had reduced fuel efficiency over time. The average car on the road gulped 18 percent more gasoline in 1973 than in 1963. With the typical driver needing to fill up once a week, Americans were spending a lot of time in gasoline lines. And spotty supplies of diesel fuel were disrupting trucking, leaving factories unable to deliver their goods and angering the drivers who moved freight across the country's vast spaces. Nixon, as keen a reader of political tea leaves as ever occupied the White House, knew it was time for decisive action. In December 1973, he appointed an energy czar.[1]

That appointment was, in many ways, a typical government reaction in the early 1970s. The idea that the economy might adjust on its own to changing prices was not widely accepted in the Golden Age. Distrust of market forces was endemic; in almost every country, the most mundane details of economic life, from interest rates on savings accounts to the opening hours of grocery stores, were subject to law, regulation, and bureaucratic whim. Governments also used regulations to reinforce certain social policies without the need for political battles. Stockbrokers were allowed to agree on the commissions investors had to pay when buying or selling shares; this price-fixing ostensibly protected small punters who might make bad bets if they tried to invest without a stockbroker's advice, but it mainly served to fatten brokers' profits. Large businesses communicated by telex, a cumbersome teletype system, because regulators deliberately made long-distance phone calls costly to subsidize cheap local calls. US banking was controlled in such a way that when interest rates rose, home mortgage lending would dry up while loans would keep flowing to business. Such strictures had been in place for so long that they had come to seem entirely normal.

The man Nixon chose to restore order to the unruly energy market did not see things that way. William Simon, the deputy treasury secretary, was an unabashed defender of dog-eat-dog capitalism. Then forty-six, Simon had made his fortune trading municipal bonds, the tax-exempt securities issued by US state and local governments. Unlike many top Treasury officials, he possessed neither an Ivy League pedigree nor a graduate degree.

More interested in athletics than intellectual pursuits, he had studied at a small college, started his career at a little-known bond house, and rose on his merits to become a senior partner of the prestigious investment bank Salomon Brothers. Life in the markets, where opportunity was always fleeting, had conditioned him to act, not to temporize; he was nothing if not decisive, "a human buzzsaw," as a journalist once called him. Simon was a devout Catholic, but he bristled at the notion that he understood Catholicism to be a right-wing ideology. "I am a non-interventionist," he told an interviewer. "I believe in Thomas Aquinas's concept . . . that the community should not do for the individual what the individual can and should do for himself."[2]

Simon had turned down lesser government posts during Nixon's first term, holding out until Nixon appointed him to the Treasury in January 1973, at the start of his second term. With oil prices already on the rise, Nixon soon asked him to chair a committee to revise controversial restrictions on oil imports. Simon had no expertise in energy, and the posting would be his introduction to a sector dominated by state and federal regulations, many of which he openly regarded as bizarre. Congress was eager for Nixon to ask for new powers over the oil market. Simon disagreed vehemently, declaring that the Nixon administration did not want or need additional authority over petroleum production or refining. Market forces, he thought, would eliminate the shortage as high prices prompted risk takers to drill for more oil. The only power that might bring prices back down, he said bluntly, was "the power to create a barrel of oil or gasoline."[3]

Nixon already had a testy relationship with Congress. He was enmeshed in the Watergate scandal, which would soon drive him from office, and his vice president, Spiro Agnew, had been forced to resign in late 1972 after pleading guilty to tax evasion. While some officials might have sought to make peace with the administration's critics, the new energy czar enjoyed goading them. Simon's fief, formally known as the Federal Energy Office, would be housed within the Executive Office of the President, above the many federal agencies and departments that could pose obstacles to decisive action and sheltered from congressional committees that might want to dictate energy policy. Simon was to run the Energy Office while keeping his job as deputy treasury secretary, giving him extraordinary influence over the economy. Energy, Nixon thought, posed tough problems that only a strongman could fix. The analogy, he told his cabinet, was Albert Speer, the architect who took charge of Germany's armaments industry in 1942. Had Hitler not given Speer total control over weapons production, Nixon said, Nazi Germany would have lost the war much earlier.[4]

The obvious way to defuse public anger about gasoline lines and natural gas shortages was to increase production. But Simon soon learned that despite his extensive reach, this was out of his control. All drilling off US coasts, on federal lands, and in Alaska was governed by federal law, and with the memory of the 1969 blowout of an offshore well near Santa Barbara, California, still fresh, Congress was in no hurry to make drilling easier. Legislators were similarly disinclined to change laws that constrained the energy market. One of those laws required the administration to develop plans for allocating petroleum supplies in the event of a national energy shortage. Simon did so three weeks after taking charge of the energy sector, laying out a plan to ration gasoline, jet fuel, and other oil and gas products if necessary. His scheme came with a free-market twist: if rationing were ordered, each licensed driver over age eighteen would be entitled to thirty-two to thirty-five gallons of gas per month, but the ration coupons would be freely tradable. The market, not the government, would set the price.

The proposed rationing plan was a charade. Simon was philosophically opposed to rationing, and he had no intention of putting his scheme into force. After winning plaudits from Congress and headline writers by announcing the plan, Simon consigned it to a shelf. Instead, he set out to encourage private companies to increase oil and gas production by reducing regulation. In the early months of 1974, the energy czar began to take advantage of his ready access to the media to preach loudly against government controls over energy. Simon's highly public assaults on bureaucracy and regulation opened a wide-ranging debate over the economic role of government.

ENERGY WAS AMONG THE MOST HEAVILY REGULATED OF ALL economic sectors in the United States, and the complexity of its regulation was second to none. A 1938 law directed the Federal Power Commission to ensure that natural gas prices were "just and reasonable." The commission did so by regulating pipelines transporting natural gas from wells to storage tanks in other states; it had no power over pipelines that did not cross state borders. In 1954, the Supreme Court ruled that the commission should regulate not just pipelines but also the prices that producers charged for their gas, drastically increasing its reach and its workload. However, as with pipelines, the federal government had no authority over gas produced and used within a single state—meaning that an in-state power plant and an out-of-state power plant could pay different prices for gas from a single well. The Federal Power Commission thus found itself regulating the price of natural gas from tens of thousands of wells when the gas entered *inter*-state pipelines while ignoring the identical product flowing into *intra*-state pipelines.[5]

Never having regulated a gas well, the commission was flummoxed. In 1955, it settled on a process in which the owner of each well would have to submit documents disclosing its costs. The owner would then be required to price the gas high enough to show a reasonable profit. The commission was stealing a time-tested idea, as this was pretty much the way railroads and electric companies had been regulated since the early 1900s.

Yet there was a small problem with this approach: operating a gas well was nothing like running a railroad. Many wells produced both gas and oil, requiring complicated judgments about which exploration and development costs should count in setting gas prices and which should be charged to oil. Some wells were farther from major markets than others and needed to charge lower gas prices to make up for higher transportation costs. New wells had higher drilling costs than wells drilled decades earlier; cost-based pricing made this so-called new gas more expensive than gas from an older well nearby, rendering the "new gas" hard to sell. Moreover, with 4,700 producers submitting reams of cost data, the commission estimated in 1960 that figuring out the correct price for the gas from each well would keep it busy for eighty-three years, assuming no new wells were drilled. And those investigations would not resolve the politically sensitive question of whether cheaper "old gas" should be reserved for consumers to heat their homes or sold to chemical producers that wanted to reduce their input costs.[6]

If the natural gas market had been muddled before, federal regulation of some (but not all) wellhead prices tied it up in knots. By the middle of the 1960s, producers in Texas, Oklahoma, and other gas-rich states could earn far more selling within the state than to customers in other states. Naturally, they tried to sell their gas locally whenever possible. Users in states without gas wells, including the utilities that supplied gas to households and businesses, could not get all the natural gas they needed. Customers willing to pay extra to protect their supplies could not do so, because prices for interstate sales were set by the government, not by negotiations between buyers and sellers.

In Cleveland, thirty thousand workers at seven hundred companies were laid off for ten days in January 1970 when the local natural gas storage tanks hit empty. Gas deliveries nationally fell about 2 percent short of demand in 1971, 5 percent in 1972, and more than 6 percent in 1973. Eastern states from New York to North Carolina, which produced no natural gas but consumed large amounts to heat homes and fuel factories, were hardest hit. Even the *Washington Post*, normally a sharp critic of the energy industry, accepted the American Gas Association's contention that government price-setting was discouraging the search for new gas. The reliably conservative *Reader's Digest*, circulated monthly to eighteen million US households, told readers in April 1973, "We're running out of gas needlessly."[7]

THE US OIL MARKET WAS, IF ANYTHING, EVEN MORE IRRATIONAL than the gas market. The rates charged by oil pipelines that crossed state lines had been under federal regulation since the early years of the twentieth century, and in 1932 Congress had imposed taxes on imported petroleum, gasoline, and lubricating oil to guarantee that domestic producers would be able to sell their oil. Regulation tightened in 1955 after a committee appointed by President Eisenhower recommended holding imports below 10 percent of domestic demand in the interest of national security. When refiners ignored this recommendation—imports in the second half of 1956 exceeded 12 percent of demand—Eisenhower ordered major refiners in all regions except the Pacific coast to "voluntarily" reduce their imports of crude oil by 10 percent, while smaller refineries were asked to seek federal approval of their imports. What this meant, in practice, was that the US Department of the Interior decided how many barrels of imported crude should go to Standard Oil of Indiana's refinery in Virginia or to the Hess refinery in New Jersey.[8]

Bizarrely, this attempt to limit oil imports by voluntary action led to more imports rather than fewer. Refineries that could not get enough imported oil had to buy more domestic crude, forcing up the price of domestic oil. US oil sold for 18 percent more than imported oil, but all refiners received the same prices for their gasoline and diesel fuel no matter where the oil came from, meaning that a refiner more reliant on domestic oil would face a profit squeeze. Refiners thus had an enormous incentive to import as many barrels as they could. Those that had previously used oil from Texas and Louisiana now sought permission to use Middle Eastern and Venezuelan oil, claiming that competitive conditions left them no choice.

After his "voluntary" program failed to hold down oil imports, Eisenhower made import controls mandatory in 1959. Under the mandatory program, each refiner was supposed to receive an import quota equal to at least 80 percent of its last allocation under the voluntary program. But there were many complications. As the domestic price rose above the price of oil from western Canada—normally an expensive source—refineries in the Midwest began importing Canadian oil. To keep the total amount of imports unchanged, the government had to reduce the quotas of refineries on the Atlantic coast, which brought in oil from the Middle East and Venezuela. These large refineries, desperate to avoid having to purchase expensive domestic oil, found a way around the problem by striking deals with small refiners, which were entitled to special import quotas for political reasons. The small refiners signed up to become "concubines" of larger ones, reselling their import quotas at a markup without bothering to refine the oil themselves.

In another circumvention, the New England states that relied heavily on oil for heating won the right to import heating oil outside the quota system, so distributors elsewhere siphoned up cheap heating oil in the Northeast and shipped it west. The strangest arrangement of all was known as the Brownsville Loop. This involved sending heavy Mexican crude by ship to Brownsville, Texas, heating it so it could be pumped into tanker trucks, and sending the trucks across the border into Mexico. There, trucks would go around a traffic circle, cross the Rio Grande back into the United States, and return to the Brownsville docks to pump the oil aboard a ship that would carry it to a refinery—all to qualify it for special quotas granted to imported oil arriving by land.[9]

The oil import quota system was not only Byzantine; it was extraordinarily inefficient. By 1969, import restrictions effectively required East Coast refiners to buy domestic oil for $3.90 per barrel instead of importing Middle Eastern crude for $2.30. Of course, this higher price was passed through to consumers, even as Nixon's anti-inflation program was trying to hold down price increases. And the mandatory use of domestic oil depleted US oil reserves, increasing dependence on reserves abroad—precisely the opposite of the program's intended purpose. Nixon's anti-inflation bureaucracy made matters worse. In the summer of 1972, officials encouraged refiners to maximize their output of gasoline to make driving cheaper. Refining more gasoline from each barrel of oil meant cutting back on other products, such as heating oil. Predictably, heating oil supplies ran short when winter arrived.[10]

Even well-informed citizens were unfamiliar with the intricacies of oil import quotas, and they couldn't make much sense of the battles over new gas and old gas. On the other hand, gasoline lines and heating oil shortages struck close to home. During the anxious months of 1974, Americans frequently heard an unaccustomed explanation: regulation might be causing the energy problem, and deregulation might resolve it.

Deregulation was not an entirely new concept in 1974. Congress had briefly considered rolling back some of the regulations governing trains and trucks in 1957, and in 1968 the Federal Communications Commission had allowed customers to connect some of their own equipment to the telephone network, a tiny step toward deregulation of the telecommunications sector. More consequentially, economists such as George Stigler and Ronald Coase, both of the University of Chicago, had been laying the intellectual framework for deregulation since the 1950s by arguing that the economy would be better off if prices for particular goods and services were determined by competition rather than the dictates of government agencies. The Ford Foundation had jumped into the fray in 1967, granting the Brookings Institution, a Washington think tank, $1.8 million for a program of studies that resulted in 125 books, journal articles, and dissertations on regulation or deregulation by 1975. Warning of an energy "crunch," the oil and gas industry had called for price deregulation in 1971, and its allies at the American Enterprise Institute, a conservative think tank, created their own program to study deregulation. Yet none of this had much practical impact. "Procompetitive regulatory reform was well articulated as a policy prescription; but it remained a solution in search of a widely perceived problem," political scientists Martha Derthick and Paul J. Quirk wrote in 1971.[11]

In truth, politicians of both parties were ambivalent about energy deregulation. They wanted more oil and gas production in the United States, but they did not want to allow the price rises that might encourage wildcatters to drill more wells. Energy policy swayed back and forth with the political needs of the moment, haplessly piling regulation upon regulation in a futile effort to accomplish the impossible.

In March 1973, Nixon's Cost of Living Council, charged with fighting inflation, set controls on the price of oil and on the profit margins of major oil companies. One month after approving these sweeping new regulations, Nixon reversed course, calling for deregulation of "new gas" and announcing that oil import quotas would be phased out over seven years, which would undermine price regulation. In June, the administration changed course again, ordering a sixty-day freeze on prices, including prices of petroleum products, bringing sporadic shortages of gasoline. When the freeze expired in August, the price of oil from new wells was decontrolled but the price of oil from existing wells was not; as with gas, "new oil" could sell for a higher price than "old oil," even when the "new" and "old" wells were just a mile or two apart.

If Nixon's ideas about regulation were inconsistent, those advanced in Congress were even harder to make sense of. Even as legislators called for more drilling, committees drafted bills to strengthen the Federal Power Commission's authority to hold natural gas prices down, which would discourage drilling. In November 1973, seven weeks after the start of the oil embargo, Congress extended federal control over petroleum prices and supplies through August 1975, even though price controls were bound to discourage well owners from pumping oil that was readily available. Federal law dictated that energy prices should remain low, regardless of the law of supply and demand.[12]

This was the situation when Simon took charge of the Federal Energy Office in December 1973. He shared none of his boss's ambivalence about deregulation; later, he would acknowledge that he found Nixon's economic policies "insane." He discovered that, Nixon's public statements notwithstanding, the position of energy czar included none of the dictatorial powers of Albert Speer. "I immediately learned that my plans to operate in an efficient, businesslike manner had nothing on earth to do with the centralized allocation of resources by a government agency," he later wrote. Unable to transform Washington with the stroke of a pen, he tried haranguing it instead. He made himself a prophet of deregulation, using any occasion to advocate freeing the energy sector from layers of government controls.[13]

His first chance came in January 1974, when he pointed out to Congress that federal price regulations enabled some households to buy heating oil for twenty-three cents per gallon while their neighbors were forced to pay twice as much. In March, he successfully urged Nixon to veto legislation that, among many other things, sought to codify the price of oil in law. Soon thereafter, Nixon told Republican Party leaders that he wanted to end federal regulation of natural gas prices. "Do you want natural gas at a higher price or no more natural gas?" he asked them. But his plans went nowhere. The Republicans were well in the minority in both houses of Congress; even if they had been united in support of energy deregulation, they lacked the votes to achieve it. And they certainly were not united. The priorities of Republicans from the Northeast, where oil was the major fuel for heating and for mass transit systems that ferried many workers to their jobs, were very different from those of Republicans from rural oil-and-gas states like Oklahoma, or from a state like Florida, where the cost of electricity for air-conditioning mattered far more than the cost of wintertime heat.[14]

Oil and gas deregulation proved to be very tough nuts to crack. An enormous number of investment decisions, supply arrangements, and pricing formulas were based on the existing regulations. Some factories and power plants had contracted to buy natural gas at fixed prices years into the future; if immediate deregulation enticed owners of old wells to bring more gas to market, the average price of gas would fall, and users with fixed-price contracts would be stuck paying far more than their competitors. On the other hand, if the price of new gas were set free but the price of old gas remained capped, owners of old wells might simply shut them rather than selling their gas at below-market prices. Would oil prices fall if price controls went away entirely, or would they rise to the level set by the Persian Gulf exporters? No one could be certain. And what if US natural gas reserves were so depleted that deregulation failed to stimulate new production? In that case, Congress was warned, Americans' heating bills would soar.[15]

Instead of abolishing regulation with a single big bang, Congress and four successive presidential administrations would vacillate, acting to encourage drilling while holding down consumer prices and assuring various interests, from farmers to transit systems to chemical manufacturers, that they would have enough energy. Although the National Energy Act, passed in 1978, supposedly deregulated energy prices, federal controls on natural gas prices would not fade away until the 1990s. Restrictions on oil exports, designed to assure ample domestic supplies and thus to keep prices low, would survive well into the twenty-first century, even after new discoveries transformed the United States from an importer into an exporter of oil.[16]

SIMON'S TENURE AS ENERGY CZAR WAS BRIEF, BECAUSE NIXON AP-
pointed him secretary of the treasury in May 1974. In his new role, he
continued his impassioned attacks on the harm caused by excessive regulation. He found an important ally in President Gerald Ford, who took
office after the Watergate scandal forced Nixon's resignation in August
1974. On September 10, one month into Ford's administration, Simon
called for "an all-out effort to remove government restraints" on energy,
including price controls on oil and natural gas. "The government," Simon
said, "has posed, and continues to pose, the major obstacle in the short
and medium term to efficient market allocation in energy." Ford extended
the argument to government regulation in general, listing it among the
factors that were propelling inflation to the highest rate since the end of
World War II price controls in 1947.[17]

Amid public anger at gasoline lines and cutoffs of natural gas shipments, such verbal assaults transformed deregulation from an academic
debating topic to a practical concern. Simon missed no occasion to
pound the drum. Federal regulation and inflation "are malignant forces
that are subtly, quietly, but very busily eating away at the foundations of
our society," the treasury secretary proclaimed in February 1975. "We
must lift the heavy hand of government regulation, which cramps so
much of our economy," he wrote two weeks later. But where to start?
With energy deregulation stalled, the Ford administration turned its attention to an industry where the political outlook for deregulation was
more promising: transportation.[18]

Transportation had been the first part of the US economy to be sub-
jected to heavy government control; the Interstate Commerce Act of
1887, which created a new federal agency with jurisdiction over the railroads, was a landmark in the history of regulation. Over time, the Interstate Commerce Commission and agencies much like it took charge of
pipelines, coastal ships, river barges, buses, trucks, and airplanes.

The regulations had two main purposes: to promote stability in the
transportation sector and to ensure that carriers did not discriminate by
treating one shipper, product, or community differently from any other.
Only one or two airlines were allowed to fly each domestic route, charging

fares authorized by the government; airlines' applications to serve new routes were rarely approved. A truck owner wishing to carry cargo between two cities had to prove that the public "convenience and necessity" would be served by his entry into the market—a point the truck lines already serving the route would engage lawyers to dispute. A trucking company also had to obtain approval of the products its trucks could carry and the rates it could charge, to ensure it would not unfairly grab business from other truck lines or from railroads. There were endless investigations of whether changes in railroads' freight rates were justifiable. Coastal ship lines had to charge less for every type of freight than the railroads they paralleled, but not so much less that their competition might undermine the rail industry.

Most other governments had similar regulations, or else they owned transportation companies directly. And almost every country had a "flag carrier," a national airline whose interests the government protected by limiting international competition. Brazil, to take one of many examples, had signed a treaty with the United States specifying how many airlines could fly between the two countries, which airports they could serve, how many flights they could offer, what size planes they could use, and what fares they could charge—all to make sure that Pan American World Airways, the US carrier, and Varig, its Brazilian counterpart, divided the passenger traffic evenly. If a newcomer wanted to offer flights between Atlanta and Rio de Janeiro, the door was closed.

Regulation of prices and market entry had protected transportation companies' profits for decades. High prices and inefficiency were built in, burdening not just users of the transportation system but the entire economy. Airline travel was a luxury, priced beyond the reach of many Americans, even as half of all domestic airline seats went unoccupied. A truck carrying television sets from Memphis to Kansas City might have to return empty if it could not locate cargo it was authorized to carry for the backhaul. Two percent of railroads' revenues went to pay damage claims, and railroads had no particular incentive to reduce that figure because regulators let them pass the costs on to shippers. But by the 1970s, the transportation system was in distress because of high fuel prices and the

loss of business from manufacturers and retailers who found it more profitable to own truck fleets than to deal with regulated truck lines and railroads. Major freight railroads were collapsing into bankruptcy, and airlines
were warning they would need government subsidies to survive.[19]

In this situation, Ford and Simon found an ally from the other end of
the political spectrum: Senator Edward Kennedy of Massachusetts. Kennedy, among the most liberal of Democratic senators, became convinced
that government regulation of the transportation sector, far from aiding
the disadvantaged, benefited some companies and their well-paid workers
at the expense of consumers. In the winter of 1975, he organized a six-part
hearing at which academics, consumer advocates, and Ford administration
officials blamed regulation for high airfares, empty planes, inadequate service on some routes, and excessive service on others. A few months later,
the administration unveiled a plan to eliminate regulation of the airlines—
and, for good measure, of trucks and trains as well.

So drastically had Simon's preaching changed the public mood, and so
dire was the financial situation of the railroads, that support for deregulation transcended ideology. Jimmy Carter, the Democrat who took office
as president in 1977, named Cornell University economist Alfred Kahn to
head the Civil Aeronautics Board, which regulated the airlines. Kahn
promptly began lobbying Congress to put his agency out of business.
Congress was happy to oblige. Later that year, it did away with price regulation of domestic air cargo. In 1978, Congress eliminated federal authority to control passenger fares and to decide which routes airlines could
fly. Economic deregulation of trucking, bus service, railroads, and ocean
shipping would follow. In all, a Congress rabid with deregulatory fervor
passed eight laws in nine years drastically curbing the government's power
over the transportation market.[20]

TRANSPORTATION WAS MERELY THE BEGINNING. CONGRESS PASSED
a law in 1980 deregulating the interest rates banks could pay depositors;
against all expectations, that law led to massive growth of the financial
industry and deprived government officials of the ability to decide which
sectors of the economy were most deserving of credit. US regulations

limiting competition in telecommunications, electricity, and other industries quickly came under scrutiny, and deregulation of oil and natural gas soon returned to the political agenda as well. The movement quickly spread abroad, as critics took aim at laws restricting shop hours, limiting the products stores could sell, allowing companies to form price-fixing cartels, and protecting high international airfares. By 1978, the tide of deregulation had advanced so far that in France, where the state had dominated the economy since the age of Louis XIV, the government abolished controls on the price of bread for the first time in 185 years.[21]

In aviation and telecommunications, deregulation triggered waves of innovation, from overnight package delivery to discount airlines to the mobile phone revolution, which provided precisely the economic stimulus that advocates like William E. Simon had promised. Deregulation infused new life into European cities where the law had required commerce to cease at 6:30 in the evening, revived the moribund US railroad industry, and allowed Japanese consumers their first experience of discount shopping.

In other cases, though, deregulation failed to work as expected. Among them was the US energy industry, where Simon had begun the deregulatory push. While gasoline lines vanished and emergency cutoffs of natural gas were forgotten as consumers learned to adjust to volatile prices, deregulation did not trigger the drilling boom Simon had predicted. Domestic oil production trended downward from 1970 until 2008, long after producers were free to charge whatever they wished, and it took twenty-three years before natural gas production exceeded the level of the early 1970s.

Deregulation brought enormous benefits, but they did not come free. The deregulation of interest rates on deposits and loans made the US banking industry less stable, contributing to the failure of more than a thousand savings and loan associations, which specialized in home mortgage lending, between 1986 and 1995. Taxpayers were forced to cover most of the cost. In other industries, regulated companies, facing little or no competition, had earned steady profits that supported stable, well-paid jobs. As their monopolies crumbled and artificially high prices plummeted, workers and shareholders who had thrived under regulation found themselves far worse off. Dramatically lower airfares allowed hundreds of millions of people to fly for the first time—but competition from new budget airlines brought pay cuts and job losses at long-established carriers. Traffic at the venerable Greyhound bus line in the United States fell 40 percent in six years as air travel became cheap; sharp cuts in bus drivers' pay followed, leading to bitter strikes and, in 1990, the company's bankruptcy. Across the Atlantic, British Telecom shed one hundred thousand jobs after deregulation arrived in 1991.[22]

On balance, however, the results of deregulation were undeniably positive. Where old jobs and old companies vanished, new ones appeared, and new products that had been delayed by regulation—variable-rate savings accounts, mobile phones, privately owned television channels appealing to golfers or gourmets—brought benefits to consumers. Economic growth got a boost as firms, able to negotiate prices and services previously dictated by regulators, found ways to run their own businesses more productively. But without the enveloping structure of regulation, the stability and security that had been such fundamental aspects of the Golden Age were seriously undermined. As governments tried to restore productivity growth and reinvigorate their economies, stability had become an unaffordable luxury.

CHAPTER 8

The Export Machine

It may have been the toilet paper situation that awoke Japan to the dangers ahead. In late October 1973, just as the Arab oil producers were raising prices and cutting back supplies, a rumor made the rounds in Osaka that the country was running out of toilet paper. A newspaper picked up the story, and mobs of housewives soon set upon grocery stores to buy every roll in sight. A government statement that there was no shortage only increased the panic. In Amagasaki, an elderly woman broke her leg when a crowd of shoppers pushed her to the floor. In Shizuoka, one man purchased a thousand rolls, just in case. In Tokyo, stores capped sales to individual customers. As tiny Japanese apartments filled up with boxes of paper, the government stepped in, ordering wholesalers to empty their warehouses of toilet paper in order to stem the frenzy.[1]

With turmoil pervading even the market for toilet paper, no one in Japan could doubt that the country was in dire straits. The soaring price of oil threatened Japan more than any other wealthy economy. During the Golden Age, when its economic growth far surpassed that of any other country, Japan had transformed itself from a beggar into the world's second-largest economy. But the oil shock endangered the dreams of a society that had unexpectedly grown rich. The government in Tokyo was desperate to sustain Japan's unprecedented achievements. Its efforts to do so would reshape the pattern of world trade and contribute to the growing sense of crisis across the rest of the industrialized world.

The 1960s had been an incredible decade. At its start, more Japanese had worked on farms (12.8 million) than in factories (9.4 million), and many of the latter had earned their living hunched over sewing machines or mindlessly watching molding machines spit out cheap plastic dolls. Over the ensuing ten years, manufacturers had invested massively in the latest Western machinery, raising output per work hour more than 10 percent per year, compounded, even as they added millions of jobs. After adjusting for inflation, Japan's income per person had more than doubled, enabling millions of consumers to buy refrigerators, cars, and color televisions. Work was to be had for the asking. Companies were so desperate to hold on to labor that they promised restive workers jobs for life, a new practice that was soon deemed a venerable tradition.[2]

By 1970, though, the elite bureaucrats responsible for planning Japan's future at the Ministry of International Trade and Industry, known as MITI, began to worry that the economy would soon fall to earth. They had good reason for concern, for the foundations of prosperity were not nearly as solid as they looked.

Japan's headlong growth could be traced largely to three factors. One was the embrace of European and American technology. Japanese companies binged on foreign patents and used them to make their factories as efficient as those abroad. By one estimate, new technology alone, almost all of it imported, boosted Japan's economic growth by about 2 percent per year before the onset of the oil crisis. A second contributor was heavy capital investment. Encouraged by low tax rates on interest income, Japanese households' savings rates soared in the late 1950s. Banks recycled that family money into loans to manufacturers. The third big factor, closely related to the first two, was economies of scale, as artisans' tiny workshops gave way to huge factories stuffed with modern equipment.[3]

Japan's "high growth period," as it was officially known, was almost entirely a manufacturing story. By 1970, 45 percent of national income was produced on the factory floor. But high growth could not go on forever. The big gains to be had from updating factories with Western technology were past. Cheap loans and excessive enthusiasm had led to more capital investment than the country needed. And once big plants had squeezed out the less efficient small ones, that boost to productivity could not recur; already in 1970, more than half of Japan's industrial production came from plants with more than three hundred workers.

Meanwhile, other parts of the economy were still extremely inefficient. Japan had 711,269 food shops in 1970, one for every forty-three households. The average bakery employed two workers, the average drug store only three. Thanks to laws that restricted the size of retail stores, thousands more tiny shops were opening each year. At a bank, exchanging a few hundred dollars for yen could take fifteen or twenty minutes and involve encounters with multiple employees, each of whom had to approve the transaction before the Japanese currency could be handed over. While productivity in industries like electronics and metal products had raced ahead during the miracle years, productivity in trucking and railroads had hardly improved at all.[4]

MITI's planners foresaw the 1970s as a time of modernization. They spoke of strengthening Japan's service sector. They favored allowing bigger retail stores so that the hundreds of thousands of mom-and-pop proprietors would have to find more productive work. And they urged manufacturers to move away from metal bashing into high-technology products befitting an advanced economy with an educated workforce, such as computers and aircraft engines. The collapse of the Bretton Woods system in the early 1970s made their efforts to move Japan away from labor-intensive manufacturing look prescient, as the soaring yen left Japanese industry reeling. In just two years, from 1971 to 1973, the cost of one hour of factory labor rose 38 percent in dollar terms, rendering a wide swath of Japanese exports uncompetitive on the world market. Workers' double-digit pay raises were not enough to keep up with inflation, which topped 18 percent in 1973, but they made Japan's exports even costlier abroad. By the time the oil shock slammed the Japanese economy in the autumn of 1973, Japan's industrialists were starting to fear for their future, while housewives were up in arms over what the newspapers described as "crazed prices."[5]

Cheap oil had made it practical for energy-intensive chemical, aluminum, and steel plants to thrive in a country that produced hardly any petroleum or natural gas, so OPEC's price hikes instantly threatened the core of Japanese industry. Seemingly overnight, the mood turned from worried to downright grim. Two years earlier, when companies had still been desperate to staff assembly lines and sales counters, fifteen-year-old boys fresh out of middle school had received an average of 5.8 job offers apiece. Now, in the final months of 1973, unwanted workers faced the ax. At first, women bore the brunt of "operation scale-down," as firms dismissed temporary and part-time workers, most of them female, in order to keep fathers and husbands employed. But as profits declined, men, too, were sloughed off to lower-paying contractors, put on part-time schedules, or forced into early retirement. As the government ordered businesses to use less energy to conserve precious oil, industrial production fell precipitously. Police officials warned of the potential for violent conflict come March, when labor unions would launch their annual "spring offensive" to demand higher pay.[6]

The government tried its best to encourage optimism. In January 1974, it forecast growth of 2.5 percent through March 1975. Had the forecast come true, Japan would have experienced its worst economic performance since 1945, a year when American bombers were setting entire cities aflame, but there still would have been enough growth to fund pay raises. Reality was far bleaker. With the oil shock dramatically increasing import prices, the trade balance turned sharply negative, leaving doubts as to whether Japan had enough foreign currency to pay for oil to keep the lights on. At the same time, soaring prices belied the government's forecast that inflation would subside. As the annual inflation rate headed above 20 percent, the Bank of Japan saw no choice but to raise interest rates, despite the weakening economy. The inflation problem simply had to be solved, Eimei Yamashita, the powerful vice minister of MITI, told the press. If not, he warned, "The Japanese economy will completely collapse."[7]

The anti-inflation campaign hit consumers and businesses hard. In 1973, Japan had still been an international superstar. By the middle of

1974, its economy was underperforming that of every other wealthy country, and its social peace was at risk. Japan urgently needed to bring in enough dollars to pay its oil bill. Government leaders saw no choice but to power up exports.[8]

EXPORT-LED GROWTH WAS HARDLY A NOVEL IDEA. DURING THE 1950s and 1960s, Japan had rebuilt its manufacturing sector by exporting first blouses and radios, then textiles and steel. It ran annual trade deficits almost every year, as its imports of oil and factory equipment cost more than the exports brought in. Those imported capital goods, though, laid the groundwork for a large increase in factory production. The first-ever Japanese auto exports, small in number, appeared on streets in the United States and Thailand. Once containership services to California opened in September 1968, lowering transport costs, the shelves of US appliance stores groaned under the weight of Japanese-made televisions, stereos, and microwave ovens. Japan's chronic trade deficit turned into a surplus.[9]

The political backlash in the United States was immediate. American car companies, steelmakers, and electronics manufacturers were up in arms about the sudden competition from across the Pacific. In the spring of 1968, the State Department demanded that Japan and Europe "voluntarily" limit steel exports to the United States. A few months later, American makers of color televisions petitioned the government to levy punitive import duties on televisions from Japan. And in August, Richard Nixon, seeking southern votes in his campaign for US president, promised the region's textile makers he would try to limit imports of woolen and synthetic fabrics.

Nixon followed through on his promise. Shortly after taking office in January 1969, he put a leading campaign adviser in charge of textile matters. When reporters asked whether he would crack down on Japan, he responded that he would "prefer to handle this on a voluntary basis." The clear implication was that if Japan did not limit its textile exports, Congress would pass a law setting quotas on the quantity of Japanese textiles the United States would accept. Tokyo could not ignore the hint: the United States was Japan's largest trading partner, buying more than a third of its exports by the late

1960s, and also its ally and protector; while Japan spent relatively little on its military, tens of thousands of US troops were housed on the Japanese mainland and the outlying island of Okinawa. When Japanese prime minister Eisaku Sato visited Washington in November 1969, mainly to discuss the return of Okinawa to Japanese control, textiles were on the agenda; improbably, the leaders of the world's two largest economies spent more than two hours discussing woolens and synthetic fibers. After two years of difficult bargaining at the highest levels of government, the two countries finally struck a deal in early 1972 in which Japan agreed to hold down the growth of its companies' textile shipments to the United States.[10]

The intensity of US anger shocked Japan. Who would have expected a president to berate a prime minister about apparel fabric? In reaction, MITI revised its guidance to Japanese companies: "The concept that, 'No matter what may be involved, we must expand exports' can no longer be considered appropriate," it announced in 1972. "Depending on the circumstances, such a policy tends to cause dissatisfaction on the part of other nations." Japan, MITI counseled, should upgrade to exporting knowledge-intensive goods rather than simply shipping larger quantities of the products it was already exporting.[11]

MITI was not simply dispensing disinterested advice. In the Japanese context, companies ignored its words at their peril, because MITI could enforce its guidance with both carrots and sticks. The carrots were grants and subsidized loans to improve energy efficiency, boost production of whichever products MITI favored, and assist workers who lost their jobs as declining industries downsized. In some cases, competitors even won permission to ignore anti-monopoly laws and agree among themselves which factories should close. The sticks were less obvious but just as important. Companies that disregarded MITI's advice might have a hard time getting bank loans. Their requests for protection against imports might not find sympathy. And the government might slap "voluntary" limits on their exports. MITI's word was not exactly law, but few businesses dared argue the point.

Starved of energy and burdened with excess capacity, the smokestack industries that had powered Japan's rise began to wither. Although unions proposed holding down wages in 1975 in an effort to avert mass unemployment, many plants making iron and steel, textiles, aluminum, and petrochemicals were beyond saving. Among business leaders, the realization set in that, as one economist said with considerable understatement in 1976, "Nine percent growth, once envisioned as a reasonable assumption for the second half of the 1970s, now looks rather unlikely." With little prospect of a revival in demand, entire factories were dismantled. Manufacturers began to shed workers by the thousands; eight hundred thousand of them lost their jobs between 1973 and 1979. In 1976 the unemployment rate climbed above 2 percent for the first time since the early 1950s, and it refused to retreat.[12]

To smooth the decline of the old economy, the government stepped in with a scheme to avert mass unemployment. It offered rebates to employers who transferred workers from declining parts of their business to growing ones. There were wage subsidies, training subsidies, and subsidies to help workers seek jobs far away from home. There were grants to supplement the wages of workers whose hours were reduced. If employers in certain industries agreed to retrain workers over age forty-five, the government paid them one-fourth of a year's wage. Yet while MITI could seem omnipotent to foreign observers, it had considerable difficulty working its will. After orders for Japan's shipbuilders fell 90 percent between 1973 and 1978, it was obvious that the industry needed to shrink. But no community wanted to lose its local shipyard, and no company wanted to close its docks. Only in 1978, five years after the shipbuilding crisis began, did the Diet, Japan's parliament, authorize the creation of a scrapping association funded by national and local governments, banks, trading companies, and shipbuilders. By the end of 1980, this cartel had bought and shut down fifty of Japan's 138 shipbuilding docks, eliminating 119,000 jobs but leaving the rest of the industry on a much more solid footing.[13]

A similar story played out in many other industries. In 1972, Japan turned out more than one million metric tons of aluminum. Ten years later, output had fallen 70 percent and half the smelters had closed. Factories making simple electric wares like drills, compressors, and fans saw demand for their products evaporate. Papermakers shut down one-seventh of their cardboard manufacturing between 1977 and 1981, and textile companies abandoned one-fifth of their nylon fiber production. The hard-fought 1972 agreement under which Japan was to limit exports of synthetic fibers to the United States turned out to be irrelevant: exports never reached the permitted level, and many of the plants that once produced them were shuttered for good.[14]

The old economy gave way to a new one, in which engineering and design mattered more than cheap energy and cheap labor. Japan would grow wealthy making cars, advanced electronics, and precision machinery, not commodity products sold by the ton.

It was in the automotive industry that the new economy was most visible. The postwar growth of Japan's carmakers is the stuff of legend. Toyota, which had gotten its start manufacturing looms and sewing machines, was debating whether to fold its tiny automaking arm in 1950 when war broke out in Korea and orders for military trucks saved the day. Honda, which started out making motorized bicycles, produced its first passenger car in only 1963. By the mid-1960s, these firms had become substantial companies, and Japan's auto industry was producing more than 2.5 million cars a year. Workers who wanted to spend their rapidly rising incomes on automobiles had little choice but to buy Japanese. Import tariffs added 30–40 percent to the cost of a US-made Ford or a German Volkswagen in Japan, and registration fees for large imported cars were far higher than for small Japanese-made ones. In any event, few retail auto dealers were willing to handle foreign models. In 1966, Japan imported all of 15,244 cars.

The spike in oil prices in 1973 played to the great advantage of Japanese automakers. While their vehicles were small and not particularly comfortable, they were far more fuel-efficient than larger American and European models. Encouraged by the government, automakers opened new assembly, engine, transmission, and parts plants across Japan. In 1966, Japan had made 5 percent of the world's cars, which earned well-deserved reputations for low quality and cheap finishes. Not until gasoline prices soared in late 1973 did Datsuns and Toyotas become big sellers overseas. When they did, the automakers' new manufacturing capacity let them rev up production quickly. Japanese auto plants increased output from 4.5 million vehicles in 1973 to seven million in 1980. Production of trucks, vehicle engines, and powerful motorcycles went into overdrive. Measured by the number of vehicles, Japan's annual auto exports nearly tripled between 1973 and 1980, and truck exports rose even faster. As quality improved, more affluent buyers in other countries were willing to give Japanese models a chance. The yen's sharp rise against the dollar in 1978 did little to dent sales. By then, Japanese cars were common sights in the United States, where they accounted for one-fourth of automobile sales in 1980.[15]

As MITI's planners had envisioned, small cars were just the leading edge of Japan's new "knowledge economy." Japan's research and development spending per worker rose 70 percent during the 1970s, after adjusting for inflation, turning Japan from a maker of copycat products to a source of innovation. As the credo "lighter, thinner, shorter, and smaller" spread across Japanese industry, high-speed computers, advanced cameras with top-notch optics, numerically controlled machine tools, and high-capacity color photocopiers began pouring out of factories. Not everything turned to gold—the effort to produce a jet engine, fostered for years by MITI, proved a bust—but there were enough successes to turn the country into an export powerhouse.[16]

The 1973 oil crisis tipped Japan's international trade balance back into deficit, as it had regularly been before 1969. The trade deficit in 1974, more than $6 billion, was easily the largest in Japanese history. But red ink was transitory. With its newly restructured export machine shifting into gear while tomes of restrictions limited imports, Japan began piling up trade surpluses of unprecedented size. Those surpluses brought the economy back from the dead. By 1975, Japan was growing again, albeit much more slowly than before 1973. Through the late 1970s and early 1980s, it would outpace every other large industrial economy. Only later would it be clear that those gains had come at some cost to Japan itself. In its laser focus on building knowledge-intensive manufacturing, the government all but ignored the country's remarkably inefficient service sector. Japanese productivity in services was lower in 1980 than it had been in

1970. In the years to come, Japan's obstacles to opening large stores, its restrictions on competition in trucking, its rules forcing banks to shut down their automated teller machines on weekends, and many similar strictures would be seen as drags on economic growth. But at the time, with manufacturing flourishing, the dire state of Japan's service sector barely drew notice.[17]

MORE THAN JAPAN'S TRADE SURPLUSES THEMSELVES, THE PATTERN of trade that emerged from the oil crisis would become a perennial problem. Japan ran steady trade deficits with the countries that supplied it with raw materials—Indonesia, Iran, Saudi Arabia, Canada, Australia—but large surpluses with the high-income countries whose sophisticated industrial products competed with Japan's. As Japan's trade shifted from deficit to surplus, the United States went from rough balance before 1975 to persistent and large trade deficits. The upper Midwest, the heartland of heavy industry, became known as the "Rust Belt," the victim of a disease that would soon be labeled "deindustrialization." Canada and Europe had their rust belts, too, and the English Midlands, the German Ruhr, and the coal and steel towns of France and Belgium would soon be just as depressed as the erstwhile industrial hotspots in the United States.[18]

Throughout the Golden Age, manufacturers in every country had benefited from seemingly unlimited demand for their products. Profits were high—far higher than in farming, mining, or the service sector—and those strong profits financed rising wages, research and development to create new products, and investment in yet more factories. The global growth slowdown after 1973, combined with Japan's forceful push into sophisticated manufacturing and the rapid industrialization of Taiwan and South Korea in Japan's wake, led to a sudden surplus of manufacturing capacity around the world even as higher oil prices were raising operating costs. As manufacturers' profits plunged, factories ran at a fraction of their capacity or closed entirely.[19]

In a representative democracy, no government could passively accept the demise of entire industries and the job losses that would go with it. The political pressure to rescue troubled industries was immense. The

United States, Canada, and the Western European countries all responded to the squeeze on manufacturing with measures to foster industry and preserve industrial workers' jobs. Although the policies differed from country to country, the argument everywhere was much the same. Manufacturing industries were said to play a special, irreplaceable role in economic growth: they typically paid above-average wages, accounted for the largest share of national productivity growth, and spent far more on research and development than service industries. Japan, it was said, was threatening this manufacturing base through its unfair methods of competition, which allegedly subsidized exports while keeping foreign products out of the Japanese market. In the face of this onslaught, supposedly coordinated by MITI, other governments needed to "level the playing field" so their own manufacturers could prosper.

In the United States, the rescue effort mainly took the form of protection against imports. In 1974, in the midst of the recession following the oil crisis, Congress eased the way for companies or labor unions to claim that they were suffering "serious injury" from imports. The government used the 1974 Trade Act to press other countries to limit their shipments to the United States, backed by the threat that if exports were not restrained voluntarily, the new law would allow injured companies to demand high import tariffs that would price the offending foreign products out of the US market. Makers of everything from shoes to typewriters lined up to argue that they were threatened with "serious injury"—a term not defined in the law—and to ask the government to fence out their foreign competitors. The end result was a strange sort of industrial policy, favoring those industries most able to exercise political influence in Washington rather than those judged to be particularly important by any economic criterion.[20]

The bolt, nut, and screw industry offers a textbook example of how the new rules worked. The United States had hundreds of nut and bolt factories, some highly automated, others so old that gloved workers held individual bolts with tongs to heat them in a forge. In December 1977, in response to petitions from companies and labor unions, the US International Trade Commission, an independent government body, determined that this little-known industry was being seriously injured by imports, about three-quarters of them from Japan. The commission urged President Carter to impose tariffs on imported bolts, nuts, and screws of up to 20 percent of the value of the goods. Carter rejected the proposal, thereby bolstering his credentials as a free trader and a friend of Japan.[21]

A few months later, in June 1978, members of Congress asked the International Trade Commission to look into the matter once again. The commission again recommended higher tariffs. This time Carter bent, agreeing to an extra tariff of 15 percent for a three-year period starting in January 1979. Higher import prices allowed domestic producers to raise their own prices, forcing American manufacturers that used nuts and bolts to pay substantially higher prices. By one estimate, limiting imports from Asia cost $550,000 per US job "saved"—at a time when the average bolt maker earned around $23,000 per year. Even then, Carter's policy could not preserve an outdated industry. Total sales of US nut, bolt, and screw factories, adjusted for inflation, were 15 percent lower in the mid-1980s than they had been in 1979.[22]

Bolt making was only one of many US industries awarded government help in the 1970s in the name of preserving jobs. Direct handouts were rare. The more common method of assisting manufacturers was to use the 1974 Trade Act to impose tariffs and quotas that drove up the cost of imports, effectively forcing US consumers to pay the cost of preserving unneeded manufacturing jobs. Makers of ball bearings and color televisions, extra-strength steel, and the machine tools used to mill and bore it all won import restraints, ostensibly to enable themselves to become more competitive.[23]

Europe took a more eclectic approach to aiding industries quaking from the Japanese export boom. Even as European governments demanded that Japan limit exports of tape recorders, textiles, cars, trucks, motorcycles, specialty steel, ball bearings, and televisions, they pumped out cash subsidies for shipyards, steelmakers, and the aircraft industry. Under European Economic Community rules that permitted "regional assistance," governments funneled aid to manufacturers in locations deemed economically challenged, such as southern Italy and West German communities along the East German border. Yet manufacturers' profits did not recover, largely because no European government was prepared to eliminate excess capacity by allowing major industrial complexes to close their doors.

In 1977, Étienne Davignon, formerly an official with the Belgian Foreign Ministry, became the European commissioner for industrial affairs and energy. Davignon was convinced that there was no free-market solution to the overcapacity problems of heavy industries like steel and chemicals. He feared that individual European countries would raise barriers to their neighbors' exports, abrogating the commitment to free trade among the nine member states in order to preserve their own heavy industries. If this occurred, he worried, the very survival of the European Community, whose original purpose in the 1950s had been to restructure the coal and steel industries, could come into question.[24]

Against strong opposition from West Germany, home to the most efficient steelmakers in Europe, Davignon pushed through a plan to create a steel cartel. The idea was that steelmakers could talk among themselves to limit capacity and fix prices, so long as companies and national governments agreed to modernize or close outdated mills. To keep imports from disrupting the arrangement, the European Community negotiated limits on imports with Japan and other countries; those imports that were permitted could be sold only at agreed prices. The Davignon Plan was enormously costly to European steel users, but it had the intended effect of forcing steelmakers to slim down. As older plants closed, one in five European steel jobs disappeared between 1978 and 1981, and even more would go in the 1980s under European Commission pressure. Similar "crisis cartels" were created to purge excess capacity in industries such as textile fibers, chemicals, and glassmaking. When European shipbuilders ran up against a highly subsidized new Asian competitor, South Korea, in 1975, European governments countered with subsidies equal to as much as half the cost of building a ship. Nonetheless, nearly a hundred European shipyards would close within a decade.[25]

THE UNITED STATES AND CANADA WERE SHARP CRITICS OF EUROPE'S fondness for cash bailouts and crisis cartels—except when it came to cars.

The two countries had created a single automobile market in 1965, and the "big three" Detroit-based automakers (General Motors, Ford, and Chrysler) operated plants in both countries and moved cars and parts freely across the border. They had the market to themselves until the late 1960s, when cheap, poorly made Japanese cars made inroads among students and young adults who could afford nothing better. As quality improved, Japanese manufacturers posted steady market-share gains—particularly after oil prices soared in 1973. The second oil-price spike, following the Iranian Revolution in 1979, brought a sharp drop in demand for the big, fuel-gulping vehicles made in North America and a surge in demand for small, fuel-efficient Japanese cars.

In 1979, Chrysler, the smallest of the three Detroit-based producers, reached the edge of bankruptcy. Its reputation for poor quality had driven away buyers, and its product line included none of the smaller vehicles that were in high demand. The company and the autoworkers union turned to Washington for help, claiming that Chrysler's failure would destroy two hundred thousand jobs at assembly and parts plants. Amid raging controversy, Congress agreed to a federal guarantee for $1.5 billion of loans to keep the company afloat.[26]

The guarantee averted Chrysler's immediate collapse, but it could not fix the industry's larger troubles. With 1980 shaping up to be one of the worst years in the history of US auto manufacturing, the autoworkers' union and Ford filed a complaint under the 1974 Trade Act, claiming that the US auto industry was suffering serious injury from Japanese imports and requesting sanctions. The International Trade Commission rejected the petition, finding that high interest rates and the US companies' lack of small vehicles, not imports from Japan, were the main causes of the industry's problems. But as domestic automakers and auto parts manufacturers shed some three hundred thousand jobs during the course of 1980, and as automobile output fell by one-fourth, the pressure for government action ahead of the November 1980 presidential election was impossible to ignore. In the midst of a closely fought campaign, Carter, who had publicly opposed sanctions against car imports from Japan, changed his stance. His opponent, Ronald Reagan, proudly heralded his support for free trade, but he told workers at a Chrysler plant in Detroit that autos were a special case; the US government, Reagan asserted, should "convince the Japanese one way or another, and in their own best interests, the deluge of their cars into the United States must be slowed while our industry gets back on its feet."[27]

Faced with the implicit threat of US trade sanctions, MITI announced "voluntary restraints" on car exports to the United States on May 1, 1981, barely three months after Reagan's inauguration. In each of the next three fiscal years, the Japanese promised, they would ship no more than 1.68 million cars to the United States. A month later, the Japanese government "forecast" that the year's auto exports to Canada would be 5.8 percent below the previous year's level, leaving individual automakers to adjust their export plans to match the forecast. The "voluntary" restraints would go on for years, at extremely high cost to North American consumers. Calculations by the International Trade Commission indicated that Japan's export restraints created 44,100 US jobs in 1984 but cost car buyers $8.5 billion in the form of higher prices, or $193,000 per additional job—approximately six times the annual pay of an American autoworker. The cost per job in Canada was likely even higher. It would have been far cheaper to pay unneeded autoworkers to go do something else.[28]

Japan fared much better. By selling fewer cars for higher prices thanks to the voluntary export restraints, Japanese auto manufacturers reaped perhaps $7 billion in added profit from the United States and Canada in the early 1980s. In addition to erecting assembly plants in North America, the Japanese companies used these profits to develop high-end models; if the number of vehicles they could export to North America was limited, it made sense to ship the most profitable vehicles they could sell. Japanese workers displaced by the decline of aluminum, chemical, and steel manufacturing found ready work in the auto industry, easing the pain of a difficult industrial transition.[29]

SAVING TROUBLED INDUSTRIES IN THE NAME OF HELPING THE working class became a major undertaking across the industrialized world in the decade after 1973. Under the rubric "structural adjustment," unprofitable manufacturers harvested billions of dollars in direct state aid and tens of billions more from the higher prices made possible by government policies that reduced competition, such as restricting imports and legalizing cartels. But the true cost went far beyond the higher prices and subsidies the favored firms were able to extract. At a time when the entire world was struggling with slower productivity growth, most countries' structural adjustment programs systematically assisted sluggish industries with scant growth potential rather than dynamic, innovative ones. The net result may have been to deepen the productivity slump rather than ending it.

This was evident when it came to steel. Almost every country had a steel industry for reasons of national prestige, if not economics. Steel invariably offered some of the best wages of any manufacturing industry, with powerful labor unions negotiating on behalf of the workers. By preserving steel, governments sustained some of the most attractive jobs industrial workers could have. Part of the cost was covered by taxpayers. Part was borne by workers in steel-using industries, whose employers had to pay more for steel than their foreign competitors and were thus less able to afford higher wages. But part of the cost of rescuing steel was even harder to disentangle, because it took the form of economic growth foregone. In the 1970s, steel was one of the least innovative manufacturing industries. US data show that metals companies, mainly steelmakers, spent far less on research and development, relative to sales, than the average for all manufacturers, and they held far fewer patents. Their equipment was old, and hence it often did not incorporate the latest technological advances. Eventually, starting in the mid-1980s, many of the mills that governments had preserved at such high cost were driven out of business by new methods of making and casting steel. These technologies might have developed sooner had governments not subsidized and sustained the old way of making steel.[30]

Similarly, governments in the crisis years lavished attention on the apparel sector. In many countries, garment-making employed more workers than any other industry in the 1970s. But the lack of automation—blouses and trousers were sewn one stitch at a time by poorly educated workers bent over sewing machines, paid by the piece—meant that workers in poor countries could turn out clothing far more cheaply than better paid workers in rich countries. Rather than allowing their citizens to enjoy the benefits of inexpensive clothing, first-world governments, led by the United States, signed an international pact in 1973 permitting the use of tariffs and import quotas to control the garment trade. The Multi Fibre Arrangement, as it was called, soon led to detailed agreements specifying how many brassieres and wool sweaters one country could export to another. At consumers' expense, the arrangement sustained the rich countries' low-productivity apparel industries for three decades, preserving the social peace but delaying the shift of capital and labor into industries where they might have contributed far more to economic growth.

Although it went unrecognized at the time, the end of the Golden Age was the beginning of a sweeping economic transition, in which the massive industrial complexes in vogue since the turn of the twentieth century would cease to be the drivers of economic growth. In their place, manufacturers would organize dispersed networks of much smaller factories, linked by international supply chains and employing ever smaller numbers of workers. The era of well-paid factory jobs for all was over; in the new economy, value would come from innovation, design, and marketing, not from the physical process of turning raw materials into finished goods. Japan and South Korea, the rising industrial powers, were the outliers in the late 1970s, but within a few years their manufacturing sectors, too, would begin to shed workers. Governments eager to restore past glories did not like the fact, but the industrial economy was slowly yielding to the information economy, and no amount of government assistance was going to bring it back.

CHAPTER 9

The End of the Dream

Economically, the struggles of the factory sector were challenging. Psychologically, they were devastating. When recession set in at the end of 1973, more than one-quarter of the civilian workers in the wealthy economies were engaged in manufacturing. Many more, from delivery-truck drivers to waitresses at factory-gate bars to pensioners receiving benefit checks, depended on manufacturing for their livings even if they were not directly on factory payrolls. The postwar industrial expansion had delivered this vast working class a steadily improving living standard and an unprecedented sense of economic security, buoyed by the spreading welfare state. But as well-paid jobs began to vanish and workers found themselves running in place, desperate to maintain the material gains and upward mobility of the last quarter-century, the welfare state became as much a burden as a benefit. The state's inability to deliver the ever-rising living standards it had promised would lead to a palpable social anger, with substantial political consequences.

Why, in the postwar years, had life gotten so much better for almost everyone? The best-known answer, the one that most influenced elite opinion, was advanced by the renowned American economist Simon

Kuznets. His explanation, which linked the development of an advanced industrial society to a more equitable distribution of income, became known as the Kuznets curve.

Kuznets, trained as a statistician in Bolshevik Russia, fled to the United States in 1922. He studied economics at Columbia University, earning his master's degree one year ahead of Arthur Burns, and then became a protégé of business cycle theorist Wesley Mitchell, who would also guide Burns's career. In 1927, after earning his doctorate, Kuznets joined the National Bureau of Economic Research—soon to be headed by Burns—and developed many of the statistical concepts still employed today to track national income and productivity. It is not a stretch to regard Kuznets as the father of the gross national product, a concept used since the 1930s to compare economies' size and growth—although, unlike most of the politicians who use his figures, he emphasized that many aspects of citizens' well-being are not captured in GNP. As he told Congress in 1934, "the welfare of a nation can . . . scarcely be inferred from a measurement of national income."[1]

During World War II, Kuznets turned his attention to the roots of economic growth. After assembling data on fourteen countries, he concluded that the distribution of income within a country might be related to the country's stage of economic development.

Kuznets contended that the countries whose economies were most advanced in the 1950s had passed through three stages of growth. In the first, as agrarian societies began to industrialize and urbanize, many farmworkers and artisans lost ground. Their incomes fell as their skills were devalued, while people with access to cash profited by investing in new industries. This was the age of the Industrial Revolution, starting in the late eighteenth century, when gangs of "machine breakers" destroyed the steam-powered textile looms they blamed for their poverty and government-sanctioned monopolies allowed selected factory owners to prosper at consumers' expense. As millions of workers fell into abject poverty, society became more unequal.

After several decades, Kuznets suggested, the early stresses of industrialization eased as fewer people were pushed off the land and fewer artisans driven out of business. Yet wages remained depressed in this second stage of development, as the masses of unskilled workers in the cities made it easy for employers to staff their factories without raising pay. The total absence of government assistance for the unemployed and disabled forced laborers to accept jobs regardless of the wages offered. This was the mid-nineteenth-century world of Karl Marx, in which a small number of people with capital exploited an impoverished working class that had little prospect of improving its abject lot.

Marx understood the circumstances of his time correctly, Kuznets said, but he erred in assuming that those circumstances were a permanent feature of a capitalist economy. As economies entered the third stage of development and more people moved into cities, birthrates fell. This meant that families' incomes went further to provide children with food, education, and healthy living conditions. Urban-born workers, likely to have attended school and to have acquired skills needed in a modern economy, supplanted the semi-literate migrants who had populated industrial cities in their parents' generation. They were better able to exert political influence as well, winning legislation to establish social programs that supported households toward the bottom of the income scale. Hence, Kuznets theorized, when economies reached a certain stage of development, income inequality began to recede. This had been going on in England since the late nineteenth century, and in the United States and Germany since World War I. It seemed to be happening on an even larger scale after World War II.[2]

The notion that inequality followed a U-curve, first widening greatly but eventually becoming less extreme, was comforting to the men who set economic policy during the Golden Age. Everyone knew that government guidance was helping to tame the business cycle, assuring steadier growth and lower unemployment than the world had known before. Now Kuznets's work seemed to imply that a more equal society was part of the package, at least in the industrial countries, along with regular work and higher wages. As incomes rose, almost everybody could see their lives improving from year to year. Average people could begin to amass wealth, just as the rich did. The gap between rich and poor would gradually narrow even as almost everyone grew better off. It was a seductive vision.

EVALUATING CHANGES IN INCOME DISTRIBUTION IS A HAZARDOUS enterprise. "Income" can be defined in many ways; one scholar might study changes in workers' pretax hourly wages, while another, who focuses on households rather than individuals and counts investment income rather than just wages, might tell an entirely different story. There are also many ways to measure how income is divided among a country's population. Comparing the average income of the chronically unemployed with that of the top 1 percent may yield different insights than examining changes in the share of households in the middle. Short-term trends may differ from long-term trends: a stock market downturn may mean that the wealthy receive less from selling shares for a year or two, temporarily making income look more evenly distributed; but that effect may be reversed as soon as share prices rise. And of course, measuring income does not provide a useful picture of the distribution of wealth. While almost all households receive income, a much smaller proportion own real estate, stocks and bonds, or businesses.

By any measure, there is no disputing that economic resources in the wealthiest countries were spread much more evenly in the years after World War II than in the years before. The economic elite did not starve, but in eleven of the twelve wealthiest countries for which data is readily available, the top 1 percent of households claimed a much smaller portion of total income in the 1950s and 1960s than they had enjoyed in the 1920s and 1930s. One in nine West German households survived on less than half the average household income in 1962, but only one in sixteen was in this lowest income group in 1973. A third of US households reported income below the official poverty line in the late 1940s, but only one in nine did so by 1973, the year in which the average hourly wage, adjusted for inflation, reached its all-time high. Only in Switzerland did the earners with the lowest incomes fail to gain on those nearer the top.[3]

Higher incomes made it possible for a greater number of people to buy homes and save money, so wealth, too, was spread more widely during the Golden Age. The top 1 percent of Dutch households had possessed nearly half the country's wealth in 1939, but by 1973 their share had dropped to barely one-quarter. The wealthiest 1 percent of Norwegians owned 34 percent of the country's wealth in 1948, but just 22 percent in 1973. Information from wills in France and the United States during the 1960s reveals that people of modest means accounted for a much larger share of the value of estates than in prewar years. Because wealth often produces rents, interest payments, and dividends for its owners, more widely shared wealth may well have contributed to greater equality of income.

This increased equality did not occur by magic. Many countries raised their top tax rates on income in the 1930s and early 1940s to finance the war. In some cases those high rates remained in place for many years, capturing up to 80 percent of the incomes of the highest earners. Higher inheritance taxes made it harder to pass large amounts of property from one generation to the next, evening out the distribution of wealth over time. The results could be seen at the Picasso Museum in Paris, filled with art taken by the French government in lieu of inheritance taxes, and at the stately country houses run by Great Britain's National Trust, many of which were surrendered by families that had owned them for centuries until the death of a patriarch triggered an unaffordable estate tax liability.

The strength of organized labor was another factor helping average workers improve their standing. Political leaders in many countries granted unions greater influence after the war, either from the desire to promote national unity or, in the cases of West Germany and Japan, under directives from the victorious Allied powers. The manufacturing boom contributed to the unions' strength. In the postwar world, many of the new jobs were in manufacturing. In Japan, to take but one example, manufacturing occupied one in five workers in 1950, one in three in 1970. Workers in manufacturing were far more likely to join unions than those in agriculture or service industries, so the growth of manufacturing gave unions an ever-growing pool of prospective members. Almost any type of factory work paid better than farm work, domestic service, or day labor, the other types of employment available to workers with little training or education, so the growth of manufacturing naturally raised incomes for a very large proportion of the labor force.

Powerful unions do not always bring about a more even distribution of income, because workers covered by union contracts are likely to be far from the poorest of the poor. In the postwar world, however, unions' clout extended far beyond the ability to negotiate wages with individual employers or even across an industry. They became full partners at the political bargaining table, advocating powerfully for higher minimum wages, protections from dismissal, paid sick leave and holidays, and old-age pensions. In some countries, unions played a role in raising pay for the women who entered the workforce in large numbers, giving an added boost to the incomes of two-earner families. In some cases, national union leaders even bargained with the heads of business organizations and government officials to set the share of national income that would be paid out in workers' wages and the share that would be paid out in profits, evening out the distribution of income by limiting the amount that could go to corporate shareholders or the owners of small businesses.[4]

But as the economist Thomas Piketty has shown, one of the most significant causes of greater equality in the postwar world had less to do with economic policy than with tragedy. World War II destroyed massive amounts of capital: apartments, shops, office blocks, and factories were blown to bits, along with production machinery and household furnishings. Even those business firms whose assets were not destroyed or confiscated saw their profits hurt by price controls, shortages of raw materials, and the financial problems of their customers. Those vanished assets had been owned by a select group of people, so the destruction of capital flattened out the distribution of wealth. And because much of that wealth had been used to produce rents, dividends, and interest payments that flowed into the pockets of the affluent, the loss of wealth tended to even out incomes. The gap between rich and poor narrowed not just because the poor were doing better, but also because the rich, for a brief while, were doing worse.[5]

THE TREND TOWARD GREATER EQUALITY REVERSED IN THE MIDDLE years of the 1970s, just as wage gains were beginning to slow. The timing was not the same everywhere, and the extent to which the top tier fared better than average earners or the lowest paid varied considerably from country to country. Some countries did more than others to increase the spending power of those with below-average incomes, whether by providing extra help to families with children or by encouraging banks to extend credit to homebuyers and business owners who formerly might have been rejected. But there is no doubt that the final quarter of the twentieth century was a time when those commanding high pay and investment income enjoyed a very high standard of living, while the majority of wage earners struggled to keep their footing.

It was in the United States that increasing income inequality first became visible. In 1974, amid a brutal recession, median earnings—the amount earned by a person earning less than one-half the workforce and more than the other half—rose by less than the inflation rate. Wages for female workers regained their previous level as the economy improved, but wages for men did not. Four decades later, the median full-time male worker in the United States still earned less, after adjusting for inflation, than in 1973. The share of household income received by the bottom three-fifths of households began to glide downward, while the share received by the top fifth began to climb. The take of the highest earners climbed fastest. In 1973, the top 1 percent of households received 7.4 percent of total household income. By the end of the century, their portion had more than doubled.[6]

In Great Britain as well, the average working family lost buying power between 1974 and 1979. Income inequality did not increase at first—but only because the Labour Party government's anti-inflation program clamped down tightly on pay raises for highly paid workers. Workers earning above certain limits had their pay capped, and at some points the top earners were barred from receiving any raises at all. Incomes inevitably became more equal, until the strictures came off. When they did, in 1977, the pay of managers and professionals surged, and income inequality started to increase. Even though higher pensions and other government benefits boosted the incomes of some population groups, especially retirees and single parents, income distribution grew far more skewed in the 1980s, and would continue to grow increasingly unequal for decades beyond.[7]

The disparities in other wealthy countries were less stark, in most cases because government stepped in to reduce the effects of less equal wages.

In Canada, for example, wage inequality increased from the mid-1970s but income inequality did not, thanks to government benefits that targeted low-wage workers. It was not until the 1980s that the top wage earners began to pull away. In Japan, incomes became more equal through the 1970s; but once inequality began to rise, around 1981, it advanced so steadily that by 2005 one author could write that it was "approaching the highest among advanced countries." Sweden, long thought of as a bastion of social-democratic equality, saw income disparities begin to increase around 1981, and so did Spain and Switzerland. One of the few international outliers was France, which aggressively used taxes and benefit programs to reduce income differences through the 1970s and 1980s and maintained them into the twenty-first century.

Under other circumstances, greater income disparities might not have been a significant problem; at any given time, some people inevitably fare better than others. But in the 1970s and 1980s, the widening gap between average families and those with high incomes coincided with the great global slowdown in wage growth. The precise extent of the wage slowdown is uncertain because in the 1970s most countries collected wage data only for the manufacturing sector. But the evidence on manufacturing wages is crystal clear. Of eighteen wealthy countries in Europe, North America, and the Pacific, every single one saw a sharp drop in wage growth among manufacturing workers after 1974, after adjusting for inflation. As workers saw the gulf between themselves and their better-paid neighbors widening, they saw their stable, middle-class lifestyles crumbing beneath their feet.[8]

WHAT CAUSED SUCH A DRASTIC SHIFT FROM THE GOOD TIMES OF the Golden Age? The most commonly heard explanations for the sharp slowdown in workers' wage gains and increasing income disparities have to do with political decisions—the failure to raise the minimum wage in one country, tougher regulations that discouraged hiring in another, international trade agreements that made rich-country workers more vulnerable to competition from low-wage countries, laws that made it possible for corporate bosses to set their own pay with scant regard either for the pay of their employees or their own performance on the job. It is perhaps inevitable that such conclusions became popular: people naturally attribute problems they experience firsthand to causes that seem familiar and obvious, all the more so when pundits and political opponents helpfully assign blame.

Yet purely domestic explanations are insufficient. While the social and political implications were different in every country, the phenomena of slower wage growth and widening disparities were global, affecting every high-income country and many middle-income countries. A meaningful explanation of global trends needs to be global as well. The most likely suspect lies in an economic ratio rarely mentioned in news reports, one of those figures whose year-to-year fluctuations are of no particular interest but whose longer-run movements greatly affect the state of the world. Economists know it as the "labor share."

The labor share is the amount paid out in wages to each active worker, divided by the amount of national income per active worker. In plainer language, it is the proportion of a nation's income that goes into wages, rather than to the owners of capital as dividends or profits or to the government in the form of taxes on production. Labor share is by no means a precise estimate of workers' share of the economic pie, as many workers receive capital income as well; the owner of a small business may pay herself a modest weekly wage, but she is also entitled to the firm's profits, if any. For the vast majority of workers, though, capital income is likely to be small—a few dollars of interest on a savings account, or the dividends on a handful of an employer's shares. Changes in the labor share thus are useful in understanding how well workers are faring collectively relative to owners of capital.

In the second half of the 1970s, the labor share began to fall, not just in a single country but in every part of the world. The decline began in 1974 in the United States and West Germany and hit a year later in Japan and Great Britain. It spread to Australia in 1976, Canada in 1978, and Italy and the Netherlands around 1980. By the early 1990s, even Finland and China had experienced declining labor shares. Of the forty-six countries for which at least fifteen years of reliable data is available, thirty-seven show statistically significant declines in the labor share after 1975. Globally, by one estimate, the share of income paid out in wages declined by five percentage points between 1977 and 2012. And the trend was well underway before the bursting of Japan's "bubble economy" at the end of the 1980s, the shock of German reunification in 1989, the passage of the North American Free Trade Agreement in 1994, and China's emergence as a major player in the world economy in the early 2000s.[9]

Taken alone, a declining labor share does not mean that anyone is growing poorer, and it does not necessarily reflect any change in the way employers determine wages. If an economy is growing fast enough, there can be pay raises for all even as the labor share declines. But when the pie itself is growing more slowly at the same time that the labor share is shrinking, it becomes highly likely that many citizens will receive a smaller slice. And when a declining share of national income is rewarding workers, an increasing share is probably going to owners of capital, who are overwhelmingly to be found among upper-income people. So while in theory the declining labor share need not have upset the economic balance, in practice there are good reasons why it created the feeling that the few at the top were moving ahead while the many beneath them were being left behind.[10]

The main cause of this global decline in the labor share, to the extent economists can disentangle the forces at work, was most likely a speedup in the rate of technological change. Technology contributed directly to higher unemployment during the late 1970s by reducing the number of workers needed for many tasks. Beyond that, it increased competition by permitting entire industries to operate in new ways. Established steelmakers had been sheltered from competition by the billion-dollar cost of new steelworks until the electric arc furnace allowed newcomers to build steel plants far more cheaply. And new ways of cutting and packaging beef far from urban stockyards destroyed the longstanding dominance—and pricing power—of a handful meatpackers in the United States. Greater competition pressured firms' profits, making it tougher for unions and workers to bargain for higher wages.

More fundamentally, technology changed the mix of skills required in a modern economy. As automation devalued skills and craftsmanship, it reduced workers' bargaining power in the labor market. In the 1950s, a strike by telephone workers meant that calls were not completed, disrupting users' lives. By the 1980s, a telephone strike went unnoticed by most telephone subscribers, whose service was unaffected. When factory workers demanded higher pay, it became plausible for manufacturers to threaten to shift production to countries where wages were lower, because they could now do so without sacrificing the quality of their products and the reputations of their brands. As leverage shifted in employers' favor, unions found it far tougher to bargain for better pay and job security, and workers in many industries found it impossible. At best, workers could hope to learn enough to become proficient in the new technologies that were reshaping their workplaces. At worst, they would be condemned to an early pension, their industrial skills no longer sufficient to command satisfactory pay in the information age.

For all their pompous claims to have brought permanent prosperity, the leading economists of the day had no real answers for the many people who felt they were losing ground. Politicians could offer little more than platitudes about the importance of professional training and education at a time of rapid technological change. The public, schooled to believe that the government could provide economic security for all, watched its leaders' haplessness with mounting anger—an anger that expressed itself in a revolt against the taxes that financed the welfare state.

THE CONCEPT OF THE WELFARE STATE, AND WITH IT A NEW understanding of government's role in society, had emerged during the depths of the war. The idea that government should provide a safety net was not new: Germany adopted a sickness insurance law as early as 1883, and Sweden's disability insurance scheme dates to 1901. Such programs, though, were designed mainly with urban industrial workers in mind, and they often provided little or no help to others. Sweden's vaunted unemployment insurance system, for example, covered only 70 percent of wage earners as late as 1950, leaving the remaining workers unprotected. The US old-age pension program, Social Security, excluded farmworkers, domestic workers, and the self-employed when it began in 1937. Limited coverage and highly favorable demographics allowed governments to offer such benefits at very modest cost. When the first Social Security checks were mailed out in 1940, 3.5 million retirees received payments financed by the taxes of thirty-five million workers and their employers, each paying 1 percent of the first $3,000 of income. For the average American manufacturing worker, whose annual wage was around $1,200, the tax bite came to all of $12 per year.[11]

The basic aim of the welfare state was to make such benefits universal. When child allowances were inaugurated in Great Britain and Canada in 1945 and in France a year later, payments were based only on the number of children, not on family income. Pressured by agrarian parties whose members gained little from programs designed to help urban workers, the four Scandinavian governments committed themselves to bringing health insurance and pensions to everyone, including farmers and the self-employed.

Once the middle class was firmly on board, fattening the social benefits package became politically irresistible. President Eisenhower, a conservative Republican, extended Social Security benefits to disabled workers in 1956. A year later, the West German government, controlled by the conservative Christian Democratic Union and its Christian Socialist allies, raised old-age pensions by 60 percent. In Great Britain, social benefits edged steadily higher as a share of government spending even while the Conservative Party was in power in the 1950s; in the new, more egalitarian environment of the postwar world, the party of old money and new wealth did not want to stand accused of indifference toward the working class.[12]

Through the 1960s, prosperity allowed governments to be even more generous. At the start of the decade, cash benefit payments from government directly to families, such as child allowances, pensions, and disability and unemployment compensation, averaged 6.8 percent of national income in the wealthy countries. By the early 1970s, the average was above 10 percent. Finland, the laggard among the Northern Europeans, inaugurated national sickness insurance in 1963. A year later, Italy granted all older people state-funded pensions, even if they had paid little or nothing into the pension schemes. France and Great Britain boosted child allowances much faster than inflation.[13]

The universal welfare state did not stop with direct payments. In January 1964, just six weeks after the assassination of President John F.

Kennedy, his successor, Lyndon Johnson, declared war on poverty. Congress responded by enacting food assistance for the poor and taxpayer-funded medical care for the poor and the elderly. The United States, Great Britain, and several other countries debated the virtues of a "negative income tax," which would have ensured each household a basic level of income, funded by the government, without requirements or restrictions. Spending to expand colleges and universities to welcome millions of new students was massive. In Japan, enrollment in higher education rose nearly 800 percent between 1950 and 1975, and the number of students enrolled beyond high school in Western Europe tripled. The vast majority of college and university students attended state-owned institutions that charged little or no tuition. Since the children of doctors and teachers were far more likely to score well on the entrance exams needed for university admission than the children of street sweepers and factory hands, free higher education was yet another subsidy to please the rising middle class.

Among the advanced economies, the only one that resisted the welfare state was Japan. For more than a quarter-century after their country's surrender in 1945, Japanese leaders viewed their country as an impoverished nation in the midst of reconstruction, unable to afford welfare programs. Although they were willing to invest in education because of the clear economic payoff, they were wary of the government-sponsored benefits that proliferated in Europe and North America. But after Japan's remarkable run during the 1960s, when the economy almost tripled in size, it was no longer so easy for the government to plead poverty. Amid much celebration, it rolled out new health, pension, and income supplement programs in 1973. The Japanese termed this the "first year of social welfare," the year when Japan's future glowed so brightly that citizens could at last reap rewards from their years of sacrifice.[14]

ALL THESE PROGRAMS TOOK MONEY. THE WELFARE STATE CHANGED average citizens' relationship with their government not only by providing them benefits, but also by requiring them, for the first time ever in a period of relative peace, to pay a substantial share of their incomes in the form of taxes.

Historically, few individuals had paid taxes directly to national governments. The United States was not atypical in this respect. In 1939, the year World War II erupted in Europe and Asia, all federal taxes combined came to a mere 7.6 percent of national income. Most of those taxes were indirect, and therefore largely invisible: the government collected far more from import duties and levies on whiskey and cigarettes than from taxes on workers' wages. Just one-fortieth of total national income was collected in federal income tax. Although the official tax rates on personal income reached a stiff 79 percent, only the handful of corporate chieftains and movie stars paid that rate. Around four-fifths of American families owed no income tax to the federal government because their income, after various exemptions and deductions, was below the $2,500 threshold at which taxes were due.[15]

The situation in most other countries was quite similar until war changed matters. Wartime tax burdens rose sharply as governments imposed surcharges, excess profits taxes, and a variety of other measures. In the most extreme case, Nazi Germany taxed occupied countries harshly to finance its war effort and employed its tax system to expropriate the assets of Jews and other victims who emigrated or were deported. On the Allied side, Great Britain's income tax take quadrupled between 1937 and 1943. The basic tax-free allowance was lowered so that most workers were paying income tax by the war's end; the top rate for those with high incomes was a stratospheric 98 percent.

The war made tax collectors more aggressive, too. "What I need is cash, and cash out of current income," Sir Kingsley Wood, Great Britain's chancellor of the exchequer, declared in 1940. When only a handful of wealthy people had been liable for income tax, they had usually been allowed to remit payment once or twice a year. The millions of middling folk now swept into the tax system were unlikely to have enough cash on hand to make one big annual payment, and besides, governments required a steady flow of money to pay for troops and weaponry. The United States acted first, requiring employers to withhold taxes from workers' pay packets in 1943. "We cannot get those fellows unless we have the collection-at-the-source method," a US Treasury official explained as he asked senators to approve the proposed legislation. The British christened their withholding scheme "Pay As You Earn," as if withholding gave the worker a remarkable opportunity to contribute to the government out of each week's earnings. However it was spun, there was no getting around the reality that each weekly pay stub brought a reminder of the sharper tax bite.[16]

Once the war was over, income-tax rates generally remained high, but at first they were structured so that a large number of workers paid little or nothing. In Japan, fewer than one million people had paid income tax for most years before and during the war; even after an American-imposed reform in 1947 brought the number of taxpayers to seven million, only one in seven Japanese adults had taxable income. Although 14.5 million British workers paid income tax in 1949, up from 3.8 million a decade earlier, about half of all adults still paid no tax. In 1951, the typical US family with children paid less than 3 percent of its income in federal income tax, and many families had no liability at all. In Canada, "direct taxes on persons" ate up only 6.4 percent of personal income in 1950, one-third less than during the war. Although West Germany's basic tax rate was 20 percent after a 1958 reform, allowances created to protect average workers meant that many paid less than 6 percent of their incomes in tax.[17]

Taxing average earners lightly and high earners at very high rates made after-tax incomes more equal, fulfilling an important social goal. But a system in which the vast majority of people paid little or no income tax simply could not generate enough revenue to finance the growth of the welfare state.

THE WELFARE STATE WAS A REMARKABLE ACCOMPLISHMENT. IT brought dignity to millions upon millions of pensioners who no longer faced penury in old age. Disability insurance prevented workers' families from falling into poverty following on-the-job injuries, and health benefits ensured that even the poorest children could visit the doctor. Unemployment insurance lessened the sting of recession not just for those who had lost their jobs, but for the businesses they patronized and the manufacturers whose goods they bought. Economists spoke of social insurance programs as "automatic stabilizers," and rightly so, for they kept money in consumers' hands when times got tough.[18]

But a beneficent government did not come free. Although wages, profits, and consumer spending were growing smartly, the cost of the welfare state was growing even faster. Across the advanced economies, spending on income-support programs alone increased about 150 percent, above and beyond inflation, between 1960 and 1974. Only one among the twenty-four most advanced economies, tiny Iceland, spent a smaller share of its national income on social security in 1974 than in 1960. As the growth in social spending outran the growth in workers' pay, the welfare state came to be seen as a burden as well as a benefit.[19]

As with so much else, the crisis year of 1973 was a turning point. As productivity growth declined and business profits took a tumble, the growth of workers' wages began to slow. The growth of the welfare state did not. On the contrary, millions of workers displaced amid the economic slowdown lined up to collect unemployment benefits. Millions more, convinced that they were too old to find new occupations, drew their pensions early. By 1980, most women in Western Europe were out of the workforce before their sixty-first birthday; most men were out by sixty-three. Spending on benefits that were based on income, such as housing assistance and food aid, rose as well, as more families became eligible. Outlays under the US government's food stamp program, for example, doubled between 1974 and 1976 as the number of beneficiaries rose almost by half.[20]

Social insurance bore the burden. At a time of economic difficulty, it did the job it was designed for, protecting families from the ravages of unemployment and reducing the depth of the global recession. But it accomplished that task by vacuuming up increasing amounts of money in the form of taxes and mandatory contributions and redistributing it through formulas that only the most devoted policy wonk could understand. In the first half of the 1970s, to take but one example, the West German government's spending increased 93 percent, while the economy expanded 52 percent. Across Western Europe, social security programs— not including some health programs and higher education—grew to account for almost one-sixth of the economy by the end of the decade.[21]

Aside from reducing benefits, which was political suicide almost everywhere, the only ways to make the sums add up were to raise taxes or borrow. In 1965, the twenty-four wealthiest nations collected, on average, 24.8 percent of the national income in the form of taxes. By 1973, as the welfare state grew, the average tax take approached 28 percent of national income. By 1977, the figure had reached 31 percent—a staggering increase in the span of a dozen years. The pattern of rising taxes occurred in every one of the advanced economies, without exception. In the most extreme case, Sweden, the tax collector's share rose by an astonishing thirteen percentage points in those twelve years, to the point that 45 percent of every krona Swedes earned in 1977 went to taxes.[22]

Inflation did much of the dirty work. In most wealthy countries, the income-tax laws created numerous brackets, with each increment of income taxed at a higher rate than the ones below. Australians were assessed a modest 8 percent tax rate on their first bit of income, but those whose earnings put them in the twenty-seventh bracket paid 66 percent on that last bit. In Italy, the thirty-two tax steps ranged from 10 percent to 72 percent; in Japan, low earners paid only a 10 percent tax rate, but higher earners paid as much as 75 percent on the final piece of their income. As a rule, these steps did not change with inflation, so even if a worker's annual pay raise merely kept pace with the consumer price index, the additional lira or yen or dollars might well be taxed at a higher rate than the previous year's income—leaving the worker with less take-home pay, after adjusting for inflation. Thus, although wages seemed to be rising year after year, many families felt they had less left to spend as more of their income fell into higher tax brackets.[23]

It was thus no accident that during an inflationary decade, taxes grew more painful and more controversial. The government was claiming a steadily greater share of families' incomes, even as those incomes failed to keep up with inflation. Factory workers and street sweepers felt the bite as much as their bosses did. As late as 1969, the average one-worker family in West Germany had paid nineteen pfennig in income tax on each additional deutsche mark of earnings—a marginal tax rate of 19 percent. By 1978, that family's marginal tax rate had almost doubled. British families, except for the most affluent, paid about 10 percent more of their incomes in taxes in 1979 than they had in 1969; the journalist Peter Jenkins calculated that a married Brit with two children, earning the average industrial wage, paid 26 percent of his earnings in taxes in 1976, a jump of seven percentage points in just four years. Matters in Canada were even more aggravating: the average Canadian's income-tax rate rose twenty percentage points between 1958 and 1985.[24]

Equally important, at least from a political perspective, is that the higher tax burden weighed directly on individuals' earnings. In earlier years, businesses had borne much of the bill for the welfare state through taxes on profits and fees for their employees' social insurance. Eventually, of course, businesses passed these expenses along to shareholders and workers, but so far as workers were concerned, the costs were invisible. And a very large share of government receipts in the wealthy countries, 43 percent in 1970, came from taxes on consumption, such as sales taxes, and on property and wealth, such as inheritance taxes. Between 1970 and 1980, business, consumption, and wealth taxes declined sharply relative to national income in most of the wealthy countries. Across the advanced economies, income taxes and social security charges provided 34 percent of governments' revenues in 1970, 38 percent in 1975, and almost 40 percent in 1980. The cost of the welfare state was shifted increasingly to income taxes, paid directly by workers who saw greater sums withheld from their paychecks. Wage earners' complaint that they were bearing more of the burden of government spending was entirely justified.[25]

Yet even with the average citizen paying a greater share of income to the tax collector each year, the sums did not add up. Large budget deficits became the norm as governments borrowed to cover the costs of the social benefits they had promised. The US government's deficit, insignificant during the 1960s, tripled during the 1970s despite sharp cuts in defense spending. Japanese government expenditures were roughly equal to receipts until 1973; thereafter, large deficits were an annual affair. West Germany, which had run only small budget deficits before 1973, ran big ones for the rest of the decade.[26]

The dramatic change in the financial position of governments in the wealthy countries can best be seen in the ratio of government debt to national income. From 1946 through 1974, this ratio descended without pause as countries paid down debts remaining from World War II and avoided incurring new ones. Starting in 1975, the average debt ratio began to rise, a trend that would continue well into the twenty-first century. Even as debt obligations piled up in the second half of the 1970s, interest rates soared, making interest payments on debt a significant item in government budgets. This bill, too, was presented to the wage earners whose income taxes and social security contributions provided such a large proportion of government revenue. They feared, not without reason, that the bill would now be passed to their children.[27]

IN EARLIER, CALMER YEARS, THE TRADE-OFF OF HIGHER TAXES FOR greater social benefits had been wildly popular. The United States saw sporadic campaigns against taxes during the 1960s, but these usually concerned property taxes collected by local governments to fund schools and maintain parks, not the income taxes used by the federal and state governments to provide pensions, health care, and aid to the poor and unemployed. Such protests were widely dispersed, and mattered little on a national scale. But as the economic environment grew less stable in the 1970s, with exchange rates and inflation veering out of control and the future looking very uncertain, governmental attempts to raise ever more revenue to fund the welfare state began to run into stiffer resistance. The anti-tax movement first welled up in the wealthy and bucolic kingdom of Denmark, thanks to a colorful tax lawyer named Mogens Glistrup.[28]

Glistrup's law firm, purportedly Copenhagen's largest, specialized in tax avoidance, helping clients construct chains of loans between dummy companies to take advantage of the fact that Denmark allowed taxpayers to deduct interest payments from their income. On January 30, 1971, Glistrup, then forty-four, appeared on a television show to talk about taxes. Holding up his own tax return, which showed zero tax liability, he compared tax evaders to the patriots who had sabotaged German railway lines during World War II.

Glistrup's antics made him an overnight sensation and a political force. Danish politics had long been dominated by four parties, known as the "old" parties, each linked to particular interest groups such as farmers and trade unions. The four old parties almost always agreed on social legislation, to the point that many bills passed parliament unanimously. Voters took quickly to an outsider who promised to shake things up. After the Conservatives declined to nominate him for a seat in parliament, Glistrup used his newfound fame to launch the Progress Party in 1972. The Progress Party had little formal organization, but Glistrup was a master when it came to grabbing public attention with sharp comments about the powers that be, such as his suggestion that Denmark dismantle its armed forces and replace the defense ministry with a telephone answering machine to tell callers, in Russian, "We surrender." "The most serious thing you can do in politics today is to tease the establishment," he declared.[29]

It was not a coincidence that Denmark is where the modern anti-tax movement got its start. Although the 1960s had been a prosperous decade, Denmark had the slowest economic growth in Europe in 1970 and fared little better in 1971. Its inflation rate was one of the highest among the advanced economies. And the strengthening of the Danish welfare state had brought a crushing tax burden. In 1965, Danes had paid 29.5 percent of national income in taxes. Just six years later, the government claimed 40.8 percent of the country's total income. Families were clearly feeling financial pain, and their spending was growing at a slower rate than the economy as a whole. Adding to the malaise was anxiety about their tiny country's future. In 1972, in a referendum with a 90 percent turnout, Danes voted overwhelmingly to join the European Communities. Within a year, polls showed that at least half of Danish voters regretted that decision.

Although Glistrup was not the most photogenic of men—"He is corpulent with his clothes perpetually in disarray," a US diplomat advised the State Department—he proved an effective vote getter. In December 1973, after a campaign in which he called for eliminating the income tax and promised that as prime minister he would sack one bureaucrat every ten minutes, the Progress Party became the second-largest party in parliament. The "earthquake election," as Danes called it, reshaped the country's politics overnight. Although no party was willing to bring the Progress Party into a coalition government, Glistrup's relentless attacks on the ruling powers helped his ideas gain traction. Polls in the mid-1970s showed Danes' attitudes toward social programs and income redistribution becoming distinctly more negative. "Denmark . . . is to-day beating a retreat from welfare, or at least from the tax burden that welfare necessitates. It is an unwilling and anguished retreat, but it is a retreat nonetheless," a *Financial Times* correspondent proclaimed.[30]

Glistrup had a counterpart in Norway. Anders Lange, a generation older than Glistrup, had been associated with the right-wing Fatherland League in the 1920s and 1930s but was strongly anti-Nazi during the war. After the war, he went to work for a kennel club and began publishing *Dog Newspaper*. Initially the coverage of political matters was limited to taxes on dog owners, but gradually a more political agenda surfaced. Following financial problems and embezzlement by an employee, the newspaper folded in 1953, but Lange developed a parallel career as a freelance rabble-rouser, organizing counterprotests against demonstrations by the socialist youth movement and its ilk. When Lange relaunched the newspaper in 1960, attacks on communists, politicians, and bureaucrats were regular features. Two years later, *Dog Newspaper* was rechristened *Anders Lange's Newspaper*. Broadening its horizons, it soon gave birth to a political movement of the disaffected.

Norway's economy was healthier than any other in Europe, but Lange's complaints about bureaucrats and taxes resonated nonetheless. In April 1973, a public meeting in an Oslo cinema voted to establish Anders Lange's Party for a Strong Reduction in Taxes, Duties, and Public Intervention. A month later, Glistrup traveled to Oslo to lend his support. Unlike Glistrup, Lange was a military hawk, but he shared Glistrup's distrust of the welfare state. Lange identified himself as a supporter of Milton Friedman, the American free-market economist, and a fan of libertarian novelist Ayn Rand. At the age of sixty-nine, he rode an anti-tax platform into parliament when Anders Lange's Party gained 5 percent of the vote in the 1973 nationwide elections.

The nascent Scandinavian anti-tax movement soon echoed faintly across the North Sea. There, the issue was what the British call "rates," taxes assessed on the value of real property. Under Conservative prime minister Edward Heath, who took office in 1970, tax receipts as a share of national income fell for three years running between 1970 and 1973. Although the Conservative Party had begun to distance itself from high taxes, big-city governments, largely controlled by the Labor Party, were unwilling to trim local services or cut workers. By 1974, with the economy in crisis and some ratepayers refusing to pay their local taxes, the Conservatives sensed a political opportunity. Their spokeswoman was a young minister named Margaret Thatcher. "Local authorities have been spending at a faster rate than the economy's been growing," Thatcher told a radio audience. The Conservatives, she promised, would abolish local rates and substitute "taxation based on what you can afford."[31]

In Denmark, Norway, and Great Britain, the political consensus in favor of the welfare state was slowly beginning to tear. Despite a government tax investigation that would eventually send Glistrup to prison, the Danish Progress Party defied expectations and lost only four of its twenty-eight parliamentary seats when Danes voted again in January 1975. Its voters came from many different walks of life; what they had in common, pollsters found, is that they strongly disagreed with the statement that "In general, one can trust our politicians to make the right decisions for the country." Anders Lange died in 1974, but his party, reorganized as the Progress Party by a charismatic young businessman named Carl Hagen, would become a major conservative force in Norwegian politics, finally entering government in 2013. After a prolonged internal struggle, the British Conservatives would renounce their patrician heritage, their support of the postwar welfare state, and their belief that their country was doomed to subpar economic growth. They would follow Margaret Thatcher in a new direction, toward a smaller, less enveloping government.[32]

CHAPTER 10

The Right Turn

The economic crisis that began in 1973 left voters in almost every democratic country upset and alienated. They expected government to assure jobs, better working conditions, and higher standards of living, just as it had for the previous quarter-century. Instead, they were offered austerity and insecurity, stagnant wages and shuttered factories. The old, established political parties seemed to have nothing useful to say about the new economic reality. Their programs spoke to dividing up the fruits of plenty, not to reviving productivity growth and adjusting to a world of rapid technological change.

In earlier years, voters might have accepted their party's line without objection, because their social position was likely to have determined their political preferences. In Europe, Catholic, socialist, and agrarian parties all drew reliable support from certain segments of the population. Trade unionists were the core of Canada's New Democrats, and the southern region of the United States had been a stronghold of the Democratic Party for more than a century. But by the 1970s, these once reliable voters, now more educated, prosperous, and mobile, felt less obligation to adhere to the party line. In Italy, the local bishop's opinion no longer much mattered, and American factory workers increasingly ignored the urgings of their union leaders. As voting blocs fractured, the more stable governments of the postwar era yielded to tenuous coalitions that could be toppled by the death or defection of a handful of parliamentarians.

The political scientists and sociologists who pondered such things suggested that something fundamental had changed. "At one time or another during 1974, no party had a majority in the legislatures of Great Britain, Canada, France, the Federal Republic of Germany, Italy, Belgium, the Netherlands, Norway, Sweden, and Denmark," declared a study for the Trilateral Commission, a new (and soon to be controversial) group of international business and diplomatic leaders. The experts began to speak of a new problem: "ungovernability."[1]

UNGOVERNABILITY MANIFESTED ITSELF IN SEVERAL WAYS. GOVernments seemed increasingly unable to maintain order. In Europe, headlines told of kidnappings and assassinations by gangs such as the Baader-Meinhof group in West Germany, the Red Brigades in Italy, and ETA in Spain. In America, the crime rate soared: there was one reported property crime in the United States for every twenty citizens in 1975. The nation-state itself came under attack, as parties seeking decentralization of government or even regional independence gained ground from Quebec to Scotland to Yugoslavia. And then there was the instability brought by scandal, which forced leadership changes at the top of the three largest economies in 1974. In May, West German chancellor Willy Brandt resigned after the revelation that one of his closest aides was an East German spy. In August, the Watergate scandal, stemming from Richard Nixon's attempt to cover up a break-in by Republican Party operatives at the offices of the Democratic Party during the 1972 presidential election campaign, culminated in the first-ever resignation of a sitting president. In December, Japanese prime minister Kakuei Tanaka stepped down amid claims that he had used his office to profit personally from property deals.[2]

Although the three cases differed in their specifics, what united them was that each involved the fall of a highly accomplished and highly popular political operator. Brandt, who had fled to Norway to escape the Nazis in

1933, had a long and distinguished career that had involved, among many other things, dragging the Social Democratic Party away from its Marxist roots and reshaping it to appeal to a far wider base than just industrial trade unions and their members. In his re-election campaign in 1972, West German voters had given a ringing endorsement to *Ostpolitik,* his effort to normalize relations with East Germany and Poland in order to ease international tensions and reunify families. Nixon, whose national political career dated to 1946, had chalked up an impressive re-election victory only two years earlier, winning forty-nine of the fifty states and capturing nearly 61 percent of the vote; he had built a broad base of support among middle-class and working-class white voters by capitalizing on fear of crime and resentment of racial integration. Tanaka, who was later convicted in a separate scandal for accepting bribes from American aircraft manufacturer Lockheed, had built a powerful electoral machine based on pork-barrel politics; he was so adept at turning government money into concrete that admirers called him the "computerized bulldozer."[3]

Yet even these powerful men, with their decades of experience as wheeler-dealers and their phone books full of personal contacts, could not survive scandals that, only a few years earlier, might have been met with shrugs. The political environment had changed.

Ungovernability, as the term was understood in the mid-1970s, had less to do with social unrest than with political paralysis. It was said to be the consequence of two fundamental social shifts. One was that education and prosperity had given average people the courage to find their voices. Citizens no longer blindly followed the guidance of their churches, unions, or business associations; instead they determined for themselves what was in their best interest. The other shift was that the state had grown so substantially, providing services and subsidies that directly affected so many people, that citizens kept a closer eye on its actions than ever before. Together, these two shifts meant that politicians could no longer make decisions in the name of some greater good and expect their obedient constituents to go along. The gifts of the welfare state had become entitlements; where once voters had been grateful for whatever new benefits the politicians handed out, they now mobilized to block any changes that might worsen their position, either in absolute terms or relative to others. Those increasingly articulate constituents had clear economic interests to protect, and they expected to be heard.[4]

The concern about ungovernability was directly related to economic stagnation. While economies were growing rapidly during the Golden Age, governments had been able to improve conditions for almost everyone; there was enough money to raise child allowances and build new universities offering free or low-cost education without reducing the after-tax incomes of working families without children. But now that economies were growing slowly or even shrinking, governing was a zero-sum game. Any measure that channeled more resources to one group, whether preschool toddlers or old-age pensioners, was likely to take resources away from others. Even policies that would eventually benefit almost everyone, such as reducing inflation, foundered on the public's unwillingness to accept short-term pain for long-term gain.

The welfare state promised not just steadily rising living standards but also greater equality. That promise, too, fell victim to the economic bust, as governments no longer had the cash to offer payments to all who felt disadvantaged. The British journalist Samuel Brittan pointed to a British government survey finding that 80 percent of respondents preferred to receive an extra four pounds a week along with everyone else rather than an extra five pounds a week if others were receiving six. "The more that policy concentrates on eliminating disparities and differentials, the greater the sense of outrage likely to be engendered by those that remain," Brittan cautioned, warning of "the tendency of liberal democracy to generate unfulfillable expectations." As the potential losers from changes in government policy mobilized to protect what they already had, elected governments were blocked from reforming themselves. It was this paradox that would render representative democracies ungovernable.[5]

Perhaps the best-known proponent of the view that democracy's best days were behind it was the American economist Mancur Olson. Amiable and soft-spoken in person, Olson offered a forecast for the wealthy democracies that was anything but relaxed. He saw a world in which social cohesion was weakening as large, broadly based organizations representing widely shared concerns lost ground to small groups standing for narrow agendas. The reason for this shift was simple arithmetic. If a large group influenced government policy, its members, with diverse interests, would enjoy only small average benefits. Members of a small group fighting for a single cause could obtain much more in political combat if their organization were able to affect government policy on that narrow issue. Heart surgeons, according to this line of reasoning, had far more to gain from lobbying by the cardiology association than from the work of a larger doctors' group that also represented allergists and nephrologists.

The danger, as Olson saw it, was that these specialized organizations defined their interests solely in terms of their members' immediate interests. Large organizations representing broad swaths of society were able to take a long-term view, accepting temporary setbacks for the sake of the common good. But as they lost influence and membership, Olson foresaw, power would shift to smaller organizations, each fighting tenaciously to score short-term political victories in order to keep its members engaged and happy. As these small groups gained influence, often joining one another in coalitions, they would keep government from achieving larger goals in the common interest.

One issue on which the spread of narrow interest groups would make a difference was international trade. Large organizations tended to support freer trade, because they understood that it would stimulate broad economic growth, even if individual industries or groups of workers suffered from the increased foreign competition. Smaller groups would take more parochial views; where a national labor federation might favor a trade agreement that lowered import tariffs on shoes, a shoemakers' union would almost certainly oppose it. Similarly, narrowly focused groups often tried to block new technologies that could endanger some workers' jobs and some companies' profits. As interest groups proliferated, Olson warned, economies would become more rigid and more resistant to change. Slower economic growth was an inevitable consequence. "On balance," Olson wrote, "special interest organizations and collusions reduce efficiency and aggregate income in the societies in which they operate and make political life more divisive."[6]

Olson was a political conservative, and like many on the right he especially blamed labor unions for the evident sclerosis in the wealthy democracies. But the odd thing about the ungovernability debate was that it brought together voices from across the political spectrum. Samuel Brittan, who praised many of Margaret Thatcher's economic policies, predicted that the dominance of liberal representative democracy "is likely to pass away within the lifetime of people now adult." But then Willy Brandt, a man of the democratic left, was said to have predicted much the same. In some Marxist circles, ungovernability was seen as a manifestation of "late capitalism," the stage in which the political order would lose its legitimacy before capitalism would finally collapse of its own contradictions. For libertarians, on the other hand, ungovernability was merely further evidence that governments had no means to deliver all that they had promised their citizens.[7]

IT WAS NOT JUST THE WEALTHY MARKET ECONOMIES THAT SEEMED to have become ungovernable. Behind the Iron Curtain, the Soviet client states controlled by unelected Communist parties entered a governability crisis that would prove even more severe than the one facing the democracies of Western Europe, North America, and Japan.

The Soviet bloc countries are often remembered as economic basket cases, but that is a simplistic reading of history. In fact, the state-run economies of Eastern Europe and the Soviet Union enjoyed their own versions of the postwar Golden Age. Although apples-to-apples comparisons are difficult—statistical concepts such as gross domestic product and per capita income assume that goods and services are sold at market prices, not at prices set by the state—most estimates suggest that economic growth behind the Iron Curtain was rapid. According to the British economist Angus Maddison, who attempted to filter out the effects of inflation and exchange-rate changes in order to accurately evaluate underlying economic performance, income per person increased faster in the Soviet Union and Eastern Europe between 1948 and 1973 than in Belgium and Denmark, and much faster than in Australia, Canada, and the United States. In 1948, by Maddison's estimates, the average Hungarian's income was only about one-fourth that of the average American; although per capita income in the United States grew rapidly over the next quarter-century, per capita income in Hungary grew significantly faster.[8]

The rapid economic growth of the Communist states had the same origins as the boom in the market economies. Wartime destruction left vast reconstruction needs. Millions of workers migrated from steering horse-drawn plows on farms to tending heavy equipment in new factories. Those factories were far larger and more capital intensive than the small-scale enterprises common before World War II. Communist economic planners were true believers when it came to economies of scale. From Karl Marx, they knew that industrialization was necessary to create a socialist society. From economists building on Marx's ideas, who emphasized the physical quantity of production, they learned that the most efficient way to industrialize was to build huge, centralized complexes that would be highly efficient at pouring steel, mixing chemicals, or knitting textiles.

This version of Marxist efficiency permeated the system. Planners dictated how many tons of steel or square meters of cloth should be produced, and plant managers were judged on whether they met those goals. Other state-owned factories were told how much steel or cloth to buy and how many tractors or dresses to make from it. The planners then directed state-owned farms to buy the tractors and dictated how many dresses state-owned retailers should sell. International trade often involved barter rather than cash sales. If suddenly bananas appeared on grocery-store shelves in Prague, it was probably because Czechoslovakian trade officials had arranged to export machinery to a banana-producing country and had accepted fruit in partial payment.

The communist economies were quite good at producing goods, but they were altogether hopeless when it came to producing things consumers actually wanted. Weaponry and heavy industrial goods had priority; apartments and cars for average families had a lesser claim on resources. Output was uniformly shoddy and antiquated, because there were few rewards for quality or innovation. And while planners cared greatly that shoppers purchased the correct number of dresses, they cared not at all about whether those dresses were in the colors, styles, and patterns women coveted after seeing photos of Western fashions in magazines. This latent demand for product diversity was patently un-socialist. Under centralized economic planning, every factory was assigned quotas far ahead of time in order to maximize production efficiency—a process that could not be reconciled with consumers' desire to buy according to their personal tastes. Keeping the public happy took precedence only when it was essential to defuse political unrest.[9]

Unrest was in evidence across the Soviet bloc well before the oil shock of 1973. For the first time, a nascent human rights movement in the Soviet Union was daring to speak out publicly in opposition to political repression. The state's inability to improve people's lives had already led to rebellions in Poland, where the government had contained unrest since 1970 by freezing prices, and in Czechoslovakia, which the Soviets had invaded in 1968 to put an end to political and economic reforms. In March 1974, more liberal policies in Hungary were derailed by Soviet opposition amid charges that the country was "creeping towards capitalism." Higher oil prices interfered with the Soviets' aims. By raising the cost of a vital raw material that most of the communist states needed to import and by slowing the growth of their trading partners in the West, the oil shock would make it even harder for countries in the Soviet orbit to generate the economic growth that might keep them from slipping into ungovernability.[10]

THE ECONOMIC NEWS IN THE MIDDLE OF THE 1970S WAS PERsistently negative. Yet despite the dire warnings that the world was becoming ungovernable, voters did not abandon faith in the ability of democratic governments to reform themselves. What they did abandon was faith in charismatic leaders promising milk and honey. The mid-1970s was not a time for larger-than-life figures like Charles de Gaulle and Lyndon Johnson. The call was for businesslike leaders, realistic men, capable rather than ideological, who promised steadiness in the face of economic crisis.

Compared with what had come before, this new generation of leaders was remarkable in two ways: its colorlessness and its air of competence. Helmut Schmidt, who had learned economics from Karl Schiller in

Hamburg and became West German chancellor after Willy Brandt's resignation in May 1974, was a get-things-done pragmatist who strongly advocated a tougher line against the Soviet Union; his philosophy of leadership was summed up in the oft-repeated line, "People who have visions should go see a doctor." Valéry Marie René Georges Giscard d'Estaing, universally known as Giscard, elected president of France two weeks after Schmidt's ascent in Germany, was a graduate of the prestigious École nationale d'administration and an expert in the intricate matters of international economics. Takeo Miki, who succeeded the disgraced Kakuei Tanaka as Japanese prime minister in December 1974, was unusual among Japanese politicians because he refused to curry favor with party donors and local officials by handing out construction contracts; he was renowned in Japan not only for straight talk, but also for the remarkably no-nonsense manner in which he delivered it.[11]

And then there was Jimmy Carter. The former commander of a nuclear submarine and manager of his family's peanut warehouse in rural Georgia, Carter presented himself as a competent and incorruptible leader. A Baptist Sunday school teacher, Carter was deeply religious, and his promise to infuse morality into US foreign policy struck a chord in a country riven by the Vietnam War and by American support for brutal dictatorships in Latin America. He walked rather than motoring down a frigid Pennsylvania Avenue after his presidential inauguration in January 1977 to solidify his image as a man of the people.

These leaders were serious men. They saw that inflation was corroding their economies and causing citizens to lose faith in government. They recognized the limits of the welfare state and understood the depth of public opposition to higher taxes. They were not unsympathetic to business; they readily acknowledged that only profitability would induce firms to increase investment and hire more workers. They knew that high oil prices had rendered large portions of their countries' manufacturing obsolete. And despite what they told their publics, they knew that many of the closed factories would never reopen. They were fully aware that restoring productivity growth was the greatest challenge to their efforts to restore prosperity.

Yet for all their efforts, and their frequent meetings with one another, they were able to produce only a feeble rebound. Japan's economy, under Miki and his successors, grew by an average of 2.6 percent per year between 1974 and 1979—barely one-third its growth rate during the previous six years. Germany and France grew at around the same pace; the United States, nearly a full percentage point less. Overall growth in the advanced economies over those six years averaged a modest 1.9 percent—which, after allowing for population growth, meant that the incomes of average families barely rose at all.

And that was before taxes. Political expediency required governments to hand out money to pensioners and unemployed workers, and to subsidize businesses to keep employees on the payroll. They did so, despite rising criticism, because they saw no alternative. And to fund their efforts, they continued to lay claim to a greater share of workers' earnings and consumers' spending. In Giscard's France, tax receipts soared from 34 percent of national income in 1974 to 38 percent in 1979; in Japan, the figure rose from 22 percent to 24 percent. Across twenty-three wealthy countries, the share of national income taken in taxes rose by three percentage points during those years. Yet while governments had more money to spend, unemployment everywhere was higher in 1979 than it had been six years earlier, and inflation was surging once more.

THE WORLD'S RADICALLY CHANGED ECONOMIC SITUATION HAD major political implications. High tax rates, and the political parties seen as supporting them, were about to come under fire. It was on January 30, 1976, that this first became apparent.

On that frigid Friday, the Swedish police interrupted a rehearsal of August Strindberg's *Dance of Death* at the Royal Dramatic Theater in Stockholm. As the actors looked on from the stage, plainclothes officers informed the play's director, fifty-seven-year-old Ingmar Bergman, that he was wanted for questioning about tax evasion. Bergman, an internationally acclaimed film director and the best-known symbol of modern Swedish culture, was humiliated. His passport was confiscated, his flat was searched, and he was warned not to leave the city. Facing accusations that could have resulted in a two-year prison term, Bergman checked himself in to Karolinska Hospital for "a nervous condition."

Soon after the Bergman case hit the headlines, police searched the apartment of actress Bibi Andersson. The star of nearly a dozen Bergman movies and the mother of a five-year-old girl, Andersson was jailed for thirty-six hours, without access to a telephone or a lawyer, over claims that she owed $23,000 in taxes. Then, on March 3, sixty-eight-year-old Astrid Lindgren, famed around the world for her stories about a mischievous redhead named Pippi Longstocking, published a short story called "Pomperipossa in Monismania" in *Expressen*, Sweden's most widely read newspaper. The story was a thinly veiled satire about a writer whose success caused her to face taxes of 102 percent of her income. "Are these really the wise men I so highly esteemed and admired?" poor Pomperipossa asked about the political leaders who imposed those taxes. "What are they trying to accomplish—a society as narrow-minded and impossible as possible?" The story was built on fact, as Lindgren revealed her own run-in with zealous tax collectors.[12]

The public prosecutor found no cause to charge any of the three with tax evasion, but the scandals did not simply disappear. After two months in the hospital, Bergman returned to his home on the windswept Baltic island of Fårö. There, in April, he drafted an open letter to *Expressen* announcing that he was leaving Sweden because of harassment by tax authorities. Bergman said the investigation had made him aware "that anyone in this country, any time and in any way, can be attacked and vilified by a particular kind of bureaucracy." "This bureaucracy," he added, "grows like a fast-spreading cancer." He said he would close his film studio and cancel plans to make his next movie in Sweden. He placed his assets at the disposition of the national tax board, lest "right-minded Swedish taxpayers" think he was absconding without paying his due. That same afternoon, Bergman boarded a plane for Paris and exile. Five days later, the tax auditor responded to Bergman's accusations, claiming that the tax collectors were right and Bergman was wrong. But the figures the auditor released to the press showed that the government was laying claim to 140 percent of the director's income.[13]

The three cases kindled a political firestorm. Bergman and Lindgren both were well-known supporters of the Social Democrats, a party that strongly favored high taxes to provide cradle-to-grave security and minimize inequality. Now these two cultural icons seemed to be deserting the cause. Polls showed a sudden drop in the Social Democrats' popularity going into the September 19 parliamentary election. Prime Minister Olof Palme blamed his party's decline on "a spring flood of reactionary propaganda," but in fact the celebrity scandals had left voters who were far from reactionary wondering about the justice of a tax system that routinely claimed more than half of employees' incomes and severely punished small businesses and the self-employed.

Complaints about the burgeoning bureaucracy were not unfounded. Of the one million jobs created in Sweden between 1950 and 1975, more than half were in the public sector. The number of Swedes in government employ rose 151 percent over that quarter-century—five times as fast as the labor force—as the expanding welfare state hired ever more social workers, employment counselors, and preschool teachers.

While generous social programs enjoyed broad support among the public, Swedes increasingly complained that their leaders had lost touch with the common people. The Social Democrats had become associated not with higher pensions or paid family leave, but with excessive bureaucracy. "Astrid Lindgren and Ingmar Bergman, with their protests, have opened the floodgates of querulousness, as well as more legitimate dissatisfaction," the independent newspaper *Dagens Nyheter* editorialized. Younger workers, in particular, found the welfare state stultifying, and they were turning their backs on the Social Democrats. The fact that eighteen-year-olds could vote for the first time in 1976 did not help the party's cause. Nor did another article by Lindgren in which she warned that Sweden was on the verge of becoming a "bureaucratic dictatorship."[14]

As the election approached, the end of the Golden Age unexpectedly made itself felt across the country. Sweden had weathered the 1973 oil crisis and its aftermath better than most of its neighbors. The Palme government had gone all out to stimulate the economy, cutting value-added taxes to encourage consumer spending, increasing social benefits, and paying manufacturers to keep their production lines running and their workers employed. Thanks to this aggressive stimulus, unemployment fell and wages soared, even as other economies faltered. But Sweden could not spend its way out of problems forever. Large inventories of manufactured goods clogged warehouses around the country: the government had paid factories to produce them, but no one wanted to buy them. In early 1976, as falling demand and high labor costs dragged down Swedish exports, the economy began to shrink.

The Social Democrats had ruled Sweden continuously since 1932, so long that most Swedes had never experienced another party at the country's helm. But on September 19, 1976, as the economy was slipping into what would prove a deep and painful downturn, voters swept the Social Democrats from power. Shockwaves reverberated around the world. "The Swedish model goes in for repair," London's *Financial Times* trumpeted. At least some of the voters who abandoned the Social Democrats did so to show their opposition to nuclear power, which the party strongly supported, but such nuances were largely ignored. Rightly or wrongly, the vote was interpreted as a mandate to begin paring back government. Although Sweden's nonsocialist parties were hardly sharp critics of the welfare state, their success reopened old questions about whether government was capable of delivering higher living standards and economic security at an acceptable price.[15]

GREAT BRITAIN ADAPTED TO THE NEW ECONOMIC REALITIES OF the 1970s far more reluctantly than Sweden. In fact, it hardly adapted at all.

In February 1974, the country, still in the grip of the oil crisis, was enveloped by a sense of fear. Inflation was approaching 20 percent, manufacturers worked a three-day week to save coal and power in the face of a strike by miners, and Northern Ireland was in a state of civil war. "Who governs Britain?" the Conservatives demanded, claiming that the opposition Labour Party had become so radical it might even ban homeownership. Labour, trying to oust Prime Minister Edward Heath after four years of Conservative rule, was indeed dominated by its socialist wing, in which a radical group called Militant Tendency had become highly influential.

Labour was running on a manifesto calling for "a fundamental and irreversible shift in the balance of power and wealth in favour of working people and their families" and insisting that North Sea oil and a large part of the manufacturing sector should be in the hands of state-owned companies.[16]

Angry voters granted no party a majority, delivering a hung Parliament for the first time since 1929. For three days, Great Britain was without a government, as Heath bargained for the backing of the Liberal Party's fourteen members of Parliament. When the Liberals balked, he yielded to Labour's Harold Wilson, who had been prime minister from 1964 to 1970. Wilson formed a minority government, clinging to power at the sufferance of several smaller parties until he could stage a re-vote in October. On the second try, Labour won a parliamentary majority so razor-thin that it could barely govern. The reason it won a majority at all was that many voters stayed home.

The Labour Party government that ruled between 1974 and 1979, first under Wilson and then, after March 1976, under James Callaghan, may have provided the most inept governance endured in any advanced economy since the end of World War II. Inflation raged out of control: 19 percent in 1974, 25 percent in 1975, 15 percent in 1976. The trade-off promised by the Phillips Curve, though, was nowhere to be found; rather than stemming unemployment, high inflation worsened it by driving investment away. As the economy shrank and living standards fell, the pound sterling, worth $2.43 in March 1975, performed so dismally that it bought only $1.66 by September 1976. That same month, Labour's annual party congress was shaken by the news that Great Britain, in the position of a poor country rather than a rich one, was for the first time begging for an emergency loan from the International Monetary Fund.

In his defense, Callaghan had been dealt a poor hand. Raised in poverty by a widowed mother, he had entered Parliament in 1944 and worked his way up to serve in every major cabinet post. As foreign secretary in Harold Wilson's government, he played a prominent role in renegotiating the terms of Britain's membership in the European Community, a deal that won overwhelming support in a June 1975 referendum. Wilson resigned unexpectedly the following March, and Callaghan, then sixty-four, became his successor. "Prime minister! And I never went to university!" he was said to have exclaimed after winning the internal party vote.

Three weeks after he moved into 10 Downing Street, Labour lost its majority when a member of Parliament who was about to stand trial for faking his own death quit the party. Callaghan was forced into constant bargaining with smaller Scottish and Welsh parties in order to govern. His assets included an outgoing personality, an outward calm that earned him the nickname "Sunny Jim," and close ties to the union movement, which respected the fact that after going to work as a clerk in the Inland Revenue at age seventeen, he had helped organize tax officers into a union. "No man alive better personified the old Labour Movement now dying than James Callaghan," the journalist Peter Jenkins wrote in 1988.[17]

However, the unions' respect for the prime minister did not make them any more conciliatory. Britain's labor movement had a long history of militancy, and many unions implacably opposed any and all changes proposed by employers that might eliminate their members' jobs. Unions in Germany, the Netherlands, and Scandinavia understood that innovations that improved productivity could raise their members' pay and create more jobs in other parts of the economy, but among British union leaders such talk verged on heresy. The National Union of Mineworkers fought every attempt by the state-owned National Coal Board to close even those mines that were played out after two centuries of digging. Jack Jones, head of the Transport and General Workers Union, which represented workers in construction and manufacturing as well dockworkers and truckers, was so powerful that graffiti scribbled during the 1974 elections advised, "Vote Jack Jones, cut out the middle man."

While not all British unions were so militant, rank-and-file workers overwhelmingly rejected the government's "incomes policies," which were intended to hold down inflation by restraining pay raises. By the time Callaghan moved into the prime minister's residence at 10 Downing Street, the pattern had been set: an employer would offer a pay raise within the government's limit; the union would reject the offer and strike; and the employer, with tacit government permission, would give in.[18]

At the September 1976 party conference, held in the aging coastal resort of Blackpool, Callaghan issued a blunt warning to Labour's left wing. "The cozy world we were told would go on forever, where full employment would be guaranteed by a stroke of the chancellor's pen, cutting taxes, deficit spending, that cozy world is gone," Callaghan told the party faithful. "We used to think that you could spend your way out of a recession and increase employment by cutting taxes and boosting government spending. I tell you in all candor that that option no longer exists." His call for greater productivity and tighter control of public spending was not a welcome message for a party whose most recent election manifesto, in October 1974, had advocated state ownership of manufacturers and requirements that big companies act "in harmony with national needs and objectives." The trade unions that paid Labour's bills and controlled many of its local committees translated higher productivity and tighter control of public spending to mean layoffs and less generous pensions. That was not their program.[19]

Thanks to the devalued pound, which gave a boost to exports, and to the emergency loan from the IMF, the British economy began a modest rebound in the second half of 1976. Its performance was good only by the standards of the country's recent past; among the advanced economies, Britain ranked dead last in economic growth, capital investment, and saving. Inflation still raged, and rather than telling the Bank of England to raise interest rates to stop it, Callaghan's government kept hoping that its policy of trying to limit wage increases would do the trick with less pain. It did not. In July 1977, at the annual coal miners' gala in Durham, in the far north of England, Callaghan sat on the podium as the miners' leader, Arthur Scargill, urged his members "to ignore the advice and pleas of the government for further wage restraint." When it was his turn to speak, Callaghan asked the miners to accept wage restraint "for the sake of the country—and miners are part of the whole national family." It was a difficult sell.[20]

In the summer of 1978, the Labour government announced that workers' pay should rise no more than 5 percent over the coming year. This looked like it would be barely half the rate of inflation. Union leaders, wary of workplace militants calling for unauthorized strikes, rejected the government's guideline out of hand and demanded a return to normal wage bargaining. "We'd had three years of pay restraint, and people had got fed up of it," recalled a trucker in the desolate Yorkshire city of Hull. When Callaghan refused to retreat, autoworkers, lorry drivers, railway workers, nurses, even gravediggers walked off the job. Hospitals turned away patients, and chickens died for lack of feed. The dark, snowy winter of 1978–79 would go down in history as the Winter of Discontent, the winter when Londoners' trash was piled in Leicester Square because the dustmen refused to cart it away. Output collapsed as nearly thirty million workdays were lost amid the strikes. When the disputes were finally settled, striking workers won wage hikes far above the government's 5 percent guideline. In March 1979, by the margin of a single vote, Parliament pronounced no confidence in the Callaghan government.[21]

That vote, and the ensuing collapse of the Labour Party as a driving force in British politics, owed much to Margaret Thatcher. Thatcher, who had entered Parliament in 1959, despised the postwar consensus that had built the welfare state, and she sharply criticized her own party for having joined it. In February 1975, then the Conservative Party spokeswoman on environmental affairs, she had shaken the British political establishment by ousting former prime minister Edward Heath as the Conservative leader in Parliament. She now forced Callaghan to call an election as, once again, the economy was sinking, inflation was rising, and the world was facing an oil crisis—this one in the wake of the January 1979 revolution that deposed the Shah of Iran.

Thatcher was direct and plainspoken. Her view, widely shared in the late 1970s, was that Britain was threatened with long-term economic decline. But unlike many of her compatriots—including Callaghan, who famously told Labour Party leaders in 1974, "If I were a young man, I'd emigrate"—she did not consider that decline irreversible. She blamed high taxes and the welfare state, which stifled private initiative and choked off economic growth. Thatcher was equally disdainful of unions that were resistant to change and landed gentry happy to live off their rents. She preached the virtues of hard work and entrepreneurship. "None of us is so naïve as to believe that cutting taxes will, by itself, suddenly transform everything and make our country prosperous overnight," she told a radio audience a week before the election. "But what we do believe is that there's all the difference in the world between creating a society in which it pays to work and creating one in which it doesn't. Only by becoming prosperous again can Britain become a genuinely caring society."[22]

Much has been written about the self-interested intellectual groundwork for Thatcher's ascent: the role of the Institute of Economic Affairs, a London think tank, in propagating free-market ideas in the 1960s and 1970s; the emergence of Sir Keith Joseph, then a member of Parliament, as an outspoken critic of Heath's conciliatory brand of Conservatism in 1974; the establishment of the Centre for Policy Studies as an ideas machine for a future Conservative government; Joseph's embrace of money-supply rules to squelch inflation, and of assorted other free-market ideas in which he tutored Thatcher. There is no doubt that corporate as well as ideological interests, foreign as well as domestic, were behind the new Conservative agenda. When Joseph offered a 1976 lecture with the line, "We are over-governed, over-spent, over-taxed, over-borrowed, and over-manned," he was singing a tune that industrialists in the Midlands and bankers in the City had hummed for many years.[23]

Yet while these efforts endowed the Conservative Party with a substantial intellectual base, it was not only the emergence of competing ideas that pushed the Labour Party into eclipse. Labour's fall was the result, more than anything else, of the bankruptcy of the economic model that had brought prosperity after World War II. Throughout the 1950s and 1960s, as Labour's ideas found their way into the policies that defined the welfare state, life was getting better in Britain. By the 1970s, though, no mix of economic policies could deliver the steadily rising living standards that Britons had come to expect. It was that fading dream that brought the Conservatives to power. On May 3, 1979, they gained sixty seats in Parliament, and Margaret Thatcher became prime minister.

ACROSS THE ATLANTIC, JIMMY CARTER EXUDED A FOLKSINESS much like Jim Callaghan's. Over the four years of his presidency, he came to exude a similar haplessness as well.

When Carter moved into the White House, the US economy was in much stronger condition than Great Britain's. It was soon generating the fastest growth of any major economy, and the unemployment rate, 7.5 percent in January 1977, descended steadily to 5.7 percent by the summer of 1979. But no one mistook those results to be signs of a healthy economy. The Fed, still under the control of Arthur Burns, had lowered interest rates in the second half of 1976 to help Gerald Ford win re-election, leaving Carter with the poisonous gift of rising inflation. Although Carter was able to push Burns out in January 1978, by then inflation was climbing back toward the double digits. As the Fed began raising overnight interest rates aggressively to clamp down on inflation, interest rates on the Treasury's short-term bonds rose close to those on its long-term bonds. On August 18, 1978, the lines crossed: investors earned more for lending to the government for two years than for ten. That unusual condition, known in the financial markets as an inverted yield curve, was an alarm bell, an unmistakable warning that a recession was likely in the second half of 1979.

And then came the second oil crisis, driven by the revolution in Iran and a decision by Saudi Arabia to limit oil production. After holding steady since 1974, the average cost of a barrel of crude doubled over the course of 1979. A more relevant figure for American voters, the price of gasoline, went from seventy cents per gallon to $1.11, and buying it often required a lengthy wait in line. As station owners taped "No Gas" signs to their pumps, the Carter administration printed ration coupons to distribute if supplies grew tighter. The nationwide panic turned violent when independent truckers, drivers who owned their own vehicles and hired out by the load, complained that federal regulations governing freight rates kept them from passing the higher cost of diesel fuel on to their customers. The truckers declared a strike, and some of them enforced it with stones, cement blocks, and bullets. Families moving house found their furniture hung up in transit because moving van drivers were afraid to be on the road.[24]

Carter's was a joyless presidency. Although no one blamed him for the serious economic problems he inherited, neither he nor his advisers gave the impression that they could do much to turn things around. His administration took important steps to disentangle some of the chains that restrained the economy, including the deregulation of oil prices in April 1979 and, over strong opposition, deregulation of the trucking and railroad industries in 1980. But none of this addressed what Carter himself, in a speech to one hundred million television viewers on July 15, 1979, identified as the greatest threat to the nation. "The erosion of our confidence in the future is threatening to destroy the social and the political fabric of America," he said. "For the first time in the history of our country a majority of our people believe that the next five years will be worse than the past five years." Less than a year later, in March 1980, Carter announced new requirements to raise the cost of credit cards and other forms of household borrowing. "Inflation is fed by credit-financed spending," he told Americans in a televised address. "Consumers have gone into debt too heavily." If people were to consume less, he seemed to be suggesting, that would not be a terrible thing.[25]

It was in this unhappy environment that Ronald Reagan came to the fore. Reaganism, like Thatcherism, was not a bolt from the blue. Believers in free markets had devoted years of patient investment to building an intellectual superstructure of think tanks and university research institutes to stand against the welfare state. Alongside it, starting in the 1960s, they had fostered a network of grassroots groups united by their resentment of various social and legal changes—busing of children to schools outside their neighborhoods to achieve racial integration; easier access to abortion; "affirmative action" policies to promote integration in the workplace; more widespread sex education in the schools—and committed to using the Republican Party as the vehicle to reverse those changes.[26]

But these concerns had not yet carried enough weight to swing US politics decisively to the right. In 1976, when Reagan became the conservatives' spear carrier, a more traditionally moderate Republican president, Gerald Ford, managed to deny him the party's presidential nomination. At the time, the economy was bouncing back from the debacle of the 1973–75 recession, inflation was falling, and the country was not yet consumed by the fear that America's best days were over. By the second half of 1979, as the recession predicted by the bond market arrived right on schedule, the mood was different. The conservative ascendance came only as mortgage interest rates above 11 percent made young people despair of ever buying a home and as layoff notices went out to ironworkers on construction sites and toolmakers in auto plants.

In the words he used and the self-confidence he exuded, Reagan contradicted the notion that the world had become ungovernable. He projected an image of strength and a conviction that the US government, in the proper hands, could stand up to enemies abroad and restore prosperity at home. "Are you better off than you were four years ago?" Reagan asked Americans in a televised debate against Carter in October 1980. At the presidential election a few days later, Reagan swept the country, capturing forty-four states. As in the British election the previous year, millions of working-class voters walked away from the party of the welfare state and put their faith in a candidate who rejected the narrative of inevitable decline. When Reagan promised that new ideas and hard work would bring the good times back, Americans were eager to believe him.[27]

Reagan and Thatcher were acquaintances in the 1970s, but they were hardly close friends. In 1969, during his first term as governor of California, conservative groups in Great Britain arranged an invitation for him to speak at the annual "picnic" of the Institute of Directors, a gathering of the country's most influential business leaders at the Royal Albert Hall. His speech, titled "The New Noblesse Oblige," warned against "the inexorable march and encroachment by government on what are traditionally held to be the rights of the people." Such strident language would not have caused much of a stir in America, but by the polite standards of the British upper classes, it was noteworthy. Reagan became a frequent visitor to London, where his stories about how he reduced the size of the state government in California held listeners rapt. Thatcher apparently met him for the first time at a luncheon hosted by Prime Minister Heath in 1972, and the two had an extended conversation at the House of Commons in April 1975, shortly after the end of his term as governor and her selection as Conservative leader in Parliament.[28]

Like Thatcher, Reagan sounded a few simple themes when it came to economic policy: the way to raise living standards was to stabilize inflation, cut taxes, and reduce the size of government. The technical details were of no great consequence to either of them. Thatcher's key economic advisers, Keith Joseph and Alan Walters, subscribed to the ideas of monetarist economists such as Milton Friedman, for whom the path to lower unemployment and higher incomes ran through the money supply. Reagan's advisers were a more eclectic group: they encompassed monetarists; traditional small-government Republicans, who favored a balanced budget and low interest rates; and adherents of a new doctrine called "supply-side economics," who contended that lower marginal income-tax rates would create powerful incentives for work and entrepreneurship.

The monetarists regarded the supply-siders as snake-oil salesmen. The traditionalists mocked the monetarists' obsession with the money supply, and they distrusted the supply-siders' eagerness to lower marginal rates even if that would leave the government in the red. To the supply-siders, budget deficits and the money supply hardly mattered. All three, however, shared the belief that their ideas alone could revive the American dream and restore the rising living standards Americans had come to expect.

THE WEALTHY NATIONS' TURN TO THE RIGHT WAS NOT OVER. IN September 1982, the German Social Democrats lost a confidence vote in the Bundestag. Without losing a national election, Helmut Schmidt was out after more than eight years in power.

West Germany, which had the world's third-largest economy, had outperformed almost all the wealthy countries in the late 1970s. Inflation had stayed lower there than in most of Europe, and unemployment, though far higher than it had been before the 1973 oil crisis, had not come near the levels of Italy and France. Comparatively high productivity growth had helped Germany combat the effects of a strong currency, so that its cars and factory equipment remained competitive in world markets. Throughout the decade, the living standards of German workers had continued to improve, albeit at a much slower pace than previously. But the second oil shock proved Schmidt's undoing. The price of crude oil, about sixteen dollars a barrel at the start of 1979, more than doubled by early 1981 to the unimaginable level of thirty-eight dollars. Central banks had learned their lesson since 1973, when the first oil crisis helped drive up inflation; this time around, they refused to accept that inflation might be desirable, and they tightened monetary policy sharply to keep consumer prices from getting out of control. As interest rates soared around the world, economic growth slowed, dealing a serious blow to West Germany's export-driven economy. Schmidt was widely blamed for the recession and higher unemployment. Seeing the chancellor's popularity wane, the middle-of-the-road Free Democrats, the smaller party in the coalition, switched sides, bringing down the government.

Schmidt's successor, Christian Democratic leader Helmut Kohl, was no right-wing radical, but he had learned from the Swedish and British playbooks. He railed against bureaucracy, promising to cut the "many-armed monster" of government down to size—never mind that his party had ruled West Germany for twenty of the thirty-two years since the state's founding, and that the institutions of the federal government were largely the Christian Democrats' creation. Kohl advocated lower taxes and changes in social benefits to improve incentives for work. He promised not to destroy the welfare state but to improve it. So far as voters were concerned, the Social Democrats were out of fresh ideas. They would remain out of power for sixteen years.[29]

Two months after Kohl's ascent, in November 1982, it was Japan's turn. Japan's welfare state had expanded rapidly since 1973, when the government doubled pension benefits, introduced free medical care for the elderly, and lowered the cost of health insurance for the self-employed. Government spending soared—and it kept soaring even as slower economic growth squeezed the flow of tax revenue. By 1980, the first stirrings of taxpayer revolt could be heard. "If the tax burden of Japanese citizens remains below that of many Western nations, this has not been much of a solace to Japanese at tax time," the American political scientist Ellis Krauss commented. Successive governments tried to hold down taxes by borrowing, but that, too, had its limits. In 1980, the Japanese government sold more bonds than the American, British, French, Italian, and West German governments combined, and such borrowings covered one-third of government spending.[30]

Reining in social programs proved politically impossible. Instead, the government headed off a crisis in a most Japanese way. In the fall of 1980, it set up a commission on administrative management overseen by Yasuhiro Nakasone, Japan's minister of administration. Nakasone was an unusual figure in postwar Japan. The son of a lumber dealer, he was born in Gunma, a poor prefecture in the mountains of central Japan, a couple of hours by train from Tokyo. After attending the University of Tokyo and serving as a navy paymaster during World War II, he abandoned a potential career as a bureaucrat to run for a seat in the Diet in 1946. He made his reputation as a staunch conservative in 1951 when he delivered a letter to General Douglas MacArthur, the US commander in occupied Japan, criticizing the occupation. Since then, he sat firmly on the right wing of the Liberal Democratic Party, leading one of the party's factions and running several ministries, but never garnering broad enough support to become prime minister.[31]

Thanks to Nakasone's public relations efforts, everyone understood that "administrative management" was a euphemism for slimming down the government. When the commission issued a series of reports in early 1982, the Diet enthusiastically followed its recommendations to repeal or revise 355 laws and to reduce proposed pay raises for government employees. The Liberal Democrats, who controlled the Diet, made Nakasone prime minister on November 27. His slogan, "Fiscal reconstruction without tax increases," sounded clunky in English, but to Japanese voters it sounded like words from the mouth of Ronald Reagan.[32]

In the six years since Sweden's voters had turned out the Social Democrats, conservative parties had taken power in country after country. The new crop of confident, assertive leaders put worries about ungovernability to rest. The question now was whether their program of lower taxes, freer markets, greater personal responsibility, and a less suffocating state could restore the vigorous economic health of years past.

CHAPTER 11

Thatcher

In the warm glow of memory, cherished by generations of conservative acolytes, the global ascendancy of the right brought an end to the economic crisis that had festered since 1973. The reality was quite different. The leaders who won power by campaigning against the welfare state took aim at inflation, and with persistence and the help of some determined central bankers, they eventually brought it under control—although at a far higher cost than they had imagined. They were victorious as well in the battle against Soviet communism, and some of them were still in office to celebrate the advance of democracy across Eastern Europe at the end of the 1980s. But when it came to restoring the sense of economic security that had vanished along with cheap oil, their efforts were no more effectual than those of the less market-oriented politicians they drove from office. The combination of full employment, greater equality, and economic security proved not to be within their ability to deliver.

If there was a single theme that ran through the conservative economic thinking around 1980, it was this: rules matter. This was, in the context of recent history, a radical idea. Throughout the Golden Age and beyond, from the end of World War II to the late 1970s, economic policy had been the province of brilliant men supported by armies of data collectors and number crunchers. Experts like Arthur Burns, Karl Schiller, and Raúl Prebisch were thought to possess special economic understanding, such that they could foresee an economy's future course and selflessly determine which measures would most improve the well-being of the largest number of people. The very presumption that government could steer the economy to full employment and low inflation assumed that someone was skilled enough to do the steering. But after the economic chaos of the 1970s, the public had ample reason to doubt the experts' disinterested foresight. As the economist Charles Goodhart, a longtime Bank of England insider, wrote in 1989, "the failure of the monetary authorities, whether Central Bankers or Ministers of Finance, to stem inflation in the 1970s led to reconsideration whether they were working for the public good . . . or might be swayed by other political and bureaucratic objectives."[1]

In the new conservative understanding, discretion was the heart of the problem. Discretion allowed politicians to spend and tax as they saw fit, without any accountability. So far as monetary policy was concerned, discretion enabled central bankers to tinker freely with interest rates even at the cost of higher inflation, as Burns had done to secure Richard Nixon's re-election in 1972. And discretion meant that bureaucrats could regulate as they pleased, harassing citizens and infringing on personal liberties, just as they did in Astrid Lindgren's fictional kingdom of Monismania.

In the early 1960s, the American economist Milton Friedman had laid out the case for firm rules to govern central banks' monetary policy. Friedman contended that erratic and unpredictable changes in monetary policy—now encouraging more bank lending in response to a fall-off in homebuilding, now raising short-term interest rates to counteract a big jump in wages—destabilized the economy without addressing the root cause of inflation. "Inflation is always and everywhere a monetary phenomenon," he pronounced, insisting that the only way to control it was with a rule directing the central bank to keep the money supply growing at a specific rate that would allow incomes to rise without driving up prices.[2]

So long as the world economy was booming, Friedman's ideas were of more interest to theoreticians than to public officials. In 1969, one Bank of

England official dismissed them as "wishful primitivism, born of exaspera-
tion with certain intractable economic problems of modern society." The
flood of money sloshing across borders as the Bretton Woods system collapsed seemed to make monetarism all the more impractical, as a country's
money supply could change suddenly for reasons entirely unrelated to its
domestic economic conditions. But as economic planners and central bankers flailed helplessly against the stagflation that settled in after 1973, the ideas
of Friedman and his followers took on a new prominence. West Germany's
Bundesbank, which was independent of the government, announced late in
1974 that it would try to control inflation by following a rule for the growth
of the money supply rather than by adjusting short-term interest rates.
Within two years, central banks from Switzerland to Australia followed suit.[3]

Putting monetary policy on autopilot, as Friedman recommended, required first agreeing on which measure of the money supply the central
bank should worry about. This was not a straightforward question. In
principle, monetarists thought, the concern should be the amount of
money available for spending in the near term, because decisions about
whether to spend it could affect the prices of goods or services; money tied
up in five-year certificates of deposit, on the other hand, could not readily
be spent, so the monetary rule should ignore it. But there were several
different ways to measure money. The Bank of Canada focused on what
was called M1, counting only cash and deposits in checking accounts,
while the Bank of Japan emphasized M2, which also included money in
savings accounts. Another definition of the money supply, M3, included
everything in M2 plus certificates of deposit and some short-term funds
held in money-market accounts outside the banking system. Other variants had their partisans as well.

Once the monetary target was selected, the central bank or its government overseers had to decide how rapidly the target should grow. The
theory was that if the chosen M increased too quickly, consumers and
businesses would spend more money than the economy could accommodate and inflation would rise; but if it rose too slowly, the economy would
not produce the jobs and wealth it was capable of generating. The central
bank's main job was to hit the target by adjusting short-term interest rates

and banking rules, thus inducing depositors or bankers to make more or less money available for immediate spending. The central bank should not change its policies in response to real-world events, such as a blizzard that crippled business activity or a jump in the monthly trade deficit. It was meant to watch only the Ms.

And what of other concerns, such as jobs and wages? The monetarist view was that neither governments nor central banks could ensure every citizen a job or a bigger paycheck. Aside from keeping inflation down with steady monetary policy, the best way to reduce unemployment was to avoid interfering with the labor market. Policies like minimum wage laws might make some workers too expensive to hire, and generous unemployment benefits could encourage displaced workers to lounge at home rather than find new jobs. A big government job-creation program would work only briefly, because a larger budget deficit would cause the Ms to increase more quickly, requiring the central bank to push up interest rates and ultimately slowing private investment. It was thus a small intellectual step from setting money supply rules to setting rules requiring balanced budgets and small government, on the premise that such rules would lead to the best possible economic performance.

IN OCTOBER 1977, TWO YEARS AFTER ELECTING MARGARET THATCHER its leader, Britain's Conservative Party became the party of rules. The change was quite public. A year earlier, the party's first annual policy statement issued under Thatcher's leadership had used words that could have been uttered by Conservative leaders Harold Macmillan or Edward Heath, calling broadly for "reduction and control of public expenditures" and "personal responsibility and the freedom that goes with it" without bothering about meaningless details. The 1977 policy statement struck a very different tone, redolent of discipline and rigor. It went beyond generalities to advance a novel rule for limiting the size of government: "Our intention is to allow State spending and revenue a significantly smaller percentage slice of the nation's annual output and income each year." And it laid out an anti-inflation rule straight from Milton Friedman's playbook: "strict control of the rate of growth of the money supply."[4]

Thatcher's triumph in the 1979 election allowed the Conservatives to put these ideas into action. Her chancellor of the exchequer, Sir Geoffrey Howe, announced that lowering inflation would be the government's top economic priority. He directed the Bank of England to accomplish this by holding the growth of M3, his favored money-supply target, to between 7 percent and 11 percent over the next year—disregarding the advice of the bank's governor, Gordon Richardson, who warned him that the relationship between M3 and national income "has moved in quite sharply unpredictable ways." The growth rate Howe proposed was far lower than the 17 percent inflation rate, so if the Bank of England had in fact hit the target, the British economy would have operated with much less money in 1980, on an inflation-adjusted basis, than in 1979. Businesses' borrowing costs would have gone sky-high, and soaring mortgage rates would have brought the housing market to a stop. Howe was administering nothing short of an economic shock treatment in hopes of purging inflation.[5]

The Thatcher government also laid out a rule to guide its borrowing plans over several years, intended to shrink public spending as a share of the national income. The clampdown on spending would slow the economy, at least in the short term. But monetarist theory taught that this would be a quick, cold bath from which the nation would emerge revived and reinvigorated, able to flourish without the curse of inflation. To encourage this revival, the Thatcher government hiked taxes on consumer spending but lowered income-tax rates, especially for top earners. Higher taxes on consumption were said to encourage families to save rather than spend, giving banks more deposits to lend out to businesses that could create jobs. Lower income taxes would allow workers and entrepreneurs to keep a greater share of every pound they earned, which in turn would encourage more work effort and risk-taking.[6]

The program did not work as the monetarists had promised. In disputations incomprehensible to all but those initiated to the monetary priesthood, the experts argued over whether M3 was a better target than M1, M2, or any other measure of the money supply. These arguments, of course, allowed partisans of the other money-supply measures to point the finger elsewhere if achieving the government's M3 target failed to bring results. In any event, the target proved impossible to hit. By November 1979, after six months of Thatcherism, M3 was growing at a 19 percent rate, far faster than the government wanted, and consumer-price inflation was still rising. The government's budget deficit was rising, too. Meanwhile, the foreign investment attracted by high British interest rates drove up the exchange rate, rendering British exports uncompetitive on world markets. By the end of 1979, economists at Her Majesty's Treasury were predicting the worst economic downturn since 1931.[7]

With the economy in free fall and inflation still above 15 percent, Howe doubled down, ratcheting the monetary target even lower. "There would be no question of departing from the money supply policy, which is essential to the success of any anti-inflationary strategy," the government's 1980 budget report proclaimed. Thatcher had no patience with those who, pointing to the million displaced workers forced onto the dole over the course of 1980, suggested that it might be possible to bring down inflation at less human cost. She took advice from foreign monetarists such as the American professor Karl Brunner, whom she met during a vacation in Switzerland that August, and sat through a private tutorial on the mind-numbing subject of monetary base control by experts such as Mario Monti, later to become Italy's prime minister. Their counsel bolstered her opinion that those who would compromise monetary policy were weak and irresolute, the sort of people who had gotten Britain into such a mess in the first place. Among those she despised was the very man responsible for carrying out her monetary policy: Gordon Richardson, whom she dismissed as "that fool who runs the Bank of England."[8]

It was in October 1980, amid harsh criticism over the parlous state of the economy, that Thatcher appeared before the Conservative Party conference and spoke the carefully polished words, "You turn if you want to. The Lady's not for turning." Barely a month later she turned, agreeing to Howe's proposal to suspend the monetary targets temporarily. In January 1981, a new set of experts concluded that the Bank of England, acting at the government's direction, was following the wrong monetary rule. It should have focused on a different definition of the monetary supply, they said, not on M3. The mistake was costly. In the two years between

Thatcher's election and the summer of 1981, the British economy's output shrank 6 percent, and the reality in factory towns was far worse.[9]

In the spring of 1981, after two years of dismal economic performance, Howe reluctantly threw the rule book out the window. The monetary rule, requiring the Bank of England to regulate the growth of M3, henceforth received little more than lip service. The goal of reducing government spending as a share of the economy was abandoned in a new government budget that raised taxes. "When I was not able to get public spending down as low as I wished, I took the view that if we were going to spend that amount of money, we must cover it honestly—by taxation," Thatcher said later.[10]

The budget, with its higher taxes, was immensely unpopular. In its wake, Conservative Party polling showed that 67 percent of voters disapproved of the government's record. But after it was announced, inflation finally began to fall, reaching single digits in the spring of 1982. The economy began to grow at last. It would continue to expand for eight years running. "The 1981 Budget came to be seen almost as a political equivalent of the Battle of Britain: the Thatcher Government's finest hour," trumpeted Nigel Lawson, then a Treasury official and soon to replace Howe as chancellor of the exchequer.[11]

But Thatcherism was not quite the triumph that mythmakers claimed. During Thatcher's first two years in office, with the economy starved of oxygen, Great Britain endured its most brutal contraction since the early 1930s. What brought growth back, aside from tax revenues pumped from the new oil fields off the North Sea coast, was a new, more eclectic approach to monetary policy. Without admitting that its worship of M3 had been a mistake, the government gradually renounced monetarism altogether. In 1982, Howe told Parliament that the Bank of England would henceforth focus on a combination of M3, M1, exchange rates, and other factors. "No single measures of money can fully describe monetary conditions—they must be assessed in the light of all the available evidence," he declared. It was not a line Milton Friedman would have written.[12]

AMONG TWELVE WEALTHY ECONOMIES, THE UNITED KINGDOM ranked dead last in labor productivity growth in manufacturing between

1973 and 1979. It also ranked last in net saving, the share of national income that households and businesses set aside to invest in the future. Britain had foundered for so long that politicians and business leaders treated these unhappy trends with a certain resignation, as if the fates themselves had ordained that a country that had been so dynamic in the nineteenth century should decline in the twentieth. Thatcher, however, did not believe in the fates. She attributed the country's sclerosis to out-dated institutions. Two in particular provoked her ire: trade unions and state-owned enterprises. As her monetarist experiment ended in failure, she turned her sights on both. The fact that they tended to be hotbeds of support for the Labour Party was a bonus.[13]

Trade unions had been prominent in Great Britain since the 1820s, and were the main force behind the creation of the Labour Party in 1900. At the end of World War II, after the new Labour government repealed restrictions on unions' ability to strike and picket, they grew enormously influential, representing 9.5 million workers by 1950. Although there were divergent streams within the trade union movement, the large industrial unions that dominated the Trades Union Congress pushed a traditional socialist line, calling for state ownership of heavy industry and union involvement in management. Coal mines were nationalized in 1946; power generators in 1947; railroads, some bus, truck, and barge companies, and the Thomas Cook travel agency in 1948. The government took over the iron and steel industry in 1951; Conservative governments sold it off later in the 1950s; and it was nationalized again in 1967. In the 1970s, the Conservatives, under the Heath government, took over the Rolls-Royce aircraft engine business—supposedly vital to the national defense—and thirty-one other aviation manufacturers and shipbuilders. The Labour government that took office in 1974 bowed to union pressure to add more troubled companies to the government's portfolio, from the insolvent automaker British Leyland to Drake and Scull, an engineering contractor worth less than one million pounds. It also created an entity called British National Oil Company, through which the state took direct control of a significant portion of North Sea oil.[14]

The performance of the nationalized industries had been unimpressive even when times were good, and it deteriorated sharply in the 1970s; over the course of the decade, a time when private companies were earning about 17 percent return on investment, the state-owned firms collectively earned an average return of 4.3 percent. Their unions repeatedly won large wage increases unmatched by productivity improvements. Political interference was constant: the electric generating companies were directed to buy British-designed nuclear plants and the steelworks were ordered to use British coal. Management was in disarray, because experienced private-sector executives were reluctant to take on jobs in which key decisions were determined, directly or indirectly, by the government. Billions of pounds of tax money went to sustain exhausted mines, antiquated mills, and shipyards with no commercial potential.[15]

Studies since the 1950s had repeatedly called for reform and privatization, but almost nothing had changed. The public, which well remembered how difficult working-class life had been before Labour came to power, was largely sympathetic toward state-run enterprises, even if the Post Office did take forever to install a phone. The trade unions were opposed to privatizing state-owned industry. Surprisingly, so was much of the country's business establishment. Edward Heath, whose government cheered free enterprise even as it greatly expanded the state's ownership of industry in the early 1970s, claimed in his memoirs that when he suggested privatization, "We were advised by the employers' organisations that the programme should go no further at this stage. British capitalism was at such a low ebb that no one would have taken over the major concerns which, on paper at least, might one day look like attractive candidates for privatization."[16]

By the time Thatcher took office in 1979, the nationalized industries accounted for about 10 percent of Great Britain's total output and employed 1.5 million workers. As opposition leader, Thatcher had not been particularly outspoken concerning state-owned companies. And for good political reasons: raising the issue would have amounted to waving a red flag at the unions, and such a confrontational stance would not have been endorsed by voters who were simply exhausted by labor unrest. Suggesting relatively modest reforms to labor law, such as requiring unions to obtain their members' approval in a secret ballot before calling a strike, was as far as candidate Thatcher was prepared to go.

Behind the scenes, however, forces on the right wing of the Conservative Party were laying the groundwork for a much stronger assault. In July 1977, the party's Economic Reconstruction Group, charged with thinking about how a future Conservative government might revive the country's troubled economy, received a confidential report from a committee chaired by Nicholas Ridley, a member of Parliament. The Ridley Report laid out the case against state-owned enterprises: "More and more the nationalised industries are run for the benefit of those who work in them. The pressures are for more jobs for the boys and more money for each boy." But the report deemed "a frontal attack" on nationalized industries politically unwise. It recommended instead "a policy of preparing the industries for partial return to the private sector, more or less by stealth." One potential approach would be to require each company to earn a specified rate of return on invested capital, closing or selling any unit that failed to do so. Another would be to break large enterprises like British Steel or the National Coal Board into much smaller component parts, allowing individual parts to be sold off with much less fuss than if a large entity were to be privatized in a single go. These suggestions, had they been known to the public, would have been controversial.

But of far greater consequence to the future Thatcher government was the report's confidential annex. The annex predicted that between six and eighteen months after the next Conservative government took office, its opponents would seek to mount a challenge, using a dispute over wages or layoffs as a pretext to disrupt a critical industry. The industry where this was most likely to occur, the report foresaw, would be coal. This warning probably touched a nerve, as the Conservative leaders for whom the report was written would have vividly recalled the nationwide coal strike that brought down the last Conservative government, in 1974. The Ridley Report's most sensitive advice, leaked to the press the following year, was that the government should prepare for war against the National Union of Mineworkers. It urged building large coal stockpiles at power plants, making contingency plans to import coal on short notice, installing dual-fired generators to burn oil if coal stocks ran out, and recruiting nonunion truckers to move coal if needed. The committee proposed changing the law to make striking workers ineligible for unemployment benefits. Most explosively, it called for the creation of "a large, mobile squad of police" to deal with violent picketing. The message could not be missed: if a future Conservative government wanted to fix the economy, it could not avoid facing the trade unions head-on.[17]

Thatcher had absorbed this counsel before becoming prime minister, but she was astute enough not to act on it immediately. Dealing with inflation and reducing government spending were her priorities; she would get to the unions in time. Besides, Thatcher was well aware that the Conservatives were a minority party. She owed her victory to union members, people who normally voted Labour but aspired to own their homes and send their children to university. These upwardly mobile households broke with tradition, voting Conservative in 1979 because they were tired of the Labour Party's incompetence, but they nonetheless believed in the value of trade unions. The only way the Conservative Party could stay in power was to break these voters' class allegiance. Thatcher was playing a long game. She wanted to woo Labour voters, not antagonize them.

The place to start was not by attacking the trade unions or by selling off British Steel, but by letting people own their homes. In 1979, her government introduced a bill granting tenants in housing owned by local authorities, known as "council housing," the right to buy their units at prices far below market value. This was privatization for the masses: three in ten British households lived in publicly owned housing. Those who had been council tenants for over twenty years could buy their house or apartment at a 50 percent discount; if they were uncertain, they could pay a hundred-pound deposit and preserve their right to buy at a fixed price for two years. The local authority that was selling the property was obliged to offer a mortgage.[18]

Right to Buy, as it was known, targeted a core Labour constituency. Most of the council estates had been built under Labour governments, and their residents were reliable Labour voters. By the spring of 1983, two-and-a-half years after Parliament enacted Right to Buy into law, 274,650 council tenants in England alone had acquired their homes. A poll showed that 59 percent of people who had voted for Labour in 1979 and subsequently bought their own homes would not vote for Labour again. Right to Buy was privatization conducted at a level that made sense to average people. As it went forward, gathering public support, the political obstacles to privatizing state-owned companies fell away.[19]

Privatization of state-owned enterprises was not a new idea in 1979. The Conservative government led by Winston Churchill had sold British Steel into private ownership in the early 1950s, and the government of German chancellor Konrad Adenauer had sold a majority of the shares of Volkswagen through a public offering in 1961. The term "privatization" had originated in Nazi Germany but was not widely used after World War II; the Conservative manifesto published during the 1979 campaign refrained from using it altogether. The word may have been deemed inflammatory, for when Conservative politician Nigel Lawson was given a high Treasury job in May 1979, his portfolio was defined to include "disposal of assets," not "privatization."

In the new government's first budget speech that same month, Geoffrey Howe referred to "the sale of assets" as a way of "reducing the size of the public sector," but the only plan he announced was a small reduction in the government's 51 percent holding in British Petroleum, which already traded on the London Stock Exchange. Thatcher, though, had no qualms about the term "privatization." She set up an eight-member cabinet subcommittee to pursue it. By July 19, 1979, barely two months into the new government, Lawson had come up with a list of assets, from British Steel to National Bus Company, which might be sold off. Of these, only one, the National Freight Corporation, was marked for sale in its entirety; the government would hold on to part-ownership of the other companies, "to win over employees."[20]

It was not until August 1980, when Lawson announced in a London speech that the government had "embarked on a major program of privatization of the state-owned industries," that the scale of Thatcher's intentions became clear. Even then, transactions proceeded slowly, involving the sale of government-owned shares in companies that operated in competitive industries rather than of monopolies like British Telecom and the National Coal Board. As the Ridley Report had suggested, the Conservatives acted under the radar, closing low-profile operations of state-owned companies or separating small businesses that might be sold without controversy from larger entities whose sale would be politically contentious. Even so, the government's strategy encountered strong opposition. When the National Coal Board proposed in February 1981 to close twenty-three money-losing underground mines, the National Union of Mineworkers threatened a nationwide walkout of 240,000 miners. Thatcher quickly backed down, agreeing to reinstate subsidies for the mines and to limit imports so users would have no alternative to British coal. She was not ready to risk a strike for which the government was unprepared. "Nigel," she told Lawson upon naming him energy secretary in September 1981, "we mustn't have a coal strike."[21]

By the time of the next general election, in June 1983, privatization, not counting the sales of council homes, had raised a mere two billion pounds. The Conservatives decided not to make the privatization of industry a campaign issue. The sale of council housing, on the other hand, drew hundreds of thousands of blue-collar voters to the party. That, on top of the British victory in the 1982 Falkland Islands war with Argentina and a split in the Labour Party, brought a decisive Conservative victory, freeing Thatcher to move aggressively to transform the British economy.

THATCHER SAW A DIRECT CONNECTION BETWEEN PRIVATIZATION and the weakening of trade union power; she often spoke of "the monopoly nationalized industries" and "the monopoly trade unions" as Britain's two great economic problems. Luckily for her, she drew an adversary straight from central casting. Arthur Scargill, a militant Yorkshire miner, had become president of the National Union of Mineworkers in 1982. Scargill's readiness to strike to stop the closure of unprofitable mines and to win higher wages for his members was no secret; he had tried and failed to win his members' approval of a strike three times in 1982 and 1983. The government responded first by stockpiling coal and improving relations with other unions and then, three months after the election, by naming Ian MacGregor chairman of the National Coal Board. MacGregor, a Scottish-born investment banker who had lived for years in the United States, had just come from running state-owned British Steel, where he had survived a fourteen-week strike and cut the workforce in half.

MacGregor's appointment to head the National Coal Board was a blatant challenge to Scargill, who rose to the occasion. In October, the Mineworkers announced a ban on overtime work and rejected any further mine closures. On March 6, 1984, the National Coal Board announced the closure of twenty mines, with a loss of twenty thousand jobs. Miners at several pits walked out, and on March 12, without a ballot among his members, Scargill declared a national strike.[22]

The miners' strike would be the defining moment of Thatcher's tenure as prime minister. The National Union of Mineworkers was "the enemy within," she told Parliament. Early on, physical attacks on strike-breaking miners and the killing of a taxi driver taking a strike breaker to work turned public opinion against the union. Thatcher, through careful preparation and a bit of good luck, emerged victorious. Miners who detested Scargill kept working, some power plants switched from coal to oil, and masses of police broke union blockades of working mines. Over the winter of 1984–1985, the lights stayed on. In March 1985, the Mineworkers called off the strike. The most powerful trade union in Great Britain was vanquished. More than half of the 170 collieries run by the National Coal Board when the strike began would close within five years, and 79,000 heavily subsidized jobs would go with them.[23]

The popularity of Thatcher's stand against the miners opened the way to large-scale privatization of British industry, and Scargill's defeat removed a powerful opponent from the scene. In May 1984, shortly after the coal miners' strike began, state-owned British Gas sold its half-interest in onshore oil fields. Two months later, the company's North Sea oil fields, organized into Enterprise Oil, were listed on the London Stock Exchange. In August, the carmaker Jaguar was sold as a going concern. December brought the sale of 51 percent of British Telecom, raising 3.9 billion pounds, six times as much as any previous British stock issue. Shipyards went on sale, one after the other, starting in 1985. British Gas was floated on the stock exchange in December 1986 for 5.4 billion pounds. The following year, the government shed British Airways, Rolls-Royce, and the British Airports Authority, which ran most of Britain's major airports. British Steel went private in 1988, with water and electric utilities to follow. By the end of the 1980s, the size of the state-owned sector was much reduced and billions of pounds in subsidies to industry had been cut from the budget. The government could boast that ten million people, a fifth of the population, had become shareholders by acquiring shares in newly privatized companies.[24]

Within the United Kingdom, the details of particular privatizations would be highly contested. Critics objected that the government failed to maximize its income by selling its shares too cheaply, that private monopolies replaced state-owned monopolies to no economic benefit, that the managers of some companies made unfair profits when their firms were privatized. Some privatizations undertaken after Thatcher left office in 1990—such as the sales of British Energy, operator of eight nuclear plants, and Railtrack, owner of the infrastructure used by railway trains—failed badly, requiring costly bailouts. Perhaps the most complex privatization involved replacing the money-losing service offered by state-owned British Rail with service offered by franchisees that received state subsidies and then, when they nonetheless failed to make a profit, returned their franchises to the government. The irony that some of the new operators of "privatized" businesses were in fact companies owned by other European governments did not pass unnoticed.[25]

Some state-owned companies were radically changed by privatization: stodgy old British Telecom was soon earning a better return on its investors' capital than it ever earned under state ownership, even as it faced off against new competitors. Others struggled to adapt to the new environment; worker productivity at Rolls-Royce tumbled after it was sold, in 1987, and profits were unimpressive. Blanket claims about the miraculous effects of privatization are inaccurate, for the track records of the privatized firms were decidedly mixed.[26]

What is not contested is that privatization led to a forced restructuring of Great Britain's economy. As one of its most zealous advocates, Madsen Pirie, the head of a free-market think tank, declaimed in 1988, "The privatization programme in Britain probably marked the largest transfer of power and property since the dissolution of the monasteries under Henry VIII." Some 650,000 workers were forcibly moved from state employment into the private economy as the role of state-owned enterprises faded away. The industrial sector, deprived of taxpayer subsidies, shrank quickly as marquee names closed unprofitable operations. Manufacturing employment, 30 percent of the workforce in 1979, fell to 22 percent under Thatcher as the United Kingdom shifted decisively to a service economy. Well beyond the mineworkers, the trades union movement lost power, weakened not only by changes in labor law, but also by the rapid erosion of the industries that had formed its base for more than a century. In 1979, 54 percent of British workers were union members. The corresponding figure only eight years later was 42 percent, as unions had collectively lost almost three million members.[27]

Privatization opened the way to other changes less heralded but equally profound. Pushed by Thatcher legislation, local governments put out for bid activities long considered basic public services; cricketers at the neighborhood recreation grounds had to pay a few pounds to the private contractor who trimmed the grass, and applicants for housing assistance found themselves presenting their claims to a company hired by their local authority. Private-sector workers picked up Great Britain's waste and imprisoned its undocumented immigrants. Market forces found their way into schools and public transportation systems, even if the London Underground was eventually forced to reverse its disastrous decision to hand portions of the Tube over to private operators. As Thatcher and her supporters had hoped so fervently, the country's longstanding suspicion of entrepreneurship, private enterprise, and risk-taking yielded to considerable faith in the market. When, after eighteen years of Conservative rule, the Labour Party finally regained control of Parliament in 1997, it was as "New Labour" under the leadership of Tony Blair, purged of the slightest taint of socialism.

THATCHERISM WAS, AT ITS CORE, A DESPERATION MOVE, A LAST-ditch response to economic failure. It undoubtedly left Great Britain better off than it would have been if the unhappy trends of the 1970s had continued unchecked for another decade. On a personal level, her forthrightness, her willingness to speak her mind plainly and to bulldoze obstacles and opponents to get her way, were discomfiting for many in a country where people tended to value politeness and eschew direct conflict. But Thatcher's innate optimism, her firm conviction that the United Kingdom could make itself dynamic and prosperous once more, was contagious. Thatcherism was a tonic for a nation that had convinced itself of the inevitability of economic decline. "The plain fact is that the British economy has been transformed," Nigel Lawson, then chancellor of the exchequer, declared in 1988.[28]

Yet in economic terms, the Thatcher record was far from stellar. The initial monetarist experiment, from 1979 to 1981, was a disaster from every perspective. Conditions improved after the sudden change of course in 1981, with the economy outgrowing every other in Western Europe, but it was still far from buoyant. Inflation remained high by international standards; between 1979 and 1989, consumer prices rose at an annual rate of 7.5 percent, more than in any other major economy save Italy. Not until the winter of 1988, nearly nine years after Thatcher's ascent, did British factories again produce as much as they had when she first moved into 10 Downing Street. Nor can her tenure rightly be depicted as reviving Britain's moribund productivity growth. Labor productivity rose much more slowly during her eleven years in office than it had during the previous decade. Several years of strong growth in the second half of the 1980s followed several years of poor economic performance, but the notion that the Conservative turn restored the British economy to rude health is simply not right.[29]

Some people in Great Britain fared well thanks to Thatcher's policies. Over a million working-class families had the opportunity to become homeowners thanks to Right to Buy, although large numbers of them had to sell after discovering that homeownership required more than their incomes would permit. Those with capital prospered in the friendlier investment climate, and those seeking to start businesses found their paths eased by the state's new interest in entrepreneurship. Coincidently, the eastern coast of Scotland and the isles to the north flourished thanks to the need for labor to drill for, produce, and transport North Sea oil. But in the industrial and mining towns of the Midlands and the North of England, the effects of Thatcher's policies on employment proved devastating. The number of people registered for unemployment benefits, 1.1 million upon her election in May 1979, reached two million at the start of 1981 and three million by the autumn of 1985 before finally starting to fall. During the 1980s, Britain would have the highest unemployment rate of any major high-income economy. So serious was the unemployment problem that Thatcher's personal priority, reducing government spending and taxes, was abandoned. The large number of people out of work made it impossible to cut outlays for social benefits, and Thatcher gave up trying.[30]

The fact that British unemployment fell sharply in the late 1980s, from 3.3 million in 1986 to half that number by the time of her resignation in 1990, is often taken as evidence that her policies reawakened the stagnant British economy. But the unemployment statistics do not tell the whole story. The Thatcher government made repeated changes in unemployment benefits, seventeen in all, in a deliberate effort to drive people off the unemployment rolls. This brought the official numbers down despite the lack of new jobs.

Then, starting in the late 1980s, in a blatant attempt to push down the unemployment rate, her government urged doctors to qualify displaced workers for sickness or invalidity benefits, which would mean that they would no longer be deemed unemployed. The number of people out of work because of disability rose 40 percent between 1985 and 1990, removing four hundred thousand workers from the unemployment rolls. In 1977, two years before Thatcher took office, a government survey found that 4 percent of fifty-nine-year-old women claimed that a longstanding illness limited their ability to work; in 1987, even as reported unemployment was falling, 21 percent of women that age claimed a disabling illness. Between disability and unemployment, large numbers of people exited the labor force. When Thatcher took office in 1979, eight in ten men between the ages of fifty-five and sixty-four held jobs; when she left, the ratio was six in ten. The rest had given up looking.[31]

Thatcher had no secret formula. Her policies have received much praise for reviving Great Britain's seemingly moribund economy in the second half of the 1980s. But over her entire tenure, from 1979 to 1990, the economy expanded at about the same rate as in the decade before she became prime minister. It would take until the autumn of 2000 before the jobless queues were shorter than when she took office, and they would never again be as short as they had been in the waning months of the Golden Age. Yet if her record of economic success was mixed, her conviction and her dogged determination won her admirers even among those who rejected her ideas. In the words of François Mitterrand, president of France during nine years of Thatcher's tenure, "She was an adversary, but at least she had a vision." That vision would prove so influential that it would force the hand of Mitterrand himself.[32]

CHAPTER 12

Socialism's Last Stand

Ronald Reagan's inauguration in January 1981, following the Swedes' rejection of the Social Democrats and British voters' embrace of Margaret Thatcher, seemed to confirm the triumph of small-government ideology. In truth, though, almost no one in any country really wanted the welfare state unwound; old-age pensions and low-cost health care were immensely popular everywhere. What fed the conservative reaction was not a desire for fewer social benefits but a wish for less intrusive government, based in good part on the claim that shrinking government was the only way to bring back rapid economic growth.

Voters in France, however, did not see things that way. Other countries might pin their hopes of economic revival on market forces and the animal spirits of private entrepreneurs, but in France the government would point the way, as it had since the reign of Louis XIV three centuries earlier. In May 1981, the French electorate ended a quarter-century of conservative rule. Socialist François Mitterrand moved into the Élysée Palace as president and promptly called for new legislative elections. The Socialists and their allies captured a stunning 57 percent of the vote, giving Mitterrand a large majority in the National Assembly and the backing to undertake radical economic reforms in a socialist direction.

Mitterrand was far from a new face in French politics. Born into a comfortable small-town family in southwestern France during the First World War, he had a conservative Catholic upbringing. At seventeen, he moved to Paris and enrolled at the Free School of Political Science, the prestigious institution known throughout Europe as "Sciences Po." He found a political home in the controversial Catholic movement Cross of Fire, which was both nationalist and Christian socialist in orientation. Decades later, historians still debate whether Cross of Fire and its successor, the French Social Party, which by 1940 boasted more than one million members, represented the vanguard of French fascism or were more open and progressive than other far-right French groups.

After being drafted into the army, Mitterrand was wounded in 1940 and taken prisoner by the Germans. Eighteen months later, he escaped from a prisoner-of-war camp and made his way to southern France, a region ruled by the collaborationist Vichy government but not under direct German occupation. There, while working on veterans' affairs for the Vichy government, he also helped form the resistance movement that attacked German troops and security forces across occupied France. He established ties with Charles de Gaulle, the army general who led the Free French government in exile, and joined in the liberation of Paris in August 1944. De Gaulle, highly nationalistic and intensely anticommunist, headed the first postwar French government before resigning in 1946. The general was a novice in politics, and his preference for decisive action was ill suited to a fractious and unstable political system that would see twenty-one governments led by sixteen different men over the next dozen years.

After the war, Mitterrand devoted his entire life to politics. Elected to the National Assembly in 1947 on the ticket of a centrist party, he became minister of veterans affairs at the age of thirty-one, the first of no fewer than eleven appointments as a cabinet minister. By 1953, he was head of his party. The burning issue of the day was the future of France's many overseas territories. Mitterrand, as interior minister and then justice minister between 1954 and 1957, was intimately involved in shaping the

French government's brutal but ultimately unsuccessful repression of the independence movement in Algeria, then a part of France.

De Gaulle returned to political life in 1958, ruling with emergency powers until French voters approved a new constitution designed to put an end to instability by creating a strong presidency. Alarmed by de Gaulle's seemingly authoritarian behavior, Mitterrand emerged as one of his fiercest critics. He unsuccessfully opposed the general's election as president under the new constitution in 1959. When de Gaulle sought a second term in 1965, Mitterrand became the leading opposition candidate. Square-jawed, balding, and nine inches shorter than the imperious general, Mitterrand presented himself as a man of the people, capturing an unexpected 45 percent of the vote in a two-man runoff and establishing himself as the most popular politician on the French left.

Amid the political turmoil of 1968, when battles between police and students were nightly events on the streets of Paris, Mitterrand engineered a series of back-room mergers that created the Socialist Party as a democratic alternative to France's powerful Communist Party. Mitterrand's maneuvering left bruised feelings, and he was not nominated to run in the 1969 election that followed de Gaulle's resignation. That rejection proved fortuitous. The socialist parties performed disastrously, making it abundantly clear that no other leftist politician had Mitterrand's wide appeal. Five years later, in Mitterrand's second presidential run, he came within a hair's breadth of defeating former finance minister Valéry Giscard d'Estaing.

It was Giscard's misfortune to win the presidency just as the foundations beneath the French economy were imploding. An imposing man, six feet two inches in height, he sought to profile himself as Everyman. But despite his efforts to step out of his limousine and mingle with people on the street, he came across as an aristocrat. A scholarly centrist by nature, Giscard was, by French standards, attuned to market forces and sympathetic to the needs of the private business sector. He had served as finance minister between 1969 and 1974, as the Bretton Woods system was collapsing. Giscard had spent those years dealing with one foreign exchange crisis after another, and this experience profoundly shaped his understanding of the crises facing the French economy in 1974. Aside from higher oil prices, he said, the main cause was the US war in Vietnam. The war led to large US budget deficits in the late 1960s, and the government's borrowing needs pushed up interest rates, drawing in foreign capital. The demand for dollars to invest in America, Giscard thought, caused the shake-up in the foreign exchange markets that threw the world economic order into chaos. Regaining economic stability, in his view, required stabilizing exchange rates once again.[1]

Giscard's focus on international economic problems, over which the president of France had little power, offered the advantage of allowing him to neglect domestic problems, perhaps the most pressing of which was the forced restructuring of heavy industry. France's economy was built around large factory complexes, like the Sacilor steelworks in Lorraine, near the German border, and the government-owned Renault automobile plant just southwest of Paris. These industrial flagships were known for their bloated workforces and militant unions. French law allowed multiple labor organizations in a single workplace, and the unions competed for worker support by blocking modernization plans that might eliminate jobs. When the post-1973 slump cut demand for their products, these huge factories became white elephants, viable thanks only to a rich diet of state aid. With layoffs all but impossible, the only way for factories to trim their workforces was to offer workers incentives to leave and not to replace them. Employment in manufacturing plunged, with most of the decline at the largest factories. The pain was felt most intensely by youths who had not completed high school, who found few employers eager to hire.[2]

The decay of France's industrial giants was symptomatic of a sick economy. Investment in factory equipment and other fixed capital stagnated during the Giscard years. The European Economic Community had eliminated tariffs and many other restrictions on trade within Western Europe, so companies seeking to sell their wares in Lille and Bordeaux could do so without setting up shop in a country where inflation was two or three times as high as in Germany or Belgium. With profits weak, companies already operating in the country cut back on investment and on research and development, choices that bode ill for France's future.

A more aggressive leader might have tried to slice through the thicket of rules and regulations that made it so difficult for entrepreneurs to start companies and for employers to discharge workers when business conditions changed. But Giscard was no Margaret Thatcher. Attitudes toward huge government-funded projects and state-owned industries were not matters of right and left in France; all major political philosophies shared a commitment to *dirigisme,* the direction of economic affairs by highly trained and well-informed state officials. While Giscard described himself as a conservative who liked change, he was wildly enthusiastic about the state's role in building France's first high-speed rail line, a fleet of nuclear power plants to reduce dependence, and Minitel, a video-text terminal that was installed in millions of French homes. Such projects reinforced France's prestige as a leader in advanced technology, but they did almost nothing to boost employment: France's working-age population grew nearly 1 percent per year between 1974 and 1981, but the number of people with jobs rose hardly at all. With 1.75 million workers unemployed by 1981, the president's promise of a job or a training slot for every young French worker rang hollow.[3]

Giscard's ineffectual performance opened the door for Mitterrand. During the 1970s, Mitterrand had slowly drifted to the left as he steered the Socialists into a loose alliance with the Communist Party. Despite his long history in French politics, he was able to establish himself as a maverick during the 1981 election campaign, announcing his opposition to capital punishment and refusing to rule out a role in his government for the Communists, who typically won 15 to 20 percent of the vote. The electorate, which overwhelmingly supported capital punishment and distrusted the Communists, was charmed. In May 1981, with the economy slumping, the unemployment rate headed toward 7 percent, the franc under attack in the currency markets, and the inflation rate stuck in the double digits, voters turned out in record numbers to give the Socialists a chance.[4]

IN HIS PROLONGED MIGRATION FROM CENTER-RIGHT TO CENTER-left, Mitterrand had never given much thought to economics. Not one of his many ministerial posts had involved economic affairs, and as an opposition deputy in the National Assembly, his attention was devoted mainly to internal party matters. He and his chief economic adviser, Jacques Attali, paid lip service to Karl Marx—the Socialists could succeed at the polls only by pulling in supporters of the Communists, who had yet to lose their fondness for Marxian dogma—but they saw the source of the crisis as declining profits, which, in their understanding, caused businesses to raise prices and cut back on hiring.[5]

In 1975, Attali had proposed a range of policies to create jobs, such as subsidizing the labor-intensive industries that would be most likely to hire large numbers of workers; taxing capital-intensive industries in the hope that this would prompt them to make greater use of labor instead of replacing workers with machines; nationalizing companies so the state would have direct control over their hiring and investment decisions; and gradually shortening the workweek in the hope that employers would hire additional people to do the same amount of work. These ideas reflected hopelessly naïve views about the way economies function. Subsidizing labor-intensive industries, for example, would preserve low-productivity, low-skill manufacturers rather than encouraging a shift of labor and capital investment into higher-productivity industries. Taxing capital-intensive industries would hurt precisely those firms that were most likely to succeed in a country such as France, in which wages were high. These were not the sorts of ideas that would make investors want to put their money to work in France.

Over time, however, Attali's views had matured as he worried about France's ability to adapt to a world of rapid technological change and intense global competition. He became skeptical of the extreme centralization of both the French government and the French economy. Although he advocated greater government control of key industries—almost a mandatory point of view for a Socialist Party functionary—he urged that local or regional governments take over many functions that had been run from Paris for decades. The Socialists' 1981 campaign platform, tailored to attract votes from the Communists while at the same time pulling centrist voters away from Giscard's coalition, followed a fairly orthodox socialist line. It called for the nationalization of heavy industry, new taxes on wealth, the creation of 150,000 government jobs, a large public works program, a higher minimum wage, a fifth week of paid vacation for all, and larger grants to families with children.[6]

Having approved the general policies, Mitterrand was not preoccupied with the details. He paid close attention to the political implications of the government's pronouncements, but when it came to shaping policy, he preferred to spend his time on foreign affairs, including almost nonstop summits dealing with exchange rates, trade, and the future of the European Economic Community. He kept meetings at the Élysée Palace to a minimum; his ministers and advisers were asked to put their recommendations in writing, and each morning he worked through the papers in his in-box, weighing the political implications of each proposal and writing "yes," "no," or "seen"—a euphemism for "no"—at the top. The job of delivering on campaign promises was handed to Pierre Mauroy, Mitterrand's choice as prime minister.[7]

The Communist Party, which had supplied perhaps one-fourth of Mitterrand's votes and held four ministerial posts in his cabinet, made sure the Socialists kept their word. Public spending leaped by 27 percent in 1982 as the government borrowed money to boost pensions, family benefits, and housing allowances, and to finance construction projects. That stimulus brought a burst of economic growth: after inflation, per capita income grew 1.7 percent. But below that cheery top line, most of the economic signs in 1982 were negative. Housing construction collapsed. Investment in business equipment and machinery barely grew. The unemployment rate climbed steeply, worsened by government actions that reflected a serious misunderstanding of the problem.

In France, as in other parts of Western Europe, the reigning explanation for unemployment was what economists call the "lump of labor" theory. The theory holds that a society has only a fixed amount of work that needs to be done, and therefore the only way to reduce unemployment is to share the available work. This was reflected in Mitterrand's initial program. The government lowered the retirement age to sixty to push older people out of the workforce; this was expected to create openings for youngsters, on the assumption that each employer needed only a certain amount of labor and would replace departing workers one for one. Workers who reached age fifty-five could collect pensions equal to 80 percent of their wages if their employers agreed to replace each retiree with a worker under twenty-five. The regular workweek was cut from forty hours to thirty-nine, and the maximum workweek was reduced as well, in the expectation that employers might cover those hours by adding workers. The possibility that less work for the same pay might deter hiring, or that young workers might lack the skills of the experienced workers they were replacing and therefore have lower productivity, was not widely discussed in the France of 1981.[8]

The most contentious piece of the Mitterrand program was the nationalization of privately owned companies. Important French enterprises, such as the postal and telephone services and the French National Railway, were already in state hands, and soon after their ascent the Socialists took over several private companies that could not meet payments on loans they had received from the state. The main nationalization bill, introduced in September 1981, proposed to take five industrial giants and thirty-eight financial companies into state ownership, including such famous names as Saint-Gobain, a glassmaker; Rhône-Poulenc, a chemicals manufacturer; Banque Rothschild; and Paribas, France's most influential investment bank. Many were financially weak. For some, nationalization may have been the only alternative to finding a foreign buyer, a drastic step in a country that was suspicious of foreign investment. The government could have taken control simply by acquiring a majority of outstanding shares in each firm. Instead, it sought 100 percent ownership, raising the cost to taxpayers but pleasing the Communists, who favored total state ownership of big business.

Despite the large Socialist majority, the nationalization bill quickly ran into trouble. Opponents, mainly from conservative minority parties, stalled it in the National Assembly by offering nearly 1,500 amendments. The Senate rejected the bill twice, further delaying its enactment. The Constitutional Council, charged with judging the constitutionality of laws, determined that the formula for compensating private shareholders was inadequate, raising the cost still higher. But early in 1982, the chosen enterprises finally passed into government hands, leaving the state in control of 79 percent of French steelmaking, 52 percent of basic chemical manufacturing, and 42 percent of electronics. All told, government-owned companies now accounted for one-third of all value added in French manufacturing, in addition to nearly the entire financial sector. Shareholders were forced to pay for their own expropriation, receiving compensation not in cash but in the form of bonds that would be paid off over fifteen years.[9]

The government promised that the nationalized firms would be run as independent entities. "They should have total freedom of decision and action," Mitterrand said. But total freedom meant that the firms might eliminate jobs in France, and that was something the government would not tolerate. When managers of the computer and electronics company Thomson-Brandt wanted to enter a joint venture with the Japanese company JVC to make video recorders, the ministry of industry objected; it ordered Thomson to strike a deal with a German competitor instead, with the expectation that a European company would be more likely to keep French plants open. The ministry also directed Thomson to continue producing semiconductor manufacturing equipment, which the government judged critical to France's high-technology future, and it pushed the company to make home audio equipment in competition with the Japanese. From the ministry's perspective, Thomson was a national champion. Its first priority should be strengthening the French economy, as the ministry deemed necessary; earning a return on the taxpayers' investment was secondary.[10]

Automaker Renault agreed, also under government pressure, not to trim its bloated workforce, but instead to give early retirement to 3,500 workers and replace them with an equal number of new hires. Reducing employment was out of the question. Other companies similarly received unsolicited guidance from their sole shareholder. They were told to specialize in certain products, provide loans to troubled supplier companies, and back away from product lines that, in the government's view, had too much competition. The government intervened in the state-owned firms' labor negotiations as well, urging generous wage increases and acquiescence to union proposals that made it even harder to reduce the workforce. The state-owned banks were ordered to provide loans and capital investment to state-owned industry, regardless of the likely payoff. The French taxpayer ultimately bore the cost. In the first three years of state ownership, by one estimate, the newly nationalized industrial companies collectively soaked up roughly $40 billion of government money. Very few of them made a profit, and the budget deficit soared.[11]

The expropriations and the new wealth tax unsettled investors. Mitterrand made it his highest priority to keep the franc as strong as the West German deutsche mark. "You do not devalue the money of a country when that country has just placed confidence in you," Mitterrand intoned soon after his election. But as investors pulled out of France to keep their money away from the tax collectors, they sold their francs, unavoidably pushing the currency lower. The government tried to halt currency flight by making it harder to buy foreign currencies, but this failed to deter companies and wealthy individuals from exchanging their French francs for Swiss francs and spiriting the proceeds to banks in Basel and Geneva. So much money flowed out of the country that the government was forced to devalue the currency in October 1981 and again the following June, to Mitterrand's great embarrassment. Some of Mitterrand's advisers recommended a third devaluation in August 1982, but this time Mitterrand refused: a weak currency was not compatible with his vision of France as a European power on a par with West Germany. He began to ask about other ways to support the franc and strengthen the economy.

There were no acceptable socialist answers. The economic surge triggered by the government's generous deficit spending had run its course by the second half of 1982. Employment began to fall; inflation did not. Facing nothing but bad news, the Socialist Party toned down its rhetoric and began to describe entrepreneurs as job creators instead of exploiters of the working class. Ministers quietly reopened communication with leading business executives, who pointed out that higher taxes and social security contributions were squeezing profits and reducing investment. The government lowered business tax rates and approved a plan to make it easier for small companies to raise capital by selling shares to the public on a new stock exchange, the Second Marché—an improbable move by an administration that had just nationalized the cream of French industry.[12]

In March 1983, following the Socialists' dismal showing in municipal elections, Mitterrand decided that the time for socialist orthodoxy was over. As he looked for new ideas, he considered four potential prime ministers in the span of a week. All demanded more power over the troubled economy than Mitterrand was willing to surrender. With no acceptable alternative, he asked Mauroy to stay on, but gave Finance Minister Jacques Delors free rein over the economy.

Delors declared that it was time for "rigor." This was code for giving priority to keeping the franc stable against the deutsche mark. After one more devaluation of the franc on March 21—by which point those unfortunate enough to hold French francs had lost 30 percent of their international buying power in the span of eighteen months—the government announced a combination of spending cuts and tax increases to shrink the budget deficit dramatically. Upper-income taxpayers were assessed a surtax equal to 10 percent of their tax bill for the previous year; lower-income taxpayers faced higher social security taxes. French tourists could take only limited amounts of currency abroad, where their credit cards would no longer be valid. Taxes on alcohol, tobacco, gasoline, and electric bills went up. The government's hope was that its newfound commitment to fiscal responsibility would encourage investors to hold on to their francs rather than move their money abroad, steadying the exchange rate. Critics from both right and left felt otherwise. Conservatives, predictably, objected to higher taxes on the affluent. Leftists saw a capitalist plot. The new direction, stormed the number-two official of the president's own party, was "a classical policy of deflation, favoring the entrepreneurs, the patrons, the peasants," while leaving wage earners aside.[13]

Nothing more was said about nationalizing industry and taxing wealth. The new policy, the "turn to austerity," emphasized fighting inflation, holding the franc steady against the West German mark, privatizing state-owned companies, and reducing the government deficit. Talk of capitalist exploitation and worker self-management was out; the new vocabulary emphasized "dynamism" and "modernization." "You can start a business in one month," Mitterrand boasted in February 1984. "Three years ago, it took six months." Just three years after it had nationalized much of French industry, taken over the banks, and cracked down on investors' ability to move money in and out of the country, the government welcomed foreign investment in French companies, began to deregulate financial markets, and eliminated controls on the movement of money. The new Mitterrand, urged on by Delors and Attali, sounded much more like an American Democrat or a West German Social Democrat than a traditional French Socialist.[14]

This strange new version of socialism was slow to revive the French economy, and the political response was strongly negative. In March 1984, tens of thousands of workers took to the streets of steel towns from Dunkirk in the north to Marseilles in the south to protest the government's plans to eliminate thirty thousand steel industry jobs. They pointedly reminded Mitterrand of his words from 1981: "The nationalization of the steel industry will be the point of the spear in reconquering employment." The French left was ideologically committed to extensive government ownership of business; the cathartic debates in which British, Dutch, and German socialists rejected their parties' traditional programs had never occurred in France. Longtime Socialist voters were shocked, and the Socialists' coalition partners in the Communist Party, still endorsing a Soviet-style state-run economy, were outraged.

With their ideas completely discredited by the disastrous effects of Mitterrand's nationalization program, the Communists went into a tailspin, becoming only a marginal presence in French political life. Although Mitterrand remained president, the failure of his two very different policies to produce jobs and restore growth led voters to put a center-right coalition in control of the National Assembly in 1986. In an arrangement without precedent in France, Jacques Chirac, the center-right mayor of Paris, became prime minister under a Socialist president. It was Chirac's campaign for the presidency in 1981 that had split the anti-Socialist vote, depriving Giscard of a second term; Mitterrand's decision to select him as prime minister over other conservative leaders repaid the favor. Their power-sharing arrangement—cohabitation, the French called it—left Mitterrand in charge of foreign affairs and defense policy but gave Chirac considerable authority over domestic matters.

FRANCE WAS NOT THE ONLY COUNTRY IN WHICH A SOCIALIST party was trying to chart a new course. A very similar struggle was underway in Spain, led by a socialist leader a generation younger than Mitterrand: Felipe González.

Spain was on the margins of Europe, politically and economically as well as geographically. The country had been ruled for nearly four decades by Francisco Franco, an ultraconservative military officer who had launched a failed attempt to overthrow the elected government in 1936 but emerged victorious in 1939, after three years of brutal civil war. Externally, Franco had done his best to wall Spain off from the rest of Europe, both during and after World War II. Internally, his regime had been authoritarian, repressing unions, intellectuals, and anyone else who refused to accept what Franco understood as traditional Catholic values, including the belief that God had sent him to save Spain from chaos. Franco's conservatism had not made him a proponent of private enterprise and free markets. On the contrary, he had pushed the development of a sizable state-owned sector in the name of Spanish nationalism. His government held large stakes in hundreds of companies, from chemical plants and aluminum smelters to hotels and craft shops. Most were controlled through a holding company, the National Institute of Industry, which scattered large industrial enterprises around the country to provide jobs in Spain's poorest regions.

This development model had produced miserable results from the end of the civil war until the late 1950s. As the European Economic Community brought other parts of Western Europe together into a larger, more prosperous market, Spain remained cut off: Spaniards mainly drove Spanish-made SEAT cars, barely known in the rest of Europe, and the wider gauge on the Spanish railroad made it difficult to ship freight and passengers between Spain and France. Only desperation had forced Franco to turn away from autarky, opening the country to tourism and recycling tourists' marks, francs, and pounds into infrastructure and heavy industry. This strategy fueled a period of extremely rapid economic growth between 1959 and 1974. But by the time of Franco's death in 1975, the economy was foundering. The conservative government he left in place under the newly restored monarchy kept money-losing factories open and blocked state companies from shedding unneeded workers in order to preserve the social peace.

The conservatives' main opposition came from the Spanish Socialist Workers Party, whose leaders had returned home from French exile after Franco's death. In 1979, the Spanish socialists said farewell to their party's orthodox Marxist past. After a bitter internal rift between civil-war-era leaders who had spent decades in exile and younger politicians born during Franco's long rule, the party concluded that its attacks on capitalist exploitation and support for state-owned industry had no future in a democratic post-Franco Spain. González led the Socialist Workers into a U-turn much like the one their French brethren would make in 1983. They repositioned themselves as supporters of a welfare state within a market economy and as allies of the social democratic parties in Northern Europe, and they strongly advocated membership in the European Community.

Young Spaniards were wildly eager for their country finally to become part of the new Europe. The Socialist Workers' new moderate platform made them an acceptable choice for middle-class voters who otherwise might have rejected them. With the economy stalling, the party swept to power in October 1982. González took office as prime minister, pledging to stimulate private enterprise to create eight hundred thousand jobs. Unfortunately, events did not go as the Socialist Workers had planned. Barely four months after the election, complaints of fraud at Rumasa, a holding company that controlled eighteen banks and four hundred subsidiaries, resulted in the biggest nationalization in Spain's history. Rumasa claimed to account for 1.8 percent of Spain's total economic output, but its finances were in such disarray that its auditors repeatedly refused to sign off on its financial reports. Fearing that the firm would collapse, taking sixty thousand jobs with it, the González government brought it under state control. The move, applauded by Spain's labor unions, brought the government some political cover as it plotted the elimination of even more jobs by shrinking the ailing steel industry, modernizing the docks, and launching a massive privatization program.[15]

THE FIRST MITTERRAND PROGRAM, THE ORTHODOX SOCIALIST interlude of 1981 and 1982, marked a turning point in socialist thinking. The French experience, closely watched in Spain, seemed to prove that heavy-handed state control of the economy, including government ownership of industry and finance, could not work miracles. It demonstrated as well that no country, even a major economic power like France, could chart its own course without deference to the financial markets, where investors would pass judgment on exchange rates and tax policies every day. If the hallowed socialist ideas no longer offered a viable alternative to free-market thinking, socialists had to create a new version of socialism, in which economic revival would come from the private sector, not from state enterprise. Promoting competition, advancing deregulation, helping businesses make a profit, and reducing the government's role in economic life were all part of the new socialist formula for restoring economic vitality. François Mitterrand, the longtime Socialist stalwart, now joined with Helmut Kohl and Margaret Thatcher to transform the European Community into a much tighter economic union in which market forces would play a dominant role. Mitterrand did not share Thatcher's dislike of unions and her distaste for the welfare state. But when it came to economic policy, Thatcher and the Mitterrand of 1983 were not so far apart.[16]

Mitterrand supported such changes intellectually, but in 1983 and 1984 he was hard-pressed to push them through. The state apparatus was simply too massive to sell off quickly. Nearly one in four French workers were in the employ of the government, producing 28 percent of national income and 30 percent of exports. Privatization would not happen overnight.

Felipe González was in a more favorable position. In 1985, his government sold its 69.6 percent holding in an obscure company called Textil

Tarazona. A vaccine manufacturer, a food company, and a 45 percent interest in a chemical company soon followed. Unlike in France, in Spain sales to foreigners were not taboo. The government's controlling stake in an electronics company went to a Japanese manufacturer, and a Swedish company bought a state-owned ball-bearing factory. Spain's entry into the European Community at the start of 1986 required it to open its doors wider to foreign investment: 75 percent of automaker SEAT, the closest thing to a Spanish industrial icon, was bought by Germany's Volkswagen; Amper, an electronics maker, and Gesa, an electric and gas utility, were sold through share offerings on the revived Madrid Stock Exchange, which became one of Europe's hottest stock markets. Foreign investment in the long-isolated Spanish economy quadrupled in the span of two years. Aluminum manufacturers, honey producers, paper companies all were disposed of as Spain's socialists scaled back the state.[17]

France followed suit in 1986, by which point privatization had been underway in Spain for more than two years. Chirac was eager to make his mark by selling off state-owned companies, and Mitterrand did not stand in his way. At least at first, privatization was limited to selling shares in state-owned companies to the public. Firms could not be privatized easily by selling them to other French companies, because most French companies large enough to buy large industrial enterprises were themselves owned by the government. And sales to foreign buyers were out of the question because of political sensitivities. It was uncertain that share offerings would succeed. Thatcher had been able to privatize companies by offering their shares on the London Stock Exchange, one of the world's largest and most active stock markets, with a deep investor base. The Paris bourse, by contrast, was small, and Mitterrand's nationalizations had driven investors abroad.

Finding investors took imagination and marketing savvy. The rules for the first share offering, by Saint-Gobain, offered extra shares free to investors buying fifty or fewer shares in an attempt to stoke enthusiasm among the middle class. The second offering, by Banque Paribas, followed a television ad campaign showing the bank's ornate front doors swinging open to reveal a hushed corridor and an elaborate boardroom, as a male voice hinted that now almost anyone could enter these rarified precincts: "Ladies and gentlemen, you will have the chance to become shareholders in the near future." Both stock issues were successful enough that the Chirac government raced ahead with others. TF1, a television channel; Compagnie générale d'électricité, an electrical manufacturer; and Société Générale, one of France's biggest banks, were sold by the middle of 1987. Between 1986 and 1988, some twenty-two state companies passed into private hands, bringing $12 billion into the treasury.[18]

Chirac worked quickly, because he knew his time in office might be short. In 1988, he ran against Mitterrand for the presidency. Mitterrand won a crushing victory, outpolling Chirac in every region of the country. The president promptly called new legislative elections. Thanks in good part to an economic rebound—1988 would prove to be the best year since 1973—the Socialists regained control of the National Assembly. Privatization paused. The new Socialist line was "ni-ni," literally "neither nor"—no more firms would be sold off, but the ones that had been would not be returned to the public sector. Only in the 1990s, as the European Union pushed governments to increase competition within their economies while reducing their budget deficits, would France sell off any more of its patrimony.[19]

Mitterrand's U-turn and the start of privatization in both France and Spain gave a new legitimacy to the privatization of state assets. Margaret Thatcher's enthusiasm for selling state property had been viewed cautiously in other countries because she was generally seen as a radical, a more extreme conservative than would be acceptable anywhere else. But if the French Socialists and the Spanish Socialist Workers could accept privatization, perhaps it was not so extreme after all. West Germany started selling off minority shareholdings in companies like automaker Volkswagen and Veba, an electric utility. State-owned Austrian Airlines and KLM, the Dutch airline, both went on the block. The Finnish government listed the shares of Valmet, a manufacturer of papermaking machinery. And then came the biggest deal of all. In February 1987, the Japanese government began the first of three share offerings in the national telephone monopoly, Nippon Telegraph and Telephone Company, one of the largest corporations in the world. By the time the third offering was completed in October 1988, the government had raised almost $80 billion.

The results of the privatization wave are not simple to characterize. Many companies were wildly successful when freed to operate on a commercial basis rather than as arms of the state. In general, the economic literature suggests, companies operate better under private ownership, because managers and employees face a more clearly defined objective, earning a profit for shareholders, and they tend to be more careful with private shareholders' capital than with government money. Private companies, as a rule, are freer to close unneeded facilities and discharge unneeded workers than state-owned enterprises for which politicians call the tune. And in many cases, privatization has been a boon for taxpayers, reducing state spending on subsidies while bringing in additional tax revenues.

Yet there have been many exceptions to these generalizations. In some cases, state-owned monopolies were turned into private monopolies that could extract high prices from customers while bringing neither dynamic ideas nor improved service. Other privatized enterprises failed the test of the market, pleading for additional subsidies or ending up back under state control. Private companies that provide basic government services may have interests that directly conflict with social goals: a privately owned prison operator may have good reason to report that an inmate is unsuited for release on parole, if parole might mean an empty prison cell for which the company will not receive payment. If privatization has been structured poorly, investors may renege on their promises and leave the state holding the bag, as when some of the companies that took over services from state-owned British Rail unilaterally abandoned their franchises and handed the business back to the government. Contrary to the assertions of the ideologues who have promoted privatization, there is no universal rule that private ownership offers lower costs or greater efficiency. All too often, experience has shown otherwise.[20]

So far as France and Spain were concerned, privatization and economic liberalization offered no magical elixir to cure economic stagnation. In 1980, the year before Mitterrand took office, twenty-two million French men and women held paid employment. Through strongly socialist poli-cies and strongly antisocialist policies, all pursued by the same Socialist president, that number would remain unchanged for seven years. Al-though more women joined the workforce, the number of men at work fell by more than half a million over that period, reflecting the distress of France's manufacturers and their unwillingness to replace retiring workers with new hires. Unemployment, low until the middle of the 1970s, be-came a permanent feature of the French economic landscape.

In Spain, meanwhile, the expected burst of entrepreneurial energy was nowhere to be seen. The ranks of the unemployed grew every year between 1975 and 1987, by which time nearly one in five Spanish workers were jobless. Although the influx of foreign capital set off a boom after 1986, job creation did not follow. Spain continued to have by far the highest unemployment rate in the industrial world. Its experience, like that of France, showed that the economic malaise afflicting the wealthy econo-mies was beyond the reach of ideologically driven solutions. While the statist model had failed to revive growth, stimulate investment, and raise living standards in both France and Spain, more market-oriented policies had proven no more efficacious. Neither approach offered a realistic chance of bringing back the glorious years, which were beyond the ability of any government to restore.[21]

CHAPTER 13

Morning in America

October 6, 1979, was a chilly Saturday in Washington. The coming Monday was a government holiday, Columbus Day, and much of official Washington had scattered for the long weekend. Many of those who remained, along with the news media, were keeping an eye on Pope John Paul II, who was paying the first-ever papal visit to the White House to meet with President Carter; he would lead an open-air mass at the foot of the US Capitol the following day. With almost everyone's attention elsewhere, it was a good day for a secret meeting at the Federal Reserve.

At 10:10 that morning, the central bank's top policymakers convened around the twenty-seven-foot mahogany table in the Fed's ornate board-room. The mood was grim. Six years after the sudden end of the global boom, there was still no sign that the world economy was back to normal. Although economic growth rates had picked up in some countries, inflation was roaring out of control; in many advanced economies, including the United States, consumer prices were rising at double-digit rates. The sharp oil-price increases that followed the Iranian Revolution in January 1979—US refineries had paid $15 a barrel for imported petroleum at the end of 1978, $25 nine months later—were disrupting manufacturing and transportation. Americans' total spending on motor fuel increased by one-third during 1979, sharply curtailing the amounts available to purchase everything else, and in turn destroying jobs across the economy.

The participants in the Fed meeting all had read a memorandum from the two career officials responsible for carrying out monetary policy. The opening words were ominous: "The rate of inflation continues unabated and inflationary psychology seems more and more to be generating speculative pressures—for example, in markets for foreign exchange, commodities, and bullion." The staff's most recent economic forecast, distributed three weeks earlier, was negative: recession starting in the final quarter of the year; the unemployment rate rising from 6 percent to 8.1 percent by the end of 1980. And everyone at the table was painfully aware that their previous meeting, on September 18, had been a fiasco. Eight members had voted for higher interest rates to combat inflation. Four, concerned that higher rates would make economic conditions worse, had voted against. This sharp and very public division, suggesting that the Fed lacked the stomach for an all-out fight against inflation, had sent the financial markets into a tizzy.[1]

After a full day of discussion, the central bankers agreed on a plan. As Chairman Paul Volcker told reporters at an unusual press conference that night, the Federal Reserve would stop trying to stabilize prices by adjusting short-term interest rates. Instead, it would target the total amount of reserves held by the thousands of banks in the Federal Reserve system. "By emphasizing the supply of reserves and constraining the growth of the money supply through the reserve mechanism, we think we can get firmer control over the growth in money supply in a shorter period of time," Volcker intoned. Not one in a thousand Americans could explain what that meant. But the message got through to Wall Street, where traders dissect every word of every utterance by every Fed official. Adding up banks' nonborrowed reserves was one of many ways to measure the nation's money supply. By making reserves its main gauge, the Federal Reserve, like the Bank of England four months earlier, was embracing monetarism.[2]

Neither Volcker nor any other policymaker at the US central bank was a committed believer in mechanically regulating the money supply as the monetarists counseled. Their responsibility, as all of them saw it, was to receive a stream of data and anecdotal reports, evaluate them to assess the state of the economy, and then adjust monetary policy accordingly. The October 6 announcement, known forever after as the "Volcker shock," seemed to eliminate the Fed's discretion to make those month-to-month adjustments. Henceforth the central bank would be bound by an ironclad rule governing how fast the money supply should grow.

But that was not really Volcker's intention. By appearing to put monetary policy on autopilot, the Fed was trying to sweep away two political obstacles to its goal of lowering inflation. It hoped to blunt the ceaseless attacks of its most vociferous critics, the influential monetarist economists and their allies at places like *The Wall Street Journal,* who harped constantly on the Fed's erratic policies. If perchance their Fed-bashing turned to praise, perhaps the financial markets would believe that inflation would be coming down. If that occurred, interest rates would fall, and lower interest rates on mortgages and business loans might in fact help bring inflation down. The Fed also hoped its new stance would shield it from the political assaults that were sure to come. Quelling inflation, which was running at a 12 percent rate, previously experienced only when wartime price controls were removed, seemed likely to require much higher interest rates than the United States had ever known.

If the Fed openly made interest rates the target of its policy, announcing that it was raising short-term rates to 15 or 20 percent, then auto dealers, construction workers, and corporate executives would cry foul and enraged members of Congress might strip the central bank of its independence. If, however, high interest rates were merely the byproduct of its much-praised shift to the monetary policy rules the monetarists were demanding, the Fed would have some protection from its critics. As Volcker put it to his colleagues at that Saturday meeting, "It's an easier political sale."[3]

"WHO'S PAUL VOLCKER?" JIMMY CARTER HAD ASKED ONLY THREE months earlier, when Anthony Solomon, undersecretary of the Treasury, suggested him as a possible chairman of the Federal Reserve Board. The son of a New Jersey town manager—a professional hired by the local council to oversee the day-to-day operations of the parks department and the police—Volcker had been in and out of government since joining the Federal Reserve Bank of New York as a junior economist in 1952. He was no stranger to the politics of monetary policy, foreign or domestic: in between stints at a commercial bank, he had worked in the Treasury during the Kennedy and Johnson administrations and then, although he was a Democrat, was recruited to take a high-ranking Treasury post in the Nixon administration. As the chief US negotiator during the collapse of Bretton Woods, he owned a Rolodex with the private phone numbers of central bankers and finance ministers from around the world.[4]

In early 1974, William Simon, deputy secretary of the Treasury and also Nixon's energy czar, ranked just above Volcker in the Treasury hierarchy. That April, shortly before the embattled president nominated Simon to become secretary of the Treasury, Volcker abruptly resigned. He offered no public explanation, but his disagreement with Simon's libertarian ideas was no secret. Volcker's knowledge and contacts would have brought him a million-dollar paycheck in the private sector, but Fed chairman Arthur Burns had other ideas. Volcker's Treasury job had brought the two into frequent contact, and Burns wanted Volcker close at hand. His intervention won Volcker the presidency of the Federal Reserve Bank of New York, the central bank outpost that carried out the Fed's monetary policy on a day-to-day basis and was deeply involved in foreign-exchange matters. The post also gave Volcker a vote on the Fed committee that set monetary policy.[5]

Burns departed the Fed in 1978 after Carter declined to reappoint him as chairman in favor of G. William Miller, a corporate executive. Miller, extraordinarily ill suited to the job, agreed to Carter's suggestion that he become Treasury secretary in July 1979, leaving an opening at the Fed for Carter to fill. That was the point at which the president first heard Volcker's name. Two weeks later, after a single face-to-face meeting between Carter and Volcker in the Oval Office and a lightning-fast Senate confirmation, the chairman's office was filled with the smoke of Volcker's cheap A&C Grenadier cigars.

Not particularly at home in economic matters, Carter was unfamiliar with Volcker's views in detail. Like every political leader everywhere, the president favored bringing down inflation, but he shared the widespread hope that if the Fed proceeded gradually, it might be able to achieve price stability without putting people out of work—and without endangering the president's chances of re-election in 1980. The fact that the Fed had tried this approach for more than a decade, without success, did not alter the president's opinion.

Volcker had no such illusions. In a book published in 1978, he had warned of "limits on the ability of demand management to keep the economy at a steady full employment path," an oblique way of saying that bringing down inflation would cost jobs. In early 1979, when he was serving on the Fed's policy committee by virtue of his post at the New York Fed, he had voted repeatedly for stronger action against inflation, but his views were in the minority. In the controversial September 18 vote on monetary policy, a few weeks after he had become chairman, four high-ranking Fed officials opposed his proposal to raise interest rates, representing a frontal challenge to his plans for fighting inflation. The news leaked out into the *Washington Post* the following morning: "For the first time, Fed members are wondering out loud whether it really makes sense to throw men and women out of work, and businesses into bankruptcy, in order to 'rescue the dollar' by chasing ever-rising European interest rates."[6]

The beauty of Volcker's plan to focus on banks' reserves instead of interest rates was that Fed members would not have to cast such politically unpleasant votes. All the Fed had done on October 6 was to adopt a rule intended to slow the growth of bank reserves. Thereafter, it needed merely to adhere to that rule. There would be no more contentious meetings at which central bankers debated how high interest rates should be in order to bring down inflation while supporting economic growth, for interest rates would no longer be the Fed's target.

Of course, the new Fed policy involved more than a little sleight of hand. As everyone concerned knew perfectly well, reducing the growth of banks' reserves would require pushing up interest rates on banks' overnight loans to one another, known as "fed funds" loans. The fed funds interest rate, 11.9 percent at the time of the October 6 meeting, hit 15.6 percent three weeks later and would reach 17 percent the following March. As borrowing money became more costly, banks cut back on their lending to consumers and businesses. Longer-term interest rates also rose, but not as much, a sign that the financial market's expectations of a recession, evident for more than a year, were growing stronger.

The markets were right. As high US interest rates drove up interest rates in other countries, economic growth slowed almost everywhere. In the Netherlands, unemployment would rise nine percentage points over the next four years; in Germany, it would rise more than five points. South Korea would fall into recession, and Brazil's long run of strong economic growth would crash to a stop. But it was in the United States that the Volcker shock caused the first political casualties. Construction of new homes fell by half. Auto sales, running at an annual rate of fourteen million units in October 1979, dropped below ten million. The unemployment rate jumped nearly two percentage points. Although the recession would be brief, it was enough to elect Ronald Reagan president.[7]

RONALD REAGAN WAS AN ICON OF THE RIGHT. A FORMER ACTOR and corporate pitchman, he had served two terms as governor of the fast-growing state of California. He said the right conservative things, praising free enterprise and small government, and even the blunt promise to "send the welfare bums back to work," which had carried him to the governorship in 1966, came with a smile and a friendly wave. Unlike the Moral Majority, which represented a stream of evangelical Christian thinking popular with the Republican Party's adherents in Sun Belt suburbs and small towns, he was not censorious. Unlike the bankers of the party's Wall Street wing, who treated a balanced federal government budget as a necessary dose of castor oil, he was not rigid. Although other conservatives breathed fire, Reagan personified a more compassionate conservatism motivated by a carefully articulated concern for the common man.

It was more than just the state of the economy that propelled him into the White House. The fate of Americans held hostage in Iran since

November 1979, after a conservative Islamic movement overthrew the Shah, was featured nightly on the television news, and many voters blamed Carter for the hostages' prolonged imprisonment. But Reagan took office at a time of gloom about the country's future, a sense that living standards were falling as the country was tossed about by economic storms it was powerless to control. Righting the economy was at the very top of his agenda. "The plan from the outset was to put in place the Reagan economic program as the major priority and foundation for every major initiative, domestic and foreign," his national security adviser, Richard Allen, wrote later.[8]

Beyond platitudes about small government and a boundless faith in free enterprise, Reagan had no particular economic philosophy of his own. His economic advisers were an eclectic bunch, ranging from rigid monetarists to mainstream economists who favored higher government spending to overcome the downturn. The most influential group, though, preached a new theology called supply-side economics. With a combination of religious fervor and libertarian fanaticism, supply-siders believed that the economic slump afflicting the United States since 1973 was the result of the government's efforts to make people feel prosperous by pumping up their incomes so they could buy more goods and services. Instead of trying to increase consumer demand, the supply-siders asserted, economic policy should encourage the inventors, entrepreneurs, and investors whose efforts created more goods and services for consumers to buy—in other words, those who provide the supply side of the economy. Ultimately, they asserted, supply was the only true source of demand. Only a larger supply side could increase economic output and create jobs.

Supply-side thinking had major implications for economic policy. One was that the government should spend less money, especially on social-welfare programs. "[R]eal poverty is less a state of income than a state of mind, and . . . the government dole blights most of the people who come to depend on it," George Gilder, one of the most gifted of the supply-side proselytizers, asserted in a 1981 best seller, *Wealth and Poverty*. Payments to the unemployed "deter productive work" and should be curtailed. "In fact," Gilder asserted, "nearly all the programs that are advocated by economists to promote equality and combat poverty—and are often rationalized in terms of stimulating consumption—in actuality reduce demand by undermining the production from which all real demand derives." Supply-siders thus stood front and center in the war on the welfare state.[9]

Where they differed with many other critics of Big Government was on tax policy. Traditional conservatism in the United States emphasized the importance of a balanced federal budget. Tax reductions, while generally desirable, should be measured, and should go hand in hand with reductions in public-sector spending; the worst outcome, in the traditional view, was a government swimming in red ink. For the supply-siders, in contrast, budget deficits were a side issue. Their cure for slow economic growth and stagnant living standards was cutting taxes—and not just any taxes. Taxes on investment, they argued, punished the risk-taking and entrepreneurship that created supply, so taxes on capital gains from investment in businesses and corporate shares should be cut to zero. High tax rates on the last bit of income earned by families and businesses discouraged extra work effort and drove economic activity underground. Eliminating capital gains taxes and lowering marginal tax rates would create new incentives to work and invest. The economy would flower, perhaps so effusively that tax receipts would rise.[10]

The highest marginal tax rates, of course, were paid by those with the highest incomes. This was the essence of progressive taxation, the ladder of tax rates that existed in every high-income country on the premise that those with meager incomes should pay little or nothing in income taxes, and the more prosperous should pay rates that rose as their incomes rose. Since the earliest days of income taxation, this had been accepted as the fairest way to levy taxes. The supply-siders begged to differ. Progressive taxation, they claimed, was designed to redistribute income from some people to others rather than to make the economy grow. "All this shifting of wealth is a zero sum game," Gilder asserted. Levying the highest taxes on the most dynamic people in a society, those whose creativity and entrepreneurial drive generated wealth, would kill the golden goose.

The supply-siders claimed that this was precisely what had occurred in the 1970s, as wealthy people put their money into tax shelters and gold rather than risking it in productive investments that, if successful, would allegedly have been taxed at painfully high rates. In the supply-side analysis, that flight from risk-taking by the rich, prompted by the desire to avoid punitive taxes, had caused years of slow economic growth, hurting the employment prospects and living standards of everyone else. The lesson from this experience, Gilder concluded, was that "to help the poor and middle classes, one must cut the tax rates of the rich."[11]

Supply-side economics was the creation of polemicists, not professors. Although some well-known academic names, such as Robert Mundell of Columbia University and Norman B. Ture, former head of tax research at the National Bureau of Economic Research, claimed that tax cuts would spark investment and entrepreneurship, the scholarly literature examining supply-side ideas was sparse. The fact that tax rates on owners of young, innovative companies already were much lower than those on people earning other types of income received little attention. The claims that high marginal tax rates were to blame for the slowdown of the 1970s and that lowering rates would restore the economy to its previous glory were untested. So was the assertion that lower tax rates would draw money out of tax shelters and into the sunlight, where it could be taxed.[12]

Nor was there empirical support for the so-called Laffer Curve, supposedly first drawn on a napkin at a Washington restaurant by economist Arthur Laffer. The Laffer Curve was intended as a graphic illustration of how lower tax rates could stimulate so much economic activity that government revenue would rise. As an abstract proposition, Laffer's theory was not controversial; everyone agreed that it was possible for tax rates to get so high that people would no longer bother to earn more income, at which point tax receipts would began to fall. Laffer's sketch, however, did not specify what that point was, and no one else in the supply-side camp was willing to wager a guess. The only serious study of the subject concluded that US income-tax rates would have to be much higher than they were before rate reductions would bring the government more money.

"Available evidence does not support the view that our government is currently behaving irrationally," wrote Don Fullerton, later to become a tax official in Reagan's Treasury.[13]

Evidence or not, the promise that lower taxes would reinvigorate the economy was irresistible. On February 18, 1981, less than one month after taking office, Reagan unveiled his program for economic recovery. "The most important cause of our economic problems has been the government itself," the report asserted. It laid out a package of deep reductions in personal and business taxes, along with budget cuts that would reduce federal spending, equal to 23 percent of economic output in 1981, to just 19 percent by 1986. These new policies would not merely revive a sluggish economy, the administration asserted; they would transform it. "The American economy will produce 13 million new jobs by 1986, nearly 3 million more than if the status quo in government policy were to prevail," the Reagan program promised. "The economy itself should break out of its anemic growth patterns to a much more robust growth trend of 4 to 5 percent a year." Under his plan, the president told the nation in a televised speech, "Starting next year, the deficits will get smaller, until in just a few years the budget can be balanced."[14]

Members of Congress knew better than to stand in front of a speeding train. The Economic Recovery Tax Act, enacted in August 1981, gave Reagan much of what he asked for. The fourteen personal income-tax rates were thinned to just five, so an annual pay raise that barely kept up with inflation was less likely to push a family into a higher tax bracket. The top rate facing a family with an average income fell to 24 percent of its last dollar of income from 28 percent, providing a sizable jump in take-home pay. The top rate on the highest incomes dropped from 70 percent to 50 percent. A unique property made these tax cuts particularly appealing: while the politicians could accurately crow that low-income families enjoyed the largest cuts in percentage terms, wealthy households easily received the largest tax reductions in dollar terms, in line with supply-side doctrine. A working-class family taking in $10,000 a year would save $74 in 1982, while the family of an executive earning $100,000 would save $1,897. Businesses won big tax breaks, too, with the promise that these would lead to a boom in investment, especially in new machinery and equipment.[15]

The first tax cuts took effect immediately. The planned spending cuts did not occur. Reagan's conflicting desires were the main reason: even though the president wanted to shrink government relative to the size of the economy, he sought large increases in military spending to build more than 100 new ships for the Navy, add hundreds of bombers and fighter planes, and even reactivate World War II–era battleships that had been out of service since the 1950s. His first budget proposal, offered in March 1981, two months after he took office, projected an 8 percent annual rise in defense spending through 1984, after adjusting for inflation, while all other government spending would decline about 4 percent per year. But the president's political counselors also decreed that "basic benefits" under several politically sensitive programs, including monthly Social Security checks and medical care for retirees, would not be touched. Between the sacred social programs, military spending, and interest on the national debt, a huge proportion of federal spending was exempt from budget reductions.[16]

What that meant was that holding down federal spending would require draconian cuts in almost everything else. In Room 248 of the Executive Office Building, known among Reagan advisers as the Cutting Room, the president's budget working group identified targets. Funding for a collection of forty health and social service programs was to fall by a quarter in 1982. The government was to stop providing free pneumonia vaccines to pensioners, shortening an estimated five thousand lives over four years. Many older people who had earned very low wages during their working years, and therefore received the smallest monthly Social Security checks, were to see their payments cut, a plan crafted to avoid violating the president's promise to leave "basic benefits" intact. Housing benefits for the poor, grants to poor families with children, and subsidies for school lunches all were on the chopping block. In aggregate, Reagan proposed to slash federal spending for all purposes other than defense from 17.3 percent of the nation's total income in 1981 to less than 13 percent in 1984, sharply reducing almost all the social benefits that had grown up in the years since World War II.[17]

Yet even those steep cuts would not bring the federal budget into balance. The budget for 1982 would still be deeply in deficit. The numbers for fiscal year 1984 added up only thanks to an entry of $44 billion, marked with an asterisk. The asterisk pointed readers to a note that said simply, "Future savings to be identified."[18]

Winning congressional approval of such cuts would have been difficult under any circumstances. The anti-inflation policy followed by Volcker's Fed made it impossible. The policy was having some success in restraining inflation; from a peak of almost 15 percent in the spring of 1980, consumer price inflation had fallen below 10 percent by May 1981. But the Fed thought a reviving economy would drive inflation back up, and it kept its foot firmly on the brake. The result was that interest rates moved sharply higher, even as the inflation rate was falling. The rate banks paid one another for overnight loans reached 19.9 percent in the summer of 1981, more than ten percentage points above the inflation rate—an extraordinary premium for the privilege of using money for just a few hours. With borrowing prohibitively expensive, bank lending and business investment skidded to a stop. The real estate market was all but dead; houses sold only if the seller was willing to extend a mortgage loan to the buyer. Layoffs rippled through the economy. As tax receipts fell far short of expectations, Reagan, the president who thought the US Constitution should mandate a balanced federal budget, found himself presiding over the largest peacetime budget deficit in US history.

Facing an impending flood of red ink, Congress began debating how to undo the tax cuts almost as soon as it enacted them. In 1982, a new tax law repealed some of the preferences for business investment that had been handed out in 1981. The new law made it harder for wealthy investors to avoid taxes on interest and dividend payments, and smokers faced higher taxes on cigarettes. Various tax cuts set to take effect in future years were canceled. By some measures, the 1982 tax act was the largest tax increase ever to pass the Congress. It raised the amount of revenue flowing to the federal government each year by 1 percent of the nation's income, a considerable amount of money. Even so, the top tax rates remained much lower than they had been when Reagan took office.

Reagan claimed to have extracted a price for agreeing to reverse some of the tax cuts he had won a year earlier: there were supposed to be three dollars of spending cuts for every dollar of tax increases. Yet the spending cuts that had failed to materialize in 1981 were every bit as elusive in 1982. Given the administration's commitment to enlarge and re-equip the armed forces, spending cuts of the promised magnitude would have required massive reductions in almost every other government spending program—cuts that none of Reagan's cabinet officers stood ready to propose and that no congressional committee would have endorsed. "Cutting the budget is a politically wrenching process, and the Reagan White House has never really been willing to do that," Reagan's budget director, David Stockman, acknowledged later.[19]

On balance, the 1981 and 1982 tax laws left the government collecting a far smaller share of national income than before Reagan took office, but the government's expenditures were no smaller. Voters saw little to like in Reagan's accomplishments. "National income, national income per person employed, and total hours at work were actually smaller in 1982 than in 1979," the economist Edward Denison recorded. When it came time to elect a new House of Representatives in November 1982, many of the Republicans swept into office with Reagan in 1980 were swept back out again.[20]

AUGUST 1982 BEGAN NO MORE CHEERFULLY THAN ANY OTHER recent month. The Dow Jones Industrial Average, the best-known gauge of the New York Stock Exchange, lost ground in eight consecutive sessions, dropping a total of 5.6 percent. "Stock prices continued to retreat yesterday as investors registered deep concern over the direction of interest rates," the *New York Times* reported on August 6. "We're in a bear market," a knowing stock analyst affirmed in the following day's paper. On August 13, the *Times* quoted an expert who predicted a further 5 percent drop before stocks hit bottom. At that point, an investor who had bought shares on October 5, 1973, the last trading day before the outbreak of the Yom Kippur War, would have lost one-fifth of his money over less than nine years—before figuring in the diminished buying power of a dollar. Adjusting for inflation, $1,000 invested across the thirty Dow Jones stocks back when the first oil crisis began was worth a scant $370 in 1982. Investors had cast an overwhelming vote of no confidence in the US economy.

Then, on August 13, share prices ticked up. The stock market seemed to have found a bottom. Two trading days later, the famed Wall Street economist Henry Kaufman told clients that the bond market had found a bottom as well, implying that prices of US government bonds would rise as interest rates came down. Kaufman's note drove the stock market wild, leading to the largest one-day gain ever recorded. The conventional wisdom that inflation was unbeatable was abruptly discarded; the new conventional wisdom was that Volcker's Fed was winning the battle. From beneath mattresses, out of gold vaults and foreign bank accounts, money flooded into the US financial markets. The broad index of five hundred US stocks rose 16 percent in three weeks. In October, the Fed reversed the Volcker shock of 1979, abandoning its money supply target and announcing that it would target lower interest rates instead. This move pushed up stocks once more. Between August 13 and the end of the year, share prices gained 35 percent.[21]

The run-up in US stocks—the long-awaited "bull market"—would continue for an unprecedented seventeen years; the bull market in bonds stretched for more than thirty. In America, it was a great time to be an investor.

It was a particularly good time to be a foreign investor in the United States. From 1983 through 1986, the US government posted annual deficits averaging 5 percent of national income, by far the largest, relative to the size of the economy, since the immediate aftermath of World War II. The government's huge borrowing needs kept interest rates high, by historical standards, even as inflation tumbled. And those high interest rates drew in unprecedented sums of money from abroad.

Statistically, the flow of money into and out of a country shows up in a measure called the current account. The United States had frequently run current account deficits in the past, meaning that more money was leaving the country than coming in, but these episodes were usually small and brief. In most years, the current account was in surplus, because the United States sold more goods abroad than it imported and because it lent and invested more money in other countries than foreigners placed in America. The tiny surplus in 1981, the year Reagan took office, was typical. But as foreigners chased high US interest rates by purchasing Treasury bonds, the current account deficit blew out from a negligible $3 billion in 1982 to $35 billion in 1983. By 1987 it reached $154 billion.

Foreign money was keeping the US economy afloat, but the side effects were devastating. To invest in the United States, foreigners bought US dollars in the currency market. Their demand drove the dollar's value into the stratosphere: by 1985, one dollar was worth 77 percent more against a basket of foreign currencies than it was when Reagan took office. Investors prospered two ways, enjoying the boom in the US stock and bond markets even as the rising dollar increased the value of their holdings in terms of other currencies.[22]

US manufacturers, though, faced a far more difficult situation. Traditionally, imported manufactured goods had played a relatively minor role in the US economy; in 1980, their total value equaled only 5 percent of the economy's total output, versus more than 15 percent in Europe. Thanks to the muscular dollar, which made imports much cheaper, the value of goods imported into the United States rose by 40 percent between 1981 and 1986, while the value of US exports declined. Factory towns were devastated as jobs disappeared and incomes fell; in the tire-making center of Akron, Ohio, more than one-third of rubber-industry jobs vanished in the decade after 1980, and the area's total economic output stagnated. In city after city, schools, parks, and public libraries sank into disrepair as abandoned factories ceased paying property taxes. Even workers lucky enough to keep their jobs were hit hard because their most important asset, a home on which they had made years of payments, could be rendered all but worthless when a big local employer closed up shop. When Caterpillar, the iconic maker of backhoes and bulldozers, faced a sudden onslaught from Japan's Komatsu in the early 1980s, the median price of houses near its headquarters in Peoria, Illinois, fell by 20 percent, even before adjusting for inflation.[23]

IN 1984, RONALD REAGAN'S CAMPAIGN PRODUCED A REMARKABLE television commercial for his re-election bid. It contained no harsh words about his opponent, Walter Mondale, and no promises that would make cynical voters scoff. Instead, over peaceful scenes of a fishing boat headed out to sea and a man in a business suit walking to a car, a gentle male voice recited, "It's morning again in America. Today more men and women will go to work than ever before in our country's history." As the screen showed a family moving into a new home and a young couple reciting wedding vows, the voice reminded viewers that interest rates and inflation had fallen by half, making the future bright. The commercial ended with a question that alluded to Mondale's tenure as vice president under Jimmy Carter: "Why would we ever want to return to where we were less than four short years ago?"

"Morning in America" did more than help Reagan gain an overwhelming election victory. It also helped build credence for the claim, repeated for years to come, that Reagan's tax and spending cuts had restored the economy to greatness. Yet this assertion was far-fetched. The two great economic achievements highlighted in the commercial, lower interest rates and lower inflation, were the work not of the administration but of Volcker's Fed. Reagan's ardor for cutting taxes and his willingness to tolerate huge budget deficits arguably kept interest rates and inflation higher than they would have been if the budget had been closer to balance. Indeed, it can fairly be said that the greatest economic accomplishment of Reagan's first term was his unstinting support of Volcker, without which the Fed might have found it politically impossible to wring inflation out of the US economy.[24]

Inflation and interest rates aside, the balance on Reagan's economic policies was not particularly impressive. Through the first year of the great bull market that erupted in August 1982, one in ten US workers was jobless. Even though economic growth kicked into high gear in 1983 as falling interest rates revived homebuilding and auto sales, employment gains remained sluggish; instead of the thirteen million new jobs the administration had promised between 1981 and 1986, the economy added fewer than ten million. It would take five years from the onset of the stock and bond boom, until August 1987, before the unemployment rate descended to 6 percent—a level that had indicated an economy in severe distress prior to 1973. In Richard Nixon's day, 5 percent unemployment had been so alarming that it had led Arthur Burns to back away from battling inflation. In Reagan's era, 6 percent unemployment was applauded as a major achievement.[25]

Even for many of the eighteen million Americans who joined the ranks of the employed by the end of Reagan's presidency, in 1989, the economy did not feel buoyant. The reductions in income-tax rates raised the median weekly take-home pay for full-time workers by roughly 5 percent during Reagan's presidency. But wage gains played out very differently for women than for men. The buying power of a woman earning the median wage rose 10 percent during the Reagan years, not counting the effect of lower income taxes. The buying power of a male worker earning the median wage, in stark contrast, did not rise at all. The lowest earners fared worst: the Reagan tax cuts notwithstanding, the average incomes of households in the bottom one-fifth of the income distribution fell about 4 percent between 1980 and 1989.[26]

Many families lost a large portion of their wealth during the 1980s. Homes accounted for around one-third of Americans' personal assets, and in twenty-seven of the fifty states the value of the average home, adjusted for inflation, was lower in 1990 than it had been in 1980. To buy the things they needed or wanted, consumers at all income levels had to spend a much larger share of their incomes to make payments on nonmortgage debt, such as credit cards and auto loans, leaving many households under financial stress long after the 1981–82 recession ended. Federal Reserve economists observed in 1992 that the Reagan years had brought much to some but little to most: "The small rise in the median values of income and net worth and the simultaneous substantial rise in the mean values indicate that the distributions of income and net worth became more concentrated between 1983 and 1989."[27]

Why did the Reagan revival work out so poorly for people of modest incomes? One obvious reason is that the surge in stock and bond prices after August 1982 boosted the incomes and the wealth of families that owned stocks and bonds. Not surprisingly, these were likely to be much older than the average family and to have far higher incomes. Among families headed by someone under age fifty-five, only one in fifty owned bonds in 1983 and one in five owned stocks—and those shareholdings, in most cases, were just a few thousand dollars. Wall Street's bounty trickled down to less affluent households only to the extent that financial market investors spent their windfalls in ways that created added income for auto workers, waiters, and home remodelers. The supply-siders' promise that better times for those at the top of the economic pyramid would bring greater prosperity to those below never came to pass.

Reagan's economists had insisted that allowing investors to keep more of what they earned would bring forth new investment that would modernize the economy and stimulate productivity. But supply-side economics proved to be a bust. "The fundamentals that I look at are not a miracle," Reagan budget director David Stockman said in 1986. "Our savings rate is the lowest rate in modern times. Last year our productivity growth was flat, and our whole theory was, we were going to cause an explosion of productivity growth and rising real income." On average, output per hour worked in nonfarm businesses, a key measure of productivity, grew more slowly during the Reagan years than at any time before 1977, when marginal tax rates had been far higher. Historically, productivity growth had led to higher wages and higher living standards. In the 1980s, it no longer did so.[28]

One cause of this disappointment was what sociologist Greta Krippner refers to as "financialization." As she argues, a combination of financial deregulation and high interest rates made it sensible for businesses to focus on making money from money in the rapidly expanding credit markets. This shift "took the form of nonfinancial firms withdrawing capital from long-term investments in plant and equipment and diverting resources into financial investments." This trend was noted as early as 1983, when the Reagan-appointed Commission on Industrial Competitiveness observed that the return on investment in financial assets was higher than the return on manufacturing assets, and it grew more pronounced over the course of the decade.[29]

The results can be seen in the pattern of business investment. The promised supply-side investment boom channeled capital into office buildings and shopping centers, not into making goods and providing services. In consequence, investment in business equipment was actually lower between 1981 and 1989 than it had been in the 1970s. This problem was particularly severe in the manufacturing sector. By the end of Reagan's presidency, the average age of equipment in US factories was a full year higher than when he took office—an indication that investment in manufacturing was far from robust. Many struggling manufacturers deferred installing new equipment that would have allowed them to take advantage of the latest technical innovations, forsaking the productivity gains new equipment would have delivered and making it even harder to give their workers a pay raise.[30]

The Reagan Revolution, as the president's backers called it, pointed the world's largest economy in a new direction. Inflation would no longer be tolerated. Market forces would hold greater sway, as critics of Big Government searched for new areas to deregulate. The import boom set off by the strong dollar would not be reversed; international trade and investment would continue to grow relative to the size of the economy, and the United States, with a large trade deficit year after year, would become the market of last resort for the rest of the world. Pressure to cut taxes would be ceaseless. Concern about large government budget deficits would remain in the realm of rhetoric, unmatched either by tax increases or significant spending cuts. The US government would continue to spend heavily on social welfare—but meanwhile, slowly but surely, other programs would be trimmed to make room for the ever-rising costs of pensions and medical care for the elderly, leaving less support for families struggling to care for and educate their children.

Reagan infused the United States with a new optimism about the future, a welcome change after years of despair. But what the Reagan Revolution could not do was restore the broad improvement in living standards that Americans expected. For more than half of all households, earnings were no higher in 1989 than they had been in 1981, adjusted for inflation. Meanwhile, the benefits workers received from their employers deteriorated.

More than 40 percent of private-sector employees had the right to a defined pension benefit in 1980; a decade later, fewer than 30 percent were in a pension plan. The proportion of Americans under sixty-five who had health insurance fell by five percentage points during the same period. Although the nation's total income grew nicely after 1982, almost all the gains went to those who owned businesses or held portfolios of stocks and bonds. As in several other wealthy countries, a growing number of average people were left to tread water, fearful that the state on which they had come to rely would no longer keep them from drowning.[31]

CHAPTER 14

The Lost Decade

If the 1970s were difficult years in the wealthy economies, sentiment was far more upbeat across the broad swath of poorer countries that had come to be known as the "Third World." Thanks to the events of 1973, "development" arrived in the "underdeveloped" countries far faster than Raúl Prebisch, the famed Argentine economist, had ever imagined it could. By the tens of millions, semi-literate farm families were able to flee hopeless rural poverty for the cities, where grueling days vending candy on street corners or hauling bricks on their backs allowed them to begin turning their shacks into proper houses, maybe even with electric light. The mansions along Avenida Paulista in São Paulo gave way to skyscrapers befitting one of the world's great centers of industry, and capitals from Jakarta to Cairo turned majestic boulevards into high-speed freeways to accommodate the cars of a rapidly expanding middle class. But the Third World could not escape the forces that were holding back the richer countries. The final legacy of a world economy out of gas would be the "lost decade" of the 1980s, which left many millions of people in the developing countries worse off than they had been before the boom.[1]

In terms of the world economy, the Third World had been an afterthought during the Golden Age. It accounted for three-quarters of the world's population in 1973, as crisis enveloped Western Europe, the United States, Canada, and Japan, but only a third of the world's output of goods and services. China, with an income per person one-twentieth that of the United States, had yet to launch the economic reforms that would turbocharge its growth in later decades. And Southeast Asia, far from being a critical link in global supply chains, seemed hopelessly crippled by war and internal violence. The Third World was connected to the international economy mainly as a source of raw materials. It supplied a scant 7 percent of the world's exports of manufactured goods.

The Third World's explosive growth in the 1970s was fueled by the petrodollars that were causing such worry for central bankers like Gordon Richardson and Arthur Burns. As the oil-exporting countries pumped their rapidly rising earnings into the banking system, the banks in the world's great money centers searched for ways to put these low-cost deposits to profitable use. In their home countries, there was little need: the economic slump in the wealthy economies meant weak demand for auto loans and home mortgages, and corporate customers were increasingly turning down the banks' money and choosing to raise funds directly from investors who bought their commercial paper, a sort of bond that was meant to be repaid within a few weeks. Loan demand from the Third World, on the other hand, was ravenous.

The bankers were only too glad to oblige. They were urged on by their governments, which hoped that the money would improve living standards and build a bulwark against the spread of communist ideas in the developing world. In 1972, outstanding loans from banks and bond investors to all developing countries combined were a mere $17 billion. The total reached $128 billion in 1978, $209 billion in 1981. Official lenders, such as the World Bank and the foreign aid agencies of wealthy countries, stepped up their lending as well. By the end of 1981, the foreign obligations of the developing economies reached $462 billion, five times the level of 1972. Although some of these loans were given to private borrowers, nearly four-fifths were the responsibility of the developing countries' governments, which sought the foreign financing to keep their economies humming through what they imagined would be a temporary slowdown in the world's economic growth.[2]

The commercial banks' borrowers were not the poorest of the poor. Countries like India and Sierra Leone, at the very bottom of the income league table, were deemed unacceptable credit risks even by banks that were hungry to lend, so they were forced to depend upon lenders financed by rich-country governments, such as the African Development Bank and Japan's Overseas Economic Cooperation Fund. The commercial banks' loans went to middle-income countries like Mexico and Brazil, where powerful planning ministries—following Prebisch's teachings about the need for the government to take the lead in encouraging industrialization that would raise productivity—were presumed to have the expertise to determine the best uses of the money. Some loans were explicitly tied to projects intended to generate revenue that could be used for repayment: a new mill for a state-owned textile company, planes for the state airline, roads and utility lines to serve a new industrial park. But there were also many unrestricted loans, to be spent on weaponry, government buildings, or whatever else the borrowing country's leaders desired.

In the mid-1970s, as European, North American, and Japanese banks battled for business around the world, they offered generous terms on loans. Interest rates were low. Grace periods several years long allowed the borrowers to spend the loan proceeds now and worry about repaying them later, after the investments they supported had brought faster economic growth and increased the tax base. The banks collected a sizable fee on the front end for originating each loan, boosting their profits right away, plus additional fees each time the loan was extended or rolled over into a new loan. It all seemed perfectly safe: the countries taking the money had relatively little foreign debt, their economies were growing rapidly, and the fact that their governments were standing behind the obligations seemed to limit the risk of default. As Citicorp chairman Walter Wriston explained to anyone who expressed concern about his institution's aggressive lending in Latin America and Southeast Asia, "Countries don't go out of business."

Bank regulators watched the situation warily. "Lending institutions may well be tempted to extend credit more generously than is prudent," Federal Reserve chair Arthur Burns warned in April 1977. "Commercial and investment bankers need to monitor their foreign lending with great care, and bank examiners need to be alert to excessive concentrations of loans in individual countries." The banks responded by hiring economists and political scientists to staff new risk-management departments, under the assumption that a better understanding of Argentine politics or the Korean central bank might reduce their risks. What they did not do is cut back on lending.

Indeed, they could hardly afford to. The profits of the largest US banks rose by half between 1977 and 1979, driven by business with the developing countries that accounted for more than one-sixth of their outstanding loans. Japanese banks, their domestic profits sinking, saw foreign lending as a solution. So did the big British banks, which earned one-third of their profits abroad by 1978. Institutions with no prior international lending experience jostled for a piece of the action: the big banks in New York, Tokyo, and London would arrange a loan and then allow banks in Atlanta and Utrecht and Milan to take responsibility for small pieces of it. The annual joint meeting of the World Bank and the International Monetary Fund—held each autumn, usually in Washington—was transformed from a gathering of technocrats into an obscene festival of excess as bankers competed to offer finance ministers yet more loans. Free-flowing alcohol, tables laden with crab claws and lamb chops, and strolling musicians all set the mood for dealmaking.[3]

In some places, the borrowed money was well spent; in other places, less so. Government ministers' decisions about which uses of borrowed money could best promote economic development were rarely as disinterested as Prebisch's theories suggested. Few of the borrowing countries were functioning democracies. Most were ruled by strongmen who treated their countries' treasuries as piggy banks, and who brooked no criticism, let alone investigation, from legislators or the press. Impressive economic statistics—the output of the developing countries grew at a strong annual rate of 4.6 percent between 1973 and 1980—obscured the fact that many foreign-currency loans went for prestige projects that did little or nothing to make workers more productive or improve the well-being of peasant farmers. Others supported well-intentioned goals that the recipient governments lacked the ability to accomplish, creating schools without regular teachers and clinics lacking medical supplies.

During the second half of the 1970s, the inflow of foreign money enabled many developing countries to avoid austerity. Even money that went into contracts for the well-connected trickled down, generating employment for drivers, restaurant waiters, and construction workers. New loans from international organizations like the World Bank helped bring down infant mortality, raise literacy rates, and make primary-school education almost universal. A person born in the Third World in 1979 could expect to reach the age of fifty-eight, a gain of ten years since 1960. Urban slum dwellers acquired radios, the more affluent bought televisions, and the streets of African capitals were jammed with the cars of the *waBenzi,* a term coined in Kenya to describe the well-connected elites who liked to show off their imported German sedans.

In the early 1980s, the party came to an abrupt and brutal end. As inflation rose through the late 1970s, the banks in London and New York stopped handing out fixed-rate loans and turned to variable-rate loans, whose interest rates changed according to financial market conditions. After October 1979, as the Fed's new monetary rule pushed up interest rates—the yield on one-year bonds issued by the US Treasury rocketed from 8 percent in 1978 to 17 percent by 1981—borrowers' interest payments rose as well. Locals in the know read the warning signs better than the foreign bankers did, converting whatever cash they could raise into foreign currency and sending it to Miami or Geneva for safekeeping. Much of this fleeing money, which was intended for investment in poorer countries, ended up back in the same rich-country banks that had extended the credit, leaving the borrowing government to pay interest and principal on loans that brought the country no economic benefit.[4]

Once the dollar began to rise against other currencies in 1981, the pressure became even more intense, as the borrower countries needed to export more coffee, wheat, or palm oil just to bring in the same amount of dollars as before. Peru, one of the most extreme cases, spent one-ninth of the dollars it earned from exports on debt payments in 1970. By 1981, the ratio approached one-half, leaving little of the country's foreign-currency earnings to import the machinery, generating equipment, and raw materials that might help the economy grow. At that point, as Volcker wrote later, "The debt crisis was on an express train of its own."[5]

In 1981, eight of the poorest countries, from the Central African Republic to Pakistan, needed to postpone repayment of their debts to the World Bank and other official lenders, and three more—Bolivia, Jamaica, and Sudan—renegotiated commercial bank loans they could not pay on time. Bankers around the world responded by tightening their lending standards; instead of offering to replace maturing loans with new ones, they asked for repayment. The borrowers did not have the money. "The changing composition of international capital flows, and the high level of interest rates, have placed a number of developing countries in a liquidity squeeze," the World Bank announced with considerable understatement. And then, on August 12, 1982, the bottom fell out.[6]

THE NEWS CAME VIA TELEPHONE. JESUS SILVA HERZOG, THE FINANCE minister of Mexico, called US Treasury secretary Donald Regan to report that Mexico could not pay $300 million due the following Monday. Nor did he see an obvious way for his country to find the more than $2 billion it would need each month to service its debts over the coming year. The same emergency message went out to Fed chairman Paul Volcker and Jacques de Larosière, the managing director of the International Monetary Fund.[7]

Silva Herzog knew all three men well. A longtime government official with an economics degree from Yale, he had spent years in important economic jobs in Mexico City. He had become finance minister only in March 1982, when it was already clear that a crisis was brewing. Exports by the state-owned oil company, Mexico's main source of dollars, had fallen far short of projections the previous year, while accumulated foreign debt had grown to more than $80 billion. In February, the peso had nosedived after years of stability, making it all but impossible for companies that earned pesos from domestic sales to service their dollar-denominated debts. Within weeks, Mexico's largest private company missed a $2.3 billion payment to foreign banks. In June, under a longstanding agreement, Silva Herzog had asked for a $700 million loan from the Fed. The cash was meant to demonstrate US support for Mexico, but it would barely meet Mexico's needs for a week. "It's only window-dressing money," Volcker told his Fed colleagues. "And it's all symptomatic of the international financial markets closing up pretty tightly on Mexico now." Silva Herzog's August 12 phone calls confirmed that the banks had refused to extend existing loans or offer new ones. Deadlines loomed.[8]

The calls touched off a round of tumultuous negotiations. Hundreds of banks had loans outstanding to the Mexican government. And everyone knew that Mexico was only the first domino. Across the Third World, "Development prospects . . . have worsened over the past year," the World Bank advised. The Latin American countries collectively owed $327 billion to foreign creditors at the end of 1982, and large economies elsewhere, such as Indonesia, Turkey, and Poland, owed several hundred billion more. Although Brazilian economic officials intoned, "Brazil is not Mexico," to the financial markets one developing country looked quite a bit like another. The same borrowers that had been fêted by bankers a few months earlier were now toxic. They could not borrow commercially at any rate, even for a few months; instead, they were instructed to start repaying their debts. Their financial situations turned critical, as the most common way of dealing with excessive debt, extending the repayment schedule farther into the future, was closed off. By the end of 1982, approximately forty countries were in arrears.[9]

Although it is true, as Walter Wriston had said, that countries don't go out of business, it is also true that many countries, on many different occasions, have failed to make payments on their foreign debts for years on end. Moratoriums on payments of foreign debt were common in the nineteenth century and again in the Depression-wracked 1930s. But all parties concerned had reason to avoid this option in the 1980s. If a borrower defaulted, its economy might be severed from the rest of the world. Foreign investment would come to a stop, and importing food and raw materials would become difficult. If the debtor was a state-owned company, courts in other countries might try to seize its assets abroad, from office buildings to the vessels of a state-owned ship line. Living standards would fall sharply. Unemployment would spike. And in the end, if it ever wished to borrow money again the government would still have no alternative but to bargain with its bankers.[10]

A major developing-country default would be equally ugly for the banks. Once a borrower was more than a couple of months late on a scheduled payment, the banks would have to "write down" or "write off" the value of those loans on their books, formally recognizing that some of the money was lost. The nine largest US banks held developing-country loans equal to nearly three times their capital, and German banks were heavily committed in communist Eastern Europe. If even a fraction of those loans had to be written off, the lending banks would be totally insolvent. The banks were supposed to have protected themselves against such risks by diversifying their lending. But at the same time as their government supervisors were telling them to be cautious, other government officials were urging them to support foreign policy goals by extending credit to needy neighbors. "There is some evidence that political pressure was put on bank regulators not to interfere with the Third World lending," one study concluded. Many institutions were so overextended that a large write-down of even a single country's loans could have proved fatal.[11]

The governments of the wealthy countries were on the hook, too. Many of them sponsored insurance schemes to protect banks' domestic customers and might have to dip into their budgets to pay off depositors if a big bank failed. But the potential implications of a major failure went far beyond the cost of bailing out depositors. The world economy was fragile in 1982; inflation was starting to decline at long last, but in many wealthy countries unemployment was still high and economic growth halting. It would be hard to restore growth if banks were too weak to lend to businesses seeking to expand and consumers looking to buy new cars and homes. Because banks were constantly lending to, borrowing from, and trading with one another, the failure of one major bank was likely to drag other banks down, crippling their ability to lend as well. US bank supervisors were already worried about Continental Illinois, the country's seventh-largest bank, which was on the verge of collapse after years of imprudent lending. It was imaginable that other banks would have to stop providing credit even to longtime borrowers, as they used every available dollar to deal with their troubled portfolios of Third World loans.

The world was at an impasse. Every bank wanted its money back, and many borrowers were tempted to strike deals with one or another lender. But if the government of a developing country used its scarce dollars to settle debts with a single bank, even at a discount, there would be less money available for the rest. A piecemeal resolution of the debt crisis was thus impossible. Neither the banks nor their borrowers could escape. Yet neither the banks nor the borrowers could be allowed to fail, potentially jeopardizing Western Europe, North America, and Japan. The Third World debt crisis seemed intractable.

THE FIRST PRIORITY WAS TO STAVE OFF COLLAPSE. WITHIN A FEW days of Silva Herzog's phone calls, the Bank for International Settlements, the Swiss-based organization that was promoting cooperation among bank regulators, organized a package of emergency loans from various central banks, and the US Treasury cobbled together more money so Mexico could pay its loans for a few more weeks. Bank presidents from around the world were summoned to the Federal Reserve Bank of New York on August 20, where they were asked to agree to a "standstill" of Mexican loan payments. What "standstill" meant, so far as bank supervisors were concerned, was that the banks had voluntarily agreed that Mexico should not make payments. The purportedly voluntary aspect was critical; the Mexicans had not declared a moratorium, a default, or any other condition that would force the banks to write down their loans, so the banks could still pretend to be strong. The emergency loans and the standstill were designed to buy time to put together a longer-term agreement that might allow Mexico to stay current on its debts and keep the banking system afloat.[12]

The final months of 1982 were a blur of negotiations, with sleep-deprived bankers and finance ministers commuting between Mexico City, Washington, Basel, London, and New York from one bargaining round to the next. Once the International Monetary Fund took charge of the talks, officials discovered that Mexico had a startling 1,400 bank creditors. The larger ones urgently needed a deal: the shareholders of Wriston's Citicorp stood to lose more than half their investment if Mexico went bust, assuming the bank could even stay in business. Many smaller banks, on the other hand, had no interest in postponing Mexico's loan payments, much less lending more money. They were afraid, not without reason, that the IMF and the finance ministers who governed it would serve the interests of the big banks and leave small ones high and dry.

The IMF, one of the institutions created in the Bretton Woods agreement back in 1944, had originally been set up to help countries that were unable to keep their pledges to hold their currencies fixed against the dollar. When that occurred, the finance minister of the troubled country would come hat in hand to the IMF's modernistic headquarters in Washington, conveniently located midway between the Treasury and the Federal Reserve. The Fund, as it was universally known, might authorize a change in the exchange rate and lend the country money to put its economic house in order. After the wealthy economies shifted to a floating-rate system in 1973, many smaller countries still pegged their currencies to the US dollar or the French franc, and they could call on the Fund for aid when the currency markets turned against them. The IMF's most notable venture had come in 1976, when it had lent $3.9 billion to Great Britain to help stabilize the crumbling pound. Its usual clients were finance ministries and central banks; restructuring commercial bank loans was not its normal business.

IMF loans came with strings attached. Before turning over a penny to a would-be borrower, the Fund sent out a team of experts to develop an economic reform program. If the government did not agree to the Fund's conditions, it would not get the money. Even then, the loan was disbursed in pieces, known as tranches, so the flow of cash could be cut off at any point if the borrower failed to make promised reforms. Although the Fund was heavily staffed with economists who considered themselves nonpolitical technocrats, it was very much a political organization, and the conditions it imposed on would-be borrowers reflected the views of US and European officials. Its head, by custom, was European; Jacques de Larosière, the managing director since 1978, had been a high official in the French Treasury. Representatives of twenty-two countries sat on the executive board, which had the final say on loan proposals, but the United States, with the greatest voting power by far, usually called the shots. At the time the Mexican crisis broke, the IMF was running short on funds, and the Reagan administration was opposing de Larosière's efforts to increase the amounts that governments put at the IMF's disposal.[13]

On November 16, de Larosière unveiled the IMF's plan to assist Mexico. It would lend $3.9 billion, provided the Mexican government implemented the sorts of reforms the Fund frequently required: sharply cutting the budget deficit, reducing subsidies, increasing its tax take, and strictly controlling the money supply. But there was a catch. De Larosière insisted that Mexico could not use the IMF's money to repay its commercial bankers. There would be no IMF loan until the banks agreed to make $5 billion in new loans to Mexico: instead of a bailout, there would be a bail-in. Under pressure from their governments, the banks reluctantly acceded, each agreeing to share in the new loans in proportion to its share of Mexico's debt. The Reagan administration sealed the deal by agreeing that the IMF should receive more money. When it was all over, Mexico had won a year's reprieve—and the banks had won assurance that, at least for the next year, supervisors would consider their loans to the Mexican government to be as good as gold. The banks divided a $200 million fee for originating the loan, immediately boosting their profits. And Mexico's on-time interest payments in 1983 went straight to the banks' bottom lines, even though it was the banks' own money that Mexico was using to make those payments.[14]

Just as Mexico's loan package was being signed and sealed, the Brazilian government made known that it, too, wanted the IMF to help restructure its debts. Brazil's plea came as a surprise to international financiers, for it had disclosed no looming problems. "In September of 1982," economist John Makin recalled, "Brazil was still the apple of every banker's eye." Its debts were soon revealed to be even larger than Mexico's. The banks were bailed in there, too, to the tune of a $4.9 billion loan for three years. The arrangement quickly fell apart when the Brazilians failed to bring inflation down, as the IMF had ordained, and the banks refused to hand over more money. Through 1983 and 1984, Brazil tottered on the edge of default.[15]

In the queue behind Brazil was Argentina, whose military government had left the country a basket case. Unusually among the major debtors, Argentina had not prospered during the 1970s; much of its borrowing had gone for weapons and aircraft rather than roads and pipelines. Its national income had grown an imperceptible 2 percent between 1974 and 1982. Inflation was running at 16 percent a month, households' consumer spending had fallen for three years running, and much of the private economy was effectively bankrupt. In April, desperate to distract public attention from the disastrous economic situation, the generals and admirals had decided to invade the Falkland Islands and other British South Atlantic territories over which Argentina claimed sovereignty. The venture had ended in a humiliating Argentine defeat. The generals, suddenly eager to relinquish power, had built up a foreign debt of $38 billion, and war-related sanctions had already caused the government to miss debt payments. With half its foreign loans payable by the end of 1983, Argentina desperately needed the bankers to agree to stretch out its debts.[16]

A default by any one of these three big debtors would have brought down many large foreign banks. And behind the big three marched a parade of countries whose debt problems were equally serious, relative to the sizes of their economies: Peru and Ecuador, Poland and the Philippines, Venezuela and Yugoslavia. Country after heavily indebted country came to the Fund, promised economic reforms, and negotiated a loan. The Fund, in turn, bailed in the banks, insisting that they defer payments or extend new loans. A year or two later, the borrowing country would return for another round of negotiations and a new package of loans. Commercial banks' loans to developing countries, totaling $232 billion at the end of 1981, reached $427 billion by the end of 1986. Considering the fees the banks collected for originating each loan and the double-digit interest rates they charged, loan restructuring looked to be a very profitable business.

It was all a bit of a shell game. The banks' earnings appeared strong, because they were effectively lending money to themselves. Their balance sheets looked increasingly healthy because, especially in the United States and Japan, their supervisors looked the other way rather than requiring big banks to acknowledge that certain loans would never be repaid; between 1982 and 1985, US banks wrote off barely 1 percent of the amount they were owed. From the wealthy countries' point of view, a financial catastrophe had been averted. As their domestic businesses began to pick up in 1985, Third World loans accounted for a smaller share of big banks' loan portfolios and profits, and many of the smaller banks were able to extricate themselves from developing-country loans altogether. The banks seemed to be stepping back from the edge of the abyss.[17]

IN THE WEALTHY COUNTRIES, THE PANIC IN BANKS' LAVISH OFFICE towers and the evident worry on the faces of finance ministers meant nothing to the man on the street. Systemic risk—the risk that the entire banking system might come tumbling down—was not something the public worried over so long as bankers still offered loans and automated teller machines spat out cash.

The effects of the Third World debt crisis made themselves felt in the First World in quite a different way. Factory towns bore the pain. In the late 1970s, developing countries' orders for construction equipment, power stations, and consumer goods had helped keep plants in the wealthy countries busy. But in the 1980s, the only way the debtor countries could hope to service their debts was by running large trade surpluses, which would allow them to amass desperately needed foreign currency. Orders for imports dried up or were simply blocked by debtor countries' finance ministries, which might refuse to make dollars or yen available to importers. Meanwhile, aided by favorable exchange rates, manufactured goods from poor countries were exported to rich countries in significant quantities for the first time. The United States was particularly hard hit as traders in the currency markets dumped developing countries' currencies and drove up the dollar, making imports cheaper and US exports much more expensive. In 1982 alone, by one estimate, the $9 billion drop in US exports to Latin America cost 250,000 US manufacturing jobs. The debt crisis was by no means the greatest blow to industrial workers in the wealthy economies, but it was one more source of pressure on their living standards.[18]

On the streets of the developing world, though, the export boomlet did little to alleviate the sense of crisis. More exports and more debt restructuring had kept the heavily indebted countries from defaulting on their loans, but it had brought their citizens nothing but austerity. Wages were sharply lower, and already tenuous living standards spiraled downward; people who had been living on two dollars a day had to learn to make do on one. Poverty rates soared as income per person in Latin America and Africa fell 5 percent in 1983 alone. A landscape of half-finished bridges and padlocked factories revealed economies that had crashed to a stop. As foreign investment dried up, workers who had finally found a place in the formal economy in the 1970s, sweeping floors or loading trucks at a factory, were reduced again to informal labor, struggling to earn a few coins by shining shoes in a public park or juggling for motorists at a busy traffic light. A bottle of cognac became a status symbol, demonstrating that the host had the connections and the cash to obtain a forbidden import. The IMF's adjustment programs made no one feel better. To the Fund's economists, eliminating subsidies was a way to curb government budget deficits. To the poor, it simply meant an increase in the price of bread.[19]

New loans were piled atop old ones as economies shrank, making the debt burden even heavier. Africa's foreign debt equaled less than one-third of its total income in 1981; five years later, it equaled one-half. By the end of 1986, if the countries of Latin America had magically been able to halt imports altogether and devote every single cent of their export earnings to debt repayment, they would still have required three-and-a-half years to pay off their debts. Perversely, more money was flowing out of the debtor countries than flowing in, stifling the investment that was the only hope for a better future. The lack of investment had very real consequences: there were fewer new roads to take farmers' crops to market, fewer new transmission lines to bring power to remote areas, fewer new university buildings to educate the next generation.[20]

As a recipe for economic growth, austerity was an abject failure. And failure led to a change in the conversation. In 1985, officials in the wealthy countries began to suggest that management of the debt crisis should move from the IMF, whose short-term loans were meant to deal with immediate currency crises, to the World Bank, which was specifically mandated to support the economic development of poorer countries. In October 1985, James Baker, recently named US Treasury secretary, put forth an alternative "program for sustained growth." Baker said what many in Latin America and Africa had been saying for three years: the way for developing countries to overcome their debt problems was for their economies to grow. Although the details were vague, Baker proposed that the commercial banks and the World Bank lend more money to the fifteen most troubled countries—but only if they adopted "comprehensive macroeconomic and structural policies . . . to promote growth."[21]

Baker's plan went nowhere—the last thing the big banks desired was to lend more money to countries that already were hopelessly mired in debt—but his speech pushed the discussion in a direction consistent with the Reagan administration's ideological inclinations. The underlying cause of the debt crisis, in this view, was not the banks' unwise lending or the decline of commodity prices or the spike in interest rates after 1979, but rather the actions of the debtor countries themselves. Their governments, Washington now proclaimed, were too big and too intrusive, stifling private initiative and killing prosperity. Big Government was the problem, and smaller government would be the solution. The policies Baker had in mind to "promote growth" were much the same as those Reagan had advocated for the United States: less government spending, lower marginal tax rates, free trade, openness to foreign investment, privatization.

In a world suffering from debt fatigue, these ideas played well. The IMF and the World Bank spread the new wisdom that free-market policies would enable the debtor countries to grow at long last, sharply reversing their past positions favoring top-down planning and government-directed investment. Many people in the debtor countries came to the same conclusion, recognizing that state-managed industrialization backed up by import barriers, as advocated for so long by Raúl Prebisch, had failed to bring sustained prosperity. The new market-oriented thinking would become known as the Washington Consensus, a semi-official compendium of principles the experts said would help the developing countries outgrow their debts.[22]

The experts, their advice framed by the ideological battles over the role of government in Washington and London, failed to recognize that the economic problems of developing countries generally had less to do with high tax rates and Big Government than with large-scale tax avoidance and incompetent government. Privatization brought little economic boost when it meant nothing more than turning a state-owned monopoly into a privately owned monopoly, and opening the door to foreign investment was of little consequence when would-be investors encountered a parade of corrupt officials demanding bribes or contracts. In countries where shockingly low literacy rates stood in the way of improving worker productivity, simply rolling back government could not improve the ability of education ministries to provide an adequate education to children for whom private-school tuition was beyond reach. Such shortcomings, ignored by advocates of the Washington Consensus, turned out to be serious drags on developing countries' economic growth.

When it came to surmounting the debt crisis, there was only one poster child: South Korea. The country's foreign debts were nearly $47 billion at the end of 1985; relative to the size of its economy, it was more indebted than Mexico. The Koreans flatly rejected the advice being dispensed from Washington. Theirs was in no sense a free-market economy; five-year plans determined which industries would grow and which would shrink, and the state decided which companies could borrow money from Korean banks. Import barriers protected industries the government deemed vital. The government sharply restricted sales of cars and kept prices of other goods high, inducing families to save a large share of their incomes; those savings funded business investment without further need for foreign borrowing. The Koreans raised taxes in order to run a budget surplus, directly contrary to supply-side teachings, and they constantly tinkered with taxes and spending to "fine-tune" economic performance. Deregulation, privatization, and openness to foreign capital were not on the political agenda; instead, the government spent massively on education. Despite the Koreans' contraventions of the new conventional wisdom, their economy performed so strongly that the country was beginning to outgrow its foreign debt even as it made the tricky transition from a harsh military dictatorship to a raucous electoral democracy.[23]

Only a very few places, all of them small—Singapore, Taiwan, the British territory of Hong Kong—were able to emulate South Korea by essentially forcing their citizens to postpone consumption and save more than one-third of their incomes. Almost every other debtor country staggered through the 1980s, waiting for Washington's free-market growth agenda to bear fruit. In 1987, the commercial banks, still healing after five years of international efforts to keep the debtor countries afloat, finally began to write off some of their Third World loans. Yet even with some debts now partially forgiven, "The international debt crisis is now entering its seventh year with no end in sight," Pedro Pablo Kuczynski, a former World Bank economist and Peruvian cabinet minister, wrote in 1988. Productivity growth in most of the heavily indebted countries remained dismally low, job creation sluggish.

Their economic woes had serious political ramifications as well. Military rulers, no longer able to generate the economic improvements their citizens expected, were ejected from power in many debtor countries, and Mexico's authoritarian government was forced to allow honest elections that eventually drove it from office. Yet the newly elected governments had no greater success improving economic conditions than the autocrats they replaced. It would take until 1997, according to economist Angus Maddison's calculations, before the average Mexican was as well off as at the onset of the debt crisis in 1982. For the average Filipino, full recovery would take until 2002; the average Peruvian would have to wait until 2005. In poorer countries as in richer ones, the satisfaction of enjoying rapidly improving living standards remained elusive long after the economic crisis was past.[24]

CHAPTER 15

The New World

The economic slump that began in 1973 lasted much longer than any-one had imagined. By the second half of the 1970s, it was clear that the tougher economic times were related to lagging productivity growth not just in one or two countries, but all around the world. The result, put simply, was that workers were not creating wealth as quickly as they had in the recent past, leaving fewer gains to be shared.

Economists have many ways to measure productivity, of which the best understood is the amount of output produced by a single hour of labor. From 1959 through 1973, labor productivity in twelve of the world's largest, most prosperous economies grew at a stunning average rate of 4.6 percent a year, creating the wealth that raised living standards all around and financed the expansion of the welfare state. In 1974, immediately after the oil crisis, productivity growth plummeted. For the next quarter-century, the mean labor productivity growth of those same twelve countries averaged 2 percent, less than half the pace of the Golden Age. Japan's average tumbled from 8.5 percent per year to 3 percent, Sweden's from 4.6 percent to 1.2 percent. The same was true in poorer countries. With only a few exceptions—Chile, Malta, South Korea—the productivity slowdown affected every country in the world for which data can be found.[1]

Other productivity measures take a broader look, considering the efficiency with which economies use available resources by raising workers' skill levels, installing more and better equipment for each worker to use, and improving technology. Looked at in this way, too, productivity in the wealthy economies grew much more slowly in the 1970s and 1980s than before. Estimates for the United States, which has the most complete measures for this period, tell the shocking tale. Over the thirteen years from 1960 to 1973, multifactor productivity—a measure that counts labor productivity, the productivity of capital, and technological advances—increased 34 percent across the US business sector. In the thirteen years from 1973 to 1986, in sharp contrast, multifactor productivity in US business increased only 7 percent. Instead of vast increases in efficiency, businesses made halting gains, hardly enough to notice.[2]

Intuitively, it made sense that poor productivity growth would hold down wages and contribute to the spreading malaise. But *why* productivity growth was lagging, and what could be done to revive it, were mysteries.

Theories were a dime a dozen. The movement of workers from low-productivity farm jobs to higher-productivity industrial jobs had contributed powerfully to productivity growth in the 1950s, but it was slowing by the 1970s because there were far fewer workers left on the farm. Another explanation was that the unprecedented numbers of young people entering the workforce two decades after the baby boom of the 1950s lacked the skills of veteran workers; with time, as their abilities improved, perhaps their productivity would increase. Or perhaps the large supply of young, low-wage workers was making it less attractive for employers to invest in labor-saving technology. Maybe soaring oil prices were to blame, because they particularly affected the industries that had seen the greatest productivity growth in earlier years, such as chemical and textile manufacturing; as firms adjusted to higher energy costs by installing more energy-efficient equipment, productivity might rebound.

And then there was the global decline in the rate of business profits. Canada, Great Britain, the United States, and West Germany all saw profitability decline through the 1960s, especially in the manufacturing sector. Japanese companies followed the same trend, as the cost of paying for the investments they had made in the 1960s became an increasing burden. Profits in France, too, fell sharply after 1973. With weaker profitability, businesses had fewer resources to invest in improving productivity, much less to meet the demands of workers who felt entitled to a larger share of the economic pie. As companies held on to their old equipment longer, productivity growth slowed further.[3]

Adding to the pressure on businesses was the emerging demand for environmental protection. Clean air and clean water had been low priorities in the postwar world. Government authorities rarely measured emissions, and if a factory or power plant encountered complaints from nearby communities, it might respond by extending a smokestack or a drain line, solving the local problem by transporting the pollution further away. The crop of new environmental laws that came into force in many countries in the late 1960 and early 1970s put an end to that game, mandating pollution controls on new facilities, and often on existing ones. Over time, by reducing illness, discomfort, and property damage from environmental pollution, these controls improved the quality of life in ways that were not measured in statistics on productivity and national income. But installing power-plant scrubbers and water filtration systems consumed business capital that could otherwise have gone toward achieving higher productivity. In the United States, private-sector spending for environmental protection, adjusted for inflation, doubled between 1972 and 1978. Economists' warnings that environmental standards should be carefully calibrated to avoid economic harm were largely disregarded in the political tug of war that accompanied the new environmental rules.[4]

Poorer productivity growth was visible not just in factories, but also on farms and in the service sector. Agricultural output in the wealthy countries had increased sharply during the 1960s. Aided by heavy spending on inputs like fertilizer, pesticides, and hybrid seeds, farmers were able to coax roughly 2 percent more grain and soybeans from an average acre of land each year. In the 1970s, output per acre grew more slowly, and in the 1980s it barely grew at all. The advances that had made French sugar-beet growers and Canadian wheat farmers prosperous were harder to come by. Meanwhile, the service sector burgeoned, because once consumers had filled their homes and garages with cars and appliances and furniture, they began spending more of their incomes on services rather than goods. Unlike factories, which could always install new and better machines to raise productivity, service businesses such as manicure salons, law offices, and vacation resorts found productivity increases challenging. As more workers came to earn their livings in the service sector, the explanation went, the average growth of labor productivity across the economy inevitably slowed.[5]

None of these explanations sufficed to explain the productivity bust afflicting countries with vastly different economies and divergent approaches to economic policy. The more deeply the scholars mined the data, the more confused they became. What the data could not yet show was that the world had moved to a new stage of economic growth, one that would develop in a far different way.

SIR KEITH JOSEPH, MEMBER OF PARLIAMENT, PERFECTLY TAILORED business executive, and the man most responsible for tutoring Margaret Thatcher in free-market economics, had a reputation for speaking out of turn. He burnished that reputation in June 1974, at a meeting of Conservative Party regulars in Upminster, on the eastern fringe of London. Not four months earlier, with the economy in free fall, the Labour Party under Harold Wilson had knocked the Conservatives from power in a tightly contested election. Labour's minority government was shaky, and another election seemed unavoidable. Most politicians would have seized the opportunity to broaden the base, appealing to swing voters who might help the Conservatives regain power. Joseph did the opposite, attacking not just Labour's mistakes, but his own party's failures as well. "During thirty years we have tried to force the pace of growth," he asserted. "Growth is welcome, but we just do not know how to accelerate its pace."[6]

Such perplexity revealed an uncomfortable truth: there was no obvious way to counteract the forces that brought the Golden Age to an end. The world's wealthy economies were no longer flourishing as they had; that much was indisputable. Through the 1970s, the standard tools—adjusting short-term interest rates, tinkering with government spending, offering a subsidy here or a tax break there—failed to control inflation, create jobs, or raise living standards in almost every one of the wealthy economies. Inflation was finally slain in the 1980s, but the unemployment rate seemed permanently higher than it had been before, and income gains were much slimmer. Income per person in the wealthy countries, after adjusting for inflation, grew barely half as fast in the years after 1973 as in the years before. Japan, guided by a strong government hand that pushed manufacturers to sell abroad and shielded them from import competition at home, seemed to be a unique exception—until, in the early 1990s, with far too much factory capacity and extraordinarily inefficient retailing and service sectors, it entered two decades of stagnation even more severe than what Western Europe and North America had endured.[7]

In 1966, American economist Walter Heller, who had served as one of President Kennedy's top advisers, famously pronounced that the "new economics" could assure full employment, low inflation, and steady economic growth. Within a decade, his teachings already seemed laughable. The happy economic balance of the "magic square," dictated by West German law and promoted with such effort by economy minister Karl Schiller, seemed entirely beyond reach—not just in West Germany, but everywhere. No matter what governments and central bankers tried, whether trimming the welfare state or expanding it, whether following a strict monetary rule or adjusting interest rates month to month, whether lowering top tax rates or holding them steady, nothing could bring back the all-but-universal belief that life was good today and would be even better tomorrow. During Jimmy Carter's presidency, "It was just almost impossible to say what good economic policy would have been," Alice Rivlin, head of the Congressional Budget Office from 1975 to 1983, told an interviewer in 1991. "It was easy to criticize what they were doing, but it wasn't clear, even in hindsight, what should have been done." The same could have been said for almost every country in the world.[8]

No politician could have admitted the fact, but there was little that anyone could have done to set the world economy to rights. The tools that governments have at their disposal often work well to provide a short-term boost: the stimulus of a big tax rebate or a cut in interest rates can quickly get a recession-bound economy moving again. Similarly, easy credit from poorly supervised banks may support a spending binge that makes everyone feel good for a while, as with the developing country boom of the 1970s and early 1980s.

But once stimulus has run its course, an economy's long-run growth potential depends overwhelmingly on higher productivity. In every wealthy economy, productivity growth after the early 1970s was markedly slower than before, for reasons having little to do with economic policy. The huge reservoir of underutilized labor that had shifted into more productive work in the postwar years could not be tapped again: peasant farmers and sharecroppers had long since moved to the cities, and the flow of previously unemployed women into the labor force was over. The sorts of public-sector expenditures that could bring almost immediate gains in productivity, such as building superhighways and modernizing ports, had been made. Although young people entering the labor force invariably had more schooling than their parents, the years of an extremely rapid rise in average education were past now that literacy was almost universal in the wealthy economies. Future advances in well-being would depend heavily on developing innovations and putting them to effective use.

GOVERNMENTS ARE NOT MERE BYSTANDERS WHEN IT COMES TO influencing innovation. Funding research makes new discoveries more likely. Education and immigration policies may create a larger pool of technically trained workers able to advance the frontiers of knowledge. Policies that encourage competition and make it easy for new firms to grow may speed the development of innovative equipment, software, and ideas. Yet the rate at which innovations affect productivity is almost totally beyond the ability of governments to control. Turning an innovative idea into commercially useful products and services may involve years of trial and error, as with mobile telephones, which came into widespread use only in the 1990s, two decades or more after many of the essential technologies were developed. Some innovations become economically useful only after complementary innovations occur; color television sets first went on sale in the United States in the early 1950s, but few people purchased them until color programming was readily available a decade later. Even a proven technology may proliferate slowly: the invention of a more efficient boiler will improve energy efficiency only as older boilers are replaced over time.[9]

Productivity growth and innovation both seem to move in long cycles. In the United States, for example, the effects of innovation on the economy were slight in the early twentieth century, very strong from the 1920s to 1973, quite weak between 1973 and 1995, fairly strong between 1995 and 2003, and considerably weaker in the years thereafter. Intense spending on research can bear no economic fruit for years before unexpectedly triggering a deluge of commercially viable products and services. This is what happened with the microprocessor, a tiny piece of silicon that was invented in November 1971 but did little for productivity for two decades, until managers began to figure out how to reshape their businesses to take advantage of the cheap computing power the device made possible. Conversely, the sudden embrace of a technology, often years in development, can fuel a productivity boom when none is expected. Telecommunications costs began to fall steeply in the 1970s, but it was only in the late 1990s that the commercialization of the Internet contributed to a burst of productivity growth across the wealthy economies—a burst that exhausted itself in just a half-dozen years.[10]

The years after World War II saw the upswing of just such a cycle, bringing a quarter-century of robust productivity growth. The gains thereafter were far more modest. While some wealthy countries seemed to have found formulas that allowed them to defy the global trend—France and Italy for a few years in the late 1970s, Japan in the second half of the 1980s—their economies revived only briefly before productivity growth waned, jobs became scarce, and improvements in living standards came far more slowly. There were innovations aplenty during those years, but their overall economic effect was modest. As the economist Robert Gordon points out, "the productivity advances since 1970 have tended to be channeled into a narrow sphere of human activity having to do with entertainment, communications, and the collection and processing of information. For the rest of what humans care about—food, shelter, transportation, health, and working conditions both inside and outside the home—progress slowed down." Gordon's research pertains to the United States, but his conclusions are relevant to the other wealthy countries as well.[11]

And unlike the innovations of the 1950s and 1960s, which seemed to benefit almost everyone, those of the final quarter of the twentieth century had costly side effects. Giant industrial complexes became dinosaurs. There was no longer a need to have tens of thousands of workers in a single place whose sheer size inevitably led to militarized management practices that alienated workers and disrupted operations, and which brought complications, such as the need to recruit, house, and feed thousands of employees. With the increasing reliability of communications and freight transportation, and with the development of computers that could relay information back and forth, it was feasible to break large organizations into smaller parts, locating each to take advantage of labor supplies, airports, rail routes, government subsidies, or other attractions, or to contract out certain tasks to companies that were now easier to supervise from afar. Whether it involved making a car or approving a mortgage, work could be distributed more widely. Research and development might go to places where there was a large supply of engineers and scientists, and routine production tasks—like processing beef carcasses for a meatpacker or transferring an airline's data from paper tickets to computer tapes—could be shifted out of urban areas to smaller towns, where wages and rent on office space likely were lower.

The economic logic behind this radically different division of labor was readily apparent. But the changes involved were often traumatic. Workers whose jobs were relocated found that their years of experience and training were of little value in other industries, leaving them the choice of lower-paid work or unemployment. Communities that lost major employers hemorrhaged income and tax revenue, losing the resources that funded public services and amenities and, in many cases, entering a prolonged cycle of decay. And firms discovered that restructuring their operations to take maximum advantage of new technologies was anything but painless. As many corporate executives learned at great cost, closing a plant in Ohio on Friday and opening a new one in Alabama on Monday was a recipe for disaster, regardless of the new computer, communications, and transportation links that were supposed to make the transition seamless.

By the 1980s, these shifts were transcending national boundaries, marking the beginning of what later came to be called globalization. To be sure, there had been a few cross-border supply arrangements since the 1950s, when six European countries eliminated all barriers to trade in steel and coal. In the 1960s, a trade agreement between Canada and the United States had made it practical for auto parts manufacturers on one side of the border to supply assembly plants on the other, and a handful of Japanese electronics companies fought rising labor costs at home by having circuit boards soldered in Hong Kong. But it was only the spread of intermodal transportation and cheap communications that made it practical for manufacturers and retailers to stretch their supply chains across the oceans and for financial and transportation companies to send routine data-entry work abroad. There were many kinks to work out. Globalization came with a learning curve, and the learning often entailed a considerable loss of productive efficiency.[12]

The greatest beneficiaries of globalization were the fast-growing "tiger" economies of East Asia. In the 1990s and early 2000s, they seemed to defy the productivity slowdown that was plaguing Europe, North America, and Japan, but they, too, found their momentum impossible to sustain. After riding five decades of explosive growth to achieve per capita incomes on a par with Italy and Spain, Korea and Taiwan saw productivity growth slow sharply in the early years of the twenty-first century. The investments that followed China's economic reforms, starting in 1978, created hundreds of millions of new jobs and unleashed a vast migration of rural peasants to higher-productivity work in the cities, but after a thirty-five-year boom China's productivity miracle ended in 2012.[13]

In the 1970s and 1980s, even as businesses were struggling with rapidly changing technologies and the first stirrings of globalization, they were straining to cope with an exceedingly difficult economic environment—one in which inflation and interest rates were high, exchange rates and energy prices volatile, and profitability well below past norms. Managers saw risks all around, and they responded by putting off long-term investments whose payoff seemed highly uncertain. Across the wealthy economies, business investment, which had increased an average of 5.6 percent per year between 1960 and 1973, grew at a far slower rate, barely 4 percent per year, for the next two decades. Sluggish investment left steel mills operating antiquated blast furnaces and insurance offices using high-speed computer printers to spit out form upon form for clerks to organize in file cabinets. Technological innovations usually arrive in the business world incorporated in new equipment and facilities. With firms deferring such investments at every turn, their workers' productivity improved at less than half the rate in the decades after 1973 as in the decades before. The reason families no longer sensed that their lives were getting better is no mystery.[14]

IN EVERY COUNTRY WHERE IT OCCURRED, THE PRODUCTIVITY bust left families' incomes stagnant or creeping higher at rates that would have been deemed unacceptably slow a few years earlier. This was the new normal, the unhappy trend that neither the tonic of free markets nor the strong hand of government seemed able to alter. For the average family, slower income growth meant slower improvements in living standards. To be sure, incomes stretched a bit farther than they had in earlier years because families were smaller, and almost everyone benefited from widespread material advances: smartphones and household computers became ubiquitous; boxy television sets were replaced by wide screens showing programs in stunning high definition; formerly incurable health problems could be diagnosed and treated with high-tech equipment. But as weak growth undermined the financial viability of the welfare state, unemployment benefits grew less generous, pensions were frozen or vanished altogether, and tuition bills rose. One means of salving the anger was to make credit easier to come by, so people who could no longer afford to purchase life's luxuries outright could more readily borrow to enjoy them. In the United States and Europe, that experiment ended badly in 2008.[15]

For the most part, the modest income gains in the wealthy countries were captured by a small share of households. The causes of greater income inequality lie partly in technological changes that favor some types of workers over others, partly in the incontrovertible fact that capital can move fluidly around the world in search of higher returns while labor is tied to particular occupations and particular places. Yet the underlying economic trends were so powerful that even governments with a deep suspicion of capitalism had difficulty moderating them. From Spain to Japan, government interventions to secure rising wages for workers with regular, full-time jobs obscured the fact that large numbers of workers had neither, making do with short-term contracts and temporary jobs and facing an insecurity their parents never knew.

As productivity growth slowed in one country after another, rising anger at the state's inability to deliver average citizens the prosperity it had promised manifested itself in uncomfortable ways: resentment of immigrants blamed for taking supposedly scarce jobs; vociferous opposition to paying sufficient taxes to maintain roads and public buildings; relentless criticism of public services that had once been treated as proud achievements, such as schools and health programs. Most of all, stagnant living standards played out in the rise of dissident movements on the fringes of the political mainstream, drawing support from the large number of disaffected voters: parties seeking independence for Quebec and Catalonia; ultranationalist movements in France, Hungary, and Great Britain; wealthy political outsiders, such as the American computer-services tycoon Ross Perot, who won nearly one-fifth of the popular vote in the 1992 presidential election, and the media magnate Silvio Berlusconi, who parlayed his domination of Italy's newspapers and television stations into nine years as Italy's prime minister. The theme of ungovernability, much discussed in the 1970s, emerged again in the twenty-first century as political leaders struggled to communicate convincing visions of a better future.

It is easy to read the economic changes that began around 1973 as a perversion of the postwar social contract. The German sociologist Wolfgang Streeck, for example, interprets what he calls "the crisis of late capitalism" in the final decades of the twentieth century as "an unfolding of the old fundamental tension between capitalism and democracy—a gradual process that broke up the forced marriage between the two after the Second World War." But the evident popular despair about economic decline in Japan, North America, and Western Europe reflected an entirely different problem: the difficulty of writing a social contract able to respond to demographic change and technological innovation.[16]

The arrangements that brought peace and prosperity after World War II have often been portrayed as imposing limits on the power of capital for the benefit of labor. That was part, but not all, of the story. The postwar compromises were a gift to bosses as much as to their workers. Even the most rabid anticapitalists of the day understood that generous social benefits could be sustained only if employers could provide stable jobs and rising wages. Competition makes it difficult for employers to keep those promises by depressing profits and driving firms out of business. Creating the postwar social contract thus required limiting competition throughout the economy—by enforcing state monopolies in some industries; tightly regulating firms' operating hours, business locations, licenses, and prices in others; and giving governments a firm hand on the market through credit controls, import restrictions, and investment barriers. Damping competition allowed firms to earn sufficient profits to support steadily rising pay and, in many cases, lifetime employment.

This arrangement made many people better off—for a while. But as they came of age in the 1980s and after, people far too young to have been involved in writing the postwar social contract found themselves bearing its cost. In many countries they could find no jobs, because laws crafted in earlier times to provide ironclad job security left businesses unwilling to hire workers they might never be able to discharge. Private pension schemes in the United States and Great Britain, rendered unviable by the large number of workers eligible to retire at age sixty-two or even earlier, were closed to new employees or wound down altogether. A low-income American couple born in 1920 earned a generous average annual return of 5.3 percent on the taxes they paid into the Social Security retirement program during their working years. Their children's children, born in 1965, could expect a far leaner 3.3 percent annual return. The social contract, it turned out, involved a compulsory gift from grandchildren to their grandparents. It should come as no surprise that the grandchildren were unenthusiastic.[17]

The Golden Age was an extraordinary time, and the generation that lived through it enjoyed extraordinary opportunity. But as economist John Fernald observed after delving deeply into American productivity data, "It is the exceptional growth that appears unusual." The same applies to every other country in the world. Economic miracles do happen, but in most times and most places, economies grow slowly, bringing a gradual improvement in living standards punctuated by sudden bursts of euphoria and by recessions that throw unneeded workers on the street. Neither market-oriented economic policies, such as those championed by Margaret Thatcher and Ronald Reagan, nor statist reforms, such as those initially undertaken by François Mitterrand, have proven able to alter that reality. In Japan and Korea, massive state-guided investment booms, once the objects of breathless admiration around the world, brought explosive economic growth followed by rapid improvements in living standards—again, for a while. But those economies, too, eventually fell from orbit, their political leaders no longer able to deliver miracles.[18]

Just as eighteenth-century scientists sought to capture electricity in a bottle, their modern descendants are wont to suggest that economic dynamism can be captured and dispensed at will. In truth, though, the forces that sustain faster economic growth and prosperity are rarely set in motion with the flip of a switch or the passage of a law. Golden ages usually arise suddenly and end unexpectedly. While it may turn out that a particular government action or private innovation raised living standards dramatically for a generation, the connection may not be clear until well after the fact—and a similar policy or innovation, unleashed at a different moment or under different circumstances, might have no far-reaching consequences at all.

Indeed, policies advanced for their purported power to increase long-run economic growth may have precisely the opposite effect. This was the case with the structural adjustment programs of the 1970s, which channeled public and private resources into troubled industries unlikely ever to regain their previous heights, such as shipbuilding and steelmaking, rather than helping workers and communities prepare for the economy to come. Cuts in taxes on capital, measures to weaken labor unions, stricter limits on corporate mergers, regulations to encourage or discourage the formation of large banks—all may enhance economic performance at one point in time but weaken it at another. Hope that wise, well-considered measures will propel an economy to a higher growth trajectory is eternal, but there are no foolproof recipes. After studying eighty sustained periods of unusually high economic growth, three Harvard University economists found the episodes had little in common. "The vast majority of growth accelerations are unrelated to . . . political change and economic reform," they wrote, "and most instances of economic reform do not produce growth accelerations."[19]

The aftereffects of the crisis of the 1970s would reverberate for decades. The asset price bubble that decimated Japanese households' finances in the 1990s; the thousands of bank failures in the United States between 1980 and 1994; the deep downturn, fed by excessive lending to unqualified borrowers, that began in Europe and the United States in 2008, bringing painfully high unemployment and threatening the very survival of the European Union—all can be traced to political efforts to make economies grow faster than productivity advances would allow. It was a fool's errand. The American economist Paul Samuelson put it well: "The third quarter of the Twentieth Century was a golden age of economic progress. It surpassed any reasoned expectations. And we are not likely to see its equivalent soon again."[20]

Acknowledgments

This book, I suppose, began with my own personal history. I was a student in West Germany at the time of the 1973 oil crisis, and I experienced both the euphoria of car-free Sundays and the queues of ill-tempered drivers desperate for gasoline. West Germany, in those days, had far more jobs than available workers, and in consequence many of my fellow students felt no particular urgency to enter the workforce. Tuition was free, housing was cheap, and rumors that the state government intended to cap the number of semesters for which an individual could enroll were a predictable cause of student protest. The good life in a miracle economy was the only life most of my classmates knew. They were in for a rude awakening.

The rediscovery of the 1970s as a critical period in economic history has spurred an outpouring of research around the world. Much of this, however, peers through the lens of domestic politics, losing sight of larger forces and imputing to politicians and public officials far more power to affect events than they ever possessed. This book represents an effort to correct this misperception by focusing attention on aspects of the crisis that transcended national borders. Writing history in this way can be a challenge: names that are famous in one place are often unknown elsewhere; the details of economic policy and performance inevitably vary greatly from one country to another; the statistics can overwhelm even the committed reader; and the minutiae of international negotiations over exchange rates and banking regulations can be mind-numbingly boring.

Yet without an international context, our understanding of important historical events is shallow or incomplete.

I would like to extend my thanks to archivists and librarians at the Bank for International Settlements, the Bank of England, the Bundesarchiv Koblenz, Library and Archives Canada, and the Library of Congress for their assistance with my research, and to the many people who gave of their time to discuss aspects of this story with me or to comment on portions of the text over a period of many years. At the risk of omitting some, I would particularly like to thank Ralf Ahrens, Richard Baldwin, Alex Brummer, Bill Cassidy, Martin Chick, Peter Cooke, Charles Freeland, Charles Goodhart, John Heimann, Louis Hyman, Doug Irwin, Torsten Kathke, Henry Kaufman, David Lascelles, Danièle Nouy, Julia K. Ott, Arturo Porzecanski, Brian Quinn, Richard Sylla, Stig Tenold, Laurent Warlouzet, and William R. White. The American Historical Association, the Business History Conference, the Centre for Contemporary History Potsdam, the Council on Foreign Relations, the German Historical Institute, and the Keizei Koho Center all offered me opportunities to present my work in progress and receive helpful comments. I am also grateful to my agent, Ted Weinstein, for his steadfast guidance. Responsibility for errors of fact or interpretation is mine alone.

Notes

INTRODUCTION

1. For an evaluation of the first car-free Sunday, see Duco Hellema, Cees Wiebes, and Toby Witte, *The Netherlands and the Oil Crisis: Business as Usual*, trans. Murray Pearson (Amsterdam: Amsterdam University Press, 2004), 107–108. Film of the occasion can be found at www.youtube.com/watch?v=iyJbg-4NKZs, viewed June 30, 2013. Queen Juliana soon traded in the Cadillac for a more fuel-efficient and less conspicuous Ford Grenada; see "Royal Family in Firing Line on Spending Cuts," *NRC Handelsblad*, September 21, 2009, http://vorige.nrc.nl/article2365311.ece.

2. The war began on October 6. On the origins of the embargo against the Netherlands, see Hellema et al., *The Netherlands and the Oil Crisis*, 53; Paul Kemzis, "Europeans Move to Conserve Oil," *New York Times*, November 7, 1973; Terry Robards, "Oil-Short Europe Is Facing Hardest Winter Since War," *New York Times*, December 11, 1973; "Wen ich nicht kenne, der kriegt nichts," *Der Spiegel*, November 26, 1973.

3. Richard Halloran, "Japan Is Stunned by Arab Oil Cuts," *New York Times*, October 19, 1973; "Japan to Slash Supplies of Oil to Industry in Crisis Program," *New York Times*, November 9, 1973; Fox Butterfield, "Aide Says Curb May Cut Gain of Economy," *New York Times*, November 12, 1973; Fox Butterfield, "Japan to Ration Fuel and Power," *New York Times*, November 16, 1973.

4. M. A. Adelman, "The First Oil Price Explosion, 1971–1974," MIT-CEPR working paper 90–013, May 1990.

5. Angus Maddison, *The World Economy: Historical Statistics* (Paris: OECD, 2003), 260–263.

6. Julius Shiskin, "Long-Term Economic Growth: A Statistical Compendium," *Business Cycle Developments* 66–10 (October 1966): 71.

7. For econometric analysis of 1973 as a break year, see Michael Bruno and Jeffrey D. Sachs, *Economics of Worldwide Stagflation* (Cambridge, MA: Harvard University Press, 1985), chap. 12; Maddison, *The World Economy*, 237.

8. Recession dates provided by the National Bureau of Economic Research. The average compensation of US production workers rose at an annual rate of 0.24 percent between 1873 and 1997; see Samuel H. Williamson, "Annualized Growth Rate and Graphs of Various Historical Economic Series," MeasuringWorth, at www.measuring worth.com/growth, viewed November 20, 2015.

9. Edmund Phelps, *Mass Flourishing: How Grassroots Innovation Created Jobs, Challenge, and Change* (Princeton, NJ: Princeton University Press, 2013). Phelps asserts that the rate of innovation has declined in Europe and the United States.

10. Paul M. Romer, "Mathiness in the Theory of Economic Growth," *American Economic Review* 105 (2015): 89–93. For a less technical exploration of the debate over the sources of economic growth, see David Warsh, *Knowledge and the Wealth of Nations* (New York: Norton, 2006).

11. George F. Will, "Defining Economic Failure Down," *Washington Post,* February 5, 2015.

12. Paul M. Romer, "Crazy Explanations for the Productivity Slowdown," in Stanley Fischer, ed., *NBER Macroeconomics Annual 1987, Vol. 2* (Cambridge, MA, 1987), 163–210; Dale W. Jorgenson, "Productivity and Postwar U.S. Economic Growth," *Journal of Economic Perspectives* 2 (Fall 1988): 23–41; Steven Englander and Axel Mittelstädt, "Total Factor Productivity: Macroeconomic and Structural Aspect of the Slowdown," OECD *Economic Studies* 10 (Spring 1988): 28; Zvi Griliches, "Productivity Puzzles and R&D: Another Nonexplanation," *Journal of Economic Perspectives* 2 (Fall 1988): 19.

13. Jefferson Cowie, *Stayin' Alive: The 1970s and the Last Days of the Working Class* (New York: New Press, 2010); Dominick Sandbrook, *State of Emergency: The Way We Were: Britain, 1970–1974* (London: Penguin, 2010); Serge Bernstein and Pierre Milza, *Histoire de la France au XXe siècle: Tome 5, De 1974 à nos jours* (Paris: Editions Complexe, 2006).

14. George Packer, "The Uses of Division," *The New Yorker,* August 11–18, 2014.

1. THE NEW ECONOMICS

1. US Bureau of the Census, *Sixteenth Census of the United States–1940–Population,* vol. 2, part 6, 994, and *Sixteenth Census of the United States–1940–Housing,* vol. 1, 586; City of Arlington, "Preserving Arlington: Past Visions, Future Realities," 2010; Vickie Bryant and Camille Hess, *Top O' Hill Terrace* (Charleston, SC: Arcadia Publishing, 2012).

2. US Census Bureau, *United States Census of Agriculture—1950,* vol. 5, part 6, 99; Statistics Japan, *Historical Statistics of Japan,* at www.stat.go.jp/english/data/chouki /index.htm, Tables 2–17 and 11–4.

3. On French farm output, see Jean-Pierre Dormois, *The French Economy in the Twentieth Century* (Cambridge, UK: Cambridge University Press, 2004), 17. Figure of 4.5 million strikers is from Jack Barbash, "Unions and Rights in the Space Age," in

Richard B. Morris, ed., *The U.S. Department of Labor Bicentennial History of the American Worker* (Washington, DC: US Government Printing Office (USGPO), 1976), at www.dol.gov/dol/aboutdol/history/chapter6.htm.

4. See "War Cabinet: Social Insurance and Allied Services: Summary of Report by Sir William Beveridge," November 25, 1942, United Kingdom National Archives (NA), cab/66/31/27.

5. Dennis Guest, *The Emergence of Social Security in Canada*, 3rd ed. (Vancouver, BC: UBC Press, 2003), 123–126; J. Van Langendonck, "Belgium," in *International Encyclopedia of Laws* (Alphen aan den Rijn, Netherlands: Wolters Kluwer, 2007), 17; Robert H. Cox, *The Development of the Dutch Welfare State: From Workers' Insurance to Universal Entitlement* (Pittsburgh: University of Pittsburgh Press, 1993), 105–110; Philip Nord, *France's New Deal* (Princeton, NJ: Princeton University Press, 2010). The new Japanese law was Act No. 164 of December 12, 1947.

6. Barry Eichengreen, *The European Economy Since 1945* (Princeton, NJ: Princeton University Press, 2007), 55; United States Strategic Bombing Survey, *Summary Report (Pacific War)* (Washington, DC: USGPO, 1946), 17–18.

7. Howard B. Schonberger, *Aftermath of War: Americans and the Remaking of Japan, 1945–1952* (Kent, OH: Kent State University Press, 1989), 166–177; Herbert Giersch, Karl-Heinz Paqué, and Holder Schmieding, *The Fading Miracle* (Cambridge, UK: Cambridge University Press, 1994), 39.

8. US education data are from Thomas D. Snyder, ed., *120 Years of American Education: A Statistical Portrait* (Washington, DC: National Center for Educational Statistics, 1993), 19, 55. The average home in Tokyo provided 2.79 tatami units of dwelling space per person, which equates to 4.3 square meters or 46.5 square feet; *Historical Statistics of Japan*, Table 21.7. French refrigerator ownership data are in Dormois, 21. The average South Korean calorie intake was 1,236 calories per day; see Jinwung Kim, *A History of Korea: From "Land of the Morning Calm" to States in Conflict* (Bloomington: Indiana University Press, 2012), 387. As of 2014, the US Department of Agriculture recommended 2,400–3,000 calories per day for males sixteen to thirty-five and smaller amounts for females. On rationing in Spain, see Instituto Nacional de Estadística, *Annuario 1949*, 648–652. On epidemics, see Australia Government Department of Health, *Notifiable Diseases Surveillance, 1917 to 1991*, 2003. The country's age-standardized death rate jumped from 1,681 per 100,000 people in 1947 to 1,751 in 1948; see Australian Institute of Health and Welfare, General Record of Incidence of Mortality books, 1907–2011.

9. For consistency, this discussion relies on the work of Angus Maddison, who developed a time-series estimate of income in 1990 US dollars adjusted for purchasing power parity, allowing comparisons among as well as within countries. The United States had 42.5 million occupied units and 23.4 million homeowners in 1948; *Statistical Abstract* 1951, 721. In 1974, there were 70.8 million occupied units and 45.8 million homeowners; *Statistical Abstract* 1976, 736. On improved living standards in Great Britain, see Sandbrook, *State of Emergency*. On changes in average retirement

ages, see DICE Database (2010), "Average Age of Transition to Inactivity Among Older Workers, 1950–1995," Ifo Institute, Munich, at www.cesifo-group.de/DICE/fb/3M8 mHhFq7.

10. On French students, see Georges Lavau, "The Effects of Twenty Years of Gaullism on the Parties of the Left," in William G. Andrews and Stanley Hoffmann, eds., *The Fifth Republic at Twenty* (Albany, NY: State University of New York Press, 1981), 165.

11. James N. Gregory, *The Southern Diaspora: How The Great Migrations of Black and White Southerners Transformed America* (Chapel Hill: University of North Carolina Press, 2005), 21. Gregory estimates that 2.6 million blacks left the American South during the 1940s and 1950s. On Macmillan, see http://news.bbc.co.uk/onthisday/hi /dates/stories/july/20/newsid_3728000/3728225.stm.

12. Diego Comin and Bart Hobijn, "Technology Diffusion and Postwar Growth," Harvard Business School working paper 11–027 (2010). The authors emphasize the importance of US economic assistance programs in diffusing technology internationally.

13. Nicholas Crafts and Gianni Toniolo, "Postwar Growth: An Overview," in Crafts and Toniolo, eds., *Economic Growth in Europe since 1945* (Cambridge, UK: Cambridge University Press, 1996), 9, 18. The authors argue that capital investment was the driving force in Europe. Data on US investment in manufacturing equipment are from *Historical Statistics of the United States, Millennial Edition Online*, series Dd707. UK investment statistics are from Tim Congdon, "Productivity Could Be the Key," *The Times* (London), November 7, 1973. According to the OECD, 34 percent of British workers were employed in manufacturing in 1971. This was approximately the same share of the workforce as had worked in manufacturing in the 1840s. On Japan, see Takafusa Nakamura, *The Postwar Japanese Economy*, 2nd ed. (Tokyo: University of Tokyo Press, 1995), 149. The growth in investment was widespread. For France, see Dormois, *The French Economy in the Twentieth Century*, 19. In Germany, the useful life of investment declined through the 1950s as many companies brought in new technologies even before older equipment was fully depreciated; see internal memorandum by Dr. Demand, Bundesministerium für Wirtschaft (BMWi), "Perspektiven des Wirtschaftswachstums in der Bundesrepublik Deutschland bis zum Jahre 1990," October 1976, Bundesarchiv Koblenz (BA), B102/306599.

14. There is no precise information on average tariffs; the estimate here is drawn from Douglas Irwin, "The GATT's Contribution to Economic Recovery in Post-war Europe," in Barry Eichengreen, ed., *Europe's Postwar Recovery* (New York: Cambridge University Press, 1995), 138. For an estimate of export growth, see ibid., 129. On scale economies in manufacturing, see Eichengreen, *The European Economy Since 1945*, 115–129.

15. Alexander Field, *A Great Leap Forward: 1930s Depression and U.S. Economic Growth* (New Haven, CT: Yale University Press, 2011), 120. Field argues that the construction of the US Interstate Highway System, starting in 1956, was key to the rapid productivity growth of the 1960s and early 1970s.

16. For growth in labor productivity, I rely on a series developed by Angus Maddison, "GDP per Hour, in 1990 GK $," published as "The Conference Board Total Economy Data Base, Output, Labor and Labor Productivity Country Details," www.conference-board.org/data/economydatabase/. The labor productivity growth story is widely accepted among specialists, but its causes are hotly debated. The key variable at issue is "total factor productivity," or "multifactor productivity," which is the portion of productivity growth that remains unexplained after factors such as improved education and greater fixed capital are taken into account. Total factor productivity growth is usually attributed to technological innovation. Relevant statistics for most countries are lacking before the 1960s, but Nicholas Crafts contends the United Kingdom, the United States, France, Germany, and Japan all had significantly faster multifactor productivity growth over the 1950–73 period than before or since. See Crafts, "A Perspective on UK Productivity Performance," *Fiscal Studies* 22 (2001), 283, and his 2008 conference paper, "What Creates Multifactor Productivity?" Some economists assert US multifactor productivity growth was greater before World War II than after; see Robert J. Gordon, "Two Centuries of Economic Growth: Europe Chasing the American Frontier," Working Paper 10662, National Bureau of Economic Research, August 2004, and Field, *A Great Leap Forward.*

17. Ludwig Erhard, West German economy minister from 1949 to 1963, was a strong opponent of economic planning. See Giersch et al., *Fading Miracle*, 63–116.

18. Ruth Ellen Wasem, *Tackling Unemployment* (Kalamazoo, MI: Upjohn Institute Press, 2013), 55–67.

19. Henry C. Wallich, "The German Council of Economic Advisers in an American Perspective," *Zeitschrift für die gesamte Staatswissenschaft* 140 (1984), 360; Walter W. Heller, *New Dimensions of Political Economy* (Cambridge, MA: Harvard University Press, 1966), 9.

2. THE MAGIC SQUARE

1. Matthias Hochstätter, *Karl Schiller—eine wirtschaftspolitische Biographie*, Ph.D. dissertation, University of Hannover, 2006, 9, 47, 51, 60, 64.

2. Alexander Nuetznadel, *Stunde der Oekonomen: Wissenschaft, Politik und Expertenkultur in der Bundesrepublik 1949–1974* (Göttingen: Vandenhoeck & Ruprecht, 2005), 243–244; Karl Schiller, "Neuere Entwicklungen in der Theorie der Wirtschaftspolitik," in Karl Schiller, *Der Ökonom und die Gesellschaft* (Stuttgart: G. Fischer, 1964), 21.

3. Tim Schanetzky, *Die große Ernüchterung: Wirtschaftspolitik, Expertise, und Gesellschaft in der Bundesrepublik 1966 bis 1982* (Berlin: Akademie Verlag, 2007), 55–57.

4. Torben Luetjen, *Karl Schiller (1911–1994), "Superminister" Willy Brandts* (Bonn: Dietz, 2007), 209.

5. Memo, BMWi, "Mittelfristige Zielprojektion 1967/71 und tatsächliche Entwicklung, Abschlussbericht," April 29, 1974, BA, B102/248424; Hochstätter, *Karl Schiller*, 162.

6. Karl Schiller, "Runder Tisch der kollektiven Vernunft," *Die Berliner Wirtschaft*, December 21, 1968. According to a January 29, 1969, speech by Hans Tietmeyer, then secretary of state in the economics ministry, the need for a mechanism to resolve conflicts over economic policy had been discussed since the early 1960s; BA, B102/278282. The seating plan described here was used after Schiller left government; BA, B102/303302.

7. Description of Schiller is from unlabeled notes of a December 14, 1967, meeting of Konzertierte Aktion, apparently written by Johannes Prass, a senior official in the chancellor's office. For objections by Labor Minister Hans Katzer and Finance Minister Franz Josef Strauss and Kiesinger's directive, see "Auszug aus dem Kurzprotokoll über die 1. Sitzung des Kabinettsausschüsses für Sozialbudget und soziale Strukturfragen am 9. Oktober im Bundeskanzleramt," BA, B136/7406.

8. Gabriele Metzler, "Am Ende aller Krisen," *Historische Zeitschrift* 275 (2002): 91–97.

9. Luetjen, *Karl Schiller*, 281.

10. For assessments of the five-year plans, see two economics ministry memos, "Mittelfristige Zielprojektion 1967/71 und tatsächliche Entwicklung, Abschlussbericht," April 29, 1974, BA B102/248424, and "Die wirtschaftspolitischen Ziele der Projektion 1970/1974 und ihre Realisierung," March 15, 1974, BA, B102/248 423.

11. Luetjen, *Karl Schiller*, 280.

12. For an eloquent argument on this point, see William Easterly, *The Tyranny of Experts* (New York: Basic Books, 2014).

13. This biographical sketch relies on Edgar J. Dosman, *The Life and Times of Raúl Prebisch, 1901–1986* (Montreal: McGill-Queen's University Press, 2008).

14. Argentina's industrial productivity fell 7.5 percent between 1935 and 1943, largely because domestic manufacturers were protected from import competition. See especially Irene Brambilla, Sebastian Galiani, and Guido Porto, "Argentine Trade Policies in XX Century: 60 Years of Solitude," working paper, Washington University, August 2010.

15. Raúl Prebisch, "El desarrollo económico de la América Latina y algunos de sus principales problemas," *El Trimestre Económico* 16 (1949): 347–431. For the English translation of Prebisch's speech, see United Nations Department of Economic Affairs, Economic Commission for Latin America, "The Economic Development of Latin America and Its Principal Problems," 1950.

16. Dosman, *Life and Times of Raúl Prebisch*, 276.

17. "Final Communiqué of the Asian-African Conference of Bandung (24 April 1955)," in *Texts of Selected Speeches and Final Communiqué of the Asian-African Conference, Bandung, Indonesia, April 18–24, 1955* (New York: Far East Reporter, 1955).

18. The literature on dependency theory is quite large and varied. Among important examples are Paul A. Baran, *The Political Economy of Growth* (New York: Monthly Review Press, 1957); Celso Furtado, *Development and Underdevelopment* (Berkeley:

University of California Press, 1964); Andre Gunder Frank, *Capitalism and Underdevelopment in Latin America* (New York: Monthly Review Press, 1967); Guillermo O'Donnell, *Modernization and Bureaucratic-Authoritarianism* (Berkeley: University of California Press, 1973); Immanuel Wallerstein, *The Modern World-System* (New York: Academic Press, 1974).

19. *Trends in International Trade: Report by a Panel of Experts* (Geneva: General Agreement on Tariffs and Trade, 1958), 11, 104–114. This report was widely known as the Haberler Report after Gottfried Haberler, the chairman of the group of authors. High duties and taxes on coffee, tea, and cocoa beans, in some cases exceeding 60 percent of the value of the product, exemplified the barriers to tropical products; see Appendix, Table D.

20. For an economic discussion of such schemes, see David M. G. Newbery and Joseph E. Stiglitz, *The Theory of Commodity Price Stabilization* (Oxford: Oxford University Press, 1981), and David G. Gill et al., "Access to Supplies and Resources: Commodity Agreements," American Society of International Law, *Proceedings of the Annual Meeting* 71 (1977): 129–144.

21. United Nations Conference on Trade and Development, *The History of UNCTAD 1964–1984* (New York: UNCTAD, 1985), 56–58.

22. See, for example, M. Ataman Aksoy and Helena Tang, "Imports, Exports, and Industrial Performance in India, 1970–88," World Bank Policy Research Working Paper WPS 969 (2001).

23. Industry grew at an annualized rate of more than 7 percent in developing countries from 1950 to 1975. For data on growth rates, see World Bank, *World Development Report 1978* (Washington, DC: World Bank, 1979), 27, 75–79, 88–89.

24. For a clear statement of his views, see Raúl Prebisch, "Joint Responsibilities for Latin American Progress," *Foreign Affairs*, July 1961, 622–633.

25. Statistics from UNCTAD statistical service.

3. CHAOS

1. Wyatt C. Wells, *Economist in an Uncertain World: Arthur F. Burns and the Federal Reserve, 1970–78* (New York: Columbia University Press, 1994), 13–19.

2. John Ehrlichman, *Witness to Power* (New York: Simon and Schuster, 1982), 248; Burton A. Abrams, "How Richard Nixon Pressured Arthur Burns: Evidence from the Nixon Tapes," *Journal of Economic Perspectives* 20 (2006): 185; Arthur Burns, *Inside the Nixon Administration: The Secret Diary of Arthur Burns, 1969–1974*, ed. Robert H. Ferrell (Lawrence: University Press of Kansas, 2010), 28, 44, 72–73; "Memorandum of Discussion," Federal Open Market Committee, March 10, 1970, 61. On Burns's temper, see Stephen H. Axilrod, *Monetary Policy and Its Management, Martin Through Greenspan to Bernanke* (Cambridge, MA: MIT Press, 2009), 60.

3. Arthur F. Burns, *Prosperity Without Inflation* (New York: Fordham University Press, 1957), 65; Christina D. Romer and David H. Romer, "The Most Dangerous

Idea in Federal Reserve History: Monetary Policy Doesn't Matter," *American Economic Review* (May 2013). In a January 30, 1978, speech to the National Press Club, his final public appearance as Fed chairman, Burns reaffirmed his belief that high inflation was "chiefly traceable to fundamental mistakes of governmental policies made in the mid-1960s," compounded by both Republican and Democratic administrations since; he assigned no responsibility to the Fed's conduct of monetary policy.

4. Robert L. Hetzel, "Arthur Burns and Inflation," *Federal Reserve Bank of Richmond Economic Quarterly* 84 (Winter 1998): 21–84.

5. The description of the Bretton Woods agreement in this paragraph is extremely simplified. For more background, see Barry Eichengreen, *Globalizing Capital: A History of the International Monetary System*, 2nd ed. (Princeton, NJ: Princeton University Press, 2008), 91–133.

6. Michael D. Bordo, Ronald MacDonald, and Michael J. Oliver, "Sterling in Crisis, 1964–1967," *European Review of Economic History* 13 (2009): 437–459; Barry Eichengreen, *Exorbitant Privilege: The Rise and Fall of the Dollar and the Future of the International Monetary System* (Oxford: Oxford University Press, 2011). Many of the problems that would develop from the Bretton Woods arrangements were described in 1959 by the economist Robert Triffin; see his book *Gold and the Dollar Crisis* (New Haven, CT: Yale University Press, 1960).

7. *OECD Economic Outlook* 12 (December 1972): 18–19. On the importance of fixed exchange rates in resisting political pressures to inflate, see Helmut Schmidt, "Dank an einen Hanseaten," *Die Zeit*, April 20, 1984, at www.zeit.de/1984/17/dank-an -einen-hanseaten.

8. For a thorough discussion of Fed deliberations in 1971 and 1972, see Allan H. Meltzer, *A History of the Federal Reserve, Vol. 2* (Chicago: University of Chicago Press, 2009), 795–800. Schiller headed both the finance and economy ministries. Robert L. Hetzel, "German Monetary History in the Second Half of the Twentieth Century: From the Deutsche Mark to the Euro," Federal Reserve Bank of Richmond, *Economic Quarterly* (Spring 2002): 40; Wells, *Economist in an Uncertain World*, 85; Burns, *Inside the Nixon Administration*, 72; "Transcript of a recording of a meeting between the President and H.R. Haldeman in the Oval Office on June 23, 1972, from 10:04 to 11:39 am," 12, Nixon Presidential Library and Museum, Yorba Linda, CA, National Archives and Records Administration (NARA).

9. In technical terms, some countries had negative real short-term interest rates.

4. CRISIS OF FAITH

1. Donella H. Meadows et al., *The Limits to Growth* (New York: Universe Books, 1972), 23.

2. Robert Gillette, "The Limits to Growth: Hard Sell for a Computer View of Doomsday," *Science* 175 (March 10, 1972): 1088; William Nordhaus, "World Dynamics: Measurement Without Data," *The Economic Journal* 83 (1973): 1157; Jean

Matteoli, "Les ressources mondiales et l'économie française," Conseil Économique et Sociale 197/S.G./13 (1975): 11; Christopher Freeman, "Malthus with a Computer," in H. S. D. Cole et al., eds., *Thinking About the Future: A Critique of* The Limits to Growth (London: Chatto & Windus, 1973), 11.

3. Frank Uekoetter, *The Age of Smoke* (Pittsburgh: University of Pittsburgh Press, 2009), 118–119, 132–136.

4. Quotation is from a representative of Enjay Chemical Company, cited in Gerald Markowitz and David Rosner, *Deceit and Denial* (Berkeley: University of California Press, 2002), 144.

5. Paul R. Ehrlich, *The Population Bomb* (New York: Ballantine Books, 1968), xi. On precursors, see Pierre Desrochers and Christine Hoffbauer, "The Post-War Intellectual Roots of the Population Bomb," *Electronic Journal of Sustainable Development* 1 (2009): 37–61.

6. Russell W. Peterson, the Republican governor of Delaware from 1969 to 1973, recounted how the state's Republican-controlled legislature approved a law in 1971 limiting industrial development within two miles of the state's coastline over the opposition of supposedly more progressive Democrats. See Peterson, *Rebel with a Conscience* (Newark, DE: University of Delaware Press, 1999), 147–149.

7. Tape of conversation among President Nixon, Lido Anthony Iacocca, Henry Ford II, and John S. Ehrlichman in the Oval Office, April 27, 1971, Nixon Presidential Library and Museum, NARA; Richard Nixon, "Remarks on Signing Bill Establishing the Commission on Population Growth and the American Future," March 16, 1970, online by Gerhard Peters and John T. Woolley, *The American Presidency Project*, at www .presidency.ucsb.edu/ws/?pid=2911; Commission on Population Growth and the American Future, *Final Report* (Washington, 1972), 12, 52; Richard Nixon, "Statement About the Report of the Commission on Population Growth and the American Future," May 5, 1972, *The American Presidency Project*, at www.presidency.ucsb.edu/ws/?pid=3399.

8. Edward Goldsmith and Robert Allen, "A Blueprint for Survival," *The Ecologist* 2 (1972); United Nations Environmental Program, "Declaration of the United Nations Conference on the Human Environment" (June 1972); Jean Bourgeois-Pichat, "In 200 Years So Many Things Can Happen," *Population Index* 38 (1972): 306; Walter E. Hecox, "Limits to Growth Revisited: Has the World Modeling Debate Made Any Progress?" *Boston College Environmental Affairs Law Review* 5 (1976): 65–96.

9. The unidentified Israel diplomat is quoted in John Brooks, "A Reporter at Large: Starting Over," *The New Yorker*, October 23, 1971. The term "stationary state" was taken from the English philosopher John Stuart Mill. See John Harte and Robert H. Socolow, "The Equilibrium Society," in John Harte and Robert H. Socolow, eds., *Patient Earth* (New York: Holt, Rinehart and Winston, 1971), 203.

10. Herman E. Daly, "Toward a Stationary-State Economy," in Harte and Socolow, eds., *Patient Earth*, 228–231.

11. On weight-to-output trends, see Grecia Matos and Lorie Wagner, "Consumption of Materials in the United States, 1990–1995," US Geological Survey, 1999.

12. Edward F. Denison, "Effects of Selected Changes in the Institutional and Human Environment Upon Output per Unit of Input," *Survey of Current Business* 58 (January 1978): 21–44; Gary L. Rutledge, "Pollution Abatement and Control Expenditures in Constant and Current Dollars, 1972–77," *Survey of Current Business* 59 (February 1979): 13–20. In 1972, approximately 6 percent of capital spending by US businesses went to environmental abatement; by 1977, the figure was 8 percent.

5. THE GREAT STAGFLATION

1. Allen Matusow, *Nixon's Economy* (Lawrence: University Press of Kansas, 1998), 220.

2. *The Guardian*, December 21, 1972; David Gumpert, "Rise in Demand Causes Shortage of a Variety of Materials, Parts," *Wall Street Journal*, December 8, 1972; President's Council of Economic Advisers, *Economic Report of the President*, 1973, 82; Bank of Japan, *Monthly Economic Review*, January 1973, 1; "Commentary," *Bank of England Quarterly Bulletin* 13 (March 1973): 6; John L. Hess, "Forecasters' Word Is 'Boom,'" *New York Times*, January 7, 1973; Charles Reeder, *The Sobering Seventies* (Wilmington, DE: DuPont, 1980), 101.

3. E. Philip Davis, "Comparing Bear Markets—1973 and 2000," *National Institute Economic Review* 183 (2003): 78–89.

4. Paul Samuelson, "Science and Stocks," *Newsweek*, September 19, 1966; memo from Dr. Ranz, BMWi, to various cabinet ministers, "Angepasste mittelfristige Zielprojektion bis 1976," March 20, 1973, BA, B 102/248423; Don Oberdorfer, "Japanese Economy Is Booming Again," *Washington Post*, January 14, 1973.

5. *OECD Economic Outlook* 13 (June 1973): 102.

6. Memorandum of discussion, Federal Open Market Committee, February 13, 1973, 17; US Central Intelligence Agency, Office of Economic Research, "Oil Companies Compensate for Dollar Devaluation: The Geneva Agreement," *Foreign Relations of the United States* (FRUS), vol. 36, 264.

7. Jeffrey Robinson, *Yamani: The Inside Story* (New York: Atlantic Monthly Press, 1988), 4, 40.

8. Matthew R. Simmons, *Twilight in the Desert: The Coming Saudi Oil Shock and the World Economy* (Hoboken, NJ: Wiley, 2011), 49, 55.

9. "Saudi Arabia Seeking Ownership Participation in Giant Oil Producer," *Wall Street Journal*, June 27, 1968; US Department of State, Bureau of Intelligence and Research, "The Middle East: Relations Between Governments and Petroleum Concessionaires—The Participation Issue," June 10, 1969, FRUS, vol. 36, 11; Telegram, US Embassy in Saudi Arabia to Department of State, February 17, 1972, FRUS, vol. 36, 270; Bernard D. Nossiter, "New Oil Talks Could Reshape World Economic, Political Map," *Washington Post*, January 29, 1972; Robinson, *Yamani*, 67, 70; Ray Vicker, "Persian Gulf Nations This Week May Sign 25% Oil-Interest Accords Effective Jan. 1," *Wall Street Journal*, December 18, 1972.

10. Robinson, *Yamani*, 77–80; Daniel Yergin, *The Prize: The Epic Quest for Oil, Money and Power* (New York: Simon & Schuster, 1991), 577–578.

11. Memorandum from Rogers to Nixon, "Petroleum Developments and the Impending Energy Crisis," March 10, 1972, FRUS, vol. 36, 284; Memorandum from Peter Flanigan, President's Assistant for International Economic Affairs, to George Shultz, secretary of labor, and Henry Kissinger, President's Assistant for National Security Affairs, June 29, 1972, FRUS, vol. 36, 301; Government of Canada, Cabinet Conclusions, "Canada-USA discussions on security of oil supply," February 15, 1973, Canada Archives, RG2, Privy Council Office, Series A-5-a, vol. 6422, 10. The United States maintained import quotas on Canadian oil; Canada allowed producers in Alberta to ship only small quantities of oil to the United States while allowing imported oil only in Quebec and the Maritime Provinces, effectively creating a protected domestic market for Alberta's expensive oil. US contingency planning in early 1973 assumed that all oil imports would be suspended for one year, while Canadian planning assumed only a 25 percent reduction in imports for six months.

12. There was also said to be, in Nixon's words, "an enormous national security aspect of the issue." In Nixon's mind, this appears to have had more to do with the prospect that erratic leaders in countries such as Libya and Iraq would have more resources with which to cause trouble for other countries. See "Memorandum of Conversation," February 8, 1973, FRUS, vol. 36, 410. For an example of the assumptions widespread at the time, see William D. Smith, "A Gasoline Shortage Soon Is Predicted," *New York Times*, April 3, 1973.

13. Ibid.; Clyde H. Farnsworth, "OPEC and Oil Companies Avert Showdown on Prices," *New York Times*, May 27, 1973.

14. "Commentary," *Bank of England Quarterly Bulletin*, June 1973, 271; Bank of Japan, "The Short-Term Business Outlook for Major Manufacturing Corporations," *Monthly Economic Review* (June 1973): 6; *OECD Economic Outlook* 13 (June 1973): 6. The West German government's forecast had the economy expanding 6 percent in 1973 and 4 percent the following year, with inflation subsiding. BMWi, "Vermerk: Ein denkbarer Konjunkturverlauf der mittelfristigen Wirtschaftsentwicklung bis 1977," May 9, 1973, BA, B 102/248423.

15. Reeder, *The Sobering Seventies*, 119; Bank of Japan, *Monthly Economic Review*, September 1973; BMWi, "Sprachzettel zur Problematik der mittelfristigen Wirtschaftsentwicklung," September 3, 1973, BA, B 102/248423; Clyde H. Farnsworth, "Oil Nations, at Vienna Meeting, Seeking More Price Increases," *New York Times*, September 16, 1973.

16. Robinson, *Yamani*, 83.

17. Bank of Japan, *Monthly Economic Review*, September 1973; Federal Reserve, "Current Economic Comment by District," October 10, 1973; BMWi memo, "Probleme bei der Fortschreibung der mittelfristigen wirtschaftlichen Perspektiven bis 1978 für die Bundesrepublik Deutschland," January 2, 1974, BA, B 102/248423.

18. A. W. H. Phillips, "The Relation Between Unemployment and the Rate of Change of Money Wage Rates in the United Kingdom, 1861–1957," *Economica* 25 (1958): 283–299.

19. Edmund S. Phelps, "Phillips Curves, Expectations of Inflation and Optimal Employment over Time," *Economica* 34 (1967): 254–281; Milton Friedman, "The Role of Monetary Policy," *American Economic Review* 58 (1968): 1–17; Interview with Charles Schultze, *The New Yorker,* September 13, 1976.

20. "Japan agrees measures to control inflation," *The Guardian,* September 1, 1973.

21. "Memorandum of Discussion," Federal Open Market Committee, October 2, 1973, and October 16, 1973.

22. Peter Jay, "Super-growth period is over," *Times* (London), October 19, 1973. France foresaw 5.5 percent growth; see Charles Hargrove, "French budget aims at strong growth," *Times* (London), October 24, 1973.

23. The Bank of Japan cut its forecast for the year ending in March 1974 from nearly 11 percent to less than 6 percent—and since the fiscal year was mostly over, the new figure implied no growth at all in the coming months. Bank of Japan, *Monthly Economic Review,* December 1973, 4; Rupert Cornwell, "French Oil Fears Grow," *Financial Times,* December 13, 1973; Federal Open Market Committee, "Memorandum of Discussion," November 19–20, 1973; Craig R. Whitney, "Bonn Aides Fear Major Recession," *New York Times,* November 30, 1973; BMWi, Memorandum, "Auswirkungen einer Energieverknappung auf die mittelfristige gesamtwirtschaftliche Entwicklung," November 23, 1973, BA, B 102/248423. As an example of the delay in recognizing the seriousness of the economic situation, on October 10, 1973, the Fed forecast that the economy would grow 2.5 percent in 1974. On November 14, it raised that forecast to 2.9 percent; "Current Economic and Financial Conditions," Federal Reserve Board, November 14, 1973. Then, on December 12, it lowered its growth forecast for the coming year to 0.8 percent.

24. The apparent originator of the term "stagflation" was Ian Macleod, a Conservative member of the British Parliament, who would briefly serve as Chancellor of the Exchequer in 1970 before his unexpected death. See Hansard, *House of Commons Debates,* November 17, 1965, vol. 720, 1165. For an example of a prominent economist looking ahead to 1974 from a traditional macroeconomic perspective, see Paul Samuelson, "Declining output and more inflation," *Financial Times,* December 31, 1973.

25. When Hendrik S. Houthakker, a prominent Harvard University economist and former member of Richard Nixon's Council of Economic Advisers, spoke to the American Economic Association in January 1974 on "Policy Issues in the International Economy of the 1970's," he did not mention productivity; see *American Economic Review* 64, no. 2 (May 1974): 138–140.

26. On the spurious connection between oil price shocks and US economic performance, see Robert B. Barsky and Lutz Kilian, "Oil and the Macroeconomy Since the 1970s," *Journal of Economic Perspectives* 18 (Autumn 2004): 115–134.

6. GOLD BOYS

1. Richard Halloran, "Japan Braces for a Full-Scale Oil Crisis," *New York Times*, December 8, 1973.

2. On Richardson's background, see the official City of Nottingham website, www.nottinghamcity.gov.uk/index.aspx?articleid=4116#R, viewed October 26, 2011. See also Anthony Loehnis, "Lord Richardson of Duntisbourne Obituary," *The Guardian*, January 24, 2010; "Lord Richardson of Duntisbourne, KG," *The Telegraph*, January 24, 2010; William Keegan, "Lord Richardson of Duntisbourne: Governor of the Bank of England During the Troubled Times of the 1970s and Early 1980s," *The Independent*, February 9, 2010.

3. Forrest Capie, *The Bank of England, 1950s to 1979* (Cambridge, UK: Cambridge University Press, 2010), 519.

4. Clyde H. Farnsworth, "Force on Monetary Scene: Oil Money from Mideast," *New York Times*, March 16, 1973; Michael Blanden, "NatWest weighs in with bumper £92m. profit," *Financial Times*, July 25, 1973; *International Financial Statistics Yearbook* (Washington, DC: International Monetary Fund, 2000), 980, 986.

5. On fringe banking, see Daniel O'Shea, "Role of secondary banks," *Financial Times*, September 11, 1972, and Kenneth Lewis, "Secondary Banks," *Financial Times*, September 10, 1973. On the crisis, see Capie, *Bank of England*, 531–577; Michael Flanden, "Secondary banks: an end to freewheeling," *Financial Times*, December 24, 1973; Margaret Reid, "How the 'Bankers Lifeboat' came to the rescue," *Financial Times*, January 29, 1974; and Derek Matthews, "London and County Securities: A case study in audit and regulatory failure," *Accounting, Audit and Accountability Journal* 18 (2005): 518–536. On legal authority, see the statement by Sir Geoffrey Howe, the minister responsible for fringe banks, in Hansard, *House of Commons Debates*, December 3, 1973, vol. 865, 909.

6. Paul Thompson, "The Pyrrhic Victory of Gentlemanly Capitalism: The Financial Elite of the City of London, 1945–90, Part 2," *Journal of Contemporary History* 32 (1997): 433; Capie, *Bank of England*, 532, 596–597.

7. Capie, *Bank of England*, 499–507, 824.

8. Ibid., 605–614.

9. Otmar Emminger, "Probleme der Stabilitätspolitik," address to the Association of Public Credit Institutions, Frankfurt, November 9, 1973, BA, B102/165947.

10. Henry C. Wallich, "Notes on BIS Meeting of March 11–12, 1974," March 18, 1974, in Federal Open Market Committee, "Memorandum of Discussion," March 18–19, 1974, Attachment B; Federal Open Market Committee, "Memorandum of Discussion," April 15–16, 1974.

11. Joan Spero, *The Failure of the Franklin National Bank* (New York: Columbia University Press,1977), 46–51.

12. Ibid., 53–57, 64–66, 81–83.

13. "Bankencrach: Die Bilder sind bedrückend," *Der Spiegel*, July 1, 1974.

14. Meir Heth, Bank of Israel, "The Failures of Israel-British Bank, Tel-Aviv, and Israel-British Bank (London): Some Preliminary Conclusions," Bank for International Settlements archive (BISA), BS75/47, 1/3A(3), vol. 19.

15. Richard Redden, "Probe May Prove a Classic Example," *The Guardian*, September 16, 1975; Gil Sedan, "Bank Scandal Hits Israel," *Jewish Telegraphic Agency*, July 11, 1974.

16. The names of the Swiss banks were suppressed in most news reports but were reported in "Banking Scandal Hits Israel," *Washington Post*, July 21, 1974. See also Paul J. Green, "When a Bank Is Not a Bank," *Brooklyn Law Review* 43 (1976): 899.

17. "Israel-British Bank (London) closes doors," *Financial Times*, July 12, 1974.

18. "Israelis to Allow Pooling of British Bank's Assets," *New York Times*, June 25, 1975. On the British liquidity guidelines that Israel-British was evading, see BISA, BS/75/3, "Regulations governing the commercial banks' foreign currency transactions: Summary of replies received from the central banks," March 26, 1975, BISA, 1/3A(3), vol. 18; "Liquidity Crunch Gets New Victims at Foreign Banks," *Wall Street Journal*, July 10, 1974.

19. Eric Silver, "12 years for Bension," *The Guardian*, February 24, 1975; "Anger at Begin move to pardon banker," *The Times* (London), September 10, 1977; "Fraud convictions quashed after judge's 'unclear' summing up," *The Guardian*, January 13, 1981; David Lane, *Into the Heart of the Mafia: A Journey Through the Italian South* (London: Profile Books, 2009), 4.

20. The two agreed on the committee's mandate before asking the other central bank governors to authorize it.

21. According to one story, the representative of the German Bundesbank hastened to introduce himself to his counterpart from the German Federal Supervisory Office for Credit Institutions; although their responsibilities overlapped, the Bundesbanker from Frankfurt and the supervisor from Berlin had never met. Cable, US Mission to the EC, Brussels, to Secretary of State, NARA, RG 59, Central Foreign Policy Files, Electronic Telegrams, https://aad.archives.gov/aad/, 1975ECBRU02657, March 25, 1975; George Alexander Walker, *International Banking Regulation: Law, Policy and Practice* (Kluwer Law International: The Hague, 2001), 36; Charles Goodhart, *The Basel Committee on Banking Supervision: A History of the Early Years, 1974–1997* (Cambridge, UK: Cambridge University Press, 2011), 43; confidential interviews. I am grateful to Paul Volcker for emphasizing the committee's lack of legal authority.

22. Goodhart, *Basel Committee*, 53; Alex Brummer, "Bank of England names supremo in wake of crises," *The Guardian*, July 19, 1974; Alex Brummer and Tom Tickell, "Adding up the list of 'don'ts'," *The Guardian*, September 27, 1976. George Blunden's father, also George Blunden, worked in the bank's accountant's department until he retired in 1955; see Bank of England, *Old Lady Magazine*, March 1955, 58.

23. "Informal record of the first meeting of the Committee on Banking Regulations and Supervisory Practices held at the BIS on 6th-7th February 1975," April 3, 1975, BISA, 1/3A(3), vol. 18; "Informal record of the fifth meeting of the Committee on

Banking Regulations and Supervisory Practices held at the BIS on 11th-12th December 1975," BISA, 1/3A(3), vol. 22.

24. "International co-operation in banking supervision," *Bank of England Quarterly Bulletin* 17 (1977): 325. George W. Mitchell, "How the Fed sees multinational bank regulation," *The Banker* 124 (1974): 757–760; "International Banking Survey," *The Economist*, March 20, 1982; Colin Campbell, interview with Don Templeman, Colin Campbell Collection, Special Collections Department, Georgetown University Library, Washington, DC, box 2.

25. "Report to the Governors on the supervision of banks' foreign establishments," September 26, 1975, BISA, BS/75/44, 1/3A(3), vol. 20; "Informal record of the third meeting of the Committee on Banking Regulations and Supervisory Practices held at the BIS on 19th-20th June 1975," BISA, BS/75/40, 1/3A(3), vol. 19. Ethan B. Kapstein, "Resolving the Regulator's Dilemma: International Coordination of Banking Regulation," *International Organization* 43 (1989): 330. Kapstein described the Concordat as a "gentleman's agreement" rather than as a "regime for dealing with bank failures." This is accurate as far as it goes, but neglects provisions that sought to lay out regulatory responsibilities in a way that might avert failures of international banks, and did so in an excessively vague way. "Strictly confidential: Note on the Committee's discussion of the paper, 'The failures of Israel-British Bank, Tel-Aviv and Israel-British Bank (London): Some Preliminary Conclusions' by Dr. Heth of the Bank of Israel," November 3, 1975, BISA, BS/75/56, 1/3A(3), vol. 20; "Informal record of the fifth meeting of the Committee on Banking Regulations and Supervisory Practices held at the BIS on 11th-12th December 1975," BISA, 1/3A(3), vol. 22; BIS staff paper BS/76/3, "Possibilities for international co-operation in a problem bank situation," distributed to the committee on March 5, 1976, BISA, BS/75/56, 1/3A(3), vol. 22.

26. OPEC production of crude oil ranged between 10 billion and 11.4 billion barrels per year between 1973 and 1978. See William L. Liscom, ed., *The Energy Decade, 1970–1980: A Statistical and Graphic Chronicle* (Cambridge, MA: Ballinger, 1982), 372.

27. Philip Green, "Citibank's Apostle of Innovation," *Washington Post*, July 28, 1974; confidential interviews.

28. Arthur F. Burns, "Maintaining the Soundness of Our Banking System," address to American Bankers Association, Honolulu, Hawaii, October 21, 1974.

29. See comments by F. R. Dahl, Federal Reserve Board, in BISA, BS/76/37 Banking Supervision 1976/4; "Informal record of the fourteenth meeting of the Committee on Banking Regulations and Supervisory Practices held in Basel on 26th and 27th October 1978," BISA, BS/78/42, Banking Supervision: Informal Records 01/78–11/79; "Cost to International Banks of Supervision and Regulation: Maintenance of Reserve and Capital Ratios," BISA BS/79/49, 1979/10; Ronald Kessler, "Citibank, Chase Manhattan on U.S. Problem List," *Washington Post*, January 11, 1976; "Citibank, Chase Listed as 'Problem' Banks But Regulators Say Neither Is in Danger," *Wall Street Journal*, January 12, 1976; confidential interviews.

30. "Informal record of the eighth meeting of the Committee on Banking Regulations and Supervisory Practices held at the BIS on 28th-29th October 1976," BISA,

Banking Supervision: Informal Records, BS/77/1, 02/75–06/77; "Cost to International Banks of Supervision and Regulation: Maintenance of Reserve and Capital Ratios," BISA, BS/79/49, 1979/10.

7. QUOTAS AND CONCUBINES

1. The fuel efficiency of the average car on US roads was 14.3 miles per gallon in 1963, but only 13.3 miles per gallon in 1973. Total US gasoline consumption rose 58 percent over that period. In 1972, the last full year before the oil embargo reduced supplies, the average American purchased 785 gallons of gasoline. Assuming an average tank capacity of around 18 gallons and an average purchase per gas station visit of sixteen gallons, the average vehicle owner would have purchased gasoline forty-nine times per year. See US Energy Information Administration, *Annual Energy Review 1995* (Washington, DC, 1996), tables 2.15 and 5.12b. See also US Environmental Protection Agency, *Factors Affecting Automotive Fuel Economy* (Washington, DC, 1976).

2. Quotations are from Philip Shabecoff, "The Simon Years at the Treasury," *New York Times,* November 7, 1976.

3. The quotation comes from Simon's congressional testimony in May 1973. See "Nixon's Decisive New Energy Czar," *Time,* December 10, 1973.

4. William E. Simon, *A Time for Truth* (New York: Reader's Digest Press, 1978), 51.

5. Richard L. Strout, "Gas Vote Near in Tense Senate," *Christian Science Monitor,* February 6, 1956; American Enterprise Institute, "Natural Gas Deregulation Legislation," December 28, 1973, 10–11, 27.

6. Ronald R. Braeutigam and R. Glenn Hubbard, "Natural Gas: The Regulatory Transition," in Leonard W. Weiss and Michael W. Klass, eds., *Regulatory Reform: What Actually Happened* (Boston: Little, Brown, 1986), 141.

7. I. C. Bupp, "The New Natural Gas Business," in I. C. Bupp, ed., *U.S. Natural Gas After Deregulation: A New Business* (Cambridge, MA: Cambridge Energy Research Associates, 1985), 9, 143; Federal Energy Administration, "The Natural Gas Shortage: A Preliminary Report," August 1975, 3–5 and fig. 2; "Your Gas Bill and the Shortage," *Washington Post,* December 23, 1972; Patricia E. Starratt, "We're Running Out of Gas Needlessly," *Reader's Digest* (April 1973).

8. R. O. Kellam, "Regulation of Oil Imports," *Duke Law Journal* 10, no. 2 (1961): 177–187; Kenneth W. Dam, "Implementation of Import Quotas: The Case of Oil," *Journal of Law and Economics* 14 (1971): 1–60; Executive Order No. 10761, in *Federal Register* 23 (1958): 2067.

9. Interview with Julius L. Katz by Charles Stuart Kennedy, May 12, 1995, Association for Diplomatic Studies and Training Foreign Affairs Oral History Project, 43. The Brownsville Loop was eliminated after regulatory changes in 1971.

10. Cabinet Task Force on Oil Import Control, *The Oil Import Question* (Washington, DC: USGPO, 1970), 19; US Treasury, Office of Economic Stabilization,

Historical Working Papers on the Economic Stabilization Program Vol. 2 (Washington, DC: USGPO, 1974), 1237.

11. Martha Derthick and Paul J. Quirk, *The Politics of Deregulation* (Washington, DC: Brookings Institution, 1985), 36. There are many other explanations for the onset of deregulation. See Kim Phillips-Fein, *Invisible Hands: The Making of the Conservative Movement from the New Deal to Reagan* (New York: Norton, 2009). Phillips-Fein sees deregulation as part of a conservative counterthrust against the social-democratic consensus that reigned in the years after World War II. See also Meg Jacobs, *Panic at the Pump: The Energy Crisis and the Transformation of American Politics in the 1970s* (New York: Hill and Wang, 2016), 26–27. Jacobs suggests that the high cost of meeting new environmental requirements and drilling offshore was cited by the energy industry and the US Chamber of Commerce in calls for oil and gas price deregulation well before the 1973 oil crisis. Paul W. MacAvoy and George C. Eads, among others, contend that rapid technological advances and changes in relative prices led regulated industries to seek deregulation. The present author has emphasized the unwillingness of customers to accept the consequences of regulation as a cause of change. See Marc Levinson, "Evasion as a Driving Force in U.S. Transport Deregulation," in *Regulation between Legal Norms and Economic Reality: Intentions, Effect, and Adaptation: The German and American Experiences* (Tübingen: Mohr Siebeck, 2012), 187–196. One matter that is not in doubt is the political irrelevance of deregulation before 1973. Between 1969 and 1972, the *New York Times* mentioned "deregulation" in only fifteen articles, roughly one every three months.

12. Executive Order 11723, June 13, 1973; Paul W. MacAvoy and Robert S. Pindyck, "Alternative Regulatory Policies for Dealing with the Natural Gas Shortage," *Bell Journal of Economics* 4 (1973): 454–457; R. Glenn Hubbard, "Petroleum Regulation and Public Policy," in Weiss and Klass, eds., *Regulatory Reform*, 113. The most widely debated energy bill in the spring and summer of 1973 was S. 2506. The Emergency Petroleum Allocation Act was enacted as Public Law 93-159.

13. Simon, *A Time for Truth*, 3, 51.

14. William Robbins, "Simon Pledges Northeast Equitable Treatment in Oil," *New York Times*, January 29, 1974. The vetoed bill was the National Energy Petroleum Act, S. 2589. Jack Anderson, "Nixon Insists on Deregulating Gas," *Washington Post*, March 18, 1974.

15. Exemplifying the perverse effects of regulation, although US oil drilling jumped by one-third in 1974 and the number of new gas wells was the highest ever recorded, US oil output was the smallest in eight years and natural gas production was the lowest since 1969. The owners of old wells, it seemed, saw no reason to sell their production at the below-market prices set by the government. US Energy Information Administration, "U.S. Crude Oil Developmental Wells Drilled," "U.S. Natural Gas Exploratory and Developmental Wells Drilled," "U.S. Field Production of Crude Oil," and "U.S. Natural Gas Gross Withdrawals," all on the agency's website, www.eia.gov. See also Edward Cowan, "Oil Hangup—The Split-Price Rule," *New York Times*, September 22, 1974.

16. Regarding concerns about the possible price effects of deregulation, see US House of Representatives, Committee on Interstate and Foreign Commerce, Subcommittee on Energy and Power, *An Economic Analysis of New Gas Deregulation* (Washington, DC: USGPO, 1976. The first major step toward energy deregulation came in the Energy Policy and Conservation Act of 1975, which created the first fuel economy standards for automobiles, established a strategic petroleum reserve, and, in a clause buried deep in the text to avoid public attention, authorized the president to raise the maximum price of old oil under various circumstances. The law gradually brought US prices closer to those on the world market through the late 1970s. A second step was the National Gas Policy Act of 1978, which lifted price controls on some gas in 1979 and other gas in 1985 or 1987, but left some "old gas" under control indefinitely. For good measure, that law also gave the president authority to allocate supplies among gas users—just in case partial deregulation failed to lead to production of more gas. On the politics behind the law, see Jacobs, *Panic at the Pump,* 161–190.

17. "Simon Urges Removal of Energy Restraints," *Chicago Tribune,* September 11, 1974; "Simon Urges Steps to End Price Curbs on Oil, Natural Gas," *Los Angeles Times,* September 11, 1974; President Gerald R. Ford's Address to a Joint Session of Congress on the Economy, October 8, 1974, Gerald R. Ford Presidential Library & Museum, NARA.

18. Daryl Lembke, "Simon Sees Peril in Big Government," *Los Angeles Times,* March 1, 1975; William E. Simon, "Game Plan for a Sound Economy," *Chicago Tribune,* March 19, 1975.

19. US Senate, Judiciary Committee, Subcommittee on Administrative Practice and Procedures, *Oversight of Civil Aeronautics Board Practices and Procedures*, vol. 2, February 6–March 21, 1975 (Washington, DC: USGPO, 1075), 1315; Marc Levinson, "Two Cheers for Discrimination: Deregulation and Efficiency in the Reform of U.S. Freight Transportation, 1976–1998," *Enterprise and Society* 10 (2009): 178–215; "Airlines Urge Simon to Impose Price Curbs on Jet Aviation Fuel," *Wall Street Journal,* January 9, 1974.

20. On Kahn, see Thomas K. McCraw, *Prophets of Regulation: Charles Frances Adams, Louis D. Brandeis, James M. Landis, Alfred E. Kahn* (Cambridge, MA: Harvard University Press, 1986). The laws included the Railway Revitalization and Regulatory Reform Act of 1976 (P.L. 94–201), the Air Cargo Deregulation Act of 1977 (P.L. 95–163), the Airline Deregulation Act of 1978 (P.L. 95–504), the Motor Carrier Regulatory Reform and Modernization Act of 1980 (P.L. 92–296), the Staggers Rail Act of 1980 (P.L. 96–448), the Household Goods Transportation Act of 1980 (P.L. 96–454), the Bus Regulatory Reform Act of 1982 (P.L. 97–261), and the Shipping Act of 1984 (P.L. 98–237).

21. On US interest rate deregulation, enacted in the Depository Institutions Deregulation and Monetary Control Act of 1980, see Greta R. Krippner, *Capitalizing on Crisis: The Political Origins of the Rise of Finance* (Cambridge, MA: Harvard University Press, 2011), 58–85.

22. Peter T. Kilborn, "Money Isn't Everything in Greyhound Strike," *New York Times,* April 9, 1990; Gautam Naik, "U.K. Telecom Deregulation Delivers Nice Surprise: Jobs," *Wall Street Journal,* March 5, 1998.

8. THE EXPORT MACHINE

1. Yoshikuni Igarashi, *Narratives of War in Postwar Japanese Culture, 1945–1970* (Princeton, NJ: Princeton University Press, 2000), 201. See also Jayson Makoto Chun, *A Nation of a Hundred Million Idiots: A Social History of Japanese Television, 1953–1973* (New York: Routledge, 2007), 291. Photos of panic buying from *Asahi Shimbun,* November 1, 1973, at http://ajw.asahi.com/reliving_the_past/leaf/AJ2011110116049, viewed December 16, 2014.

2. Employment data are from US Department of Labor, "Comparative Civilian Labor Force Statistics, 10 Countries, 1960–2004," May 13, 2005. Dale Jorgenson and Masahiro Kuroda estimated that capital investment accounted for 60 percent of economic growth in Japan during the 1960s; see their chapter, "Productivity and International Competitiveness in Japan and the United States, 1960–1985," in Charles R. Hulten, ed., *Productivity Growth in Japan and the United States* (Chicago: University of Chicago Press, 1991), 50. Estimates of Japanese productivity growth and real output per hour are from the Conference Board's Total Economy Database, at http://www .conference-board.org/data/economydatabase/. Figures in OECD *Historical Statistics* are similar. Kazutoshi Koshiro, "Lifetime Employment in Japan: Three Models of the Concept," *Monthly Labor Review* (August 1984): 34–35. Koshiro reported that the lifetime employment system in large companies began around 1910, but it was only after 1955 that employers began hiring recent graduates with the implicit promise that they could remain with the firm until retirement.

3. Hugh Patrick, "Prospects for Longer-Run Productivity Growth in Japan," Economic Growth Center, Yale University, Discussion Paper No. 257, December 1976, 11; Edward F. Denison and William K. Chung, *How Japan's Economy Grew So Fast* (Washington, DC: Brookings Institution, 1976), 52, 54; M. Iyoda, *Postwar Japanese Economy* (New York: Springer, 2010), 20. For examples of purchases of foreign technology that reshaped Japan's textile industry, see Robert M. Uriu, *Troubled Industries: Confronting Economic Change in Japan* (Ithaca, NY: Cornell University Press, 1996), 151. There is a considerable literature debating the behavior of savings rates in Japan. See, for example, Fumio Hayashi, "Is Japan's Saving Rate High?" and Lawrence J. Christiano, "Understanding Japan's Saving Rate: The Reconstruction Hypothesis," both in *Federal Reserve Bank of Minneapolis Quarterly Review* 13, no. 2 (spring 1989), and Charles Yuji Horioka, "Why Is Japan's Saving Rate So High? A Literature Survey," *Journal of the Japanese and International Economies* 4 (1990): 49–92.

4. For data on capacity utilization, output by factory size, and number of food shops, see Ministry of International Trade and Industry, *Statistics on Japanese Industries 1973,* 20, 26–27, 31, 47–49. In 1970, Japan had 30.3 million households; see

Statistics Bureau, Ministry of Internal Affairs and Communications, *Statistical Handbook of Japan 2014*, Table 2.3. Data on productivity change by industry are in Dale W. Jorgenson and Koji Nomura, "The Industry Origins of Japanese Economic Growth," National Bureau of Economic Research working paper 11800, November 2005, Table 19.

5. On the anxieties of economic planners, see Kozo Yamamura, "Joint Research and Antitrust: Japanese vs. American Strategies," in Hugh Patrick, ed., *Japan's High Technology Industries: Lessons and Limitations of Industrial Policy* (Seattle: University of Washington School of Business, 1986), 183. Figure on relative labor costs is from President's Council of Economic Advisers, *Economic Report of the President 1974* (Washington, DC, 1974), 192.

6. Ibid.

7. Bank of Japan, *Monthly Economic Review*, February 1974, 4; Fox Butterfield, "In Japan, Oil May Expose Ills of Growth," *New York Times,* January 6, 1974.

8. G. John Ikenberry, "The Irony of State Strength; Comparative Responses to Oil Shocks in the 1970s," *International Organization* 40 (1986): 113–116.

9. Marc Levinson, *The Box: How the Shipping Container Made the World Smaller and the World Economy Bigger* (Princeton, NJ: Princeton University Press, 2006), 186–188. Japan ended 1968 with a trade deficit of $16 million, and had a surplus of nearly $1 billion in 1969; see Ministry of Finance, Customs and Tariff Bureau, http://www.customs.go.jp/toukei/suii/html/nenbet_e.htm.

10. I. M. Destler, Haruhiro Fukui, and Hideo Sato, *The Textile Wrangle: Conflict in Japanese-American Relations, 1969–1971* (Ithaca, NY: Cornell University Press, 1979), 66; Henry Kissinger, *White House Years* (Boston: Little, Brown, 1979), 336. The Japan–US Memorandum of Understanding was signed January 3, 1972; see "Agreement on Wool and Man-made Fibers," in US Department of State, *United States Treaties and Other International Acts*, vol. 23, part 3 (Washington, DC: USGPO, 1972), 3167.

11. Japan Industrial Structure Council, *Japan in World Economy* (Tokyo, 1972), 48–50.

12. Nakamura, *Postwar Japanese Economy*, 224; Konosuke Odaka, "Are We at the Verge of a Stagnant Society?" in Hisao Kanamori, ed., "Recent Developments of Japanese Economy and Its Differences from Western Advanced Economies," center paper 29, Japan Economic Research Center, September 1976, 33.

13. Chiaki Moriguchi and Horishi Ono, "Japanese Lifetime Employment: A Century's Perspective," in Magnus Blomström and Sumner La Croix, eds., *Institutional Change in Japan: Why It Happens and Why It Doesn't* (London: Routledge, 2006), 152–176; Uriu, *Troubled Industries*, 191–209. The shipbuilding industry accounted for 1.2 percent of Japan's economic output in 1975; its share slid to 0.2 percent by 1986. See OECD Council Working Party on Shipbuilding, "Peer Review of Japanese Government Support Measures to the Shipbuilding Sector," C/WP6 (2012) 26, 7.

14. Yoshimitsu Imuta, "Transition to a Floating Exchange Rate," in Mikiyo Sumiya, ed., *A History of Japanese Trade and Industry Policy* (Oxford: Oxford University Press,

2000), 528; Sueo Sekiguchi, "Japan: A Plethora of Programs," in Hugh Patrick, ed., *Pacific Basin Industries in Distress* (New York: Columbia University Press, 1990), 437.

15. William Diebold Jr., *Industrial Policy as an International Issue* (New York: McGraw-Hill, 1980), 162; Japan Automobile Manufacturers Association, *Motor Vehicle Statistics of Japan 2014*, 16, 32.

16. Imuta, "Transition to a Floating Exchange Rate," 527. Data on Japanese R&D spending are from Steven Englander and Axel Mittelstädt, "Total Factor Productivity: Macroeconomic and Structural Aspects of the Slowdown," *OECD Economic Survey* 10 (1988): 36.

17. Dale W. Jorgenson and Masahiro Kuroda, "Productivity and International Competitiveness in Japan and the United States, 1960–1985," in Hulten, ed., *Productivity Growth in Japan and the United States*, 45.

18. The term "deindustrialization" was popularized by Barry Bluestone and Bennett Harrison, *The Deindustrialization of America* (New York: Basic Books, 1982).

19. James Chan Lee and Helen Sutch, "Profits and Rates of Return in OECD Countries," OECD Economics and Statistics Department, working paper 20, 1985.

20. See US International Trade Commission, *Bolts, Nuts, and Screws of Iron and Steel* (Washington, DC, 1975). It is noteworthy that none of the law's proponents identified improving productivity as one of its purposes. See, for example, House of Representatives, Committee on Ways and Means, *Prepared Statements of Administration Witnesses, Submitted to the Committee on Ways and Means at Public Hearings Beginning on May 9, 1973* (Washington, DC: USGPO, 1973).

21. US International Trade Commission, *Bolts, Nuts, and Large Screws of Iron and Steel* (Washington, DC, 1977); Jimmy Carter, "American Bolt, Nut, and Large Screw Industry Memorandum from the President," February 10, 1978.

22. Jimmy Carter, "American Bolt, Nut, and Large Screw Industry Memorandum from the President," December 22, 1978; "Proclamation 4632–Temporary Duty Increase on the Importation into the United States of Certain Bolts, Nuts, and Screws of Iron or Steel," January 4, 1979; US Department of Commerce, International Trade Administration, "An Economic Assessment of the United States Industrial Fastener Industry (1979 to 1986)," March 1987; Gary Clyde Hufbauer and Howard Rosen, *Trade Policy for Troubled Industries* (Washington, DC: Institute for International Economics, 1986), 20.

23. Hufbauer and Rosen, *Trade Policy for Troubled Industries*, 23. Hufbauer and Rosen identify twenty-three examples of "special protection" affecting the manufacturing sector during the 1970s and early 1980s. This does not count industries that successfully claimed to be suffering from imports that were being subsidized or sold in the US market below cost. See also W. Carl Biven, *Jimmy Carter's Economy: Policy in an Age of Limits* (Chapel Hill, NC: University of North Carolina Press, 2002), 228–234.

24. See Étienne Davignon, interview with Étienne Deschamps, Brussels, January 14, 2008, Centre virtuel de la connaissance sur l'Europe, at www.cvce.eu.

25. See Laurent Warlouzet, "The Golden Age of EEC Industrial Policy: Managing the Decline of Steel from 1977 to 1984," and Christian Marx, "A European Structural Crisis Cartel as a Solution to Structural Depression?," both presented at a conference on "The Practices of Structural Policy in Western Market Economies Since the 1960s," Zentrum für Zeitgeschichte, Potsdam, May 28–29, 2015; Götz Albert, *Wettbewerbsfähigkeit und Krise der deutschen Schiffbauindustrie 1945–1990* (Frankfurt am Main: P. Lang, 1998), 200–201; Lars C. Bruno and Stig Tenold, "The Basis for South Korea's Ascent in the Shipbuilding Industry," *Mariner's Mirror* 97 (2011): 201–217.

26. Jimmy Carter, "Remarks on Signing into Law H.R. 5680, the Chrysler Corporation Loan Guarantee Act of 1979," January 7, 1980. For detail on the Canadian auto industry during this period, see Michel Côté, "The Canadian Auto Industry, 1978–1986," *Perspectives on Labor and Income* 1 (Autumn 1989).

27. Stephen D. Cohen, "The Route to Japan's Voluntary Export Restraints on Automobiles," working paper no. 20, National Security Archive, 1997; US International Trade Commission, *A Review of Recent Developments in the U.S. Automobile Industry Including an Assessment of the Japanese Voluntary Restraint Agreements* (Washington, DC, 1985), 4–11. The Reagan quote appeared in Richard J. Cattani, "Carter, Reagan Cast for Votes Among Blacks, Auto Workers," *Christian Science Monitor*, September 3, 1980.

28. Shailendra J. Anjaria, Naheed Kirmani, and Arne B. Petersen, *Trade Policy Issues and Developments*, International Monetary Fund occasional paper no. 38 (Washington, DC, 1985), 47. The International Trade Commission estimated that Japan sold one million fewer cars in the United States in 1984 than it would have sold without the restraints, but received an average of 17 percent more for each vehicle sold—a transfer of $3.3 billion from US consumers to Japan. The commission estimated that domestic automakers took in an additional $5.2 billion from price rises made possible by the higher prices of Japanese-made vehicles. The average pay of an autoworker in the first half of 1984 was $15.33 per hour, or roughly $32,000 per year. See *A Review of Recent Developments in the U.S. Automobile Industry*, 10, 41. Estimates of the cost per job saved in Canada ranged from C$200,000 to over C$1 million in 1985, equivalent to approximately US$145,000 to $730,000. See Margaret Kelly, Naheed Kirmani, Clemens Boonekamp, Miranda Xafa, and Peter Winglee, *Issues and Developments in International Trade Policy*, International Monetary Fund occasional paper no. 63 (Washington, DC, 1988), 79.

29. Kelly, Kirmani, Boonekamp, Xafa, and Winglee, *Issues and Development in International Trade Policy*, 41. The authors estimate that the Japanese manufacturers' increased revenue from US sales was $6.1 billion between 1981 and 1984. As this revenue was obtained by making and selling fewer cars, the increase in profitability must have been larger. Japanese manufacturers would have reaped additional profits because of the restraints on exports to Canada.

30. National Science Foundation, *National Patterns of R&D Resources: 1994* (Washington, DC, 1995), Table 3; Zvi Griliches, Ariel Pakes, and Bronwyn H. Hall, "The

Value of Patents as Indicators of Inventive Activity," working paper no. 2083, National Bureau of Economic Research, 1986, Table 2. The average age of equipment in the primary metals sector was ten years in the mid-1970s and reached 11.8 years in 1985. Allan Collard-Wexler and Jan De Loecker, "Reallocation and Technology: Evidence from the U.S. Steel Industry," NBER working paper 18739, January 2013. The authors show that much of the industry's productivity increase following the introduction of electric arc furnaces came from the closure of antiquated facilities.

9. THE END OF THE DREAM

1. *National Income 1929–32: Letter from the Acting Secretary of Commerce Transmitting in Response to Senate Resolution No. 220 (72nd Congress) a Report on National Income, 1929–32* (Washington, DC, 1934), 7. Gross national product was for many years the most widely followed measure of economies' size. It has largely been supplanted by gross domestic product, a measure that excludes net income from foreign sources.

2. Simon Kuznets, "Economic Growth and Income Inequality," *American Economic Review* 45 (1955): 1–28. Kuznets acknowledged that his findings pertained to the economies of Europe, North America, and Japan, and that the distribution of income in "underdeveloped" countries might not even out in the same way.

3. The data on income distribution in this paragraph are taken from Anthony B. Atkinson and Salvatore Morelli, "Chartbook of Economic Inequality," at www.chartbookofeconomicinequality.com, accessed January 8, 2014. The other countries for which Atkinson and Morelli provide relevant data for the 1950s and 1960s are Australia, Canada, Finland, France, Great Britain, Japan, New Zealand, Norway, South Africa, Sweden, and the United States. In Japan, the Gini coefficient, a measure that would equal 0 if each household had an equal share of the nation's income and 1 if all income belonged to a single household, fell from around 0.3 before the war to 0.04 in 1953, indicating a very high degree of equality. See T. Mizoguchi, "Long-run Fluctuations in Income Distribution in Japan," *Economic Review* 37 (1986): 152–158, cited in Toshiaki Tachibanaki, *Confronting Income Inequality in Japan* (Cambridge, MA: MIT Press, 2005), 59.

4. Facundo Alvaredo, Anthony B. Atkinson, Thomas Piketty, and Emmanuel Saez, "The Top 1% in International and Historical Perspective," *Journal of Economic Perspectives* 27 (2013): 7; Richard T. Griffiths, "Economic Growth and Overfull Employment in Western Europe," in Richard T. Griffiths and Toshiaki Tachibanaki, eds., *From Austerity to Affluence: The Transformation of the Socio-Economic Structure of Western Europe and Japan* (New York: St. Martin's Press, 2000), 68–72; Takenori Inoki, "From Rapid Growth to the End of Full Employment in Japan," in Griffiths and Tachibanaki, eds., *From Austerity to Affluence*, 87.

5. Thomas Piketty, *Capital in the Twenty-First Century* (Cambridge, MA: Harvard University Press, 2014).

6. Carmen DeNavas-Walt, Bernadette D. Proctor, and Jessica C. Smith, *Income, Poverty, and Health Insurance Coverage in the United States: 2012*, US Census Bureau, Current Population Reports, P60–245 (September 2013), Table A-4; Atkinson and Morelli, "Chartbook of Economic Inequality." In the United States, the Gini coefficient of household gross income reached its lowest level in 1974.

7. Alissa Goodman and Steven Webb, "For Richer, for Poorer: The Changing Distribution of Income in the United Kingdom, 1961–91," Institute for Fiscal Studies, 1994, 15–17, 40, 56–60; Mike Brewer, Alastair Muriel, and Liam Wren-Lewis, "Accounting for Changes in Inequality Since 1968: Decomposition Analyses for Great Britain," Institute for Fiscal Studies, 2009; UK Office for National Statistics, "Middle-Income Households, 1977–2011/12," December 2, 2013; A. B. Atkinson, "Bringing Income in from the Cold," *Economic Journal* 107 (1997): 297–312. See also Gregory Clark, "What Were the British Earnings and Prices Then? (New Series)" Measuring-Worth, 2015, at http://www.measuringworth.com/ukearncpi/.

8. Bruce Western and Kieran Healy, "Explaining the OECD Wage Slowdown: Recession or Labour Decline?" *European Sociological Review* 15 (1999): 234.

9. Data on the labor share for six large economies from 1960 are reported in the German council of economic advisors (Sachverständigenrat), *Jahresgutachten 2012/13*, 318–341; very similar figures for the period from 1975 onward are reported by Loukas Karabarbounis and Brent Neiman, "The Global Decline of the Labor Share," *Quarterly Journal of Economics* 129 (2014): 61–103. There is a considerable literature exploring the meaning of the decline. See, for example, Roberto Torrini, "Labour, profit and housing rent shares in Italian GDP: long-run trends and recent patterns," Banca d'Italia occasional paper 318, March 2016, and Benjamin Bridgman, "Is Labor's Loss Capital's Gain? Gross Versus Net Labor Shares," working paper, US Bureau of Economic Analysis, October 2014. Bridgman asserts that the fall in the labor share is much lower than widely believed because economists' models misstate depreciation.

10. Some evidence on this point, for a later time period, appears in Martin Adler and Kai Daniel Schmid, "Factor Shares and Income Inequality—Empirical Evidence from Germany 2002–2008," discussion paper 82, Institut für Angewandte Wirtschaftsforschung, University of Tübingen, May 2012.

11. Urban Lunberg and Klas Åmark, "Social Rights and Social Security: The Swedish Welfare State, 1900–2000," *Scandinavian Journal of History* 26 (2001): 161.

12. Leif Hannes-Olsen, "Children's Allowances: Their Size and Structure in Five Countries," *Social Security Bulletin* (May 1972): 17–28; Matti Alestalo, Sven E. O. Hort, and Stein Kuhnle, "The Nordic Model: Conditions, Origins, Outcomes, Lessons," working paper 41, Hertie School of Governance, Berlin (2009).

13. OECD, *Historical Statistics 1960–88* (Paris: OECD, 1990), 67.

14. On Japan, see Toshiaki Tachibanaki, "Japan Was Not a Welfare State, But . . . " in Griffiths and Tachibanaki, eds., *From Austerity to Affluence*, 203.

15. Tax receipts as a share of US national income are taken from www.usgovernment revenue.com, viewed February 15, 2015. Rates are from Tax Foundation, "U.S.

Individual Income Tax Rates History," October 17, 2013. Jacob Fisher, "Earners and Dependents in Urban Families in Relation to Family Income," *Social Security Bulletin* 10, no. 4 (April 1947): 14; US Treasury Department, Internal Revenue Service, "Instructions for Form 1040A, United States Individual Income Tax Return, 1939."

16. B. E. V. Sabine, *A History of Income Tax* (London: Allen & Unwin, 1966), 196; Charlotte Twight, "Evolution of Federal Income Tax Withholding: The Machinery of Institutional Change," *Cato Journal* 14 (1995): 371.

17. On Japan, see Chiaki Moriguchi and Emmanuel Saez, "The Evolution of Income Concentration in Japan, 1885–2002: Evidence from Income Tax Statistics," *Review of Economics and Statistics* 90 (2005): 713–734. On Great Britain, see Tom Clark and Andrew Dilmont, "Long-term Trends in British Taxation and Spending," Institute of Fiscal Studies briefing note 25 (2002). In the United States, the median earned income of families with two children in 1951 was $3,270. The federal income tax on that amount would have been $112. Calculated from US Census Bureau, Current Population Reports, "Consumer Income," Series P-60, no. 10, September 26, 1952, and Internal Revenue Service, "U.S. Individual Income Tax Return for Calendar Year 1951, Form 1040." On Canada, see Roger S. Smith, "The Personal Income Tax: Average and Marginal Rates in the Post-War Period," *Canadian Tax Journal* 43 (1995): 1059, 1065. On Germany, see Giacomo Corneo, "The Rise and Likely Fall of the German Income Tax, 1958–2005," *CESifo Economic Studies* 51 (2005): 159–186.

18. On the appeal of social spending to economic planners, see Hans-Peter Ullmann, "Im 'Strudel der Maßlosigkeit'? Die 'Erweiterung des Staatskorridors' in der Bundesrepublik der sechziger bis achtziger Jahre," *Geschichte und Gesellschaft* 22 (2006): 255–263, and Werner Ehrlicher, "Deutsche Finanzpolitik seit 1945," *VSWG: Vierteljahrschrift für Sozial-und Wirtschaftsgeschichte* 81 (1994): 10–19.

19. On the changes in Italy, see Daniele Franco, "A Never-Ending Pension Reform," in Martin Feldstein and Horst Siebert, eds., *Social Security Pension Reform in Europe* (Chicago: University of Chicago Press, 2002), 213–214.

20. Data on food stamps from US Department of Agriculture Food and Nutrition Service, at www.fns.usda.gov/sites/default/files/pd/SNAPsummary.pdf, viewed June 1, 2015.

21. The average retirement age for women in the OECD countries fell from 63.4 years in 1970 to 61.4 in 1980; the average retirement age for men in OECD countries dropped from 65 years to 63.3 during the same time period. OECD, "The Retirement Decision in OECD Countries," Ageing working paper 1.4 (2000); Bo Strath, "The Politics of Collective Consumption in Europe," in Griffiths and Tachibanaki, eds., *From Austerity to Affluence*, 178–185.

22. OECD dataset, "Tax revenue as % of GDP," stats.oecd.org, viewed February 9, 2015. The 1977 figure for Iceland has been interpolated, as that country did not report annual data.

23. Deborah Mitchell, "Taxation and Income Distribution: The 'Tax Revolt' of the 1980s Revisited," Public Policy Program working paper 36, Australian National

University, September 1993, 33–34, at https://digitalcollections.anu.edu.au/bitstream /1885/7301/1/Mitchell_Taxation1993.pdf; Hiromitsu Ishi, *The Japanese Tax System*, 3rd ed. (Oxford: Oxford University Press, 2001), 82.

24. Gebhard Kirchgässner, "Die Entwicklung der Einkommensteuerprogression in der Bundessrepublik Deutschland," *FinanzArchiv*, new series, 43 (1985): 333; Deborah Mitchell, "Taxation and Income Distribution," 18; Peter Jenkins, *Mrs. Thatcher's Revolution* (Cambridge, MA: Harvard University Press, 1988), 9; Smith, "The Personal Income Tax."

25. OECD, "Tax on Personal Income, Total, % of GDP," and "Social Security Contributions, Total, % of GDP," stats.oecd.org, viewed February 9, 2015.

26. President's Council of Economic Advisers, *Economic Report of the President* (Washington, DC, 1995), 366–367; Ishi, *The Japanese Tax System*, 51.

27. National debt measures were taken from the International Monetary Fund Public Debt Database, http://www.imf.org/en/Data#data.

28. Isaac William Martin, *The Permanent Tax Revolt* (Stanford, CA: Stanford University Press, 2008), 52–55. Martin points out that attacks on property taxes in the United States in the 1960s came from both ends of the political spectrum.

29. Jørgen Goul Andersen and Tor Bjørklund, "Structural Changes and New Cleavages: The Progress Parties in Denmark and Norway," *Acta Sociologica* 33 (1990): 195–217; Lars Nørby Johansen, "Denmark," in Peter Flora, ed., *Growth to Limits: The Western European Welfare States Since World War II, Vol. 1* (Berlin: W. de Gruyter, 1986), 351–352; Malcolm Rutherford, "Burning Tax Records," *Financial Times*, April 6, 1973; Hilary Barnes, "Backlash against welfare," *Financial Times*, November 8, 1974.

30. Johansen, "Denmark," 368; Confidential memorandum, US Embassy in Copenhagen to Secretary of State, COPENH 00349 01 OF 02 071311Z, February 7, 1975, NARA, RG 59, Central Foreign Policy Files, Electronic Telegrams, at http://aad .archives.gov/aad/.

31. Christopher Warman, "Conservatives accused of making local government 'fall guys' as part of election preparation," *The Times* (London), January 14, 1974. Thatcher first attacked rates in a parliamentary debate on June 27, 1974; see Hansard, *House of Commons Debates*, June 27, 1974, vol. 875, 1750. The text of her August 28, 1974, broadcast on the BBC can be found at http://www.margaretthatcher.org/document /102391.

32. Andersen and Bjørklund, "Structural Changes," 203.

10. THE RIGHT TURN

1. Michael J. Crozier, Samuel P. Huntington, and Joji Watanuki, *The Crisis of Democracy: Report on the Governability of Democracies to the Trilateral Commission* (New York: New York University Press, 1975), 166.

2. US crime data from the Federal Bureau of Investigation, Uniform Crime Reporting Statistics, http://www.ucrdatatool.gov.

3. James Sterngold, "Kakuei Tanaka, 75, Ex-Premier and Political Force in Japan, Dies," *New York Times*, December 17, 1993.

4. Suzanne Berger, "Politics and Antipolitics in Western Europe in the Seventies," *Daedalus* 108 (1979): 27–50.

5. Samuel Brittan, "The Economic Contradictions of Democracy," *British Journal of Political Science* 5 (1975): 156–158.

6. Mancur Olson, *The Rise and Decline of Nations* (New Haven, CT: Yale University Press), 47, 74, 181–237.

7. Sir Keith Joseph, "This Is Not the Time to Be Mealy-mouthed: Intervention Is Destroying Us," speech at Upminster, June 22, 1974, at www.margaretthatcher.org /archive/displaydocument.asp?docid=110604. See also Hugo Young, *The Iron Lady* (New York: Farrar, Straus & Giroux, 1989), 85; Armin Schäfer, "Krisentheorien der Demokratie: Unregierbarkeit, Spätkapitalismus und Postdemokratie," *Der Moderne Staat* 2, no. 1 (2009): 159–183. On Brandt's purported prediction, see Crozier et al., *The Crisis of Democracy*, 2.

8. Angus Maddison, *Historical Statistics of the World Economy: 1–2008 AD*, www .ggdc.net/maddison/Historical_Statistics/horizontal-file_02-2010.xls, viewed May 8, 2016.

9. Judd Stitziel, *Fashioning Socialism* (Oxford: Berg, 2005); Eichengreen, *European Economy Since 1945*, 131–162.

10. "Memorandum Prepared by the Office of Current Intelligence of the Central Intelligence Agency, Washington, August 13, 1974," *FRUS 1969–1976*, vol. E-15, part 1, document 11, and "Memorandum of Conversation," December 4, 1973, ibid., document 28.

11. The original source of the Schmidt quote is unknown. In a subsequent interview, he commented, "I spoke that sentence just once, and it's been cited a thousand times. Once would have been enough." See "Verstehen Sie das, Herr Schmidt?" *Die Zeit*, March 4, 2010.

12. I have used the translation of Lennart Bilén. Roger Choate, "Ingmar Bergman Tax Ordeal Swings Swedes Against Government," *The Times* (London), May 10, 1976; William Dullforce, "Strong Swing Against the Government in Sweden," *Financial Times*, May 11, 1976; William Dullforce, "Have Swedish Taxes Reached Saturation Point?" *Financial Times*, May 21, 1976.

13. "Bergman says farewell to Sweden," *The Times* (London), April 23, 1976; William Dullforce, "Ingmar Bergman Goes into Tax Exile," *Financial Times*, April 23, 1976; Birgitta Steen, *Ingmar Bergman: A Reference Guide* (Amsterdam: Amsterdam University Press, 2005), 956.

14. Sven Olson, "Sweden," in Flora, ed., *Growth to Limits*, vol. 1, 15.

15. Olof Petersson, "The 1976 Election: New Trends in the Swedish Electorate," *Scandinavian Political Studies* 1 (New series, 1978): 109–121; "Modell in Gefahr," *Der Spiegel*, September 13, 1976; Gerard Caprio, "The Swedish Economy in the 1970's: The Lessons of Accommodative Policies," Federal Reserve Board international finance discussion paper 205, April 1982.

16. Labour Party Manifesto, February 1974; Sandbrook, *State of Emergency,* 611–645.

17. David McKie, "Lord Callaghan," *The Guardian,* March 28, 2005; "Lord Callaghan of Cardiff," *The Telegraph,* March 28, 2005; Peter Jenkins, *Mrs. Thatcher's Revolution* (Cambridge, MA: Harvard University Press, 1988), 24.

18. Graffiti cited in Andy Beckett, "The Most Powerful Man in 70s Britain," *The Guardian,* April 22, 2009.

19. Prime Minister James Callaghan speech to Labour Party Conference, Blackpool, September 1976, http://www.britishpoliticalspeech.org/speech-archive.htm?speech =174; October 1974 Labour Party Manifesto, http://www.labourmanifesto.com/1974 /oct/.

20. Joel Krieger, *Reagan, Thatcher, and the Politics of Decline* (New York: Oxford University Press, 1986), 9.

21. Andy Beckett, *When the Lights Went Out: Britain in the Seventies* (London: Faber, 2009), 486.

22. Margaret Thatcher, "Party Election Broadcast," April 30, 1979, Margaret Thatcher Foundation Archives (MTFA), document 104055. On fears about Britain's long-term decline, see Jenkins, *Mrs. Thatcher's Revolution,* 30–49. The Callaghan quotation circulates in several variants, none authoritative.

23. For example, see Daniel Yergin and Joseph Stanislaw, *The Commanding Heights: The Battle Between Government and the Marketplace* (New York: Simon & Schuster, 1998).

24. US Energy Information Administration, *Monthly Energy Review,* February 2015, Tables 9.1 and 9.4.

25. Stacy L. Schreft, "Credit Controls: 1980," in Federal Reserve Bank of Richmond, *Economic Review* (November–December 1990): 25–55.

26. Phillips-Fein, *Invisible Hands*; Hugh Heclo and Rudolph Penner, "Fiscal and Political Strategy in the Reagan Administration," in Fred I. Greenstein, ed., *The Reagan Presidency: An Early Assessment* (Baltimore: Johns Hopkins University Press, 1983).

27. Transcript of presidential debate between Ronald Reagan and Jimmy Carter, Cleveland, Ohio, October 28, 1980, http://www.debates.org/index.php?page=october -28-1980-debate-transcript.

28. John Antcliffe, "40 Years Ago Today: Governor Reagan at the Royal Albert Hall," *Wall Street Journal,* November 5, 2009. Margaret Thatcher did not attend the speech at the Institute of Directors, but was told about it by her husband, who was present, and obtained a printed copy. See January 8, 1990, interview of Thatcher by Geoffrey Smith, MTFA, document 109324.

29. Bundesministerium für Wirtschaft, "Perspektiven des Wirtschaftswachstums in der Bundesrepublik Deutschland bis zum Jahre 1995," December 6, 1979, appendix Table 12, BA, B102/306599.

30. Yasuo Takao, "Welfare State Retrenchment—The Case of Japan," *Journal of Public Policy* 19 (1999): 265–266; Ellis S. Krauss, "Japan in 1983: Altering the Status

Quo?" *Asian Survey* 24 (1984): 89; James Elliott, "The 1981 Administrative Reform in Japan," *Asian Survey* 23 (1983): 765.

31. Martin Fackler, "Japan's Elder Statesman Is Silent No Longer," *New York Times,* January 29, 2010.

32. Toshiaki Tachibanaki, "Japan Was Not a Welfare State, But . . . " in Griffiths and Tachibanaki, *From Austerity to Affluence,* 205; Kumon Shumpei, "Japan Faces Its Future: The Political-Economics of Administrative Reform," *Journal of Japanese Studies* 10 (1984): 143–165.

11. THATCHER

1. Charles Goodhart, "The Conduct of Monetary Policy," *Economic Journal* 99 (1989): 296.

2. Milton Friedman, *A Program for Monetary Stability* (New York: Fordham University Press, 1959); Milton Friedman and Anna J. Schwartz, *A Monetary History of the United States* (Princeton, NJ: Princeton University Press, 1963); Friedman, "The Role of Monetary Policy," speech to the American Economic Association, Washington, DC, December 29, 1967, published in *American Economic Review* 58 (March 1968): 2–17.

3. The official was John Fforde, the Bank of England's chief cashier. See Duncan Needham, *UK Monetary Policy from Devaluation to Thatcher* (Basingstoke: Palgrave Macmillan, 2014), 34.

4. Friedman was by this time a well-known figure in the United Kingdom; see Edward Nelson, "Milton Friedman and U.K. Economic Policy: 1938–1979," working paper 2009–017A, Federal Reserve Bank of St. Louis, April 1979. The Conservative Party platforms appeared in the pamphlets "The Right Approach," October 4, 1976, MTFA, document 109439, and "The Right Approach to the Economy," October 8, 1977, MTFA, document 112551.

5. The Bank of England had used money-supply targets since the early 1970s, but this was announced publicly only in 1976. Even then the targets were rarely met, in good part because the government often wanted the Bank of England to use its control of short-term interest rates to support the pound sterling in the currency markets, making domestic inflation a secondary issue. See Needham, *UK Monetary Policy,* chaps. 2–4. Richardson staked out his views on monetary and exchange-rate policy in a secret letter to Howe on May 4, 1979, the day following the election, MTFA, document 113156. Quotation is from a document appended to that letter, "Problems of Monetary Control," April 30, 1979.

6. G. K. Shaw, "Fiscal Policy Under the First Thatcher Administration, 1979–1983," *FinanzArchiv/Public Finance Analysis,* New Series, 41 (1983): 321–322.

7. Nigel Lawson, *The View from Number 11* (New York: Doubleday, 1993), 50.

8. UK Treasury, *Financial Statement and Budget Report 1980/81* (London: H.M. Stationery Office, 1980), 19; letters, Karl Brunner to Thatcher, September 10, 1980, MTFA, document 115641; Allan Meltzer, Carnegie-Mellon University, to Thatcher,

October 7, 1980, MTFA, document 113291; and "Note of a meeting between the Prime Minister and foreign participants in a seminar on monetary base control: 1430 hours 30 September at 10 Downing Street," MTFA, document 113259; Charles Moore, *Margaret Thatcher* (New York: Knopf, 2013), 462. The unemployment figures cited here are based on internationally harmonized figures reported by the OECD and are lower than those reported in the United Kingdom at the time. For comparison, see James Denman and Paul McDonald, "Unemployment Statistics from 1881 to the Present Day," *Labour Market Trends* (January 1996): 5–18.

9. Thatcher's speech to the Conservative Party Conference, Brighton, October 10, 1980, is in MTFA, document 112637. On suspension of the target, see "Chancellor of the Exchequer Minute to the PM," November 14, 1980, MTFA, document 113302; Needham, *UK Monetary Policy*, 156–162.

10. *The Sun*, September 30, 1983, quoted in Nelson, "Milton Friedman and U.K. Economic Policy," 66.

11. Letter, D. K. Britto, Conservative Research Department, to Derek Howe, March 24, 1981, MTFA, document 114281; Lawson, *The View from Number 11*, 98.

12. The transcript of the 1982 budget speech is in MTFA, document 111447.

13. "Trends in Manufacturing Productivity and Labor Costs in the U.S. and Abroad," *Monthly Labor Review* (December 1987); OECD, *Historical Statistics 1960–1990* (Paris 2001), 73.

14. Michael Heseltine, "Drake and Scull Holdings Ltd. (DSH)," Ministerial Committee on Economic Strategy Sub-committee on Disposal of Public Sector Assets," July 17, 1979, CAB 134/4339, MTFA, document 116489.

15. David Parker, *The Official History of Privatisation, Vol. 1: The Formative Years 1970–1987* (Abingdon, UK: Routledge, 2009), 15–17.

16. Edward Heath, *The Course of My Life: My Autobiography* (London: Bloomsbury, 1998), cited in Parker, *The Official History of Privatisation*, 30.

17. "Final Report of the Nationalised Industries Policy Group," July 8, 1977, MTFA, document 110247.

18. Paul Pierson, *Dismantling the Welfare State* (New York: Cambridge University Press, 1994), 76.

19. U.K. Department of Communities and Local Government, Table 671, "Annual Right to Buy Sales for England," November 20, 2014; Patrick Cosgrave, *Thatcher: The First Term* (London: Bodley Head, 1985), 158.

20. On the origins of "privatization," see Germà Bel, "The Coining of 'Privatization' and Germany's National Socialist Party," *Journal of Economic Perspectives* 20 (2006): 187–194. Lawson, *The View from Number 11*, 22, 199–200. On the subcommittee, see Nigel Lawson, "Disposals in 1980/81," MTFA, document 116843; Ministerial Committee on Economic Strategy Sub-committee on Disposal of Public Sector Assets," July 17, 1979, MTFA, document 113709, and Minutes, Ministerial Committee on Economic Strategy, Sub-Committee on Disposal of Public Sector Assets, July 19, 1979, CAB 134/4339, MTFA, document 116821.

21. For the speech, see Lawson, *The View from Number 11*, 1039–1054; the quotation from Thatcher is at 140. See also John Burton, "Privatization: The Thatcher Case," *Managerial and Decision Economics* 8 (1987): 24.

22. "Brief for the Prime Minister: NUM Special Delegate Conference: 21 October 1983," PREM19/1329 f213, MTFA, document 133124.

23. UK Department of Energy & Climate Change, "Historical Coal Data: Coal Production, 1853 to 2013," July 31, 2014.

24. U.K. Treasury, "Implementing Privatisation: The U.K. Experience" (n.d.), 20.

25. Burton, "Privatization," 25–27; Robert Jupe, "The Privatisation of British Energy: Risk Transfer and the State," working paper 221, Kent Business School, 2010.

26. Stephen Martin and David Parker, "Privatization and Economic Performance Throughout the UK Business Cycle," *Managerial and Decision Economics* 16 (1995): 225–237.

27. Madsen Pirie, *Privatization* (Aldershot: Wildwood House, 1988), 4; Brian Towers, "Running the Gauntlet: British Trade Unions Under Thatcher, 1979–1988," *Industrial and Labor Relations Review* 42 (1989): 175–177.

28. Nigel Lawson budget speech, March 15, 1988, Hansard HC 129/993–1013.

29. "Production in Total Manufacturing for the United Kingdom" and "Registered Unemployment Level for the United Kingdom," both seasonally adjusted quarterly data, OECD Main Economic Indicators database, accessed May 10, 2015. See also Nigel M. Healey, "Fighting Inflation in Britain," *Challenge* 33 (1990): 38, and Graeme Chamberlin, "Output and Expenditure in the Last Three UK recessions," *Economic & Labour Market Review* 4 (August 2010): 51–64. Labor productivity, as measured by the OECD, rose 22 percent during Thatcher's eleven years in office; it had risen 30 percent between 1970 and 1979.

30. Supporters of the Thatcher government have claimed that its policies contributed to an increase in entrepreneurship, but a very large number of the new businesses formed during the 1980s had no employees other than the proprietor. According to David Goss, "It is clear that the expansion in the numbers of self-employed is responsible for the bulk of growth in small enterprises." See David Goss, *Small Business and Society* (Abingdon, UK: Routledge, 1991), 34. See also Paul Dunne and Alan Hughes, "Age, Size, Growth and Survival: UK Companies in the 1980s," *Journal of Industrial Economics* 42 (1994): 115–140. The authors found that only the smallest British companies, those with net assets of less than four million pounds, were unusually dynamic in the 1980–1985 period; companies with net assets of four million pounds or more performed very much as they had in the 1970s.

31. Pierson, *Dismantling the Welfare State*, 105; James Denman and Paul McDonald, "Unemployment Statistics from 1881 to the Present Day," *Labour Market Trends*, January 1996, 11; UK Office of National Statistics, Freedom of Information Request 2013–1822, published May 16, 2013; James Banks, Ruchard Blundell, Antoine Bozio,

and Carl Emmerson, "Disability, Health and Retirement in the United Kingdom," Institute for Fiscal Studies working paper W11/12 (2011), 10, 21.

32. Jacques Attali, *C'était François Mitterrand* (Paris: Fayard, 2005), 92.

12. SOCIALISM'S LAST STAND

1. Valéry Giscard d'Estaing, speech at the École polytechnique, Paris, October 28, 1975, published as Giscard d'Estaing, *Le nouvel ordre économique mondial* (Paris: Centre de recherches européennes, 1975), 7.

2. Most of the employment decline occurred at plants with more than five hundred workers; see Guy De Méo, "La crise du système industriel en France au début des années 1980," *Annales de Géographie* 93 (1984): 328. According to OECD data, manufacturing accounted for 28.4 percent of France's employment in 1974, when Giscard took office, but only 25.1 percent by 1981.

3. Research spending went from 2.1 percent of GDP in 1969 to 1.8 percent in 1980, and most of that was at state-owned companies; by the end of the period, private spending on research and development had all but dried up. De Méo, "La crise du système industriel en France," 327. On Giscard's responses, see his comment during the presidential debate, "Face à face télévisé entre MM. Valéry Giscard d'Estaing et François Mitterrand, lors de la campagne officielle pour le second tour de l'élection présidentielle, Paris, mardi 5 mai 1981," at http://discours.vie-publique.fr/notices /817005300.html, viewed April 19, 2015.

4. Jacques Attali, *C'était François Mitterrand*, 54–55.

5. Jacques Attali, *La nouvelle économie française* (Paris: Flammarion, 1978), 113, 226–250.

6. See "Intervention de M. François Mitterrand," and Jacques Attali, "Principes et Techniques d'une politique economique Socialiste," to the Socialist Party meeting, *Entretiens*, no. 75, June 6, 1975; and Parti Socialiste, "110 propositions pour la France," April 1981. See also Jean-Gabriel Bliek and Alain Parguez, "Mitterrand's Turn to Conservative Economics: A Revisionist History," *Challenge* 51 (2008): 97–109.

7. Attali, *C'était François Mitterrand*, 108.

8. On the retirement programs, see Daniel Frank, Raymond Hara, Gérard Magnier, and Olivier Viller, "Entreprises et contrats de solidarité de préretraite-démission," *Revue du Travail et Emploi* 13 (1981): 75–89.

9. Bela A. Balassa, *The First Year of Socialist Government in France* (Washington, DC: American Enterprise Institute, 1982), 3.

10. Richard Holton, "Industrial Policy in France: Nationalization Under Mitterrand," *West European Politics* 1 (1986): 72–75; Balassa, *The First Year of Socialist Government in France*, 3–4.

11. Vivien A. Schmidt, *From State to Market: The Transformation of French Business and Government* (Cambridge, UK: Cambridge University Press, 1996), 108. See also Bertrand Jacquillat, "Nationalization and Privatization in Contemporary France,"

Hoover Institution Essays in Public Policy (Stanford, CA: Hoover Institution Press, 1988).

12. Elliot Posner, *The Origin of Europe's New Stock Markets* (Cambridge, MA: Harvard University Press, 2009), 80–88.

13. Thomas Rodney Christofferson, *The French Socialists in Power, 1981–1986* (Newark, DE: University of Delaware Press, 1991), 124.

14. Mitterrand quotation in Attali, *C'était François Mitterrand*, 157; Schmidt, *From State to Market*, 97–106.

15. John Darnton, "Spain's Stunning Takeover," *New York Times*, February 25, 1983; Justino Sinova, "Para qué sirve la nacionalización," *Diario 16*, February 28, 1983.

16. Andrew Moravcsik, *The Choice for Europe: Social Purpose and State Power from Messina to Maastricht* (Ithaca, NY: Cornell University Press, 1998), 341–343; James E. Cronin, *Global Rules: America, Britain, and a Disordered World* (New Haven, CT: Yale University Press, 2014), 129.

17. Laura Cabeza García and Silvia Gómez Ansón, "The Spanish Privatisation Process: Implications on the Performance of Divested Firms," *International Review of Financial Analysis* 16 (2007): 390–409; Álvaro Cuervo García, *La privatización de la empresa pública* (Madrid: Ediciones Encuentro, 1997), 146; Sofía A. Pérez, *Banking on Privilege: The Politics of Spanish Financial Reform* (Ithaca, NY: Cornell University Press, 1997), 151–154; Keith Salmon, "Spain in the World Economy," in Richard Gillespie, Fernando Rodrigo, and Jonathan Story, eds., *Democratic Spain: Reshaping External Relations in a Changing World* (London: Routledge, 1995), 80.

18. Arrêté du 21 novembre 1986 fixant les modalités de la privatisation de la Compagnie de Saint-Gobain, https://www.legifrance.gouv.fr/affichTexte.do?cidTexte=LEGI TEXT000006070659&dateTexte=.

19. Michel Berne and Gérard Pogorel, "Privatization Experiences in France," CESifo Dice Report 1/2005, 33.

20. William L. Megginson and Jeffry M. Netter, "State to Market: A Survey of Empirical Studies on Privatization," *Journal of Economic Literature* 39 (2001): 321–389. Spain's private companies were persistently more profitable than state companies between 1985 and 1995, earning twice the average return on capital; see Cuervo García, *La privatización*, 76.

21. For employment and unemployment data, see OECD, Main Economic Indicators, and The Conference Board, "International Comparisons of Manufacturing Productivity & Unit Labor Cost Trends," https://www.conference-board.org/ilcprogram /#LaborForce.

13. MORNING IN AMERICA

1. Memo to Federal Open Market Committee (FOMC) from Stephen Axilrod and Peter Sternlight, October 4, 1979; FOMC, "Summary and Outlook" ["Greenbook"],

September 12, 1979; Transcript, FOMC meeting, October 6, 1979, all available at https://www.federalreserve.gov/monetarypolicy/fomchistorical2010.htm. For background, see David E. Lindsey, Athanasios Orphanides, and Robert H. Rasche, "The Reform of October 1979: How It Happened and Why," Federal Reserve Board Finance and Economics Discussion Series, working paper 2005-02, December 2004.

2. Federal Reserve Board, "Meeting of Federal Open Market Committee, October 6, 1979, Minutes of Actions"; Federal Reserve Board press release, November 23, 1979.

3. Transcript, FOMC meeting, October 6, 1979, 8, 17. The observation that the shift would propitiate the Fed's critics was offered by Robert Mayo, president of the Federal Reserve Bank of Chicago and former budget director under Nixon.

4. William R. Neikirk, *Volcker: Portrait of the Money Man* (New York: Congdon & Weed, 1987), 59; Joseph B. Treaster, *Paul Volcker: The Making of a Financial Legend* (Hoboken, NJ: Wiley, 2004).

5. Treaster, *Paul Volcker,* 32.

6. Paul A. Volcker, *The Rediscovery of the Business Cycle* (New York: Free Press, 1978), 61–62; John Berry, "Fed Lifts Discount Rate to Peak 11% on Close Vote," *Washington Post,* September 19, 1979.

7. For a practical explanation of how the Fed's reserve targeting worked, see Richard W. Lang, "The FOMC in 1979: Introducing Reserve Targeting," *Federal Reserve Bank of St. Louis Quarterly Review* (March 1980): 2–25.

8. Allen quotation from Cronin, *Global Rules,* 93.

9. George Gilder, *Wealth and Poverty* (New York: Basic Books, 1981), 12, 45. Other important books by supply-siders include Jude Wanniski, *The Way the World Works* (Washington, DC: Regnery, 1978); Paul Craig Roberts, *The Supply-Side Revolution* (Cambridge, MA: Harvard University Press, 1984); Bruce R. Bartlett and Timothy Roth, eds., *The Supply-Side Solution* (London: Macmillan, 1983); and Victor A. Canto, Douglas H. Joines, and Arthur B. Laffer, *Foundations of Supply-Side Economics—Theory and Evidence* (New York: Academic Press, 1983).

10. Many supply-side advocates subsequently disclaimed having predicted that lower marginal tax rates would lead to higher tax receipts. Bruce Bartlett, a deputy assistant Treasury secretary in the Reagan administration, eventually traced the claim to work done in 1975 by Norman B. Ture, then an economic consultant and later undersecretary of the Treasury during Reagan's first year in office. See Bruce Bartlett, "The Laffer Curve: Part 1," *Tax Notes,* July 16, 2012. On the irrelevance of budget deficits, see Robert Ortner, *Voodoo Deficits* (New York: Dow Jones Irwin, 1990), 41–80.

11. Gilder, *Wealth and Poverty,* 12, 20, 45, 188.

12. The top US tax rate on investment income was 70 percent during the 1970s, and the top tax rate on wage income was 50 percent. Rates on capital gains, such as profits on the sale of stock held for more than one year, were lower throughout that decade, and a portion of capital gains income was excluded from taxation. While dividends on shares were taxed at the higher rates, this did not affect investments in startup companies, which often do not pay dividends.

13. Arthur Laffer, "The Laffer Curve: Past, Present, and Future," Heritage Foundation Backgrounder 1765, June 1, 2004; Don Fullerton, "On the Possibility of an Inverse Relationship Between Tax Rates and Government Revenues," working paper 467, National Bureau of Economic Research, April 1980.

14. "America's New Beginning: A Program for Economic Recovery," (Washington, DC: White House, 1981); Reagan address to Congress, July 27, 1981.

15. Tax Foundation, "Special Report: The Economic Recovery Tax Act of 1981," September 1, 1981.

16. Congressional Budget Office, "Building a 600-Ship Navy," March 1982, and "Future Budget Requirements for the 600-Ship Navy," September 1985; David A. Stockman, *The Triumph of Politics: How the Reagan Revolution Failed* (New York: Harper & Row, 1986), 130.

17. Congressional Budget Office, "An Analysis of President Reagan's Budget Revisions for Fiscal Year 1982," March 1981, A-54-A78.

18. Stockman, *Triumph of Politics,* 132.

19. The Stockman quotation is from an interview on the television program *Frontline,* April 20, 1986.

20. Edward F. Denison, *Trends in American Economic Growth, 1929–1982* (Washington, DC: Brookings Institution, 1985), 5.

21. For the text of Kaufman's influential note to clients, see Henry Kaufman, *On Money and Markets: A Wall Street Memoir* (New York: McGraw-Hill, 2000), 168.

22. There are numerous measures of exchange-rate changes. The one used here is the Federal Reserve Board's trade-weighted foreign exchange index, which went from 91 in January 1981 to 162 in March 1985 (in March 1973 it was 100). Using a Fed index that is adjusted for inflation rates in various countries, the dollar's value climbed 42 percent over the same period.

23. Trade data are from the World Bank, *World Development Report 1982,* 12. On Akron, see Larry Ledebur and Jill Taylor, "Akron, Ohio: A Restoring Prosperity Case Study," Brookings Institution, 2008; Federal Housing Finance Agency, "All-Transactions House Price Index for Peoria, IL (MSA)," available from Federal Reserve Bank of St. Louis, https://research.stlouisfed.org/fred2/series/ATNHPIUS37900Q.

24. For praise of Reagan's economic policies, see Robert L. Bartley, *The Seven Fat Years* (New York: Free Press, 1992). Henry Kaufman recounts that the Reagan administration objected strongly to his view that heavy federal government borrowing left interest rates higher than they would have been otherwise, and that Republican congressional leaders urged him to support the administration's position. See Kaufman, *On Money and Markets,* 270. On the importance of Reagan's support for Volcker, see Robert J. Samuelson, *The Great Inflation and Its Aftermath: The Past and Future of American Affluence* (New York: Random House, 2010), 112.

25. See Nixon comments at March 21, 1970, press conference, *Public Papers of the Presidents of the United States: Richard Nixon, 1970* (Washington, DC: USGPO, 1971), 87.

26. Congressional Budget Office, *Trends in the Distribution of Household Income Between 1979 and 2007* (Washington, DC, 2011), supplemental data for Figure 4; US

Bureau of Labor Statistics, Current Population Survey, http://www.bls.gov/cps. Determining the effect of lower tax rates on the inflation-adjusted value of the median wage is difficult, as a wage is received by a single individual whereas married couples often pay income taxes jointly. The average rate of federal income tax on the median household income—not the median wage—fell from 11.8 percent in 1981 to 9.3 percent in 1989, according to the Tax Policy Center. Applying that decline to the inflation-adjusted median wage yields an increase in the wage of approximately 5 percent during Reagan's term. Households earning below the median income saw smaller declines. Data from the Tax Policy Center, at http://www.taxpolicycenter.org /taxfacts/Content/PDF/family_inc_rates_hist.pdf, viewed August 4, 2015. On the real incomes of the lowest 20 percent of households, see the underlying data for Figure 2 in Congressional Budget Office, *Trends in the Distribution of Household Income Between 1979 and 2007.*

27. US Census Bureau, "Historical Census of Housing Tables Home Values," median home values adjusted to 2000 dollars; Arthur B. Kennickell and Janice Shack-Marquez, "Changes in Family Finances from 1983 to 1989: Evidence from the Survey of Consumer Finances," *Federal Reserve Bulletin* (January 1992): 1–18. Installment debt reached a record level, measured against income, in 1986; see Robert B. Avery, Gregory E. Elliehausen, and Arthur B. Kennickell, "Changes in Consumer Installment Debt: Evidence from the 1983 and 1986 Surveys of Consumer Finances," *Federal Reserve Bulletin* (October 1987): 761–778.

28. *Frontline*, April 20, 1986.

29. President's Commission on Industrial Competitiveness, *Global Competition: The New Reality* (Washington, DC, 1985), 12.

30. Krippner, *Capitalizing on Crisis*, 37. Productivity growth, investment and average age of equipment are taken from US Bureau of Economic Analysis, National Income and Product Accounts. The investment measure used is net investment, which takes into account the rate at which existing equipment depreciates.

31. Employee Benefit Research Institute, "What Are the Trends in U.S. Retirement Plans?" at http://www.ebri.org/publications/benfaq/index.cfm?fa=retfaq14, viewed August 1, 2015. See also William J. Wiatrowski, "The Last Private Industry Pension Plans: A Visual Essay," *Monthly Labor Review* (December 2012): 4; Robin A. Cohen et al., "Health Insurance Coverage Trends, 1959–2007," *National Health Statistics Reports* 17 (2009): 9.

14. THE LOST DECADE

1. World Bank, *World Development Report 1982* (Washington, DC, 1982), 24, 190–196.

2. Debt figures are taken from the World Bank's annual publication, *World Debt Tables*. See also World Bank, *World Development Report 1982* and *1983*. The 1970–1980 growth rate appears in *World Development Report 1982*, 35. On the growth of the

commercial paper market in the 1970s, see Peter A. Abken, "Commercial Paper," Federal Reserve Bank of Richmond, *Economic Review* (March/April 1981): 11–21.

3. Arthur F. Burns, "The Need for Order in International Finance," address at Columbia University, April 12, 1977; Federal Deposit Insurance Corporation (FDIC), *An Examination of the Banking Crises of the 1980s and Early 1990s* (Washington, DC, 1997), 196–197. On the British banks, see Philip L. Cottrell, "The Historical Development of Modern Banking Within the United Kingdom," in Manfred Pohl and Sabine Freitag, eds., *Handbook on the History of European Banks* (Aldershot, England: Elgar, 1994), 1157.

4. Anne O. Krueger, "Debt, Capital Flows, and LDC Growth," *American Economic Review* 77 (May 1987): 159–164.

5. Paul Volcker and Toyoo Gyohten, *Changing Fortunes* (New York: Times Books, 1992), 180.

6. *World Development Report 1982,* 16.

7. Philip L. Zweig, *Wriston* (New York: Crown, 1995), 756–761.

8. Alan Riding, "Survivor: Jesus Silva Herzog," *New York Times,* August 21, 1982; Federal Reserve Board, "Transcript of Federal Open Market Committee Meeting of June 30–July 1, 1982," June 30, 1982, Afternoon Session, 23, and "Record of the Policy Actions of the Federal Open Market Committee, Meeting Held on August 24, 1982"; James M. Boughton, *Silent Revolution: The International Monetary Fund, 1979–1989* (Washington, DC: International Monetary Fund, 2001), 281–317.

9. *World Development Report 1982,* 2; Graciela L. Kaminsky and Alfredo Pereira, "The Debt Crisis: Lessons of the 1980s for the 1990s," Federal Reserve Board, international finance discussion paper 481, September 1994; FDIC, *An Examination,* 206.

10. For a history of the many instances in which governments defaulted on their foreign debts, see Carmen M. Reinhart and Kenneth S. Rogoff, *This Time Is Different: Eight Centuries of Financial Folly* (Princeton, NJ: Princeton University Press, 2009), 68–118.

11. Federally chartered banks in the United States were prohibited by law from lending more than 10 percent of their capital to a single borrower, but their lead supervisor, the Comptroller of the Currency, allowed them to circumvent that law by deciding that a country's national government was a separate borrower from a state-owned oil company or a state development bank. Interestingly, Congress raised the 10 percent limit to 15 percent in 1982, just as the crisis struck. See FDIC, *An Examination,* 203–204. In *Changing Fortunes,* 195, Volcker emphasizes that the State Department strongly opposed efforts to limit banks' lending to Latin America.

12. For a description of the events in the first days after August 12, see John Makin, *The Global Debt Crisis* (New York: Basic Books, 1984), 11–15.

13. International Monetary Fund, *Annual Report 1983* (Washington, DC, 1983), 177.

14. FDIC, *An Examination,* 197; John E. Young, "Supervision of Bank Foreign Lending," Federal Reserve Bank of Kansas City, *Economic Review* (May 1985): 36.

15. Makin, *The Global Debt Crisis,* 238.

16. José Maria Dagnino Pastore, "Progress and Prospects for the Adjustment Program in Argentina," in John Williamson, ed., *Prospects for Adjustment in Argentina, Brazil, and Mexico* (Washington, DC: Institute for International Economics, 1973), 7–25; Boughton, *Silent Revolution,* 8.

17. Barbara A. Bennett and Gary C. Zimmerman, "U.S. Banks' Exposure to Developing Countries: An Examination of Recent Trends," Federal Reserve Bank of San Francisco, *Economic Review* (Spring 1988): 14–29.

18. Richard E. Feinberg, "Comment: Debt and Trade in U.S.-Latin American Relations," in Kevin J. Middlebrook and Carlos Rico, eds., *The United States and Latin America in the 1980s* (Pittsburgh: University of Pittsburgh Press, 1986), 300.

19. Growth in real per capita incomes, from IMF data, is taken from Martin Feldstein et al., *Restoring Growth in the Debt-Laden Third World* (New York, Trilateral Commission, 1987), 7.

20. IMF, *World Economic Outlook* (April 1987), Table A50. From 1975 to 1980, Latin American countries devoted almost 23 percent of their total incomes to investment; in the 1980s, the figure fell below 18 percent. See José Antonio Ocampo, "The Latin American Debt Crisis in Historical Perspective," Initiative for Policy Dialogue, Columbia University (2013).

21. Boughton, *Silent Revolution,* 418–429.

22. Don Babai, "The World Bank and the IMF: Rolling Back the State or Backing Its Role?" in Raymond M. Vernon, ed., *The Promise of Privatization* (New York: Council on Foreign Relations, 1988), 260.

23. Susan M. Collins and Won-Am Park, "External Debt and Macroeconomic Performance in South Korea," and Edward F. Buffie and Allen Sangines Krause, "Mexico 1958–86," in Jeffrey D. Sachs, ed., *Developing Country Debt and the World Economy* (Chicago: University of Chicago Press, 1989), 121–140, 158. According to the authors, Mexico's foreign debt was 55.1 percent of national income in 1985, while South Korea's was 56.3 percent.

24. Jeromin Zettelmeyer, "Growth and Reforms in Latin America: A Survey of Facts and Arguments," working paper 06/210, International Monetary Fund, September 2006.

15. THE NEW WORLD

1. Conference Board Total Economy Database, at www.conference-board.org/data/economydatabase/, May 2015. The twelve wealthy countries cited in this paragraph were Australia, Belgium, Canada, France, Italy, Japan, Netherlands, Sweden, Switzerland, United Kingdom, United States, and West Germany.

2. The technical name for the measurement described in this paragraph is "total factor productivity," sometimes referred to as "multifactor productivity." Its main components are usually referred to as "labor quality" (related to education, training, and

experience), "capital deepening" (measured in terms of the amount of capital, such as business machinery and structures, per worker, but then adjusted for depreciation), and "technological change," which is usually defined as whatever portion of productivity growth is not explained by changes in labor quality and capital deepening. For primers and data on various economies, see Nicholas Crafts, "What Creates Multifactor Productivity?" presentation to European Central Bank, 2008, and Wolodar Lysko, "Manufacturing Multifactor Productivity in Three Countries," *Monthly Labor Review* (July 1995): 39–55. See also Sachverständigenrat, "Zu den gesamtwirtschaftlichen Auswirkungen der Oelkrise," December 17, 1973, BA, B136/7459. For US productivity estimates, see *Historical Statistics of the United States, Earliest Times to the Present: Millennial Edition,* (New York: Cambridge University Press, 2006), series Cg290. See also Jean Acheson, "Multi-factor Productivity: Estimates for 1970 to 2009," UK Office for National Statistics, *Labor Market Review* (May 2011): 80, and Giersch, Paqué, and Schmieding, *The Fading Miracle,* 220.

3. OECD, *Historical Statistics, 1960–1980,* Tables 7.1–7.4. With profits in 1960 set equal to 100, the German economics ministry determined in 1975, profits had been below 80 in almost every subsequent year, after adjusting for inflation, and had fallen to 60 in 1973; see Deutscher Bundestag, 7.Wahlperiode, Drucksache 7/2848. On Japan, see Nakamura, *The Postwar Japanese Economy,* 226. See also BMWi, "Fortschreibung der mittelfristigen Zielprojektion bis 1977," unsigned draft memorandum, March 8, 1973, BA, B102/306599. On France, see Institut National de la Statistique et des Études Économiques, "Partage de la valeur ajoutée, partage des profits et écarts des rémunérations en France" (2009), 67.

4. *Historical Statistics of the United States,* Series Cf182. For cautions about the potential economic impact of environmental regulations, see Council of Economic Advisors, Economic Report of the President, 1972 (Washington, DC, 1972), 123; BMWi, "Fortschreibung der mittelfristigen Zielprojektion bis 1977," which advised, "The greater the legal requirements in this area in the coming years, the more they will limit growth potential."

5. Keith O. Fuglie, "Productivity Growth and Technology Capital in the Global Agricultural Economy," in Keith O. Fuglie, Sun Ling Wang, and V. Eldon Ball, *Productivity Growth in Agriculture: An International Perspective* (Wallingford, UK: CAB International, 2012), 335–367; OECD, *Historical Statistics, 1960–1980,* Tables 2.9 and 5.4. In the OECD countries, manufacturing declined gradually as a share of total economic output, from 29.6 percent in 1960 to 22.2 percent by 1990. For a readable summary of the convoluted and highly technical debate over measuring productivity growth, see Paul S. Adler, "The Productivity Puzzle: Numbers Alone Won't Solve It," *Monthly Labor Review* (October 1982): 15–21.

6. Sir Keith Joseph, "This Is Not the Time to Be Mealy-Mouthed: Intervention Is Destroying Us," speech at Upminster, June 22, 1974, MTFA, document 110604.

7. Fumio Hayashi and Edward C. Prescott, "The 1990s in Japan: A Lost Decade," *Review of Economic Dynamics* 5 (2002): 206–235.

8. For Rivlin quotation, see Biven, *Jimmy Carter's Economy*, 206.

9. Diego Comin and Martí Mestri, "If Technology Has Arrived Everywhere, Why Has Income Diverged?" National Bureau of Economic Research working paper 19010, 2013. The authors find that new technologies are diffusing more quickly than in the past.

10. Sumon Bhaumik, "Productivity and the Business Cycle," UK Department for Business Innovation and Skills, economics paper no. 12, March 2011; Robert Shackleton, "Total Factor Productivity Growth in Historical Perspective," US Congressional Budget Office, working paper 2013–01, March 2013; Shane Greenstein, *How the Internet Became Commercial: Innovation, Privatization, and the Birth of a New Network* (Princeton, NJ: Princeton University Press, 2016), 249–300.

11. Robert J. Gordon, *The Rise and Fall of American Growth: The U.S. Standard of Living Since the Civil War* (Princeton, NJ: Princeton University Press, 2016), 2.

12. David Koistinen, "The Origins of Offshoring," paper presented to the Business History Conference, Miami, Florida, June 27, 2015.

13. Zuliu Hu and Mohsin S. Khan, "Why Is China Growing So Fast?" International Monetary Fund *Economic Issues* 8 (1997); Conference Board, "Conference Board Total Economy Database, Summary Tables," May 2015, Table 10.

14. Englander and Mittelstädt, "Total Factor Productivity," 17–18. Robert Brenner, *The Economics of Global Turbulence* (London: Verso, 2006), 6–7, 101–109. Brenner identifies manufacturers' declining profits as a major cause of poor productivity growth.

15. Raghuram G. Rajan, *Fault Lines: How Hidden Fractures Still Threaten the World Economy* (Princeton, NJ: Princeton University Press, 2010).

16. Wolfgang Streeck, *Buying Time: The Delayed Crisis of Global Capitalism* (London: Verso, 2014), 4.

17. Retirement ages are from OECD estimates of the average effective age of retirement. On Social Security, see Orlo Nichols, Michael Clingman, and Alice Wade, "Internal Real Rates of Return Under the OASDI Program for Hypothetical Workers," Social Security Administration *Actuarial Note*, no. 2004.5 (March 2005). Returns are adjusted for inflation.

18. John G. Fernald, "Productivity and Potential Output Before, During, and After the Great Recession," Federal Reserve Bank of San Francisco working paper 2014–15, June 2014.

19. Ricardo Hausmann, Lant Pritchett, and Dani Rodrik, "Growth Accelerations," *Journal of Economic Growth* 10 (2005): 303–329.

20. Some 1,617 federally insured banks in the United States failed between 1980 and 1994, in addition to numerous thrift institutions and state-chartered banks without federal insurance. Quotation is from Paul A. Samuelson, "To Protect Manufacturing?" *Zeitschrift für die gesamte Staatswissenschaft* 137 (1981): 407.

Index

Adenauer, Konrad, 24, 190
administrative management, 178
Africa, 35–36, 243; debt crisis in, 252–253;
    income per person in, 6; population
    growth in, 60–62
African-Asian conference (Bandung,
    Indonesia, 1955), 41
African countries: Cold War and, 40–41. *See
    also specific countries*
African Development Bank, 241
Agnew, Spiro, 101
agriculture, 22, 37, 42, 137, 259–260. *See
    also* farming
Algeria, 4, 44
Allen, Richard, 225
American Bankers Association, 96
American Enterprise Institute, 107
American Gas Association, 104
Andersson, Bibi, 165
Andreotti, Giulio, 88, 91–92
anti-inflation campaigns/programs, 106,
    118–119, 139, 183, 184. *See also*
    inflation
anti-inflation policy, 53, 106, 230. *See also*
    inflation
anti-tax movements, 151–154. *See also*
    income tax; taxes/tax rate/tax policy
Arab-Israeli conflict, 69, 70–71
Aramco, 69–70, 71
Argentina: boom-and-bust cycles in, 37;
    central bank in, 37, 38; debt crisis in,
    250; economic planning in, 39;
    economy of, 36–38; loans to Third
    World and, 242; political parties in, 36;
    rapid industrialization in, 37–38, 39
Arlington, Texas, 15–16

Asia, 35–36; economy at close of World War
    II in, 16, 19–20; income tax in, 146;
    population growth in, 60–62
Asian countries: Cold War and, 40–41. *See
    also specific countries*
Attali, Jacques, 204, 210
Australia, 81, 124, 181; economy at close of
    World War II in, 20; income per person
    in, 160; income tax in, 149
automation, 130–131; unemployment and,
    142–143
automobile industry, 127–129, 202; and
    bailouts in United States, 127–128; in
    France, 207; in Japan, 122–123
aviation, deregulation of, 113

Baker, James, 253–254
balanced budget, 176, 182, 224, 226, 228,
    229–231, 234, 236, 237
Bank for International Settlements, 86, 247
Bank of Canada, 181
Bank of England, 37, 51, 66, 74, 87–88, 89,
    91, 93, 170, 180–181, 183, 184–185,
    220; oil crisis impact on, 82–86
Bank of Japan, 66, 92, 94, 181
Bankhaus Herstatt, 89–90, 91, 92, 95, 96
banks/banking systems, 12; bank failures of
    1980s and 1990s and, 270; bank
    regulators/regulation and, 92, 93–94, 95;
    Basel banking meetings (1975) and,
    92–95; capital and, 95–97; expansion
    breathing spell and, 96; impact of oil
    crisis of 1973 on, 81–97; loans to Third
    World by, 240–243; systemic risk and,
    251; Third World debt crisis and,
    243–256. *See also* central banks; global

financial system; International Monetary
Fund; *specific banks; under specific
countries;* World Bank
Banque Parabas, 214–215
Basel banking meetings, 1975, 92–95
Basel Concordat, 95
Begin, Menachem, 92
Belgium, 1–2, 23, 30, 124, 127; anti-
inflation policy in, 53; income per
person in, 160; welfare state in, 17–18
Bension, Joshua, 90–91, 92
Bergman, Ingmar, 164–166
Berlusconi, Silvio, 10–11, 267
Beveridge, William, 17
Bismarck, Otto von, 17
Blair, Tony, 194
Blunden, George, 93
Bolivia, 44, 244
Brandt, Willy, 34, 35, 156–157, 160, 163
Brazil, 46, 111, 224; bank loans to, 241; debt
crisis in, 245, 249–250; economy of, 37;
Prebisch and, 38
Bretton Woods conference (July 1944),
52–55
Bretton Woods system: collapse of, 67, 72,
83, 117, 181, 201–202, 222; foreign-
exchange rates and, 52–55, 117, 248
British Telecom, 114
Brittan, Samuel, 158, 160
Brookings Institution, 107
Brunner, Karl, 184
Bucher, Jeffrey, 67
budget deficits, 9, 176, 249, 252; in France,
202, 208, 209, 215; in Great Britain,
182, 184; in Japan, 150; in United
States, 47, 150, 226, 230, 234; in West
Germany, 32, 150
Burns, Arthur, 48, 65, 75, 77, 82, 86, 92, 96,
134, 173, 180, 222, 240; economic
policy of, 47–49; inflation and monetary
policy and, 51–56; loans to Third World
and, 242; public psychology and, 51;
wage and price controls and inflation
and, 53–54
business sector, 201, 258–259

Callaghan, James, 168, 169–171, 172
Canada, 124, 125; anti-inflation policy in,
53; auto industry in, 127, 129; banks/
banking systems in, 94 (*see also* Bank of
Canada; banks/banking systems);
economy at close of World War II in, 18;
environmentalism in, 62; income

distribution in, 140; income per person
in, 160; income tax in, 147, 150;
inflation and buying power in, 56; labor
share in, 141; oil crisis of 1973 in, 2, 71,
240; productivity bust in, 258–259, 260;
ungovernability in, 155, 156; welfare
state in, 17, 144
capital: banks/banking systems and, 95–97;
destruction of, and income distribution,
138
capitalism, 25, 101, 162, 187; late, and
ungovernability, 160; late, crisis of,
267–268
car-free Sundays, 1–2, 3
Carson, Rachel, 60
Carter, Jimmy, 75, 126, 163, 172–174, 175,
234; economic policy of, 219–224, 261;
Iranian hostage crisis and, 225; trade
sanctions against Japan and, 128–129
central banks: foreign-exchange rates and, 67.
See also banks/banking systems; Federal
Reserve
Central Europe, 29, 81
Chase Manhattan Bank, 91, 96
Chile, 43, 257–258; economy of, 37
China, 4, 265; hardship and poverty in, 21,
44; income per person in, 240; labor
share in, 141–142
Chirac, Jacques, 210–211, 214–215
Churchill, Winston, 190
Citicorp. *See* First National City Bank
Clean Air Act, 62
Club of Rome, 57
Coase, Ronald, 107
Cold War, 40–41
collective rationality, 32, 34
Commission on Industrial Competitiveness,
236
Committee for Economic Development, 26
Committee on Banking Regulations and
Supervisory Practices, 93
commodity prices: stabilization of, 42–43
commonality: among developing countries,
41
communism, 63
Communist Bloc. *See* Soviet Bloc
communist economies of 1970s: in Soviet
Union, 161–162
Communist Party, in France, 201, 203,
204–205, 206, 210. *See also* political
parties
computers, 58, 64, 93, 117, 123, 264, 265,
266

concerted action (government and nongovernmental cooperation), 32–34
Congo, 44
conservatism: move to the right and, 10, 155–178
conservative economic policy, 179–182; discretion and, 180; employment and, 179, 180, 182; inflation and, 180–182; rules matter and, 179–180; of Thatcher, Margaret, 182–197. *See also under specific conservative leaders*
conservative political parties: welfare state and, 24. *See also* political parties
Cost of Living Council, 107
cost-push inflation, 75–77
Council of Economic Advisers, 48, 65–66
crisis cartels, 127
Czechoslovakia, 19

Dai-ichi Kangyo of Tokyo, 91
Daly, Herman E., 63
Dance of Death (Strindberg), 164
Davignon, Étienne, 127
Davignon Plan, 127
de Gasperi, Alcide, 24
de Gaulle, Charles, 24, 162, 200, 201
de Larosière, Jacques, 244, 249
debt crisis, 243–256; cause of and solution to, 253–256; emergency loans and, 247–249; impact on First World, 251–252; inflation and, 246; unemployment and, 246
deindustrialization, 124
Delors, Jacques, 209, 210
demand-pull inflation, 75–76
democracy, 268
Denison, Edward, 231
Denmark: anti-tax movement in, 151–153, 154; income per person in, 160
dependency theory (government intervention re: raw materials and manufacturing), 42
Der Spiegel, 89
deregulation, 12, 99–114, 237; of aviation, 113; of electricity, 113; of energy sector, 99–109, 110, 113; of gas, 99–100, 102, 103–104, 107–108, 109, 113; of interest rates on deposits and loans, 112, 113; of natural gas, 103, 104, 108–109, 110, 113; of oil, 99, 101, 102, 103, 104–106, 107–108, 109, 110, 113; positive and negative results of, 113–114; of telecommunications sector, 107, 113; of

transportation sector, 106–107, 110–112, 113–114. *See also* regulation
Derthick, Martha, 107
developing countries, 35–46; commonality among, 41; debt crisis in (*see* Third World debt crisis); economic growth in, 44, 45–46; economies of, and Prebisch, 40–43; hardship in, 44; income per capita in, 44; industrialization in, 36; new industries vs. raw materials and, 45–46. *See also specific countries;* Third World
Diefenbaker, John, 24
discontents, 21
Dresdner Bank, 94
DuPont, 66

Earth Day, 61, 62
East Asia, 265
East Germany, 29; ungovernability in, 156, 157
East Pakistan, 44
Eastern Europe, 29; debt crisis in, 246; democracy in, 179; income per person in, 160–161; ungovernability in, 160–162
ECLA. *See* Economic Commission for Latin America
The Ecologist, 61–62
Econ-Bank of Switzerland, 89
economic boom, postwar (1948–1973), 3–5, 20–26; causes of, 22; economic planning and, 25; government programs and, 21–22; manufacturing and, 22–23; in the 1950s and 1960s, 4; productivity and, 22–24; productivity growth and, 263–264; social contract and, 267–269; as unique, 9–10. *See also under specific countries*
Economic Commission for Latin America (ECLA), 38–39, 39–40
economic crisis of 1970s, 164–178, 201–203, 257–258; aftereffects of, 270; income tax and, 164–167; productivity bust and, 258–262, 266–268. *See also* oil crisis of 1973; *under specific countries*
economic crisis of 1990s in Japan, 270
economic development: income distribution and, 134–135
economic growth: accelerations, failure of, 269–270; contributors to, in Japan, 116–117; environmentalism and, 57, 59–63; government's inability to control,

9, 261–262; innovation and, 9; limits to, 57–64; productivity and, 78–79; productivity growth and, 7–8, 262; slow, vs. economic miracles, 269; stages of, 134–135; in United States (1873–1897), 7. *See also* productivity growth

economic management: economy based on cheap oil and, 79; traditional methods of, 79

economic miracles: vs. slow economic growth, 269

economic moderation: political moderation and, 24

economic outcomes: government's inability to control, 9, 261–262

economic planning: in communist economies of 1970s, 161–162; as cruel hoax, 46; economic success and, 25. *See also under specific countries*

economic policy: move to the right and, 10, 155–178. *See also* conservative economic policy; *under specific countries, economists, Federal Reserve chairmen, presidents, prime ministers, etc.*

Economic Recovery Tax Act, 228

economic slowdown: restructuring and, 264–265; unemployment and, 264. *See also* productivity bust

economic slowdown (1973–end of century), 3–4, 6–13; banks/banking systems and, 12; factors that influenced, 12–13; loss of faith in the future and, 13; manufacturing and, 12; as normal, 9–13; unemployment and, 11, 12; workers' skills vs. technology and, 12–13

economic stagflation, 78, 181

economic stagnation, 78, 158, 261

economists. *See specific economists*

economy: role of government in, 24. *See also under specific countries, economists, presidents, etc.*

economy, world, at close of World War II, 15–20; obstacles to recovery and, 18–19; rebuilding vs. reparations and, 19–20; reverse course and, 19–20. *See also under specific countries*

Ecuador, 250–251

education, 145; ungovernability and, 155, 157

Egypt, 1, 69, 73

Ehrlich, Paul, 61

Eisenhower, Dwight, 24, 48, 105, 144

electricity, deregulation of, 113

Emminger, Otmar, 86

employment/unemployment. *See* full employment; Full Employment Act; magic square; Phillips Curve; *under specific countries, economists, Federal Reserve chairmen, presidents, prime ministers, etc.;* unemployment

endogenous growth theory, 9

energy sector, 99–100, 101, 102, 103–109, 110, 113

England, 170, 190, 196; income inequality in, 135

entitlements, 157–158

environmental protection, 259

environmental regulation, 64

environmentalism: economic growth and, 57, 59–63; technology and, 63–64. *See also* pollution; population growth

Erhard, Ludwig, 30–31

Europe, 124, 140; bank loans to Third World and, 241; crisis cartels in, 127; Davignon Plan and, 127; debt crisis in, 247; deregulation in, 113; economic slowdown in, 3–4; economy at close of World War II in, 16–17, 19–20; financial crisis of 2008 in, 270; income per person in, 6; income tax in, 146; manufacturing and trade with Japan in, 125–127; oil crisis of 1973 in, 1–2, 3; postwar productivity in, 24; productivity slowdown in, 265; unemployment in, 176; welfare state in, 144

European Community, 152, 168, 213, 214, 215; regional assistance and, 126–127

European countries: economic forecasts in 1973 and, 66–67; economy at close of World War II in, 18–19; postwar trade in, 23. *See also specific countries*

European Economic Community, 202, 205, 211

European Union, 30, 215; financial crisis of 2008 and, 270

exchange rate. *See* foreign-exchange rate

Faisal, King, 69, 70–71

farming, 124, 258, 259–260. *See also* agriculture

Federal Communications Commission, 107

Federal Power Commission, 103, 108

Federal Reserve, 173–174, 219–224, 232; Basel banking meetings (1975) and, 92; chairmen (*see* Burns, Arthur; Greenspan, Alan; Miller, G. William; Volcker, Paul);

Franklin National Bank and, 87–89; loans to Third World and, 242; monetarism and, 220–221; monetary policy, 49–56, 180–182, 220–221, 222, 223–224; oil crisis of 1973 and, 72, 74, 77, 78, 94, 96; Redbook and, 74; Third World debt crisis and, 243–244, 244–245. *See also* banks/banking systems; central banks
Federal Reserve Bank of New York, 222, 247
Fernald, John, 269
financial assistance from foreign countries, 43
financial crisis of 2008, 270
Financial Times (London), 167
financialization, 236
Finland, 56, 215; labor share in, 141; welfare state in, 144
First National City Bank, 96
food production, 58
Ford, Gerald, 110, 173, 174
Ford administration, 112
Ford Foundation, 107
foreign-exchange rate, 11–12, 47, 51–55, 66, 67, 87, 90, 151, 184, 185, 252, 266; Bretton Woods agreement and, 52–55; France and, 202, 205, 209, 213; International Monetary Fund and, 38
foreign investors, 232–233
France, 19, 30, 62, 124, 163, 176, 199–211, 213–217; automobile industry in, 202, 207; banks/banking system in, 93, 206, 214–215 *(see also specific banks)*; budget deficits in, 202, 208, 209, 215; Communist Party in, 201, 203, 204–205, 206, 210; *dirigisme* in, 203; economic crisis of 1970s in, 164, 201–203; economic planning in, 25; economic policies of the 1970s in, 204; economy at close of World War II in, 16; foreign-exchange rate and, 202, 205, 209, 213; income distribution in, 137, 140; income tax in, 164; inflation and buying power in, 55–56; inflation in, 202, 208–209; labor/trade unions in, 202, 208, 213; "lump of labor" theory in, 205–206; manufacturing in, 202; market-oriented economic policies of, 217; modernization in, 202; nationalism in, 206–208, 209, 210, 267; new version of socialism in, 210, 213–217; oil crisis of 1973 in, 72–73, 77, 78; political parties in, 199–200, 201, 203, 204–205, 206, 208–209, 210–211, 215, 217;

postwar economic boom in, 20, 21; postwar economy of, 29; privatization in, 213, 215, 216–217; productivity bust in, 259; productivity growth in, 263; Socialist Party in, 199–200, 201, 203, 204–205, 206, 208–209, 210–211, 215, 217; taxes in, 208–209; technology in, 203; trade in, 202; "turn to austerity" policy in, 209–210; unemployment in, 202, 203, 207, 208, 209, 210, 217; welfare state in, 18, 144, 213. *See also specific presidents and prime ministers*
Franco, Francisco, 211–213
Franklin National Bank, 87–89, 91, 95, 96
free enterprise, 224, 225
free-market economics, 30, 31, 254–255; Thatcher and, 172, 260
French Republic, 4
Friedman, Milton, 75, 76, 153, 176, 180–181, 185
full employment, 6, 25–26, 30, 35, 170, 179, 180, 233, 261; tax cuts, easy money, government programs and, 75. *See also* employment/unemployment; unemployment
Full Employment Act, 25–26
full-employment budget, 26
Fullerton, Don, 228

G-77, 43
gas: deregulation of, 99–100, 102, 103–104, 107–108, 109, 113
GATT. *See* General Agreement on Tariffs and Trade
General Agreement on Tariffs and Trade (GATT), 42
German Bundesbank, 28, 51, 55, 86, 181
Germany, 19, 224; banks/banking system in, 28, 91, 94 *(see also* banks/banking systems); debt crisis in, 246; economic crisis of 1970s in, 164; economic planning in, 28, 29–30; economy at close of World War II in, 16–17; economy policy in, 27–35; formal division into two zones in, 28–29; income inequality in, 135; inflation and buying power in, 55–56; labor/trade unions in, 169; political parties in, 27–28; postwar occupied zones in, 28; postwar productivity in, 23; welfare state in, 17. *See also* East Germany
Ghana, 43
Gilder, George, 225–227

Giscard d'Estaing, Valéry Marie René Georges (aka Giscard), 163, 164, 201–203, 204–205, 210–211
Glistrup, Mogens, 151–153, 154
global financial system (banks and brokerage houses): impact of oil crisis of 1973 on, 81–97. *See also* banks/banking systems
globalization, 11–12, 265–266
GNP. *See* gross national product
González, Felipe, 211, 212–213, 213–214
Goodhart, Charles, 180
Gordon, Robert, 263–264
government: inability to control economic outcomes, 9, 261–262; role in economy, 24
government debt: ratio of, to national income, 151
government spending, 229–230, 237; Thatcher and, 189, 196
Great Britain, 16, 19, 65, 66, 124; anti-inflation policy in, 53; anti-tax movement in, 151–154; bank loans to Third World and, 242; banks/banking system in, 37 (*see also* Bank of England; banks/banking systems; Israel–British Bank of Tel Aviv); budget deficits in, 182, 184; conservative economic policy in (*see under* Thatcher, Margaret); debt crisis in, 248; deregulation in, 114; economic crisis of 1970s in, 167–172; environmentalism in, 62; income distribution in, 139; income tax in, 149, 150; inflation in, 167, 168, 169, 170, 171, 172; labor share in, 141; labor/trade unions in, 169–171; manufacturing in, 167, 168, 169, 170; nationalism in, 267; oil crisis of 1973 in, 72, 74–75, 77, 167; political parties in, 167–172, 182, 184–191, 194, 260; pollution and, 59–60; population growth in, 61–62; postwar economic boom in, 20–21, 268–269; postwar productivity in, 22; productivity bust in, 258–259; tax rate in, 137; ungovernability in, 156, 158; wartime tax burden in, 146, 147; welfare state in, 18, 144, 145. *See also* Thatcher, Margaret
Great Depression of 1930s, 7
Great Migration (African American), 21
Greece, 19, 81; postwar economic boom in, 20
Greenspan, Alan, 65

Griliches, Zvi, 9–10
gross national product (GNP), 134
Guardian, 65
"guns and butter" model, 48–49

Hagen, Carl, 154
Haldeman, H. R., 55
Heath, Edward, 82, 154, 167–168, 171, 172, 175, 182
Heimann, John, 97
Heller, Walter, 26, 27, 35, 58, 261
Herstatt, Iwan, 89, 92
Hitler, Adolf, 27, 102
Hong Kong, 255
Howe, Sir Geoffrey, 183, 184–185, 190
Hungary, 160–161; nationalism in, 267

Iceland, 148
IMF. *See* International Monetary Fund
import substitution, 40, 43, 45
income: defined, 136
income distribution, 136–138, 235–236; destruction of capital and loss of wealth and, 138; economic development and, 134–135; explanations for increasing disparities in, 140–143; income equality reversal in mid-1970s and, 138–140; labor share and, 141–142; labor/trade unions and, 137–138; tax rate and, 137
income equality: reversal of, in mid-1970s, 138–140
income inequality: U-curve and, 135
income per capita, 265; in developing countries, 44; in Japan, 116
income per person, 5, 160–161; productivity bust and, 261
income tax: economic crisis of 1970s and, 164–167; individual earnings and, 150; inflation and, 149; welfare state and, 145–147, 149–151. *See also* taxes/tax rate/tax policy; *under specific countries*
India, 241; hardship/poverty in, 21; license raj and, 45
Indonesia, 46, 124, 245
industrialization, 37–38, 58, 134–135, 161; in developing countries, 36
inflation, 11–12; cost-push inflation, 75–77; debt crisis and, 246; demand-pull inflation, 75–76; income tax and, 149; jawboning and, 76–77; monetary policy and, 51–56; oil crisis of 1973 and, 74–77, 78; political pressure and, 76; price and wage controls and, 53–54;

price controls and, 76–77; productivity bust and, 261; Third World debt crisis and, 246; as unavoidable nuisance, 75; varieties of, 75–77. *See also* anti-inflation campaigns/programs/policy; magic square; Phillips Curve; *under specific countries, economists, Federal Reserve chairmen, presidents, prime ministers, etc.*

innovation: economic growth and, 9; in the late-twentieth century, 264; in the 1950s and 1960s, 264; productivity growth and, 262–265, 266

input-output analysis, 30

Institute of Economic Affairs, 172

interest rates: on deposits and loans, deregulation of, 112, 113; unemployment and inflation and, 55–56

International Monetary Fund (IMF), 52, 170; bank loans to Third World and, 242; foreign-exchange rate and, 38; Third World debt crisis and, 244, 248–254

International Trade Commission, 125–126, 128, 129

Internet, 12, 24, 263

Interstate Commerce Act of 1887, 110

Interstate Commerce Commission, 110

Iran, 124

Iranian hostage crisis, 224–225

Iranian Revolution, 128, 171, 173, 219–220

Iron Curtain, 4, 19

Israel, 1, 2, 3; Arab-Israeli conflict, 69, 70–71; foreign-exchange rates and, 90

Israel-British Bank of Tel Aviv, 90–91, 92, 95

Italy, 1–2, 16, 19, 23, 30, 55, 88, 126–127, 176, 267; income tax in, 149; oil crisis of 1973 in, 72; per capita income in, 265; postwar economic boom in, 21; postwar economy of, 29; productivity growth in, 263; ungovernability in, 155–156

J. Henry Schroder & Co., 82

Jamaica, 244

Japan, 63, 66–67, 81, 115–129, 163, 164, 233; administrative management in, 178; anti-inflation campaign in, 118–119; automobile industry in, 122–123; bank loans to Third World and, 241, 242; banks/banking system in, 94 (*see also* Bank of Japan; banks/banking systems); budget deficits in,

150; debt crisis in, 247, 251; decline of old economy of cheap labor and energy in, 118, 121–122; deregulation in, 113; economic crisis of 1990s in, 270; economic growth in, contributors to, 116–117; economic inefficiency in, 117; economic planning in, 25, 117, 123; economic slowdown in, 3–4; economic stagnation in, 261; economy at close of World War II in, 17, 18, 19; education in, 145; environmentalism in, 62; income distribution in, 140; income per person in, 6, 116; income tax in, 147, 149, 164; inflation and buying power in, 56; inflation in, 164; knowledge economy in, 123; labor productivity in, 257; labor share in, 141–142; manufacturing and trade in, 11, 116, 118, 119, 123, 124–129, 131, 137, 261; Ministry of International Trade and Industry, 25, 116, 117, 118, 120, 121, 123, 125, 129; modernization in, 117; new economy of engineering and design in, 122; oil crisis of 1973 in, 2–3, 72, 74, 77–78, 115–119, 122–124, 240; oil crisis of 1970s in, 177–178; operation scale-down in, 118; political parties in, 178; postwar economic boom in, 20; postwar productivity in, 23, 24; privatization in, 215–216; productivity bust in, 259, 268; productivity growth in, 263; productivity slowdown in, 265; service sector in, 117, 123–124; textile/apparel sector in, 119–120; trade with United States and, 119–120; unemployment scheme in, 121; ungovernability in, 156–160; US trade sanctions against, 128–129; wage, training, and job seeking subsidies in, 121; welfare state in, 18, 145

jawboning, 76–77

Jenkins, Peter, 150, 169

John Paul II, 219

Johnson, Lyndon, 145, 162; "guns and butter" model and, 48–49

Johnson administration, 222

Jones, Jack, 169

Jordan, 69

Joseph, Sir Keith, 176; free-market economics and, 172, 260

Kahn, Alfred, 112

Kaufman, Henry, 66, 232

Kennedy, Edward, 112
Kennedy, John F., 26, 144–145; inflation and, 261; unemployment and, 261
Kennedy administration, 222
Kenya, 44
Keynes, John Maynard, 31
Kiesinger, Kurt Georg, 33
Kissinger, Henry, 70
Klasen, Karl, 55
Kleinwort Benson, 84
knowledge economy, 123
Kohl, Helmut, 10, 177, 213
Korea, 242, 265
Korean Peninsula, 44
Korean War, 4, 20, 122
Krauss, Ellis, 177
Krippner, Greta, 236
Kuczynski, Pedro Pablo, 255
Kuwait, 70
Kuznets, Simon, 133–136; gross national product and, 134; stages of economic growth and, 134–135
Kuznets curve, 134–135

labor productivity, 257–258. *See also* productivity
labor share, 141–142
labor/trade unions, 10, 270; in France, 202, 208, 213; in Germany, 169; in Great Britain, 169–171; income distribution and, 137–138; manufacturing and, 137; in the Netherlands, 169; in Scandinavia, 169; in Spain, 211, 213; state-owned companies, privatization, Thatcher and, 190, 191–194, 214; state-owned companies and Thatcher and, 186–191; ungovernability and, 160; in West Germany, 137
Laffer, Arthur,227–228
Laffer Curve, 227–228
Landy, Harry, 90–91, 92
Lange, Anders, 153, 154
late capitalism, 160, 267–268. *See also* capitalism
Latin America, 35–36, 241; cause of poverty in, 39; Cold War and, 40–41; debt crisis in, 245, 252–253; economic slowdown in, 4; economic survey of, 38; economy of, 37; importance of industrialization in, 39–40; income per person in, 6; population growth in, 60–62. *See also* ECLA; *specific countries*
Lawson, Nigel, 185, 190–191, 195

leaders: new generation of, 162–163
license raj, 45
The Limits to Growth (Meadows et al.), 57–59, 61, 62, 63–64
Lindgren, Astrid, 165, 166, 180
London and County Securities, 83–84
Louis XIV, 199
"lump of labor" theory, 205–206
Luxembourg, 23, 30, 94

MacArthur, Douglas, 178
MacGregor, Ian, 192
Macmillan, Harold, 22, 24, 182
Maddison, Angus, 5, 160–161, 256
magic square (full employment, economic growth, low inflation, international balance of payments), 30, 31–32, 34–35, 261
magic triangle, 30
Malta, 257–258
Malthus, Thomas, 58
manufacturing, 12, 133, 140, 143, 258–259; government intervention and, 42; labor/trade unions and, 137; postwar boom and, 22–23; structural adjustment and, 129–130. *See also under specific countries*
Marshall Plan, 19
Marx, Karl, 135, 161, 204
Massachusetts Institute of Technology, 57
Mauroy, Pierre, 205–209
medical care, 229
Mexico, 46; bank loans to, 241; debt crisis in, 244–245, 247, 255–256
Miki, Takeo, 163, 164
Militant Tendency, 167–168
military spending, 229
Miller, G. William, 222
minerals price index, 45
mining sector, 4, 42, 124, 196
Ministry of International Trade and Industry (MITI), 25, 116, 117, 118, 120, 121, 123, 125, 129
Mitchell, Wesley, 48, 134
MITI. *See* Ministry of International Trade and Industry
Mitterrand, François, 197, 199–201; economic policy of, 203–211, 213–217; labor/trade unions and, 213; nationalism and, 206–208, 209, 210, 214; new version of socialism and, 210, 213–217; Socialist Party under, 199–200, 201, 203, 204–205, 206, 208–209, 210, 215, 217; welfare state and, 213

modernization, 117, 202, 210
Mondale, Walter, 234
monetarist theory/monetarism, 27, 176, 181, 182, 183–185, 186, 195, 220–221, 225
monetary inflation, 75–76
monetary policy, 183–184; Federal Reserve, 49–56, 180–182, 220; inflation and, 51–56; jobs and wages and, 182
Monti, Mario, 184
Mozambique, 44
Multi Fibre Arrangement, 131
multifactor productivity, 258. *See also* productivity
Mundell, Robert, 227

NAFTA. *See* North American Free Trade Agreement
Nakasone, Yasuhiro, 178
National Bureau of Economic Research, 48, 134
National Energy Act, 109
national income: ratio of government debt to, 151
National Westminster Bank, 82, 84
nationalism, 267; in France, 206–208, 209, 210, 214; in Spain, 211
natural gas: deregulation of, 102, 103, 104, 108–109, 110, 113
Nazi Germany, 146, 190
Nazi Party, 27–28, 29
Nehru, Jawaharlal, 41
Netherlands, 1, 23, 30, 224; labor share in, 141; labor/trade unions in, 169; ungovernability in, 156; welfare state in, 18
new economics, 26, 261
new industries: vs. raw materials, 45–46
New International Economic Order, 43
The New York Times, 54, 231
Newsweek, 70
Nixon, Richard, 2, 3, 70–71, 119–120, 157; anti-inflation policy of, 106; Cost of Living Council and, 107; economic forecasts and, 65, 66; economic policy of, 47–49; employment and, 50; energy czar appointment by, 100, 108 (*see also* Simon, William); energy sector and, 102; environmentalism and, 61; inflation and, 48, 50; interest rates, unemployment, and inflation and, 55–56; monetary policy and, 51; oil crisis of 1973 in, 99–100; population growth and, 61; re-election of, 56, 180;

regulation and, 108; Smithsonian agreement and, 55; Speer analogy and, 102, 108; treasury secretary appointment by, 101, 110 (*see also* Simon, William); unemployment and, 48, 235; Vietnam and, 48; wage and price controls and inflation and, 53–54; Watergate scandal and, 156; Watergate scandal and resignation of, 101, 110
Nixon administration, 222
Nixon Shock, 53
Nordhaus, William, 59
North America, 140; bank loans to Third World and, 241; debt crisis in, 247; economic slowdown in, 3–4; economy at close of World War II in, 17; income per person in, 6; postwar productivity in, 24; productivity bust in, 268; productivity slowdown in, 265; ungovernability in, 156–160
North American Free Trade Agreement (NAFTA), 142
Northern Europe, 81, 212
Northern Ireland, 4, 167
Norway, 1–2; anti-tax movement in, 153, 154; income distribution in, 136–137
nuts and bolts industry, 125–126

Obama, Barack, 9
oil: deregulation of, 99, 101, 102, 103, 104–106, 107–108, 109, 110, 113
oil crisis of 1973, 1–3, 68–79, 81–97, 155; Arab-Israeli conflict and, 69, 70–71; Aramco and, 69–70, 71; in Canada, 2, 71, 240; economic stagnation and stagflation and, 78; economy based on cheap oil and, 79; in Europe, 1–2, 3; Federal Reserve and, 72, 74, 77, 78, 94, 96; in France, 72–73, 77, 78; in Great Britain, 72, 74–75, 77, 167; impact on global financial system (banks and brokerage houses) and, 81–97; inflation and, 74–77, 78; in Italy, 72; in Japan, 2–3, 72, 74, 77–78, 115–119, 122–124, 240; oil price increases and production cuts and, 72, 73–74, 95; productivity bust and, 78–79; Saudi Arabia and, 1, 67, 68–71, 73, 95; Seven Sisters (US and European oil companies) and, 68–69; in Soviet Union, 162; in Sweden, 166; Third World development and, 239–240; UN Security Council Resolution 242 and, 71; in United

States, 1, 2, 3, 67, 68–79, 99–100, 240; welfare state and, 148; in West Germany, 72, 74, 177; Yom Kippur War and, 73. *See also* economic crisis of 1970s

oil crisis of 1979 (or second oil crisis), 171, 173, 174, 176–177, 219–220

oil production cuts and price increases: oil crisis of 1973 and, 72, 73–74, 95

oil shortages, 58. *See also* oil crisis of 1973; oil crisis of 1979

Olson, Mancur, 158–160

OPEC. *See* Organization of Petroleum Exporting Countries

OPEC oil crisis of 1973. *See* oil crisis of 1973

operation scale-down, 118

Organisation for Economic Co-operation and Development, 72–73

Organization of Petroleum Exporting Countries (OPEC), 67, 69. *See also* oil crisis of 1973

organizations: small vs. large, and ungovernability, 158–160

Overseas Economic Cooperation Fund of Japan, 241

Pacific, 140

Packer, George, 11

Pakistan, 44

Palme, Olof, 166

Perot, Ross, 267

Peru, 244, 250–251, 256

Phelps, Edmund, 75

Philippines, 250–251

Phillips, A. W. H., 74

Phillips Curve (full-employment and higher inflation), 74–75, 78, 168

Piketty, Thomas, 138

Pirie, Madsen, 194

Poland, 11, 94, 157, 245, 250–251

political moderation: economic moderation and, 24

political paralysis, 157

political parties: conservative, and welfare state, 24; ungovernability and, 155–156, 156–157. *See also* Communist Party; Socialist Party; *under specific countries*

political pressure: inflation and, 76

political scandals, 101, 110, 156–157

pollution, 58, 59–60, 62. *See also* environmental protection; environmentalism

The Population Bomb (Ehrlich), 61

population growth, 58, 59, 60–62. *See also* environmentalism

Portugal, 74, 81

Prebisch, Raúl, 36–39, 39–43, 180, 239, 241, 242, 254; attack on free trade by, 38–39; dependency theory (government intervention re: raw materials and manufacturing) and, 42; economic policy failures and, 45–46; economic principles of, 41; economies of developing countries and, 40–43; ex-colonies as industrialized powers and, 40; financial assistance from foreign countries and, 43; import substitution and, 40, 43, 45; importance of industrialization and, 39–40; New International Economic Order and, 43; stabilization of commodity prices and, 42–43

price controls: inflation and, 76–77; wage controls and inflation and, 53–54

price increases and oil production cuts: oil crisis of 1973 and, 72, 73–74, 95

private investment, postwar, 23

privatization, 12; in France, 213, 215; in Japan, 215–216; pros and cons of, 215–217; in Spain, 213, 215; state-owned companies, labor/trade unions, Thatcher and, 190, 191–194, 214; in West Germany, 215

production efficiency: vs. product diversity, in communist economies, 161–162

productivity, 7–8; of capital, 258; economic growth and, 78–79, 262; globalization and, 11–12, 265–266; innovation and, 262–265, 266; postwar, 22–24; tax and spending policies and, 8; technology and, 8; ways to measure, 257–258. *See also* labor productivity; multifactor productivity; productivity bust

productivity bust, 258–262; innovation as answer to, 262–265, 266; low-productivity theories and, 258–260; as new normal, 266–268; oil crisis of 1973 and, 78–79; search for solutions to, 260–262. *See also* productivity

Project Independence, 2

public psychology, 51

Quirk, Paul J., 107

racial discrimination, 4

Rand, Ayn, 153

rational governance, 27
raw materials: government intervention and, 42; vs. new industries, 45–46
Reader's Digest, 104
Reagan, Ronald, 10, 174–176, 178, 269; balanced budget and, 224, 226, 228, 229–231, 230, 234, 236, 237; economic failures and successes of, 234–238; economic policy of, 175–176, 224–231, 231–238; financialization and, 236; foreign investors and, 232–233; free enterprise and, 224, 225; government spending and, 229–230, 237; income distribution and, 235–236; inflation and, 176, 230, 233, 234, 235–236, 237; manufacturing and, 233, 237; military spending and, 229; monetarists and, 225; "The New Noblesse Oblige" speech of, 175; re-election victory of, 234; small government and, 175, 176, 199, 224, 225; social programs and, 229; social security and medical care, 229; social welfare and, 237; stock market and, 231–232; supply-side economics and, 225–229, 236–237; tax and spend policy of, 234; tax policy of, 176, 226–231, 235, 237; Third World debt crisis and, 249, 253–254; trade and, 233, 237; trade sanctions against Japan and, 128–129; unemployment and, 225–226, 234–235; welfare state and, 224; worker benefits and, 237–238
Reagan Revolution, 237
redistribution of income, 226
Reeder, Charles, 66, 73
Regan, Donald, 244
regional assistance, 126–127
regulation: of banks/banking systems, 92, 93–94, 95; environmental, 64; purposes of, 110–111. *See also* deregulation
resource depletion, 58, 59
restructuring, 264–265
Richardson, Gordon, 82–86, 92, 93, 97, 183, 184, 240
Ridley, Nicholas, 188
Ridley Report, 188–189, 191
Ringelmann Scale, 60
Rivlin, Alice, 261
Rogers, William P., 70
Romer, Paul, 8–9
Roosevelt, Franklin: Depression-era social programs and, 15, 24

Salomon Brothers, 66, 101
Samuelson, Paul, 66, 270
Sato, Eisaku, 120
Saud, Prince, 70
Saudi Arabia, 124; oil crisis of 1973 and, 1, 67, 68–71, 73, 95; oil crisis of 1979 and, 173
Scandinavia: anti-tax movement in, 151–153, 154; labor/trade unions in, 169; ungovernability in, 156; welfare state in, 144
Scargill, Arthur, 170, 191–192
Schanetzky, Tim, 31
Schiller, Karl, 27–35, 39, 46, 51, 55, 58, 162–163, 180; collective rationality and, 32, 34; concerted action (government and nongovernmental cooperation) and, 32–34; economic growth rate projections and, 32; expert economists and, 31–32; inflation and, 34; input-output analysis and, 30; magic square (full employment, economic growth, low inflation, international balance of payments) and, 30, 31–32, 34–35, 261; magic triangle and, 30; stimulus programs and, 31. *See also* West Germany
Schmidt, Helmut, 28, 162–163, 176–177
Schultze, Charles, 75
Science, 59
scientific government, 31
Scotland, 196
service sector, 137, 259–260, 261; in Japan, 117, 123–124
Seven Sisters (US and European oil companies), 68–69
Shah of Iran, 171, 225
Sierra Leone, 241
Silent Spring (Carson), 60
Silva Herzog, Jesus, 244–245, 247
Simon, William, 113, 222; as energy czar, 100–102, 108; as treasury secretary, 110, 112
Sindona, Michele, 88, 91–92
Singapore, 255
small government, 8, 175, 176, 224, 225
Smith, James E., 96
Smithsonian agreement, 55–56
Smithsonian Institution conference (1971), 54–55
social contracts, 11, 13; postwar economic boom and, 267–269. *See also* welfare state
social programs, 229; Depression-era, 15, 24. *See also* welfare state

Social Security, 143–144, 229, 268. *See also* welfare state

social security programs, 148, 150, 208. *See also* welfare state

social welfare, 237

socialism. *See under* France; Spain

Socialist Party, in France, 199–200, 201, 203, 204–205, 206, 208–209, 210–211, 215, 217. *See also* political parties

Solomon, Anthony, 221–222

South Korea, 124, 131, 224, 257–258; debt crisis in, 254–255

Southeast Asia, 240, 241

Southeastern Nigeria, 44

Soviet bloc, 19; ungovernability in, 160–162

Soviet communism, 179

Soviet Union, 163; Cold War and, 41; communist economies of 1970s and, 161–162; economy at close of World War II in, 17, 19; Great Depression of 1930s in, 7; income per person in, 160; oil crisis of 1973 in, 162; trade and, 162; ungovernability in, 160–162

Spain, 11, 56, 213–214; anti-inflation policy in, 53; economic policy under Franco in, 211–213; economy at close of World War II in, 20; in European Community, 214; income distribution in, 140; labor/trade unions in, 211, 213; market-oriented economic policies of, 217; nationalism in, 211; per capita income in, 265; privatization in, 213, 214, 215, 216–217; Socialist Workers Party in, 211–213, 214, 215; unemployment in, 217

Speer, Albert, 102, 108

Springsteen, Bruce, 11

stabilization of commodity prices, 42–43

state-owned companies: labor/trade unions and Thatcher and, 186–191; privatization, labor/trade unions, Thatcher and, 190, 191–194, 214

stationary-state economy, 63

steel industry, 127, 130

Stigler, George, 107

stock market: impending collapse in 1973 and, 66–67

Stockman, David, 236

Strauss, Franz Josef, 33

Streeck, Wolfgang, 267–268

Strindberg, August, 164

structural adjustment programs, 129–130, 250, 269–270

student movement: in West Germany, 34

subsidies: wage, training, and job seeking, in Japan, 121

Sudan, 244

supply-side economics, 225–229, 236–237

Sweden, 11; banks/banking system in, 94 (*see also* banks/banking systems); economic crisis of 1970s in, 164–167; income distribution in, 140; income tax in, 149, 164–167; labor productivity in, 257; manufacturing in, 167; oil crisis of 1973 in, 166; political parties in, 166–167; welfare state in, 143

Switzerland, 1–2, 62, 78; banks/banking system in, 86–87, 89, 181 (*see also* banks/banking systems); income distribution in, 136, 140

Syria, 1, 11, 69, 73

Taft, Robert A., 24

Taiwan, 124, 255, 265

Tanaka, Kakuei, 156–157, 163

tax and spending policies, 8, 30, 49, 234

taxes/tax rate/tax policy, 234, 270; in France, 208–209; government revenue and, 227–228; income distribution and, 137; Laffer Curve and, 227–228; Reagan and, 226–231, 235, 237; redistribution of income and, 226; Thatcher and, 176, 183, 185, 196; during World War II, 146–147. *See also* income tax; *under specific countries*

technology, 8, 24, 203, 258; environmentalism and, 63–64; unemployment and, 142–143; vs. workers' skills, 12–13

telecommunications sector, deregulation of, 107, 113

textile/apparel sector, 130–131; in Japan, 119–120

Thatcher, Margaret, 10, 154, 160, 171–172, 203, 213, 214, 215, 269; conservative economic policy of, 175–176, 182–197; economic policy successes and, 195–197; free-market economics and, 172, 260; government spending and, 189, 196; inflation and, 176, 182–185, 189, 195; labor/trade unions and state-owned companies and, 186–191; monetarist theory, 183–185, 186; monetarist theory, failure of, and, 195; privatization and, 190, 191–194; Reagan and, 175–176; small government and, 176, 182, 199;

state-owned companies, privatization, and labor/trade unions and, 190, 191–194; taxes and, 176, 183, 185, 196; unemployment and, 196–197

Third World: bank loans to, 240–244; development, and oil crisis of 1973, 239–240. *See also* developing countries

Third World debt crisis, 243–256; cause of and solution to, 253–256; emergency loans and, 247–249; impact on First World, 251–252; inflation and, 246; unemployment and, 246

trade, 23, 41, 159, 162; with Japan, and European manufacturing and, 125–127; with Japan, and US manufacturing and, 11, 124–127, 127–129; and manufacturing in Japan, 116, 118, 119, 123, 124–129, 131; removing obstacles to, 23; in United States, 51–52, 119–120, 128–129, 233. *See also* GATT; International Trade Commission; NAFTA; UNCTAD; *under specific countries*

Trade Act of 1974, 125, 128

trade unions. *See* labor/trade unions

transportation sector: deregulation of, 106–107, 110–112, 113–114

Treaty of Rome, 30

Trilateral Commission, 156

Truman, Harry, 19

Ture, Norman B., 227

Turkey, 81, 245

UN Conference on Trade and Development (UNCTAD), 43; minerals price index and, 45

UN Environment Program, 62

UN Security Council Resolution 242, 71

UNCTAD. *See* UN Conference on Trade and Development

unemployment, 8; automation and, 142–143; financial crisis of 2008 and, 270; income tax and, 164; 1950–1960, 21; productivity bust and, 261; technology and, 142–143. *See also* employment/unemployment; full employment; *under specific countries, economists, Federal Reserve chairmen, presidents, prime ministers, etc.*

ungovernability, 155–160, 161–162, 175, 178, 267; economic stagnation and, 158; labor/trade unions and, 160; late capitalism and, 160; political paralysis

and, 157; small vs. large organizations and, 158–160; welfare state and, 157–158

United Kingdom, 185–186, 194, 195; privatization and, 193; welfare state in, 17

United States, 219–238; anti-inflation policy in, 53; anti-tax campaigns in, 151; automobile industry and bailouts in, 127–128; baby boom in, 22; bank failures of 1980s and 1990s in, 270; bank loans to Third World and, 241–242; banks/banking system in, 88, 94, 97 *(see also* banks/banking systems; Federal Reserve; Franklin National Bank *and other specific US banks)*; budget deficits in, 47, 150, 226, 230, 234; Cold War and, 41; debt crisis in, 246, 247, 249, 251, 252, 253–254; deindustrialization in, 124; economic crisis of 1970s in, 172–176; economic forecasts in 1973 and, 65–66; economic growth in (1873–1897), 7; economic planning in, 25–26; economy at close of World War II in, 17, 18, 19; environmental protection in, 259; environmentalism in, 62; financial crisis of 2008 in, 270; Full Employment Act in, 25–26; full-employment budget in, 26; government deregulation/regulation in, 99–114; Great Depression of 1930s in, 7; income distribution in, 136, 137; income inequality in, 135; income per person in, 160, 240; income tax in, 146–147; increasing income inequality in, in mid-1970s, 139; inflation in, 52, 163, 173, 174–175, 176; labor share in, 141; manufacturing and trade with Japan in, 11, 124–127, 127–129 *(see also* trade *below)*; manufacturing in, 11, 144, 157, 163, 233, 237; multifactor productivity in, 258; nuts and bolts industry in, 125–126; oil crisis of 1973 in, 1, 2, 3, 67, 68–79, 99–100, 240; oil crisis of 1979s in, 173, 174; oil prices in, 163; pollution and, 60; postwar economic boom in, 20, 21, 268–269; postwar productivity in, 22; Prebisch and, 38; productivity bust in, 258–259; productivity growth in, 264; recession following oil crisis in, 125, 133; social security in, 143–144; textile/apparel sector in, 119–120, 131; trade in,

51–52, 233 (*see also* manufacturing and trade *above*); trade sanctions against Japan by, 128–129; trade with Japan and, 119–120; ungovernability in, 155–156, 156–160; welfare state in, 18, 143–144, 144–145, 148. *See also* Federal Reserve

Venezuela, 250–251
Versailles Treaty, 86
Vietnam, 48; hardship in, 44
Vietnam War, 4, 163, 202
Volcker, Paul, 97; Carter and, 220–224; inflation and, 220–221, 223–224, 230; monetary policy of, 221–224; Reagan and, 232, 234; recession under, 224; Third World debt crisis and, 244–245; unemployment and, 224
Volcker shock, 221, 224, 232
Volpe, John, 88

wage controls, 53–54
The Wall Street Journal, 221
Wallich, Henry, 87
Walters, Alan, 176
Washington Consensus, 254
The Washington Post, 71, 96, 104, 223
Watergate scandal, 101, 110, 156
wealth: loss of, and income distribution, 138
Wealth and Poverty (Gilder), 225
welfare state, 133, 143–154, 224, 257; anti-tax movements and, 151–154; birth of, 17–18; budget deficit and, 150; conservative parties and, 24; entitlements and, 157–158; government budget deficits and, 150; growth in cost of, 147–151; income tax and, 145–147, 149–151; oil crisis of 1973, 148; role of government and, 143–145; ungovernability and, 157–158. *See also* social contracts; social programs; Social Security; social security programs; *under specific countries*
West Germany, 1–2, 23, 51, 53, 55, 66, 78, 81, 124, 126–127, 163, 261; banks/

banking system in, 91 (*see also* Bankhaus Herstatt; German Bundesbank; banks/banking systems); budget deficit in, 150; budget deficits in, 32, 150; economic crisis of 1970s in, 176–178; economic planning in, 29–30; economic policy in, 29–35; economy at close of World War II in, 19; income distribution in, 136; income tax in, 147; inflation in, 176, 177; labor share in, 141–142; labor/trade unions in, 137; oil crisis of 1973 in, 72, 74, 177; oil crisis of 1979 in, 176–177; political parties in, 29, 30–31, 33–34, 35, 176–177; postwar economic boom in, 20; privatization in, 215; productivity bust in, 258–259; scientific government and, 31; student movement in, 34; ungovernability in, 156–157; welfare state in, 143, 144, 148, 149. *See also* Germany; Schiller, Karl
Western Europe, 11, 63, 125, 240; education in, 145; productivity bust in, 268; ungovernability in, 155–156, 156–160; welfare state in, 148
Will, George F., 9
Williams, Walter Nathan, 90
Wilson, Harold, 168–169
Wood, Sir Kingsley, 146
worker benefits, 237–238
workers' skills vs. technology, 12–13
World Bank, 44, 61; loans to Third World by, 240–241, 242, 243; Third World debt crisis and, 244, 253, 254
World War II, 3, 52; postwar years, reason for prosperity during, 133–134; taxes during, 146–147; world economy at close of, 15–20
Wriston, Walter, 96, 241, 245

Yamani, Ahmed Zaki, 67, 68–70, 70–71, 73
Yom Kippur War, 1, 73, 231–232
Yugoslavia, 81, 250–251

Zhou Enlai, 41
Z.P.G. (Anglo-Danish sci-fi film), 62

KAREN SAYRE

Marc Levinson is the former finance and economics editor at *The Economist* and the author of five previous books, including *The Box: How the Shipping Container Made the World Smaller and the World Economy Bigger*. Levinson lives in Washington, DC.